Y0-CQQ-460

RACE, MANHOOD, AND MODERNISM IN AMERICA

RACE, MANHOOD, AND MODERNISM

IN AMERICA

THE SHORT STORY CYCLES OF SHERWOOD ANDERSON AND JEAN TOOMER

MARK WHALAN

THE UNIVERSITY OF TENNESSEE PRESS / KNOXVILLE

First Edition.

This book is printed on acid-free paper.

Library of Congress Cataloging-in-Publication Data

Whalan, Mark, 1974–

Race, manhood, and modernism in America : the short story cycles of Sherwood Anderson and Jean Toomer / Mark Whalan. — 1st ed.

p. cm.

Includes bibliographical references and index.

ISBN-13: 978-1-57233-580-6 (hardcover : acid-free paper)
ISBN-10: 1-57233-580-7 (hardcover : acid-free paper)

1. Anderson, Sherwood, 1876–1941. Winesburg, Ohio. 2. Toomer, Jean, 1894–1967. Cane. 3. Race in literature. 4. Race relations in literature. 5. Sex role in literature. 6. Regionalism in literature. 7. Short stories, American—History and criticism. 8. Modernism (Literature)—United States. I. Title.

PS3501.N4W577 2007
813'.52—dc22 2006034876

FOR JULIA

CONTENTS

ACKNOWLEDGMENTS

In writing this book, I have relied on the support of many institutions and individuals, gained many colleagues, and drawn on the considerable resources of my friends. It is with pleasure and gratitude that I acknowledge my debts to them.

The book would never have been written without the generous assistance of the Arts and Humanities Research Board, which provided me with a studentship and a travel grant to visit the United States. The University of Exeter has provided a supportive, friendly, and stimulating environment for my research, and the ways in which the School of English has assisted me financially, intellectually, and professionally are too numerous to mention. Thanks are due to the staff at the University Library, and also those at the British Library, the Beinecke Rare Book and Manuscript Library at Yale, and the Newberry Library in Chicago. Sections of this book have already appeared in the *Journal of American Studies* (© Cambridge University Press 2002),

Studies in American Fiction, and *Modernism/Modernity* (Johns Hopkins University Press). Permission to reprint sections of that material is gratefully acknowledged, and thanks are due to the editors and readers of those journals for their constructive and encouraging advice. Thanks are due to Jonathan Frank for his permission to quote from his father's letters, to Yale University for their permission to quote from the Jean Toomer intellectual property held at the Beinecke Rare Book and Manuscript Library, and to the Newberry Library for their permission to quote from the Sherwood Anderson Papers. Once again, Scot Danforth and Gene Adair at the University of Tennessee Press have been the kind of editors who arouse considerable envy among my academic colleagues, and the book was strengthened by the astute advice of George Hutchinson and an anonymous reviewer at the peer review stage.

I have been fortunate in my friends and colleagues at Exeter. Regenia Gagnier has proven an unfailingly helpful presence as a mentor for my doctoral studies and my professional development. My writing has also benefited from being read and commented on by Gretchen Gerzina, Angelique Richardson, and Alex Goody. The administrative staff in the school have been unfailingly both good humored and gracious with their time, and I would particularly like to thank Julia Davey, Ges MacDonald, Michelle North, Jane Roberts, and Lisa Snowdon for all their help. Elsewhere, I am grateful for the intellectual sophistication and enthusiasm for my work that Peter Nicholls brought to his role as my external doctoral examiner, and also for the encouragement and assistance shown by Richard King and Richard Gray. At Yale, Nancy Kuhl, Vera Kutzinski, and Patricia Willis have been most supportive of my attempts at transatlantic scholarship, and Barbara Foley has been extremely generous in her encouragement and advice. I would also like to offer special thanks to Grace Moore; this book would have been much the poorer without her. Thanks for things too compendious to list here are due to Dan North and Isabella Ho, Dennis and Mink Maddox, Melissa and Bruno James, Helen Vassallo, Helen Hanson, James Lyons and Karen Goldstein, Lisa Leaver and Owain Winfield—people I am truly lucky to be able to call friends.

Finally, I would like to offer my deepest thanks to my doctoral supervisor, Helen Taylor, who impressed me so much when I was an undergraduate student fourteen years ago that I never envisioned anyone else supervising my work. In a different but equally important fashion, my family, and especially Brian, Lou, and Rachael, have sustained and encouraged me with a love and generosity that I could not have wished for. I dedicate this endeavor to the memory of my mother; I hope this book would have made her proud.

INTRODUCTION

In 1934, Sherwood Anderson attempted to contact Jean Toomer for the first time since 1924, inviting him to see a baseball game in New York. Toomer never replied, but it would have been interesting to see what each man would have made of the other ten years after their last correspondence. Anderson had moved to rural Virginia to live in the kind of small town he had so often romanticized in his fiction, and had endured the extremes of depression in facing long periods of writer's block. Thematically, his fascination with lives that seemed to exist at the periphery of industrial labor in the United States had long since turned to Appalachian whites—what he called the "mountain people"—as his main point of interest. Much rarer by the mid-thirties were the idealized portraits of southern African American stevedores and field workers that so absorbed him during the early 1920s. Toomer, by contrast, having abandoned the style of writing that gave the beginning of his career such promise, was still committed to the ideas of the mystic Georges Gurdjieff. Producing writing based on Gurdjieff's systematic views of the human personality, and devoid of the subtleties and ambiguities of his earlier work, he would write in 1929 that "my main motive is to produce a to me desirable effect on living people—not to give them an experience of art" (qtd. in Kerman and Eldridge 181). The most important writing of both men's careers was behind them, and the implicit tendencies in the thought of both men in 1923—toward the spiritual on one hand and the nostalgic on the other—had been realized. Yet the invitation provided a reminder of an intellectual community, and a series of cross-racial exchanges, fantasies, and misunderstandings, which formed an important part of the story of modernism in America in the 1920s.

Anderson labeled himself a "modern" in the 1920s, and this was a verdict many concurred with—one rather misguided correspondent of his even commented on his "futurist" tendencies, because his writing "lack[ed] any romance of the past" (*Letters to Bab* 39). Yet from the distance of eighty years, it is now Toomer's career, and principally *Cane*, that is much more regularly regarded as engaged with the project of being "absolutely modern." Toomer wrote critically about the desire for nostalgia and frequently exhibited a fascination for technology, science fiction, and the new forms and features of urban American life. His friend Gorham Munson astutely identified Toomer's programmatic sense of the future in voicing his optimism in 1924 that Toomer might soon "possess an attitude that would not merely be a reaction to the circumstances of modernity, merely a reflection of the life about him, but would be an attitude that could act upon modernity" (*Cane* 174). Sherwood Anderson is connected most readily to the opposite perspective—a writer of elegiac, coming-of-age stories, most famously his 1919 cycle of 1890s small-town life *Winesburg, Ohio,* whereas Toomer is usually seen as one of the foremost writers putting the new into the New Negro. Yet both men presented a complex and in many ways complementary response to the temporal shocks, uncertainties, and possibilities of the period surrounding World War I. These responses relied upon imagined and romanticized pasts—often projected onto bodies that were somehow coded as "Other" yet were never far from what Charles Scruggs and Lee VanDemarr have called the "terrors of history." They involved technology as a force of liberation and destruction, and they involved an acute awareness of the situation of the reader of their texts, particularly in the realization that the Great War had made many people think differently about narrative. And they considered how bodies—which had undergone such violence and such new forms of what Foucault called discipline in the early years of the twentieth century—were either the repositories of a longed-for past, or the malleable raw material for building a new America.

In tracing some of these ideas, this book focuses on the two most famous texts by these authors—the short story cycles *Winesburg, Ohio,* and *Cane,* produced by Toomer in 1923. It also situates them in an intellectual and creative milieu immersed in new theorizations of regionality, culture, technology, and gender—a milieu within which the cultural critic and novelist Waldo Frank emerged as a significant figure for both men. Looking at previously unpublished manuscripts and archival material, this project reveals the extent to which Sherwood Anderson and Jean Toomer engaged with new fields of knowledge or discourses that had significant ramifications on conceptions of race and gender as America moved into an age of mass consumerism. These include developments in anthropology and ethnography, the significance of primitivism for modernist aesthetics, masculinities in a time of world war, the cult of physical culture, and the appropriation of recent advances in machine technology into aesthetics. Such discourses had considerable impact on the formal strategies of the short story cycle that Anderson and Toomer did much to advance, and yet they have generally been omitted in assessments of their work.[1] This is despite the fact that certain themes that traditional critics of these texts have often noted and discussed in historically nonspecific terms—such as the condition of alienation, gender relations and gender politics, race relations, the role of the artist, and the nature of American community—were all experiencing rapid change and intellectual scrutiny in the period 1916–25.

Bringing Anderson and Toomer together allows for a thoroughness of historical and social contextualization that is often missing from assessments of these authors. Indeed, an interdisciplinary methodology—spanning anthropology, social history, discourses of physical culture and embodiment, mass culture, genre theory, and literary history—both brings their shared intellectual concerns into sharp focus and provides a necessary counterbalance to the formalist approaches that have typified the critical history of their most famous texts. Both men were deeply engaged with conceptualizations of race and gender, yet understanding how those concepts took shape necessitates an assessment of how they were under constant renegotiation between a host of discursive and cultural locations. Crucial for both Anderson and Toomer in such considerations were the politics and cultural criticism of the Young American group, of which Waldo Frank was a prominent member. Toomer and Anderson were also both interested in racial discourses such as eugenics, primitivism, and the "vogue of the Negro." They were both attracted by the anthropology of the Boas school, particularly the overlap that existed between American traditions of regionalism and how the new anthropology sought spatial rather than temporal models for different cultures. They were both fascinated by what was often referred to as "the machine," particularly its significance for the future of masculinity in America. Working across a range of disciplines serves to accentuate why these authors deserve to be read together, when readings more narrowly focused on thematic preoccupations or organized according to the racial identity of the author have largely served to keep them apart. Moreover, in an era when—as I go on to discuss—anthropology, racial science, aesthetics, and cultural criticism were far less sequestered into highly professionalized and self-contained enclaves than exist today, and rubbed shoulders in the little magazines wherein Anderson and Toomer gained their reputations, an interdisciplinary approach is indispensable for understanding the complexities undergirding literary production in the 1920s—particularly as it relates to such expansive concepts as race and gender.

Perhaps the strongest connection between the two authors, however, was evident in Toomer's penultimate letter to Anderson—namely the fact that they shared a faith in the "emergent individual" (Toomer, *Letters* 189). Both Anderson and Toomer were committed to individualism as inherent in an archetypally American identity and held the hope that it might prove to be a solution to social divisions in the United States. Yet both were aware of the conflicting significance of social determinism, particularly when it came to economic or racial factors. What this book aims to show is some of the tensions that arose from this conflict: how both authors saw race, gender, and economics as (often problematic) factors in defining an American subjectivity, yet also how they used these factors as strategic points of leverage for their projects of cultural criticism. Their keenness in some cases for the tactical preservation of difference is often matched by the fear of its being obliterated, and yet cross-racial, cross-gender, and transracial fantasy form significant moments in their writing on the politics of identity.

In addition, an interdisciplinary model does not presuppose a sharp distinction between sociocultural history and the formal innovations for which *Cane* and *Winesburg, Ohio* are so celebrated. Rather, it demonstrates that rapidly developing fields of knowledge and aesthetics that related to gender and race were closely involved with the formal and generic choices of *Winesburg, Ohio* and *Cane*. Criticism of the short story cycle—which might briefly be defined as a collection of stories which have some structural relation or connecting element and which therefore form an integrated unit, yet wherein the stories also have a degree of significatory autonomy—has often referred to its balance between fragmentation and integration. Placing *Winesburg, Ohio* and *Cane* in an interdisciplinary and historically grounded perspective reveals just how much that balance—operative in literary form—was interrelated with social formations equally strained between atomization and coherence. Indeed, issues such as narrative structure, the relation of the artist to the object of representation, or how diversity could exist within an overarching design impacted as much on Toomer's and Anderson's thinking about subjectivity and social organization as they did on their thinking about writing fiction and poetry. Yet much of the critical reception of these two texts, while focusing primarily on their formal attributes, has failed to acknowledge these historical contexts. A more nuanced and evenhanded approach, which balances historical and formal analysis, is called for.

SHERWOOD ANDERSON, JEAN TOOMER, AND WALDO FRANK: RACE AND YOUNG AMERICA

Although the work of Sherwood Anderson and Jean Toomer has been considered together before, in light of traditional approaches to literary history this combination is unusual enough to warrant some explanation.[2] If Anderson is discussed in terms of literary communities, it has tended to be in connection with the Chicago Renaissance, and especially with reference to writers such as Edgar Lee Masters, Carl Sandburg, Floyd Dell, and Theodore Dreiser—or "Young American" critics such as Van Wyck Brooks, Paul Rosenfeld, and Waldo Frank. By comparison, although most Toomer critics have acknowledged the significance of his involvement with white intellectuals of the "Young American" group, particularly Waldo Frank, for a considerable time Toomer was predominantly discussed with reference to the Harlem Renaissance. Yet, as George Hutchinson has argued, it is the disappearance of the "Young American" critics who were so close to both Anderson and Toomer from "traditional accounts of modernism" that has been "partly responsible for the popular sense of a large gap between a monolithic Anglo-American modernism and the Harlem Renaissance" ("Foreword" vii–xi). As Hutchinson's work goes some way to demonstrating, this popular sense of a gap needs to be redressed, and exploring the connections between Toomer, Frank, and Anderson, and the literary communities they frequented, participates in this project—even as it also uncovers the misunderstandings and myopias (most often on the subject of race) that existed within their relationships.[3]

The personal interaction between Anderson and Toomer, while not extensive or particularly fruitful, illustrated their shared intellectual preoccupations and their similar positioning within a small field of nativist modernism nourished by a handful of little magazines. In 1922, Anderson, then forty-five years old and at the peak of his fame as one of the most celebrated of America's new generation of authors, had seen some of Toomer's work in the offices of the New Orleans–based little magazine the *Double Dealer.* Much enthused, he wrote to praise Toomer for having produced "a note that I have long been wanting to hear from your race," later adding that it was "the first negro [*sic*] work I have seen that strikes me as really negro" (Turner, "Intersection" 99, 102). Anderson was nothing if not generous with young authors, and he offered to write a preface for *Cane* and to help Toomer find a publisher. Toomer was flattered to have such a celebrated author interested in his work and sent Anderson a warm reply stressing how much *Winesburg, Ohio* had meant to his own artistic development. Soon, however, Anderson's stereotyped and reductive beliefs about African Americans soured their relationship; Toomer wrote to their mutual friend, Waldo Frank, that Anderson may have experienced a "deep and beautiful emotion by way of the Negro," but that "[h]e wants more. He is hungry for it. I come along. I express it. It is natural for him to see me in terms of this expression" (*Letters* 115). This tendency of Anderson to appraise Toomer and his work according to what he believed to be "really negro" soon led to Toomer's belief that their relationship could offer him nothing. Indeed, Toomer complained to Frank that he didn't think their friendship would "go very far," as "he limits me to Negro" (*Letters* 113). For a man who spent much of his career attempting to deconstruct or avoid the very American racial binary of black and white, this was not a pigeonholing that Toomer appreciated.

Of itself, this exchange was not of great import for either writer, but it does illustrate several of the reasons why they should be discussed together. It indicates Anderson's attachment to binaristic thinking about difference and also his deep interest (and investment) in the discourses of "blackness" that modernism would so often draw upon. Of all the "Young American" critics and writers, with the possible exception of Frank, it was Anderson who turned most enthusiastically to African American life and culture as a potential model for reversing what many critics had identified as the disastrous separation of culture and labor within the industrial workplace. Race also became for him a crucial mediating term for considering new formations of gender, family structure, and commodification in the emerging mass cultural landscape of 1920s America. Conversely, the exchange indicates Toomer's irritation at Anderson's view that race was a biological essence, one that determined both individual subjectivity and cultural production—a view against which he would struggle for much of his life. Indeed, it is the disavowal of this view that marks many of *Cane*'s most radical statements and underlies the possibilities it opens up for rethinking the parameters of racialized subjectivity. The exchange of letters also illustrates the significance of a new wave of little magazines in determining the shape of the cultural field and the interracial traffic this sometimes facilitated, and in this particular case, it illustrates the overlap of Anderson and Toomer in the pages of the *Double Dealer*—a magazine with a specifically southern aesthetic to develop and promote. They had a shared interest in the geography of race—and, indeed, new theories about the interaction of race, space, and culture that were being developed by U.S. anthropologists. Moreover, for both writers, these questions coalesced around the project of "writing the South," often (as here) in the same magazines.[4]

Lastly, and most important, Toomer was criticizing Anderson to Waldo Frank, who was at that point Toomer's closest intellectual contact and whose influence on the eventual shape of *Cane* has recently been convincingly argued.[5] Frank had played a signal role in Anderson's career five years earlier, when he had provided him with regular publication in a major national literary journal for the first time, and provided ecstatic critical estimations of his significance for American literature. Both writers were attracted to Frank's exhortative and lyrical brand of cultural nationalism, and his adulation of Whitman's views on the integral nature of sexuality to both the human personality and the social collective. They also admired his willingness to place the bard-prophet at the center of cultural and political life, and his determination to theorize cultural alternatives to the increasingly standardized fare of mass production. Moreover, Frank—as the son of a wealthy Manhattan Jewish business family, a graduate of Yale, and a prominent figure in the left-wing New York intellectual scene of the late 1910s—provided Anderson and Toomer with an entrance into the New York avant-garde intelligentsia that both men craved, yet remained highly suspicious of. His thinking on the constitution of national culture, on the role of racial and ethnic minorities in building that culture, and on the aesthetics of reading would have a profound effect on Toomer in particular. As a formative and linking figure between Anderson and Toomer, Frank plays a prominent role in this study—even though both men came eventually to distance themselves from Frank's plans for national cultural renewal.

Frank was only one of the key figures of the "Young Americans," a group whose significance to American modernism has been obscured by post-1930s literary histories of the period, often at the expense of expatriate writers of the *generation perdu*.[6] These "Young Americans" had close connections to the "Lyrical Left" that John P. Diggins has characterized as the first "Left" of the twentieth century, and included cultural critics such as Van Wyck Brooks, Randolph Bourne, Paul Rosenfeld, and later Gorham Munson. The group championed artists like Anderson, Theodore Dreiser, the photographer Alfred Stieglitz, and later Hart Crane, and they held editorial sway on several of the little magazines of the period, particularly the *Seven Arts*, the *Freeman*, *Secession*, *S4N*, the *New Republic*, and, to a lesser degree, the *Dial*.[7] Although generalization is problematic across what was quite a diverse group, it is fair to say that they were committed to developing models of inclusive cultural nationalism. This is typified in Bourne's famous essay "Trans-National America," which, in the words of George Hutchinson, presents a vision "in which different ethnic identities would be joined in a cosmopolitan federalism" (*Harlem Renaissance* 103). This essay helped to form Frank's vision of how to revitalize (and crucially de-Anglicize) national culture in his seminal, but often inadequately read, text *Our America*. The Young Americans also bewailed divisions in industrialized working practice between spirituality, labor, and cultural production, a critique most associated with Brooks's *America's Coming of Age* and heavily influenced by English Fabian Socialism and William Morris. Instead, they looked to a model of what Bourne called the "beloved community," a quasi-organic totality of democratic social, economic, and intellectual organization.

The intellectual tenor of the work of the Young Americans was significant to how both Anderson and Toomer shaped their creative responses to American society. Yet the differences they took within this program make them worthy of comparison also, and in ways that reflect the different backgrounds and focal points of interest of the two men. Toomer's enthusiasm for *Our America* arose from Frank's proposal that a national culture could be constituted of an "ethnic federalism," a federalism that would follow America's rejection of Anglophilic cultural forms and standards. Frank suggested that in place of this Anglophilia, the national culture should draw upon what he described in *Our America* as the "buried cultures" of Native America and Mexico—a program that drew extensively on the new methodologies then being developed in American anthropology, particularly the techniques developed under the guidance of Franz Boas. Rather than working out the implications of ethnic "federalism" at the outset of their relationship—implications that would eventually contribute to the split between the two authors—Toomer was most impressed by Frank's opulently prophetic (and self-aggrandizing) prose style, his Whitmanesque scope of vision for the nation, and his utopian ambitions for reconfiguring the way that America related cultural production to race.

Toomer's attraction to Frank's program was in large part due to the liminality of his own lived experience; he had some African American ancestry, but not to a degree of visibility that he found himself "Jim Crowed" because of his appearance. As a child he lived in both black and white communities, and attending university in Wisconsin and Chicago he decided on a policy of explaining to "real friends of both groups" his multiracial ancestry and his identity as "an American, neither white nor black" (*Wayward* 93). While attending university, he was mistaken for a Native American and an Indian. In other social, employment, or legal situations, he variously described himself as white or black as the situation demanded.[8] As he said:

> I have lived among Negroes. I have lived among Nordics and Anglo-Saxons. I have lived among Jews. I have lived among groups composed of different racial and national strains, groups formed by some common bond, such as art or literature, and existing for the pursuit of an aim which gave racial differences something like their true placement in the scale of values. ("Crock" 56)

In his personal experiences, Toomer found that he could avoid discrimination or a curtailing of his social freedoms largely by remaining silent about his racial status. Early in his life he decided to "go my way and say nothing unless the question was raised," and "if it was not the person's business I would either tell him nothing or the first nonsense that came into my head" (*Wayward* 93). This suited his oft-stated belief that "individualization" was the highest aim in personal development; to allocate a racial identity to a person was, he felt, "to [group] him with the herd, and, by implication, [deny] him individuality."[9] Frank's program in *Our America* seemed to allow plenty of opportunity for both the creative individual and the cultures of ethnic minorities; he sought both to locate the prophetic intellectual at the center of cultural renewal and to integrate marginalized ethnicities into definitions of "Americanism." Consequently, this program seemed initially to Toomer to dovetail nicely with his wish to preserve his own "individuality," and also his desire to introduce more cultural diversity into normative notions of Americanism. Frank's program also seemed to suit Toomer's long-lived attempts to replace race with either nation or class as the primary determinant of identity. This ideal was epitomized in Toomer's proclamation in 1920 that his diverse ancestry made him the "First American." As he wrote:

> [U]nderlying all of the [racial] divisions, I had observed what seemed to me to be authentic—namely, that a new type of man was arising in this country—not European, not African, not Asiatic—but American. And in this American I saw the divisions mended, the differences reconciled—saw that (1) we would in truth be a united people existing in the United States, saw that (2) we would in truth be once again members of a united human race. (*Wayward* 121)

As several recent critics have noted, this was an approach that took Toomer away from the mainstream of American social and political life, which in the 1920s was moving toward a legal and social system of increasing bifurcation between black and white. It was also a position that ultimately put Toomer on a collision course with federalist (as opposed to integrationist) theories of multiethnicity such as Frank's. Moreover, it would lead to Toomer's reluctance to be closely affiliated with the dominant aesthetic trends of the New Negro Renaissance.[10] Ultimately, Toomer would feel that "Our America" was not his, just as being labeled a "New Negro" led to him feeling "tricked and misused" by Alain Locke (*Wayward* 132).

It was Toomer's engagement with these issues of identity politics, as well as with several of Frank's aesthetic strategies for creative writing, that gave *Cane* much of its formal texture and interrogative purpose. Frank and his work therefore represent an indispensable part of any consideration of *Cane*'s politics of race, its configuration of regional identity, and its generic complexity. Ultimately, Toomer's move away from a federalist model of cultural interaction in the United States led to his famous "denial of blackness"—epitomized in his refusal in 1931 to allow poems from *Cane* to appear in an anthology of Negro poetry edited by James Weldon Johnson. Yet too often this has led to a view of *Cane* that does not take into account its nature as a testing ground within which various theories of race, formal strategies, and modes of address engage in dialogue. The intellectual exuberance of *Cane* and its willingness to play out—or play off—conflicting ideas about racial identity, representational politics, and formal strategy, is to a large degree due to Toomer's headlong enthusiasm for the intellectual circles of New York that he "discovered" in the early 1920s, circles among which the thought of Frank and "Young America" was prominent.

For Anderson, Young America also proved attractive. This was largely due to the attempts of Van Wyck Brooks and Waldo Frank to provide a cogent cultural critique of the processes of industrialization and standardization, processes that Anderson felt were degrading American life. Specifically, Anderson was attracted by the artisan-craftsman figure Brooks had admired in William Morris's work, a figure that seemed to offer a model for resistance to the division of labor in Taylorist/Fordist production methods. Anderson felt that scientific management and assembly line production had serious consequences; he argued that in the "new places, the factories, when already the work is divided in the new way . . . the men never [have] a sense of completion of self in work" (*Memoirs* 387). As this quotation implies, he felt the modern factory presented a fundamental threat to male identity and patriarchy; in his most schematic formulation of this at the outset of the Great Depression, he argued that the factory system had made men "impotent" and was transforming America into a "matriarchy."[11] Accordingly, he was drawn to the preindustrial as a model for the regeneration of community and gender relations, an attraction which—unlike Brooks's program—had by the 1920s turned to a primitivist fascination with African American culture.

However, in this fascination Anderson provides a salutary illustration of a long and often awkward history of white American male bohemia's fascination with working-class African Americans. He was generally content to treat black rural communities with platitudinous generalization, keen to see them as reservoirs of cultural authenticity that could have a potentially regenerative impact on the national culture—and was generally unconcerned by the continuing conditions of racial oppression in the United States. Just as Toomer did, he wished to present alternatives to what *Cane*'s "Seventh Street" described as the "stale, soggy wood" of Anglo-American industrial capitalism through utilizing the cultural resources of African America (*Cane* 41). Yet, in frequent contrast to Toomer, Anderson's attraction was riddled with ambivalence and hesitation—about race and sexuality, about African Americans and modernity, about the way his whiteness became visible within these contexts. This ambivalence was particularly evident in his unpublished letters and manuscripts.

Much of Anderson's fascination with African American men arose because masculinity was an area where he favored the nostalgic, a nostalgia directed particularly towards the figure that the gender historian Michael Kimmel has dubbed the "Heroic Artisan." Yet Toomer, too, was interested in the discourses of his time that produced gendered subjectivities and in their relation to the production of racial identity. In contrast to Anderson, however, it was a rapidly consolidating mass consumer culture and its reconfiguration of the gendered body that seemed to him to offer liberating potential. In particular, and as Gorham Munson noted, Toomer's search for alternatives to the economic and racial order of the day was distinguished from Anderson's by its "positive scientific character," rather than by its resulting "from a disgust or a negation" (*Cane* 174). Toomer was interested in the precursor of body-building, the physical culture movement, because it proposed methods by which masculinity could be produced and because it helped begin to reconfigure masculinity as more heavily reliant on a set of aesthetic criteria. This "externalization" of masculinity, and its linkage to both consumption and agency, led Toomer to see the body as a malleable entity, not one permanently inscribed with unalterable markers of gender and race. If the body could be "built" through answering magazine ads and a regime of training and self-discipline, then gender and race could be "built" as well—and to subjectivities extending well outside the model consumers that the American economy was aiming to produce.

Both men, therefore, wished to configure ways in which male agency could be articulated in response to constricting forces within modernity. Toomer was concerned about ways in which the increasing bifurcation of American racial politics could undercut areas of his privilege and threaten the advantages that his class and his gender afforded him. Anderson, in contrast, saw modern modes of production as inimical to the "maleness" he associated with preindustrial economies. Yet both took almost totally opposing strategies of how to imagine masculinity in modernity, a factor to a large part determined by the historical models available to them. If Anderson had "Heroic Artisans" like the aging wheelmaker Sponge Martin in *Dark Laughter* to evoke nostalgia for small-scale, craft producerism, Toomer was disturbed by the implication of figures like "Father John," the elderly and mute ex-slave who lives in the cellar of a workshop in Sempter, Georgia, in "Kabnis," the final section of *Cane*. The past here is one of enslavement, the non-differentiation of individual subjects, and abjection.

In contrast to nostalgia, Toomer looked to the emergent aesthetics and technologies of the twentieth century to imagine new processes for the social constitution of race and gender. Futurism and Dada, the new organization of urban space and the urbanization of African American life following the great migration, physical culture, and machine technology all function within this project in *Cane*. As he said of Washington's Seventh Street, which he eulogized in *Cane*, this was an African American urban environment that "Sherwood Anderson would not get his beauty from" because it was "jazzed, strident, modern." Yet it expressed the "healthy freedom" of a "new people" (*Letters* 116). Indeed, years later Anderson would complain that he had recently bought a batch of jazz records but could not bring himself to appreciate them; he also wrote an abortive, and unpublished, poem entitled "Shake That Thing," which drew on the famous jazz/blues refrain in a cringingly awkward and ill-informed fashion. Both men, therefore, saw American society as suffering from crippling divisions and believed that a new relation between hegemonic European American culture and African American culture might offer some solutions. Yet the differences between them on how this was to be achieved are instructive of the ways in which theories, experiences, and representations of African Americans and African Americanism functioned variously within the cultural criticism of the time.

GENRE, THE SHORT STORY CYCLE, *WINESBURG, OHIO,* AND *CANE*

Such tensions, debates, and endeavors are inevitably inscribed within the formal and generic outlines of Anderson's and Toomer's short story cycles. As texts which were radical and experimental in their formal choices, and which included some very explicit markers to their readers that they were self-reflexive about their own forms, it is unsurprising that primarily formalist readings have often been applied to them. Anderson himself realized that this was an important part of his legacy to American literature; in 1938, when assembling his memoirs and organizing carbon copies of his letters, he remarked about what he called "the Winesburg form" in a letter to his friend Roger Sergel that "I invented it. It was mine" (*Selected Letters* 220). This may be contentious in the light of earlier modernist texts such as James Joyce's *Dubliners* (1914), earlier American texts such as Sarah Orne Jewett's *The Country of the Pointed Firs* (1896), or American *and* modernist texts such as Gertrude Stein's *Three Lives* (1909). Yet repeating a claim that artists have made down the ages, he attested that his formal intervention realigned aesthetic practice with modern lived experience; in his *Memoirs* he would boast that these stories "broke the O. Henry grip, de Maupassant grip. It brought the short story in America into a new relation with life" (*Winesburg* 155). Moreover, many writers of the following generation were also keen to publicly acknowledge the significance of Anderson's work. For younger American writers such as Ernest Hemingway, Richard Wright, William Faulkner, Jean Toomer, Eudora Welty, Katherine Anne Porter, and John Steinbeck, it was *Winesburg, Ohio* that suggested many of the possibilities offered by an integrated short story collection. Toomer commented that *Winesburg, Ohio* and Anderson's subsequent collection *The Triumph of the Egg* "are elements of my growing. It is hard to think of myself as maturing without them" (*Letters* 102). Faulkner saw it as a gesture "commensurate with gianthood" ("Sherwood Anderson" 494). Indeed, when Anderson is included on curricula or reading lists, it is now most commonly due to his status as an important influence, or context, for the formal development of the American short story.

The distinction of being cited as an "ancestor"—as Ralph Ellison put it—also fell frequently to Jean Toomer. Although for most of his life Toomer would be completely at odds with Anderson's wish to proclaim the significance of his most famous text—Toomer would become progressively more uncomfortable with being linked to *Cane* following its publication in 1923—he has had many writers keen to acknowledge their debt to *Cane,* his experimental collection of stories, prose poems, lyrics, and drama. Wallace Thurman, noted for his cynicism about African American cultural production in the 1920s, uncharacteristically effused that Toomer was "[t]he most emancipated and intelligent Negro yet to appear. Not for him the dark morass of races. He stands on a mount . . . eyes cast alternately earthward and heavenward, relentlessly searching for some meaning in the meaningless universe."[12] Langston Hughes was to comment that *Cane* was "the finest prose written by a Negro in America. And, like the singing of Robeson, it is truly racial" ("Negro Artist" 1270). In the first introduction to *Cane* to be written by an African American writer, just two years after its reissue following an absence of forty years, Arna Bontemps could remark that "even in today's ghettos astute readers are finding that its insights have anticipated and even exceeded their own" (x).[13]

Such comments may only be fit for a publisher's blurb, were it not for what they indicate. On the one hand, they evince an admiration for Toomer's willingness to address the often painful and terrifying realities of the intersection of racial and sexual subjectivity in the United States. On the other, there is a respect for his zeal in wishing to apply new strategies of formal experimentalism to what W. E. B. Du Bois called the "criteria for Negro art"; indeed, Gorham Munson was to write that *Cane* represented "the record of [Toomer's] search for literary forms" (Du Bois, "Criteria"; *Cane* 172). This appetite for formal experimentalism was evident in his voracious reading and voluminous correspondence throughout 1922 with Waldo Frank and Gorham Munson on the subjects of literary form, reader-response, and the aesthetics of writers as diverse as Filippo Tommaso Marinetti, Anderson, Gustave Flaubert, Kenneth Burke, and the Imagist poets. These two interventions, crudely categorizable as social and formal, were highly significant to the artistic practice of subsequent writers. Moreover, these factors have often led *Cane* to assume a considerable importance in the formation of the African American, and American Modernist, canons in the years following 1923.

Despite this influential legacy, deciding on a generic term for *Winesburg, Ohio* and *Cane*—and subsequent collections such as William Faulkner's *Go Down, Moses* and *The Unvanquished,* John Steinbeck's *The Pastures of Heaven,* or Eudora Welty's *Golden Apples*—has long caused a distinct lack of agreement. It has often been recognized that these works do not fit comfortably into any of the three most frequent designations of prose fiction, namely novel, novella, or short story; as early as 1924, D. H. Lawrence's review of Hemingway's *In Our Time* for *Calendar of Modern Letters* stated that "*In Our Time* calls itself a book of stories, but it isn't that. It is a series of successive sketches from a man's life, and makes a fragmentary novel."[14] Malcolm Cowley also hypothesized a distinct aesthetic in these type of works without defining a theory of the form; in his introduction to *Winesburg, Ohio* in the 1960 Viking Press edition, he refers to it, along with *The Unvanquished, Go Down, Moses,* Steinbeck's *Tortilla Flat* and *The Pastures of Heaven,* and Erskine Caldwell's *Georgia Boy,* as "a cycle of stories with several unifying elements, including a single background, a prevailing tone, and a central character. These elements can be found in all the cycles, but the best of them also have an underlying plot that is advanced or enriched by each of the stories" (14).[15]

A number of doctoral studies in the late 1960s and 1970s applied themselves to defining a formal category to accommodate these works, producing a raft of terms with which to do so. Maggie Dunn and Ann Morris, in their extremely thorough appraisal of the critical history of what they call the "composite novel," identify the following terms that have been used: "story cycle, short story cycle, multi-faceted novel, story novel, paranovel, loose leaf novel, short story composite, rovelle, composite, short story compound, integrated short story collection, anthology novel, modernist grotesque, hybrid novel, story chronicle, short story sequence, genre of return, short story volume, and narrative of community" (4).[16] The term "short story cycle" has become the most familiar of these appellations, and it originates from Forrest L. Ingram's unapologetically formalist study *Representative Short Story Cycles of the Twentieth Century: Studies in a Literary Genre* (1971). Ingram's text deals with a number of areas that have been central to most subsequent discussions and definitions of the short story cycle. These include the existence of a tension between the overall unity of the stories and their status as individual stories; it also deals with the differentiation of the short story cycle from both the novel and the collection of short stories, which Ingram sees as representing opposite poles of a spectrum of integration and unity. Since then the term has gained a place in common critical parlance, being used in various anthology introductions, in critical articles on specific authors, and by theorists of the short story.[17] Later work, by such critics as Susan Garland Mann and Robert M. Luscher, focuses more on the site of reception than on the text as the point at which "meaning" is generated. While both critics maintain Ingram's focus on the short story cycle as an integrative, unified form, they are more interested in the readerly operations of such integration than in the architectonics of a controlling writer. Luscher, therefore, defines the genre in terms of a progressive and integrative reading experience; he sees the "short story sequence" as

> a volume of stories, collected and organized by their author, in which the reader successively realizes underlying patterns of coherence by continual modifications of his perceptions of pattern and theme. Within the context of the sequence, each short story is thus not a completely closed formal experience. (148)

Luscher also stresses the "importance of stories' sequential nature or the recurrent elements that provide more dramatic unity" (149). He agrees with Mann that connection-making is one of the pleasures of the genre; indeed, he argues that "our desire for unity and coherence is so great that we often use our literary competencies to integrate apparently unrelated material, as long as we are sustained by the faith that the work possesses formal wholeness" (155).

Such comments—which are broadly representative of much of the critical discussion of short story cycles—cannot but seem somewhat dated in light of poststructuralist critiques of aesthetics of "unity." This sentiment has been voiced by J. Gerald Kennedy, in what is perhaps the most successful application of several theories of narratology and reader-response which arose from structuralism to the consideration of this genre. He criticizes Ingram for treating "the ostensible unity of these works as an intrinsic feature of the writing rather than as a function or product of his own reading" and goes on to note that "this insistence on unity has produced a restrictive and conservative theory of form which has canonized certain collections while ignoring others," of which *Cane* may well be considered one ("Poetics" 11).[18] Indeed, Luscher's remark that stories within a sequence do not exhibit a "completely closed formal experience," in its suggestion that some texts do have such a closure—free-floating from history, author, reader, or linguistic play—waves a New Critical red rag at materialist literary critics and those interested in reading through the politics of gender, sexuality, or race. A critical practice which seeks closure at the level of the cycle as a whole is effectively a reification of the text, and a refusal of its continued involvement in *any* social process.

Deconstructionist readings of genre may have been quick to point out the ideological work underpinning much New Critical theory of the short story cycle, but several went on to question the validity of any notion of genre at all. Arguments that genre relies on an identificatory signifier that must lie outside its own generic boundaries, or that intertextuality makes all texts an inescapably heterogeneous mix of generic codes, present a serious challenge to the continuing use of genre as a meaningful category in literary analysis—as critics such as David Duff have noted.[19] Yet a significant counterbalance to such deconstructions of genre can be found in materialist theories of history, which argue for genre's continuing relevance as an element of social interaction. Raymond Williams, for example, has discussed the significance of what he calls "conventions and notations," malleable rules that effectively structure social interaction in all situations, not merely those connected with cultural production. They provide the tacit procedures whereby people within the same society share a bond of understanding about how to greet each other on the street, handle cutlery, propose marriage, or have an argument (to choose some rather random examples). Within cultural production, conventions and notations provide social "relationships," continually "expressed, offered, tested and amended in a whole social process. . ." (*Marxism* 171–72). He then links this explicitly to genre studies, seeing genre as one of the most significant conventions within which such social relationships exist in cultural production. Genres do have an important function in social interaction and inform a shared range of understanding about literary typology within specific communities of readers and writers. Genre represents a site of constant, and specific, negotiation—between author, text, and reader, between expectations that exist around collective "conventions" and individuals, between discourses and communicative forms.

It is in this tension between the social understandings that structure representation (that is, what readers *expect* from a genre) and how writers reacting to the pressure of contemporary events or discourses respond to that expectation that the concept of genre gains one of its primary critical applications in historically based analysis.[20] As Tony Bennet has commented, genre criticism gains its use "as a means for analysing historically and culturally variable systems for the regulation of reading and writing practices [rather] than as a kind of writing amenable to a socio-genetic explanation" (81). Following such a model produces a genre criticism based around seeing genre as a dynamic system and one which uses genre as a tool for *interpretation.*

This seeks to eschew the view of genre as either a mode (that is, a transhistorical *affect*, or what Fredric Jameson calls a "generalised existential experience," such as comedy, tragedy, and so forth), or a particular set of structural coordinates (168).[21] Genres do, of course, exist across historical and material formations, but the changes they undergo, and the ways in which they generate meaning, are firmly embedded in the social and economic practices of reading and writing that exist at any particular time. It is at this juncture, then, that analyzing formal (including generic) and representational strategies used by Sherwood Anderson and Jean Toomer gives insight into the organization of power relations between 1916 and 1925 (the main period of this study) and the particular struggles and tensions that operated in this process, particularly along lines of gender and race.

It is partly for this reason that this book is not a generic genealogy of which texts influenced *Winesburg, Ohio* and *Cane,* and which works they in turn influenced. Instead, in examining the relation of Sherwood Anderson and Jean Toomer to the genre of the short story cycle, I maintain a pragmatic focus on the functional and rhetorical aspects of formal textual features that have commonly been associated with the form. Yet this will be accompanied by a sociohistorical contextualization and investigation of both genre and formal convention.[22] As Jauss suggests:

> The purely diachronic perspective . . . only arrives at the properly historical dimension when it breaks through the morphological canon, to confront the work that is important in historical influence with the historically worn-out, conventional works of the genre, and at the same time does not ignore its relationship to the literary milieu in which it had to make its way alongside works of other genres.
>
> The historicity of literature comes to light at the intersections of diachrony and synchrony. (37)

My approach attempts to center on this "intersection" of historicity in several ways. It explores the generic frames of reference within which *Cane* and *Winesburg, Ohio* were received by giving extended attention to the initial reviews of these texts and by examining the early literary criticism on Anderson and Toomer. In addition, I demonstrate how these authors engaged with and contributed to discourses of subjectivity formation, particularly those related to race and gender, and the effect this had on the elements of their textual practice that made their work so distinctive. Inevitably, this approach sometimes leads to the subject of genre dropping away from the surface of the discussion, often to the point of invisibility. Yet the rewards of this approach outweigh the disadvantages. In showing how the two authors struggle to imagine and narrate subjectivities that successfully negotiate the social realities of gender, economics, urbanization, and race, I examine the interrelationship and frequent interdependence of these categories, as well as the specificities they exhibited in the time period. In terms of genre, I hope to show how the triadic relationship between narrative, patriarchy, and the progressive view of history that underwent such a traumatic interrogation in the First World War informs much of the formal innovativeness of *Winesburg, Ohio*. For Toomer, I hope to show that the generic experimentation of *Cane* is closely involved with his fascination for theories of reading, and also to demonstrate that the racialization of the American cultural field (especially little magazine culture) in the early 1920s impacted on the formal choices of the text. For both writers, genre was a supple and a provocative aspect of what was most innovative in their literary practice, and one wherein both made some of their most powerful observations on the politics of identity.

RECEPTION AND DEBATES: *CANE*

If formal analyses have often been the ground for comparative studies of Toomer and Anderson, to engage in such a comparative study at present is made both difficult and engaging by the fact that *Cane* and *Winesburg, Ohio* have developed a very different critical heritage and a very different level of current critical appreciation. However, both have received a lot of *separate* formal analyses too; indeed, Henry Louis Gates Jr. has argued that *Cane* is a text that has attracted an unprecedented level of such analysis when compared with other African American texts of the period.[23] Many of Toomer's strategies—the formal and generic variety of the work, the lack of a consistent narrator, its separation into three distinct sections—have been linked to the social divisions within American society that the work confronts: between black and white, male and female, working class and middle class, urban and rural, Northern and Southern. Of these, racial divisions and formations have attracted the most attention, and *Cane*'s critical heritage in the past thirty years is an interesting reflection of the way in which the theorization of "race" has changed within the academy. Reprinted in 1967 during the Black Arts movement's drive to reissue African American texts, and thus consolidate both the notion and the availability of an African American canon, it was reissued with an introduction by Arna Bontemps in 1969, which replaced the original foreword by Waldo Frank. The assessments that followed often reworked Robert Bone's headline in the *New York Times Book*

Review in 1967 that *Cane* was "[t]he black classic that discovered 'soul,'" which had been "rediscovered after 45 years."[24] In 1971 Rafael A. Cancel claimed that he agreed with "most critics" of *Cane* in seeing it as "an affirmation of the Negro soul in an increasingly crushing civilization" (419), and in 1974 Houston Baker would remark that *Cane* was "an examination of the journey toward genuine, liberating black art . . . *Cane* reveals Toomer as a writer of genius and the book itself as a protest novel, a portrait of the artist, and a thorough delineation of the black situation" (54). Baker's position, and that of several others, suggested that *Cane* offered positive answers to what Addison Gayle Jr. had identified as the questions that must be posed to a text by the black critic working within a Black Aesthetic:[25]

> [H]ow much more beautiful has the poem, melody, play or novel made the life of a single black man? How far has the work gone in transforming the American Negro into an African-American or black man? The Black Aesthetic, then, as conceived by this writer, is a corrective—a means of helping black people out of the polluted mainstream of Americanism. . . . (Gayle 1876)

Moreover, the fact that Toomer would later attempt to disaffiliate himself from *Cane* and "Negro" literature was linked by several critics to the fact that he never had another book accepted for commercial publication. As Robert Brinkmeyer Jr. put it, "without the touch of the black soul, Jean Toomer was not an artist but a scribbler."[26] In a more nuanced position, which stressed both the significance of Toomer's mother and his African American heritage to the aesthetics of *Cane,* Alice Walker nonetheless noted that admirers of *Cane* could not help but be disappointed with the moral choice Toomer had made in choosing to "live his own life as a white man" ("Divided Life" 62). *Cane,* she felt, was his "finest work" but also the occasion of his "saying good-bye to the Negro he felt dying in himself. *Cane* then is a parting gift, and no less precious for that" ("Divided Life" 65). Toomer's artistic ability, so the argument goes, was contingent on whether he was admitting or denying the racial essence of blackness within himself, and his failed promise following the success of *Cane* was due to his rejection of a black identity.

Such positions tended to link aesthetic value to an accurate representation of an essentialized black subjectivity or black experience. In some cases, they went on to insist on the representation of black role models as a method of countering the demeaning and degrading subjectivities available to African Americans within the "polluted mainstream of Americanism." Just as with the Black Power political movement to which it was closely affiliated, the Black Aesthetic saw essentialized black subjectivity as a powerful tool in mobilizing African Americans against American social injustice enforced along racial lines. Yet more recently the debate has shifted, in light of theories that have sought to define "race" not as an essence but the result of a *process* of racialization. Such ideas have paid more attention to ways in which the racial subject comes into being through a historically and geographically specific set of discourses and relations, rather than the earlier tendency to view race as a transhistorical and transnational category. Building on the work of Frantz Fanon, it has also shown the significance of *recognition* within the psychological mechanisms of racial formation.[27] In one of the best essays dealing with the issues which this opens up for a consideration of Toomer, George Hutchinson contends that Toomer's career, his texts, and his critical reception indicate

> how the belief in unified, coherent "black" and "white" American identities depends formally and ethically upon the sacrifice of the identity that is *both* "black" and "white," just as American racial discourse depends upon maintaining the emphatic silence of the interracial subject at the heart of Toomer's project. ("Racial Discourse" 244)

Hutchinson goes on to see *Cane* as a text that offers the critic an "ethical challenge," in that it "reveals the significant silences of our own deeply racialized social text, the gaps and absences which critics, in turn, have failed to make speak" ("Racial Discourse" 245). Critics such as Ross Posnock have gone even further, using Toomer as a historical precedent to bolster his critique of the "identity politics" that have been at the center of American social politics over the past thirty years. Posnock argues that the social model of ethnic interaction within the United States that has achieved the greatest social currency within postmodernity—that of multiculturalism—is fast approaching bankruptcy within the academy, due to a recognition of "its tribal conception of politics founded on a romance of identity" (3). In such a climate Posnock feels that "at last Toomer's day has come. He has been hailed by one contemporary political analyst as a visionary prophet of a 'trans-racial American identity'" (30).[28] Reevaluating Toomer's work in light of its possible contributions to theoretical models and practices of "post-identity" has undoubtedly increased the amount of scholarly interest in Toomer in recent years. Moreover, it has also prompted the publication of much of his previously unprinted later work, in which these ideas are developed and given much more explicit expression than anything that appears in *Cane*.[29]

The recent emphasis on the politics and processes of racialization in Toomer's work has therefore often taken this "ethical challenge" as a starting point in readings of *Cane* and has sought to avoid discussing it as a text that celebrates or memorializes an essentialized black subjectivity fitting the coordinates of what J. Martin Favor has called "authentic blackness." Instead, the emphasis has shifted to examining those identities that are "neither white nor black yet both" that appear in *Cane,* identities that represent a crisis point in American racial discourse. Other readings go further, regarding it as a text that explores and challenges the epistemological and physiological foundations of racialization in early twentieth-century America with an unparalleled thoroughness.[30] My work takes the latter path but examines discourses of race, gender, and the body that have largely been overlooked in assessments of *Cane.*

This argument also considers how *Cane* was positioned within the cultural field, a project that continues recent trends in literary histories of the period. Texts such as Michael North's *The Dialect of Modernism,* Ann Douglas's *Terrible Honesty: Mongrel Manhattan in the 1920s,* George Hutchinson's *The Harlem Renaissance in Black and White,* William Maxwell's *Old Negro, New Left: African American Writing and Communism between the Wars,* and Kathryne V. Lindberg's "Raising *Cane* on the Theoretical Plane: Jean Toomer's Racial Personae" have all been keen to retrace the interconnections, exchanges, cultural common ground, and institutional points of juncture between African Americans and European Americans in the literary culture of the late 1910s and 1920s. This is partially in an attempt to reconfigure the division between New Negro Renaissance and Anglo-American modernism as less absolute than it has been treated in earlier literary histories.[31] This recent approach has resulted in a more thorough appraisal of the intellectual circles and communities within which Toomer circulated, as the majority of the writers with whom he associated were white. As George Hutchinson has rightly asserted, *Cane* is illustrative of the phenomenon that "the texts that do most to renovate literary traditions are often subversive of the very notion of tradition; their authors are not so much unitary figures inhabiting fixed cultural coordinates as liminal figures who straddle the thresholds of social difference and, like their multivalent talents, are difficult to pin down" ("Identity" 39). As Hutchinson observes, Toomer's liminality—principally between black Washington and white Manhattan—was a generative force for the iconoclastic strategies of *Cane,* as well as being an example of how interracial connections fed the cultural production of the 1920s in ways that have often gone unacknowledged.

Of course, it is important not to fall into a kind of utopian celebration of the generative potential of such liminality, which was marked by incomprehension as well as industry. White avant-garde artists in New York in the early 1920s were not free from certain aspects of racialized thinking that served to maintain racial divisions and suspicions within the cultural field, and Toomer received his fair share of incomprehension and prejudice there. Even those closest to him were guilty of this—Gorham Munson, Waldo Frank, and his publisher, Horace Liveright. Particularly complex and double-edged was Toomer's relationship with Waldo Frank, which has recently been extensively examined by several critics often keen to castigate Frank for his racial myopia and insensitivity to Toomer's highly unorthodox and nuanced racial identification. Yet Toomer gained much from this association, and Frank is far from the exploitative primitivist that he is sometimes caricatured as. Toomer's experience is perhaps best characterized as one of the most successful examples of what an interracial modernism could achieve in the 1920s—but its attendant misapprehensions, blunders, and incomprehensions also say much about the level of racial segregation in the U.S. cultural field of the time.

One of the most thorough recent histories of Toomer's intellectual networks is Charles Scruggs and Lee VanDemarr's book *Jean Toomer and the Terrors of American History.* As Scruggs and VanDemarr explain, their title emphasizes two of the forces—"terror" and "history"—which have been missing from much Toomer scholarship, a scholarship that has often been more interested in interpreting *Cane* in light of Toomer's later turn to Gurdjieffian mysticism. The presence of Gurdjieff within the critical frame has often led to "retrospective" readings, which argue that *Cane* represents Toomer's early yearnings toward a formally integrated, spiritual totality that would be made manifest in his commitment to Gurdjieff's thought from 1924 onwards. This approach of assessing *Cane* in light of Toomer's later thought has proved attractive to many critics, as it provides the opportunity for combining formal and biographical analyses of *Cane*—formal readings often bolstered by the explicitly structural and formalistic language that Gurdjieffian interpreters such as P. D. Ouspensky used to describe Gurdjieff's theosophy, and that Toomer avidly consumed.[32] Indeed, this is the methodology followed by rigorous book-length studies of Toomer's work such as Robert B. Jones's *Jean Toomer and the Prison House of Thought* or the detailed and illuminating biography by Cynthia Kerman and Richard Eldridge, *The Lives of Jean Toomer: A Hunger for Wholeness.* It is also a central point in Jon Woodson's reassessment of the significance of Gurdjieffian thought to the Harlem Renaissance as a whole in his *To Make a New Race: Gurdjieff, Toomer, and the Harlem Renaissance,* which traces the influence of Toomer's Gurdjieffian Harlem salons on writers such as Wallace Thurman, Nella Larsen, Zora Neale Hurston, George S. Schuyler, and Rudolph Fisher.

Scruggs and VanDemarr, however, argue that this approach masks two factors. The first of these is "the social and political milieus of the post–World War I period" that conditioned much of Toomer's thinking about the relation between culture, race, and representation (2). Primary among the "milieus" they seek to recover is the significance of socialism to Toomer during the period 1918–23 and also the fact that Waldo Frank's editorial assistance and political (rather than spiritual) agenda in *Our America* was a decisive force in the formation of *Cane*. The second factor that has often been omitted, the "terrors" of American history, is the word they use to describe the "open secret" of violence, miscegenation, and sexual abuse underpinning America's racial politics, a brutally delimited nexus of sexuality, race, and class that was never allowed complete public visibility or articulation. This leads to their discussion of *Cane* in light of the genres of the detective story and the Gothic, both literary modes where concealed knowledge is central.

At all points their analysis is conducted with extensive reference to archival material, and many of their conclusions about *Cane* are similar to my own. However, I hope to show how significant the emerging discourse of anthropology was to both Frank and Toomer, particularly in the way they conceptualized the South and, more broadly, the relationship between race and geography. This is a project initiated by the work of Susan Hegeman, who argues that Frank conceptualized a "spatialization of American culture" by drawing on the work of Boasian anthropologists who were beginning to articulate more relativistic views of how cultures related to each other.[33] However, she does not link this to Toomer's thought, nor does she assess how Frank's theories underwent particular pressures as a result of his trips to the South with Jean Toomer. An assessment of the dynamics of this trip, when considered in light of both anthropological discourse and ongoing debates at the outset of the New Negro Renaissance about representations of rural African Americans, provides a useful extension and revaluation of Scruggs and VanDemarr's work.

STUDYING SHERWOOD ANDERSON: "I WANT TO KNOW WHY"

Sherwood Anderson was interested in many of the same discourses and social questions as Jean Toomer: the future of race in modernity, the possibilities for transforming models of masculinity, to what degree the reader was the site of cultural production. Yet in stark contrast to the proliferation of debates around Jean Toomer and the ways in which he is assuming renewed relevance in a postmodern (or a post-postmodern, according to Posnock) cultural climate, the main question attached to Sherwood Anderson has seemed to be: why read him at all? This was the situation outlined by Arnold Weinstein in his chapter on Anderson in *Nobody's Home: Speech, Self, and Place in American Fiction from Hawthorne to DeLillo,* which cites Anderson's perceived provincialism as the main reason he has fallen out of critical favor. Weinstein might have added the reputation Anderson received in the 1980s as a writer committed to a misogynistic and binaristic view of gender difference, the unease or offense caused by almost all of his writing about African Americans, his commitment to a tradition of republican individualism that has been savaged by poststructuralist critiques of liberal humanism, or the rapturous plaudits he received in the early 1920s from American critics—plaudits that, in the light of the later solidification of the modernist canon, seem naïve and embarrassing. These are all substantial considerations for anyone working on Anderson, and yet much can be gained in addressing them not as problems that need to be evaded or dismissed before his merits can be assessed but as constitutive factors in his aesthetic practice and, more broadly, as representative of certain dynamics within the cultural field of American literature between 1916 and 1925.

Such a move, however, is not one that Anderson's critics have been generally keen on making. For example, Weinstein's answer to his own question is to cast Anderson as a mythopoeist, a writer whose provincial settings belie the way in which his language embarks on a "new kind of poetics in which disruption and displacement rules over a mixed field, linking figuratively what is unconnected on the surface, proposing a composite figure that regroups (and recoups) its discrete parts, fashioning a startling new script" (105). Rather than the "tunnel vision of a provincial mind," therefore, *Winesburg, Ohio* represents the creation of a "mythic poet for whom the village anecdote was, if you knew how to look and compose, cosmic event, for whom language, if you knew how to write, was power" (106–7). Such a view is a variation on William Sutton's early assessment that the virtue of *Winesburg, Ohio* is that it could have been titled "Winesburg, anywhere"—that is, that it represents a sensitive and accurate depiction of human situations, encounters, desires, and frustrations not limited to specific historical or geographical reference points (441). With Anderson, the argument goes, the provincial is the gateway to the universal, and this is broadly the assumption underlying two of the most recent book-length studies of *Winesburg, Ohio:*

Duane Simolke's *Stein, Gender, Isolation, and Industrialism: New Readings of Winesburg, Ohio* (1999) and Ray Lewis White's *Winesburg, Ohio: An Exploration* (1990).

Simolke concludes his study by finding that *Winesburg, Ohio*'s merit lies in its status as "a simple framed narrative about people needing simple human contact." For Simolke, *Winesburg, Ohio*'s worth therefore lies in the fact that it is a narrative that movingly imparts a moral staple of liberal humanism, as it "clearly reveal[s] the need for people to try to understand each other—not because they will succeed but because it will force them out of their dark alleys and decayed homes. It forces them to try to enter the lives and minds of others, to see the burdens of others" (111–12). Similarly, Ray Lewis White, while giving more detail about Anderson's contemporary reception and literary historical models, often employs the same methodology as Simolke. He also discusses several "epiphanies" in the text that refer to characters' sudden understanding or appreciation of a transcendental truth, the most well-remarked of which occurs between George Willard and Helen White at the close of the story "Sophistication." Such judgments—despite the fact that White's book discusses Anderson's critical reception, the biographical and material conditions of the book's publication, and briefly the literary field at the time—mean that the progression of significance is still from the provincial to the universal in searching for the reasons why Anderson should be read and studied.

Such work clearly pays testament to what was probably the golden age of Anderson scholarship, the 1960s and early '70s. This period saw several book-length studies appear on Anderson's work, collections of critical essays, biographies, critical editions of his writing (including Ray Lewis White's invaluable edition of Anderson's *Memoirs* in 1969), and articles on him in journals such as *PMLA*. In many ways this was because of the suitability of *Winesburg, Ohio* for New Critical study: its unorthodox formal structure as a short story cycle proved attractive to critics, provoking analyses of "its various 'tensions', 'paradoxes', and 'ambivalences'" and providing an excellent opportunity to demonstrate "how these are resolved and integrated by its solid structure," as Terry Eagleton has remarked of the typical methodology of the New Critics (*Literary Theory* 49). However, as Eagleton goes on to remark, this holistic and reifying treatment of texts meant that they "became a spatial figure rather than a temporal process," necessitating a "rescuing [of] the text from author and reader" that "went hand in hand with disentangling it from any social or historical context" (*Literary Theory* 48). Disconnected from such contexts (to which I will frequently refer) as the First World War and its political aftermath, the historical specificities of gender formation, the material conditions of the text's production, the enormous demographic and social changes in race relations during the 1910s and 1920s, and the proliferation of techniques of scientific management in factories, *Winesburg, Ohio* tended instead to be seen as a study in the universalism of provincialism, or the transhistorical psychological and social formation of "grotesques." As Edwin Fussell stated in 1960, in one of the most influential essay-length assessments of Anderson:

> [U]pon the possibility of there being in Winesburg such a contribution of intelligent judgement consonant with truths of broad applicability and thus qualifying and refining the vision of grotesque isolation, would seem to depend the book's chances of survival as more than a landmark of literary history. (105)

This is not to say that all the work on Anderson conducted at this time was so keen to stress Winesburg's "broad applicability," or "universalism," at the expense of its literary or cultural contexts. Yet the general tone of this period of the text's critical history does treat it as a work that holds history at arm's length, and this is an approach that, in some quarters, lasts today. Indeed, this is the criterion by which Charles Scruggs differentiates *Winesburg, Ohio* from *Cane;* he finds that Toomer "changed Anderson's nightworld of human personality in *Winesburg, Ohio* into the nightmare of racial oppression in *Cane*," and that it is a "tension between beauty and terror, created by a historical dimension not present in Winesburg, that gives *Cane* its special visceral power" ("Reluctant Witness" 77, 96).

However, several recent assessments have sought to relocate *Winesburg, Ohio* and Anderson to some of their significant contexts. Kenny J. Williams has presented an account of how Anderson related to the tradition of Chicago novelists and to fictional accounts of Chicago; he also assesses the imaginative space of the city in Anderson's work and its relation to the subjectivities of his characters. Feminist scholars such as Marilyn Judith Atlas, Nancy Bunge, and Clare Colquitt have all published essays on *Winesburg, Ohio*'s gender politics in light of Anderson's biography and discourses of gender current in the 1910s. T. J. Jackson Lears produced a subtle essay that discusses Anderson's quest for "authenticity" in relation to the advertising jobs he held for many years in Chicago. Lears's comments on Anderson's need to differentiate his creative writing from his advertising copy as part of a republican, individualistic sense of wishing to preserve language from commercialization, and his delineation of his masculinity through his workplace activities, proved very instructive. Equally insightful was Thomas Yingling's materialist critique of *Winesburg, Ohio,* which sees it as the representation of the collective nature of small town society being eroded by the rapidly developing technologies of industrial capitalism, and the struggles of the townspeople to (unsuccessfully) recapture some form or social experience of community. Kim Townsend's biography of Anderson in 1987—the first comprehensive biography in thirty-seven years—also provides a valuable resource for treating Anderson in relation to his social and cultural contexts.

RESPONDING TO THE CRITICAL HERITAGE: SHERWOOD ANDERSON, JEAN TOOMER, THE SHORT STORY CYCLE, AND DISCOURSES OF RACE AND GENDER

My work on Anderson takes its starting point from T. J. Jackson Lears's notion that working practice and gender were central to Anderson's views on literary production. This is bolstered by Casey Nelson Blake's work on the Young American critics, who were producing their most influential early work at the same time as Anderson's emergence onto the American literary scene. These critics, most notably Van Wyck Brooks and Waldo Frank, were involved with the periodicals that initially promoted Anderson, and they represented intellectual contacts and influences that would last throughout his career. Their theories on what they saw as problematic divisions between American working practice and both cultural expression and community provided a grounding for Anderson's antimodernistic thought about the virtues of a more organic social model for America. This in turn led to his nostalgic celebration of the "heroic artisan," an ideal of masculinity whose heroism was based in the ability to integrate productive labor with aesthetic "authenticity" in the process of *craft*. This celebration had extensive bearing on his thought about African Americans and on his conception of gender identity.

In chapter 1, I discuss how the close relationship between masculinity and autonomous producerism was most evident in Anderson's own authorial persona as a craftsman/writer and how this relationship is placed under severe strain in *Winesburg, Ohio*. Although the issue of the representation of women has been assessed in *Winesburg, Ohio,* little work has been done to assess the nature of masculinity presented in the figure of George Willard and just how contingent this masculinity is on a practice of artistic and narrative control. Such a practice is polarized from both women and homosexuality; the gay subculture in Chicago at the time Anderson was working on the stories undoubtedly informed much of his thought about "authentic" writing and the portrayal of homosexuality in the text. Yet in *Winesburg, Ohio,* the figure of the confident, masculine narrator or artist—which Anderson often likened to the artisan in control of his materials—is embattled not only by the constant need to be differentiated from homosexuality and femininity but also by the historical circumstances within which it was written. The First World War, an event that, as many commentators have noted, placed pressure on the social understanding of both masculinity and narrative, provides a crucial subtext to the gender politics of *Winesburg, Ohio.* This has rarely been addressed, and yet it is a consideration that bears extensively on the formal strategies of the short story cycle Anderson went some way toward developing.

In chapter 2, I assess how Anderson's often antimodernist sentiments led to a tendency of imaginative "othering" to conceptualize alternatives to the alienating modes of production of industrial capitalism. In addition to his historical "othering" of the heroic artisan, as the 1920s progressed he would add the racial "othering" of African Americans. This was done in the belief that African American communities and working practice represented an enviable organic and patriarchal social experience, one that integrated cultural production with labor in a fashion Van Wyck Brooks felt white America had lost. Anderson spent a lot of time listening to African American work songs at the docks of New Orleans and Mobile, in sugar refineries in Louisiana, and on turpentine plantations in Mississippi, and the wistful primitivism evident in his recollections of these occasions has often led to embarrassed silence on this issue on the part of his critics. Yet Anderson's representations of African Americans provided a way of mediating a host of issues that his critical heritage has often returned to: his depictions of gender, his critique of industrialism within American modernity, his imagination of American geography. Nonetheless, within this process of mediation, Anderson exhibits the mixture of fear and desire about "blackness," the ontological need for what Toni Morrison has called an "Africanist presence" along with the compulsion to disavow that need, which has so often marked white American cultural production and which is particularly evident in white American modernism. Establishing the particulars of some of these issues therefore gives valuable insight into the nature of primitivism in the 1920s and an assessment of an element of Anderson's career that has been neglected for too long.

Chapter 3 continues this analysis of white configurations of racial and cultural difference but turns the focus onto the conceptualizations of region that fascinated Anderson, Toomer, and Waldo Frank. The anxiety Anderson felt about African American communities in the North and his praise of

New Orleans as "the most cultural town in America" both have similarities to the new spatialization of cultural difference being promoted by American anthropology in the 1910s and 1920s—a move that in many ways informed the rise in literary interest in the South. Deeply interested in anthropological methodologies of observation and textualization, Waldo Frank in particular sought geographical pockets of cultural identity distinct from what he called the "hegemony of New England," pockets he believed would assist in the forthcoming social and cultural revolution that he hoped would transform America (*Our America* 75). Such methodologies informed his trip to the South with Jean Toomer in 1922 and also his novel of that experience, *Holiday;* yet Frank's thinking about cultural authenticity, interracial observation, and the textualization of cultural difference began to concern Jean Toomer at this time—concerns that are made manifest in *Cane.*

Chapter 4 begins at this point, examining Toomer's confrontation with organicist, Romantic notions of black subjectivity in the South and also his response to the rapidly forming picture of black southerners emerging from ethnographic study. Both of these approaches tended to consolidate a view of an "authentic" black subjectivity as rural, southern, and working class, a view about which Toomer was at best ambivalent. Toomer's initial enthusiasm for Waldo Frank's model for cultural politics as outlined in *Our America* shifted into disquiet over Frank's racial politics, a process evident in Toomer's engagement with the complex issue of the status of the black voice within literature. At the time, the black voice in literature was a phenomenon connected particularly with the use of black dialect in minstrelsy and plantation fiction. However, the accurate representation of dialect was also central to the methodology of the Boas school of anthropology. Both of these discourses saw represented speech as arguably the main ground for assessing the "authentic," both in terms of the authenticity of the representation and the authenticity of the "blackness" that was its object. Toomer would eventually become suspicious of the methodology of anthropology for engaging with and ultimately textualizing discrete cultures, a suspicion that was at least partially responsible for his break with Waldo Frank. Instead, Toomer's response to the vexing question of how the black subject could speak within literature was essentially *meta-textual;* that is to say, *Cane* consciously politicizes the issue of where such literature as itself appears, and who is reading it, to a degree that virtually eclipses the significance of what the black subjects within the narratives actually say.

In the final two chapters, I examine the strategies Toomer investigated as a way out of this representational and racialized impasse. On the one hand, he sought discursive parameters that could disturb the overdetermination of the black body, which troubled the essentialization of the black subject. One such strategy emerged from Toomer's keen interest in discourses of physiology and physical training, and his engagement with new thinking about the relation between the organic and the mechanical that was evident in avant-garde European art movements. I argue that these provided him with a powerful critical model for examining the ways in which racialization operates on the body and also informed his fantasies of how this could be refused. Another point of focus in chapter 5 is the consideration of how gender interacts with race and class in *Cane*. Debates about gender—and specifically the representation of women in *Cane*—have never been far from the forefront of its critical heritage. Many initial assessments took Toomer's representation of women in *Cane* (in part one in particular) as crudely primitivistic. In assessing figures such as Karintha, Carma, and Louisa as representative of "the varying degrees of beauty found within the lives of blacks who live close to the soil," Toomer's women were often seen as embodiments of an essentialized "racial memory," in the words of Benson and Dillard (68).[34] Yet in the 1980s several feminist and womanist critics took Toomer's seeming reduction of these women's identities to their sexuality as indicative of the long history of sexual exploitation and commodification of African American women within the United States. Rather than accusing Toomer of a primitivistic essentialism that connected promiscuous sexuality among black women to a racial "soul," they argued that Toomer's presentation indicated sensitive historical insight. Specifically, they praised his awareness of the way in which African American female subjectivity had been delineated within centuries of patriarchal and racist discourse.[35]

More recently, much work on the New Negro Renaissance has examined the "intersectionality" of class, gender, and race in the formation of subjectivities, and assessments of Toomer in this regard have extended the work of critics such as Alice Walker and Nellie Y. McKay. In particular, critics such as Vera Kutzinski and Laura Doyle have developed the examination of the historicity of *Cane*'s gender politics by discussing its critical heritage in both the New Negro Renaissance and the Black Arts movement. They argue that much of *Cane*'s reception in these eras interpreted Toomer's presentation of African American female southern subjectivity as some kind of bedrock for a program of cultural nationalism, an interpretation that fundamentally misread Toomer's belief that such subjectivities were historically and culturally specific. As Kutzinski puts it, "Toomer's women, most of whom are lower-class mulattas tainted by some sort of illicit sexuality, are beautiful, innocent and pure only when situated outside of history" (169). This beautiful innocence is a product of the agenda of *Cane*'s various male narrators, who "need carefully to filter out emotionally and ideologically troubling histories of sexual and economic abuse" in order for these women to represent culturally and spiritually pure figures (169).[36] Scruggs and VanDemarr broadly concur; they perceive that "each story in *Cane*'s first section is about the pressure, communal sexual, or familial, that men put on women. . . . The women in *Cane*'s first section must attempt to negotiate an identity within the context of "relations" with both black and white men" (139).

These are valuable and insightful reassessments of *Cane*, yet they have tended to downplay the formation of masculine subjectivities in the text, and certainly have not given any sustained attention to the historical circumstances surrounding the formation of masculinity between 1918 and 1923. This has recently begun to be rectified by Siobhan B. Somerville, who devoted a chapter of her *Queering the Color Line: Race and the Invention of Homosexuality in American Culture* to an assessment of the figure of the "queer" in Toomer's writing. She sees figures such as David Teyy in "Withered Skin of Berries," Paul in "Bona and Paul," and Lewis in "Kabnis"—who are all often described in the text as "queer"—as mediatory figures exposing and channeling "the other characters' unpredictable and unconventional desires, manifested simultaneously in cross-racial and same-sex attraction" (149). Somerville is right to note Toomer's frequent textual reliance on male protagonists who orient desire across racial and same-sex prohibitions, an ability often due to their ambiguous racial or sexual identification. Yet her reading does not attend to an early experience in Toomer's life that centered around the (virtually literal) construction of masculinity, namely his involvement with physical culture, an episode that underpinned much of his later thought about the relation between the body and subjectivity.

This involvement has recently been assessed by Martin Summers in his valuable study of how black bourgeois masculinities underwent a period of transition in the 1920s—primarily as a result of a burgeoning culture of consumption, display, and physicality.[37] Yet what Summers does not explore in great detail is that the emphasis that physical culture placed on masculinity as essentially specular, as founded upon the *attainment* of a physical image, seemed to offer Toomer a discourse by which his society's ways of marking the body as gendered or racialized could be erased. Building the body offered an agency that contradicted the commonplace determinism that equated the raced and sexed body with destiny. If, as proponents of physical culture such as Bernarr MacFadden proclaimed, masculinity (or "manhood") was something that could be lost, or regained, and if (as critics such as Gail Bederman have convincingly argued) racial identity was a crucial component in the constitution of masculine subjectivities, then physical culture problematizes discourses of race that posit it as immutable and essentialized. In this way, and through these experiences, Toomer had a sense of what Judith Butler has called the "morphological imaginary" of the body. He wrote of the intersection between aesthetics, gender, race, and the body with a sophisticated understanding of the cultural semiotics of the physiological. Yet he was also aware of how American culture was troubled by bodies with multiple, or illegible, markings.

Another aspect of Toomer's "intersectionality" in relation to gender, which chapter 5 seeks to examine, is the significance of the figure of the bastard to *Cane*. The absence—or refusal, in some cases—of a patronymic legitimacy on the part of *Cane*'s protagonists is closely linked on several occasions to the aggressive rejection of either a previous generation or an existing legal/ethical situation; as Kabnis states, "a bastard son has the right to curse his maker" (*Cane* 85). Such statements function as a simultaneous admission and disavowal of kinship, which stress the existence of a paternal line of inheritance, yet emphasize the difference of their irreverent offspring. This interest in the biologically and socially illegitimate in *Cane* also functions to expose the economic and social significance of patrilineage and biological hereditary in general, especially where interracial heredity is concerned. As Scruggs and VanDemarr have noted, often the "open secret" that *Cane*'s textual structure and texture works around is that of interracial bastardy, or miscegenation: frequently, they argue, this secret suggests a hermeneutic reading strategy prompted by the question "who is the father?"

However, what they do not go on to discuss is that bastardy in *Cane* is generally something experienced or claimed by men, but which of course is conferred by women, by the many mothers in *Cane*. As is soon obvious, the power of this conferral is often countermanded by the shaming of these women within their communities for breaching the codes of public sexual conduct in having illegitimate children—exemplified most obviously by Becky, the white woman who lives in isolation with her two illegitimate, part-African sons in a portion of "eye-shaped sandy ground" between railroad and road (*Cane* 7). Yet this view of women as in a constant, if limited, negotiation of power with their patriarchal and racially segregated society provides an alternative view of the women of *Cane* that seeks not to objectify them—either as primitivistic or sexualized objects, or as aesthetic objects so constituted because male narrators had denuded them of all historical content. This, I hope, will provide a useful counterbalance to the common dichotomous thinking about gender to which *Cane* has often been subjected.

The second major strategy that Toomer explored to resituate the dilemmas inherent in representing the black voice arose from his intense interest in the racialization of readership, *Cane*'s place in the literary field, and the interaction of text-units within *Cane*—issues I explore in the final chapter. Toomer was well aware of the racially bifurcated nature of the literary audience for his work, a bifurcation James Weldon Johnson neatly summarized as the "dilemma of the Negro Author." This dilemma was facing—and writing for—"more than a double audience; it is a divided audience, an audience made up of two elements with different and often opposite and antagonistic points of view" (Johnson, "Dilemma" 477). Accordingly, one of Toomer's ambitions for *Cane,* as he wrote to Waldo Frank, was "developing a public, large or small, capable of responding to our creations," a readership that Toomer hoped would not be determined along racial lines (*Letters* 59). This ambition saw him engage in a unique practice of self-positioning within the cultural field of the little magazines proliferating in the United States at the time. This was a positioning remarkable in its diversity, and in the number of personas Toomer adopted to accord himself with the wildly various editorial policies of the little magazines to which he submitted work. This attempt at transcending the ingrained racialization of readership also drew on work among some of the Young American critics in what would now be called reception theory, and Toomer's thinking about readership and the racial dynamics of the cultural field provided some of his most subtle interrogations of American racial politics and culture.

As I have outlined, there is much in the historical and contextual analysis of these two authors that has been overlooked. In what follows I hope to combine analyses of the ways in which race and gender are constituted with a detailed level of attention to the texts, institutions, and intellectual relationships that surrounded Anderson's and Toomer's story cycles. Such a methodology—like those to which I have set my project in opposition—is inevitably partial and interpretative. It places the politics of personal identity at the center of how the relationship between cultural production and society is conceptualized. Yet by bringing both authors back into contact with the ideas of their time and with the processes that produced raced and gendered identities, what follows not only redresses omissions in the scholarship on the individual authors themselves but also illustrates much about the cultural field of the late 1910s and early 1920s. Moreover, it provides a new perspective on the innovative formal strategies that have always been at the core of critical appreciations of the texts. By examining these two authors together, I demonstrate that their ideals about the future of masculinity—particularly where this related to machine technology, racial identity, and processes of embodiment—were much more central to their respective projects of cultural criticism than has previously been argued. Both authors saw themselves as representative men; in 1923, Anderson would write Van Wyck Brooks that in his forthcoming work he was "frankly daring to proclaim myself the American man," claiming that he would "take all into myself if I can—the salesmen, businessmen, foxy fellows, laborers, all among whom I have lived," to present himself as "a kind of composite essence of it all" (*Letters* 104). Toomer, three years earlier, had proclaimed himself the "First American" (*Wayward* 120). The differences between the men—racial, intellectual, generational—caused their strategies toward formulating and defining such "representativeness" to be widely different. Yet a comparison between the methodologies, the motivations, and the results of their respective projects provides a significant contribution to the understanding of the gender and racial politics of the time, and to its relation with American literary history.

CHAPTER 1

NARRATIVE, GENDER, AND HISTORY IN *WINESBURG, OHIO*

Gender—or what he called the "man-woman thing"—was a career-long obsession for Sherwood Anderson. Much of his fiction centered on the confusion, disillusionment, misunderstanding, and lack of communication that occurs in heterosexual relationships, a preoccupation that nonetheless emphasized the significance of those relationships for individual happiness. In *Winesburg, Ohio*'s critical reception, the failure of heterosexual relationships has often been cited as the main reason for the "grotesque" nature of several of Winesburg's inhabitants, and his three novels of the 1920s—*Poor White* (1920) *Many Marriages* (1923), and *Dark Laughter* (1925)—sometimes read like quest narratives on the part of their male protagonists as they search for the right woman. Yet what was seen in the 1920s as his radicalism on sexual themes—an early review claimed his fiction was "of a character which no man would wish to see in the hands of a daughter or sister"—has in the past thirty years more often been seen as a restrictive conventionality (*Winesburg, Ohio* 164). His frequent insistence on an absolute differentiation between men and women relied on binaries such as activity/passivity, or culture/nature, which feminist criticism has long identified with patriarchal culture. Marilyn Judith Atlas accuses him of ignoring the potential of the feminists and independent-minded women he had met in bohemian Chicago, including his second wife, Tennessee Caflin Mitchell (herself named after the famous suffragist and feminist); instead, he populated Winesburg without a single woman "who wants, and is able, to form her own life" (264). Nancy Bunge has criticized Anderson's simplistic nostalgia for a supposed golden age of sexual relations, and Clare Colquitt has noted Anderson's depiction of a "community of men who in Winesburg define, exploit and understand women's desire for expression only in sexual terms" ("Motherlove" 94). Most harshly (and most famously) Susan Sontag described the tone of the book, which determines these depictions of gender, as one that condemned it to obsolescence and even unreadability; she argued that it was "bad to the point of being laughable but not bad to the point of being enjoyable," due to being "too dogged and pretentious" and lacking "fantasy" (284).

Such criticisms are substantial and well merited, and this aspect of Anderson's work has doubtlessly contributed to the decline in his critical fortunes. Yet not enough work has been done to demonstrate what contested terrain this conception of gender represents, and as a crucial structuring principle of his sense of self and his artistic practice, gender was something that affected the narrative poetics, the reading dynamics, and the racial politics of *Winesburg, Ohio* in ways that have not been significantly examined. This chapter will assess two historical factors that had considerable impact on the gender politics of Anderson's text. There has been a lack of attention to the fact that *Winesburg, Ohio* was written during the First World War—a time of what Kaja Silverman has called historical trauma, i.e., the feeling that something outside of oneself has intervened to question what had previously been a relatively stable set of "dominant fictions" of personal (and specifically gender) identity. It is this, I shall argue, that was implicated in many of the formal innovations of *Winesburg, Ohio;* it is a text that marks a distinctly different approach to narrative and gender than can be seen in the rest of Anderson's writing, even in comparison to the texts that immediately preceded and followed it.

Moreover, the binaries of male/female, masculine/feminine, and active/passive were both enabled and regulated—often in letters or memoirs revealing a mixture of anxiety and desire, or affiliation and disavowal—by the figure of the homosexual, or, as Anderson put it, the "fairy." By looking at Anderson's letters written during the war and his memoirs of life as a laborer (and later a writer) in Chicago, particularly those that address Chicago's increasingly visible gay subculture, I hope to show how Anderson's biographical experiences of the sexual culture of an industrial, urban center were vital to the narrative poetics of *Winesburg, Ohio*. This is not to say that *Winesburg, Ohio* can be understood purely biographically—although I would agree with Gertrude Stein's assessment of Anderson's novels that "you do a little tend to find yourself more interesting than your hero and you tend to put yourself in his place" (*Anderson/Stein* 27). Anderson's sense of his own gender identity was terrifically reliant on his ability to write fiction, and it is the precariousness of this relation that transfers into the character of the nascent writer George Willard in *Winesburg, Ohio* rather than any direct anecdotal correspondence between them. Moreover, this precariousness was a situation exacerbated by the challenges that World War One was offering to normative notions of gender and progressive narratives of all kinds.

"A STRANGE UNHEALTH IN MYSELF": *WINESBURG, OHIO* AND THE FIGURE OF THE FAIRY

Any account of *Winesburg, Ohio*'s engagement with the gender politics of the 1910s must recognize the centrality of homosexuality to this engagement, particularly in light of the new forms that gay culture was taking in America's urban centers in the early twentieth century. Moreover, the degree to which Anderson used homosexuality as a functional category for positioning his own masculinity has often been lost in accounts of his sexual politics, as has his recurrent celebration of homosociality in the military that World War One was to so seriously challenge. Indeed, those critics who have discussed the representation of homosexuality in Anderson's work have tended to reduce it to merely an *effect* of a masculine/feminine binary, by treating male homosexuality as essentially coextensive with feminized men. Often, these critics can then discuss this binary as resolvable in an "ideal" of androgyny. Duane Simolke, for example, remarks that George Willard's contact with gay men in *Winesburg, Ohio* leads to his ability to "transcend gender roles in order to show compassion and solace" (83), to become "more than man or woman" as described in the *Winesburg, Ohio* story "Tandy." Bidney follows a similar train of argument, seeing throughout the collection an urge towards "androgynous synthesis"; it is the general failure of this process that results in Winesburg's "grotesques" (264).[1]

However, when these critics see Anderson as striving to "transcend" gender, or "fuse" gender, they inevitably take the elements that are to be transcended or fused as in some ways naturalized, rather than produced and regulated by a set of historically specific discourses and ideologies. More to the point, they do not suggest how this "androgyny" in any way relates to the disparity in social, economic, and political power that exists between the men and women of Winesburg. These critics are right to assume the significance of homosexuality to the masculine/feminine binary in Anderson's work, but wrong to wholly subsume it within this binary by their frequent conflation of femininity with homosexuality. Instead, "homosexuality" as a socially understood category, or its historical equivalents, to a large degree enables this binary through the way it influences a wide range of social conduct. This is evident in Anderson's autobiographical writing, and it plays a pivotal role in *Winesburg, Ohio.*

The centrality of homosexuality to both Anderson's gender politics and his sense of selfhood can be seen in his comments on the open and public homosexuality within Chicago's bohemia, and also in his autobiographical account of the interrelation between homosexuality and the process of composing *Winesburg, Ohio.* The latter was included in Anderson's account of his stay in a rooming house at 735 Cass Street in Chicago during the "Robin's Egg Renaissance" of avant-garde literary production in the city. There, he lived among a bohemian community of artists, writers, and actors he later affectionately dubbed "the little children of the arts." During the winter of 1915–16, in which he stayed there, he wrote the majority of the stories in *Winesburg, Ohio,* the first work in which he was sure he had found his "vocation" (*Memoirs* 353). Yet, as with much of his writing, it was clear that the stories partly arose from a complex set of cultural and personal circumstances affecting gender subjectivity. In his memoirs, he commented, "It may be that I had been too much with business men, advertising men, laboring men, men who felt the practice of the arts in some way unmanly. These new people [of the rooming house], in some way a bit hard to explain, emphasized in me, shall I say, my maleness" (348). Significantly, earlier in this section of the memoirs, Anderson records meeting a woman on the steps of the rooming house; she was dressed as a man and crying over a failed love affair with another woman. This was part of "somewhat strange relations going on about me. . . .Whether there was actually any of what is commonly called 'perversion' in the house I don't know" (347). In identifying the space of his rooming house as "strange" and possibly "perverse," Anderson depicts an environment against which his "maleness" gains definition. Indeed, this group of people "emphasized. . . [Anderson's] maleness" through what he perceived as their difference, a difference which he admits contributed to both his psychological well-being and his artistic productivity.

Yet elsewhere in his *Memoirs*, it is clear that this "difference" was often difficult to establish, and this difficulty, which deeply unsettled Anderson, was often provoked by his encounters with Chicago's gay community. Anderson's indefinite and vague terminology in the above quotation gestures toward the often indefinite nature of precisely what types of behavior or practices indicated "perversions" within same-sex relationships and, by association, what indicated a normative notion of patriarchal and heterosexual masculinity. As Eve Kosofsky Sedgwick has discussed, it was precisely the indefinite nature of what constituted deviation from normative gender expectations that made homophobia a force capable of regulating large elements of male social activity, and Anderson records an instance of this in his *Memoirs*. It occurred when Anderson first moved to Chicago from rural Ohio as a young man and was involved in what George Chauncey has termed the "bachelor culture" of young, unmarried, and often itinerant laboring men working in American cities at the turn of the century. In this environment "fairies"—whom Chauncey describes as men who both engaged with other men in sexual congress and adopted an exaggeratedly "feminine" persona—were both visible and to a considerable degree tolerated.[2] Yet the identity of the "fairy" was determined more by his "feminine" attributes, his gender "inversion," than by his sexual object choice, and fairies often signaled their "feminine" attributes through a specific set of dress and codes of behavior.[3] It was the fairy, Chauncey argues, that formed "the central pejorative category against which men had to measure themselves as they developed their gender and their sexual style," and it was in Chicago that Anderson first became aware of such fairies' visible and public homosexuality (*New York* 61). This occurred on an occasion when he and his other workmates in a North Side warehouse jeered at a group of passing fairies:

> . . . these others, these of the city house on the street of the warehouse. They came by our platform sometimes in groups, they had painted cheeks and lips. The others, the workmen, the truckmen on the platform with me, shouted at them.
>
> "Ah, you Mable."
>
> "Why, if that isn't Sweet Little Sugar." . . .
>
> Once when I was alone on the platform (it was late fall and darkness had come) one of them stopped and spoke to me. He approached and whispered to me.

> "Don't you want to come and see me some night?"
>
> I didn't move. I was shocked and a little frightened.
>
> "I have had my eyes on you. You do not shout insults at us as the others do. You know where I live. Do come some night. There is so much I could teach you."
>
> He went off along the street, turning to throw a kiss at me, and I stood dumbly staring at him.
>
> What did it all mean? I felt a strange unhealth in myself. I was not angry and I am quite sure that, when this happened, I felt even a kind of pity. There was a kind of door opened, as though I looked down through the door into a kind of dark pit, a place of monstrous shapes, a world of strange unhealth. (My ellipsis; 339–40)

Anderson's language here reveals two things. First, it indicates his shocked and disturbed recognition of the perverse nature of desire (both his own desire, and the open expression of homosexual desire on the part of the fairy), and by perverse, I mean the ability of desire, as Dollimore puts it, both to "disturbingly unfix . . . identity" and to act as a liberating force ("Bisexuality" 258). This moment carries an anxious undertone, one that questions to what degree his vision of these "monstrous shapes" is a factor in their constitution, to what degree his recognition of this "unhealth" is implicated in his own subjectivity. Second, and within the more strictly social framework of this experience, his refusal to partake in the jeering of the fairies along with his workmates marks him as different, and possibly homosexual himself; indeed, this is the factor that initiates his solicitation. Moreover, when he refers to the "others," he means—in successive sentences—both the fairies *and* his fellow workmen, thus placing himself in an indeterminate position somewhere in between. In both of these aspects, Anderson's experience can be discussed in terms of what Eve Kosofsky Sedgwick has called "homosexual panic." She defines this as a development of secularized homophobia, a panic that effected and effects much of the "regulation of the male homosocial bonds that structure *all* [public or heterosexual] culture" ("Beast" 150). Sedgwick continues:

> [N]ot only must homosexual men be unable to ascertain whether they are to be the objects of "random" homophobic violence, but no man must be able to ascertain that he is not (that his bonds are not) homosexual. In this way, a relatively small exertion of physical and legal compulsion potentially rules great reaches of behavior and filiation.
>
> So-called "homosexual panic" is the most private, psychologized form in which many . . . western men experience their vulnerability to the social pressure of homophobic blackmail. ("Beast" 151)

This panic was to a great degree explicable by the social and legal sanctions placed upon homosexual conduct at the time, which (as Weiss and Schiller examine) could and did lead to social ostracism, dismissal from the workplace, or jail.[4] Typically, Anderson's recourse from this "homosexual panic" was to link patriarchal masculinity to working practice. As T. J. Jackson Lears has commented, "true to the republican tradition, he linked the construction of masculine identity with productive labor" ("White Spot" 27–28). For example, when Anderson was living at 735 Cass Street, the "little children of the arts" emphasized his "maleness" not merely because they were "strange" but because they became objectified within his writing, forming the models for many of the characters in *Winesburg, Ohio*. Indeed, his remasculinization was as reliant on this appropriation of their characters in his fiction as it was on what he called their possible sexual "perversion"; as he said, "The idea I had was to take them, just as they were, as I felt them, and transfer them from the city rooming house to an imagined small town . . ." (*Memoirs* 348).

This "emphasizing" of "maleness" through the labor of creative writing was part of his belief that the creative imagination must be involved in the workplace environment in order to maintain the quality of "maleness." As he wrote, "when you take from man the cunning of the hand, the opportunity to constantly create new forms in materials, you make him impotent. His maleness slips imperceptibly from him . . ." (*Story Teller* 195). This often led him to describe writing in terms of a craft, descriptions that nostalgically linked him to an imaginatively creative, producerist tradition of male labor. He described his craft as being with fragmentary observations of human behavior, which he believed represented "the materials of the story-writer's craft, these and the little words that must be made into sentences and paragraphs; now slowly and haltingly, now quickly, swiftly . . ." (*Story Teller* 292). Anderson's celebration of craft, and the establishment of its literary correlative in his commitment to resolutely noncommercial fiction, would consistently be at the center of his discussions of masculinity, as I shall discuss both in this chapter and the chapter assessing his engagement with primitivism.

As Lears has noted, at the polar opposite of this approach to story writing was the advertising copy Anderson wrote to support himself for most of his life in Chicago. This, Anderson felt, was manufactured, inauthentic writing, and a degradation of the "craft" of writing creative prose. In consequence, he linked it to homosexuality; he records an episode when he and a colleague at the Taylor-Critchfield Advertising Agency who shared this sense of contempt for their profession (and therefore themselves) would address each other as "Mable" and "Little Eva" as recognition of the fact that they were "little male whores. We lie with these business men" (*Memoirs* 414).[5] Indeed, they would deliberately go to a local working-class saloon and address each other by these names, at which they were ridiculed as fairies—a ridicule that provided "a kind of satisfaction for us" (415). He remarked to Waldo Frank at the time that "how I, living and working day after day in a business office for so long have escaped a kind of queer insanity, I don't know."[6] As Lears points out, "the basis of Anderson's ideal of literature—and the source of both its strengths and weaknesses—was his determination that his fiction would be as unlike his ad writing as possible" ("White Spot" 26).

This episode indicates the degree to which Anderson linked gender identity to writing practice but also that he was involved in a *strategic* use of the semiotics of homosexuality (or more specifically a "fairy" identity) to define himself as masculine. It could be used to demarcate aspects of his life or work that he felt to be "inauthentic" (Lears discusses Anderson's relation to homosexuality in terms of his pursuit of "the real" in his fiction), the mundane necessities of earning money, or situations where Anderson felt he had troublingly little agency. Indeed, this use of homosexuality as central to the definition of both masculinity and authentic creative writing was evident in his tributes to the contemporary writer whom Anderson (arguably) admired most, D. H. Lawrence. In America, at least, these two authors were often compared: Lawrence had a similar interest in working-class masculinity, the relations between industrial capitalism and sexuality, and the interplay between the homosexual and the homosocial. In addition—in spirit if not always in detail—the two often exhibited a shared impulse towards primitivism, misogyny, and homophobia, issues that have recurred in Lawrence's critical reception to an even greater degree than they have in Anderson's.[7] Anderson was aware of these similarities and saw the revitalization of masculinity for the modern age as being at the core of Lawrence's project. Following Lawrence's death, Anderson praised him because "[y]ou feel man flesh in his words," and for leading "a male life fighting for an old thing maleness once meant" ("Man's Mind" 22). Yet such "maleness" could only gain definition with the straw man of homosexuality in the picture; indeed, Anderson felt the need to lambaste the "homo-sexual" to add to the luster of Lawrence's "essence" of creativity and maleness. Lawrence, Anderson believed, was "the perfect antidote for the lesbian and homo-sexuality of our day."[8]

By engaging with the semiotics of "fairiness," then, as well as keeping the figure of the "homo-sexual" visible in his work, Anderson aimed to prove the solidity of his own heterosexuality. Indeed, stressing his lack of fear about being perceived as homosexual became a way of signifying his confident and self-assured heterosexual masculinity.[9] He wrote suggestively of the homoeroticism of male friendships, yet simultaneously disavowed any homosexual subtext to the nature of such a relationship; he wrote to his friend Roger Sergel that "[a] man, to be my friend, must attract me physically, not as a woman does, in a special way. We modern men are afraid of facing that fact" (*Letters* 325). This type of simultaneous encouragement and disavowal of same-sex desire was important to Anderson as a way of escaping the constricting regulation of "homosexual panic"; yet it did not indicate a view of gender as multiple, labile, or polymorphous. Instead, it served to shore up his definitions of masculinity and femininity as complementary opposites and his own identity as masculine as beyond the questioning that his culture would normally have given to such "fairy" behavior. This practice recalls remarks Judith Butler has made *apropos* the relationship between heterosexuality and drag; drag, she argues, is not necessarily a practice that subverts heterosexual hegemony. Rather, it can be

> functional in providing a ritualistic release for a heterosexual economy that must constantly police its own boundaries against the invasion of queerness. . . . this displaced production and resolution of homosexual panic actually fortifies the heterosexual regime in its self-perpetuating task. (126)[10]

This notion of a certain semiotics of "queerness" as being invoked in a ritualistic and *public* display to effectively police and consolidate heterosexual and masculine hegemony further prompts consideration of Eve Kosofsky Sedgwick's work. Specifically, it brings to mind her thesis from *Between Men: Male Desire and the Homosocial* onwards that patriarchal social formations are often underpinned by triangular relations involving two men and a woman, rather than a simpler model of binary opposition between male and female. As she remarks:

> Large-scale social structures are congruent with the male-male-female erotic triangles described most forcefully by [René] Girard . . . in any male-dominated society, there is a special relationship between male homosocial (*including* homosexual) desire and the structures for maintaining and transmitting patriarchal power. (*Between Men* 25)

This theory forms a central part of her project to explore how a homo/heterosexual definition has been a "presiding master term of the last century" in ineffaceably marking a whole series of other binary terms that underpin Western culture (*Epistemology* 11). In relation to Anderson, it can be argued that his use of a "fairy" persona, or engagement with the semiotics of "fairiness," becomes what Sedgwick has called "material or rhetorical leverage," which exerts considerable force in contests for discursive power (*Epistemology* 11).

These structures are also evident in Anderson's fiction. In *Winesburg, Ohio,* many of the binaries Sedgwick cites are highly significant, especially in George Willard's growth into adult masculinity and into being an "authentic" cultural producer—in this case, a writer. These binaries are often reducible to the association of masculinity with activity and femininity with passivity. This binary underpins various differentiations Anderson makes on the basis of gender: these include the activity of the writer/craftsman as against the passivity of the materials; geographical, social, financial, and personal mobility against stasis and stability; and a phallocentric, penetrative sexuality against a passive, receptive one.[11] George's growth to maturity and socialization provides the narrative space within which much of the constitution of these polarities takes place, as well as the potential for their subversion or self-contradiction. Moreover, as I shall go on to examine, Anderson's project to polarize masculinity and femininity in *Winesburg, Ohio,* done in the service of consolidating a patriarchal masculinity, requires the third term in the triangular structure, the "leverage" of queerness, to enact its operation.

This is nowhere clearer than in the opening story (and the fact that it starts the collection provides it with additional structural significance). "Hands" deals with a character who is socially and geographically peripheral to the town, Wing Biddlebaum. Wing was hounded out of the Pennsylvania town in which he was a teacher, after allegations by the town's parents of his sexual interest in his male students. In Winesburg, he does not "think of himself as in any way part of the life of the town where he has lived for twenty years," and he lives outside of Winesburg next to a ravine (9). As Simolke has remarked, the story shows how Anderson "exploits the human fears regarding sexuality and social identity, as well as the tendency to blame others for those fears" (29), and Simolke is right, I think, to note that Wing never regards (or recognizes) his own organization of desires as homoerotic (a point also made by Yingling). Yet homoeroticism was clearly the issue, as Simolke and William L. Phillips note; Anderson made revisions of "Hands" that toned down the language concerning Wing's desire for George Willard, and he confided to Van Wyck Brooks that "dozens of men have told me privately that they know Wing Biddlebaum" (*Letters* 60; qtd. in Simolke 76). Wing's house, outside of Winesburg's society and geography, marks him as both liminal and visible: moreover, it is sited on the edge of the ravine, which indicates his proximity to social and cultural oblivion. In this position he serves as what the critic D. A. Miller has called an "open secret":

> The open secret keeps a topic like homosexuality in the private sphere, but under surveillance; allowing it to hover on the edge of public visibility. If it gets fully into the open, it attains public recognition; yet it must not disappear altogether, for then it would be beyond control and would no longer effect general surveillance of aberrant desire. (Qtd. in Sinfield 47)

Indeed, this situation of liminality *and* visibility is evident in the first paragraph of "Hands," as Wing is observed and taunted by a group of young workers as they pass on their way home from work. Wing, therefore, clearly has a regulatory function that is significant to George's growth into "manhood," a regulation clear in the conflation of geography and sexuality. Wing's geographic marginalization effectively marks the boundary of the geography of desire within which George can operate if he is to remain within the hegemonic territory of heterosexuality. Moreover, his hands become a synecdochic representation of his "aberrant" sexuality; when he is hounded out of the town "he did not understand what had happened [but] he felt that the hands must be to blame" (13). This synecdoche comes to determine his public persona; his story is a "story of hands," and they are his "distinguishing feature, the source of his fame" (10). His identity is reduced to his sexuality, in contrast to the normalized gendering of the heterosexual inhabitants of Winesburg, and this reduction serves as a regulatory caution to the development of George's sexuality in the collection.

THE CRAFTING OF GENDER: WRITING THE BODY

Wing is a significant early figure in setting parameters for licit and illicit forms of sexuality, and throughout the collection there are moments when George or other male characters undergo extreme psychological reactions as a result of fearing that they may have somehow transgressed the lines which separate these forms. Moreover, Wing's typification as the antithesis of a normative heterosexual masculinity is partly achieved by his passivity and inactivity—he paces the veranda of his house, anxiously awaiting the arrival of George Willard, who never comes. As I shall discuss in this section, the differentiation of gender identities for Anderson was to a large degree contingent on the allocation of creative cultural activity as the exclusive property of heterosexual masculinity, an allocation that often relied on the link between craft and masculinity. Yet this presented two pressing difficulties for Anderson. First, it required women to be designated as the objects of culture, a designation Anderson perpetually struggled to maintain. Second, the World War was occurring as Anderson was writing *Winesburg, Ohio,* a war that raised the question of how men could continue to exhibit "manliness" in an essentially defensive war that relied on extended periods of enforced passivity in the trenches and destruction by the dehumanized forces of modern technology, such as long-range artillery and machine gun fire.

Within the parameters of licit sexuality defined by *Winesburg, Ohio*'s liminal positioning of same-sex attraction, male/female interaction is foregrounded in the text as the main force in structuring George's growth into adult masculine subjectivity. Indeed, the visible "open secret" of the sexuality of figures such as Wing serves an imperative function, impelling difference between masculine and feminine to be absolute to a degree that would be impossible without such a presence. For example, in the much-discussed story "The Teacher," the high school teacher Kate Swift feels she has seen a "spark of genius" in the young George Willard and "wants to blow the spark" (89). The channeling of female ambition—Kate is an intelligent, literate, traveled, independent woman—into the agency of a male author is perhaps just the most striking of many examples of the link between agency in narrative (that is, the ability to either be an active protagonist in a narrative or to engage in the writing of narrative) and masculinity that recurs throughout *Winesburg, Ohio*. As Anderson wrote later in his memoirs, "In reality women have no desire to DO. Doing is for them a substitute. Their desire is to BE. There was never a real woman lived who did not hunger to be beautiful. The male desires not to be beautiful but to create beauty" (554: see also Atlas 253). For Anderson, it follows, "real" masculinity was dependent on the idea that women could only be the object, and never the subject, of representation.[12] Moreover, if, as Chauncey has examined, "fairies" were often discussed in the same terms as women—in terms of lack, passivity, and diminutiveness—then in Anderson's rationale, becoming "like a woman" was to become like the "little Eva" of his barroom role-play. Creativity and the writing of "authentic" narrative therefore became the way to forestall homosexual panic, and in Andersonian logic, if women desire to be beautiful and men want to create beauty, then real men must want to create women.

This reinforces the link Anderson made between work and gender identity. As he said, "manhood . . . finds its full fruition only in work" ("Lawrence Again" 100). His ideal of masculinity is similar to what the historian Michael Kimmel has identified as the "heroic artisan," a remarkably durable model of masculinity based around craft, workplace autonomy, and a patrilineal apprentice system (*Manhood* 28–31). Indeed, this model was particularly attractive to antimodernist writers and critics such as Anderson, as it offered a resonant figure for nostalgia in an age of the division of labor, Fordist and

Taylorist principles of factory organization, and the continued erosion of small-scale production. The "Heroic Artisan" model draws currency from the act of transforming a precultural form of materiality—whether a piece of wood, lump of iron, or block of stone—into cultural material. This is analogous to what Peter Brooks, in his book *Body Work: Objects of Desire in Modern Narrative,* has found to be true of the relations between the body and writing. He identifies as prevalent within the Western tradition a tendency to view the body as a form of pre-cultural materiality, a view that provides a "sense of the body's otherness" which "leads to the endeavor to bring the body into language, to represent it, so that it becomes part of the human semiotic and semantic project . . ." (8). Moreover, it follows that in a patriarchal society, the female body is doubly othered—both as the "other" to "the human semiotic and semantic project" and to maleness—and hence is most sought after for representation, whereas the "male body is ostensibly deproblematized, decathected as an object of curiosity or representation" (*Body Work* 15). So, in *Winesburg, Ohio,* we are frequently given descriptions of the bodies of women, especially if they are a possible sexual partner for George Willard, whereas George's body is not an object of curiosity or representation. It is but a short step from this politics of representation to John Berger's formulaic statement about the scopic economy of patriarchy: "men act, women appear" (47).

A sense of the endeavor to bring the body into writing—or to use Anderson's schema, to "craft" the female body into fiction—is clear in Anderson's work. Brooks notes that "narrative desire, as the subtending dynamic of stories and their telling, becomes oriented toward knowledge and possession of the body," and I would argue that for writers as committed to a patriarchal order as Anderson this dynamic becomes fundamentally gendered (8). Creation, knowledge, and possession are all forms of proprietary control which promise that what is "female" can be both fixed and used in the service of male desire and patriarchal masculine identity. This writing of the female body thus becomes part of the patriarchal economy of the *propre,* what Hélène Cixous has defined as the "reductive stinginess of the masculine-conjugal subjective economy," which centers itself on notions of property and propriety (259).[13] Yet, paradoxically, the textualization of the body draws attention to its absence, "since the use of the linguistic sign implies the absence of the thing for which it stands" (Brooks, *Body Work* 8). Accordingly, in several accounts Anderson explicitly depicts this project for the representation of the female body as a compulsive one but one doomed to failure and constant repetition:

> I would have been on my bed the night before, her lovely figure floating through my mind, and then, words coming, would have jumped out of bed to put them down.
>
> The words on the paper, in the night. How lovely they seemed. Sentences marching, figure of speech, forest. . . .
>
> Where are you now, woman? (*Memoirs* 383. Anderson's ellipsis.)

Here, the female figure becomes a figure of speech. The materiality of her body is erased in the process of the substitution of sign for presence—a substitution at the heart of all representation. Moreover, this process is linked to the phallic forest and the order of masculinized, militaristic sentences. In this quotation Anderson suggests that the project of representing the female body is the dynamic force propelling his narrative, and is central to his own sense of his "manliness," but that the impossible nature of this aim compels its endless repetition. Indeed, he once stated of writing, "The struggle is never ending. There is no peace. Always you are dissatisfied, seeking and seeking" (*Memoirs* 546). As Jonathan Dollimore has noted about binary constructions of identity, "[B]ecause its terms are vulnerable to inversion and its structure (via inversion) to displacement, the continued existence of the binary is never guaranteed; it has to be maintained, often in and through struggles over representation" (*Dissidence* 64). Throughout Anderson's work the struggle on the part of his male protagonists and tacitly male narrators to represent or to know women is repeated again and again, yet it is the *process* of that struggle rather than its results that testifies most evidently to Anderson's wish to essentialize gender.

Winesburg, Ohio seems to present this process in a more direct and interrogative fashion than any of Anderson's other texts. The degree of emotional and representational energy directed toward the female body by the various male writers and narrators of *Winesburg, Ohio* testifies to the huge investment (to borrow Cixous's economic terminology) that heterosexual masculinity has in writing the female body. Moreover, by discussing gender and the project of writing fiction in a fashion that suggests their mutually constitutive nature, he tentatively edges towards the implication that an essentialized view of gender may, in fact, belong to a fictional order and not a precultural realm. His most famous *Kunstlerroman, Winesburg, Ohio* plays out this nexus of gender identity and representation, and at the time when Western modernity was undergoing one of its most intensive periods of pressure on normative definitions of gender—the First World War. As Pierre Macherey comments, literature is characterized by its tendency to gesture toward ideological formations that can never be spoken or articulated directly, and therefore it is the gaps in the novel that the critic must make speak to reveal the formulations of that ideology. It follows that at the times when that ideology is under severe strain, the gaps and the gestures will be all the more obvious. This occurs in the gender politics of *Winesburg, Ohio*, which I turn to next.

"IN EVERY LITTLE THING THERE MUST BE ORDER": ENGENDERING THE NARRATOR IN *WINESBURG, OHIO*

> There's a strange strain of the girl in [Sherwood Anderson's] brash masculinity—and hence doubtless have come not alone his beauties but as well all the troubles and contradictions.
>
> **—WALDO FRANK TO JEAN TOOMER (1923?)**[14]

Many critics have noted the compulsive search for order, or meaning, that runs through much of Anderson's work. Claire Colquitt has also linked this to Anderson's politics of gender, noting that the desire for control through art in Anderson's writing is an explicitly masculine one; she notes that for Anderson, "only the artist can impose order and meaning on an essentially meaningless world, one in which both God and mother have died" ("Motherlove" 86). In *Winesburg, Ohio* this is most evident in the story "An Awakening." Early in the story, on the night streets of Winesburg, George fantasizes about being a military inspector admonishing his men: "Everything must be in order here. We have a difficult task before us and no difficult task can be done without order" (101). In his mind, this ordering law "begins with little things and spreads out until it covers everything. In every little thing there must be order, in the place where men work, in their clothes, in their thoughts. I myself must be orderly. I must learn that law" (101). Entry into the knowledge of this law offers George the alluring possibility of imposing order on an otherwise random environment. The system of "order" shown in the quotation above, for a youth inflamed by literary pretensions, is clearly a system similar to structuralist conceptualization of language in its privileging of "place"; following the Saussurean formulation, every object, person, or word gains entry and meaning in this system of order through being in the correct "place," a place identifiable only in relation to others. Later in the story this is developed, and the system of order becomes explicitly narrative in its basis:

> For a year he had been devoting all of his odd moments to the reading of books and now some tale he had read concerning life in old world towns of

> the middle ages came sharply to his mind so that he stumbled forward with the curious feeling of one revisiting a place that had been a part of some former existence. (102)

By placing himself and his environment within this narrative sequence, George becomes even more "excited" by the sense of his own power in controlling previously unconnected phenomena; he feels "unutterably big and remade by the simple experience" (102). This intoxicating sense of his own knowledge leads him to say words "without meaning," "rolling them over on his tongue and saying them because they were brave words, full of meaning. 'Death,' he muttered, 'night, the sea, fear, loveliness'" (102). George's play with words simultaneously "without meaning" and "full of meaning" shows his double awareness of their polyvalent and potent nature as signifiers but also indicates that they become worthless as signifiers without a syntactic context. In this way he plays with the materials of his newfound mode of order, deciding where to place them in his narrative scheme, wherein they will gain significance. This heady empowerment only intensifies George's desire to create order through narrative, which centers on the objectified body of Belle Carpenter; George hopes to "achieve in her presence a position he had long been wanting to achieve" (102). The double entendre of this quotation exemplifies well the way in which Belle simultaneously becomes an object of sexual desire and a figure in a set of linguistic relations, able to be repositioned and recontextualized by George to achieve a different meaning. George feels a "sense of masculine power" (103) in his walk with Belle up the hill to the fairground, a power grounded in his certainty that masculinity has the ability to provide order to events, to write the script; at one point, quite independently of any indication on her part, he suddenly decides "that Belle Carpenter was about to surrender herself to him" (103)—clearly the necessary event to advance the story he had imagined.

However, George's self-aggrandizement and egoism are ridiculed by the fact that Ed Handby throws him into the bushes, grabs Belle Carpenter, and marches her away. Indeed, "George Willard did not understand what happened to him that night on the hillside. Later, when he got to his room, he wanted to weep and then grew half insane with anger and hate" (104). "Insanity" seems here to indicate George's fear that he has gone beyond the limits of acceptable difference, limits beyond which (as Sander Gilman and others have shown) negative stereotypes of race, sexuality, and illness overlap and reinforce one another.[15] It also seems to confirm Sedgwick's thesis that fear and shame of acting in an "inappropriate" gender role are highly effective psychological mechanisms for policing a large range of social behavior. The story clearly ridicules the possibility of one individual imposing "his story" upon others; stories and agencies interact in more complex ways than George allows for. But while ridiculing its simplicity, "An Awakening" also suggests the inevitability of George's impulse; his self-conception is reliant on narration as a mode of empowerment and gender identification. This compulsion to tell and narrate centers around the female body, and when its objectification and inscription are disturbed, George is faced with the "half insanity" of a breakdown in the normative practices of gender that structure his subjectivity.

The pattern of a futile, masculinized search for order, significance, and the legible female body is staged repeatedly throughout *Winesburg, Ohio,* particularly in the two stories that have perhaps the closest sequential and thematic links, "The Strength of God" and "The Teacher." The stories focus on successive attempts to "read" Kate Swift's body by either George Willard or Curtis Hartman in order to place it in a system of significance. Hartman, working in the bell tower of the church and looking at Kate Swift's "white shoulders and bare throat" (82), is troubled by his own "carnal desire" (83) but attempts to regain a sense of control and knowledge by placing this body in a Biblical narrative of trial: "The Lord has devised this temptation as a test of my soul and I will grope my way out of darkness into the light of righteousness" (84). However, how he interprets the body of Kate Swift on his crucial night of decision in the middle of winter provides him with "what he took to be the way of life for him" (85). With soaking feet and having sat in the cold tower for hours waiting for Kate Swift to reappear, uncertain of God and of himself, Hartman's epistemological crisis takes on a physical dimension. He had "come near dying with cold": drifting into unconsciousness, several times he needs "by an exercise of will power to force himself back into consciousness" (85). He is at risk of the ultimate loss of control and reduction to passivity, that of death—the analog to the selflessness Gilbert and Gubar found nineteenth-century patriarchal society prescribed as the ultimate feminine virtue (Moi 58). However, at this moment Kate Swift becomes "readable" and seemingly available as an object of knowledge as Hartman sees her praying naked on her bed. This scene presents her as a signifier in a narrative of transcendental truth, as a "remasculinized" Hartman explains to a bewildered George Willard:

> "I did not understand," he said. "What I took to be the trial of my soul was only a preparation for a new and more beautiful fervor of the spirit. God has appeared to me in the person of Kate Swift, the schoolteacher, kneeling naked on a bed. Do you know Kate Swift? Although she may not be aware of it, she is an instrument of God, bearing the message of truth." (85)

In Hartman's new narrative perspective of his own life, Kate Swift's naked body has become a symbol of God's truth, a narrative that both the reader and George see as delusional. However, it is the only mode by which Hartman is able to rescue himself from crisis. The "signing" of Kate's body enables him to control its threatening potential; as Brooks says, "Signing or marking the body signifies its passage into writing, its becoming a literary body, and generally also a narrative body, in that the inscription of a sign depends on and produces a story" (*Body Work* 3). Through Kate's inscription as an "instrument of God," Hartman both reads and writes her body into a narrative that reestablishes his sense of self-control and masculine identity. Although this reading is obviously erroneous and fanatical, it is clearly also a necessity in a society where the only possible role for a Presbyterian minister is one of heterosexual, monogamous masculinity.

In the subsequent story, "The Teacher," George Willard also views Kate Swift as an object of both sexual desire and knowledge; his "lustful thoughts" (86) about her are linked to his incomprehension of her character, as he "could not make out what she meant by her talk" (86). Indeed, shortly after his muttered intention to "find out about you. You wait and see" (86), he embraces a pillow and thinks of her; her staged and fetishized embodiment is inseparable from his desire to "read" her. It is also the story in which the fantasy of male control through the exercise of imaginative power seems closest to being realized. Kate's status as a doubly seen and objectified body seems to impel her to actions in which she has no control: "It was past ten o'clock when Kate Swift set out and the walk was unpremeditated. It was as though the man and the boy, by thinking of her, had driven her forth into the wintry streets" (88). Here the lines of division between the author in control of what actually occurs in his material, the narrator, and the aspirant author-character George are as thin as anywhere in the text; the fantasy of being able to write one's own life story, and write other people in and out of it at will, is momentarily indulged in during a moment where the imperative of wish fulfilment seems to override the literary codes of realism. However, this generic rupture with realism also serves as a reminder of the textuality of the story and thus the inherent fluidity and instability of its signification. As a result, the legitimation of this fantasy is called into question just as it receives its most forceful articulation.

Another voice enters the scramble for appropriation in the next paragraph by the imaginative re-creation of Kate Swift by the narrator:

> At the age of thirty Kate Swift was not known in Winesburg as a pretty woman. Her complexion was not good and her face was covered with blotches that indicated ill health. Alone in the night on the winter streets she

> was lovely. Her back was straight, her shoulders square and her features were as the features of a tiny goddess on a pedestal in a garden in the dim light of a summer evening. (88)

In such transformations, which recur consistently in Sherwood Anderson's fiction, Clare Colquitt finds that Anderson's real subject is not the nature of beauty or femininity but "the transforming power of artistic genius" ("Reader as Voyeur" 189).[16] By using the image of a woman being transformed into works of art, "the narrator/artist can effectively ignore the political realities facing [women] by making one woman's life a poetical whole" ("Reader as Voyeur" 189). Once again, however, this masculine strategy of control is revealed as flawed. At the end of the story George's quest for knowledge has been frustrated: "He could not make it out. Over and over he turned the matter in his mind" (91). Similarly, "When he became drowsy and closed his eyes, he raised a hand and with it groped about in the darkness. "I have missed something Kate Swift was trying to tell me," he muttered sleepily" (91). The ambiguity of "groping" suggests both groping for knowledge and for Kate Swift's body; both have eluded him, but the desires are conjoined.

The structure of the two stories also contributes to articulating this strategy as flawed; as J. Gerald Kennedy has noted, "By splitting a potentially single narrative into two stories, Anderson accentuates the solipsistic quality of his characters' lives" ("Winesburg" 199). Splitting the "potentially single narrative" also accentuates the polyvalency of Kate Swift's body by separating the different "readings" of it. Only briefly do Hartman's and George's readings enter into the same fictional space, and when they do, George believes "the town had gone mad" (91); their monologic desires and readings are irreconcilable. This struggle for control is staged throughout these two stories, and when we consider Hartman's view of Kate as "an instrument of God," George's belief that "she might be in love with him" (86), and the narrator's comment that her "eagerly passionate soul" (89) transforms her into a statuesque "tiny goddess" (88), we see her status as a subject recede to the point of invisibility as she is inscribed and reinscribed into various systems of male interpretation. Yet through their juxtaposition, each of these systems is recognized as inadequate, reducing a complex character to a simplistic semantic value. These attempts at apprehension of Kate Swift make her inapprehensible, and if we as readers attempt to recover the "real" Kate Swift from these inscriptions, we replicate the masculine strategies of George, Curtis Hartman, and the narrator. Kate's status as existing only in the perspective of others is foregrounded, as is the dubious nature of the voices that struggle over her.

This foregrounding of inadequacy, however, paradoxically reaffirms the desire to keep trying, to keep reaching toward representing the elusive object of desire that is both erotic and a promise of some ultimate meaning. It is this desire that animates Anderson's narrative, George's ambition to become a writer, and the reading strategies the text holds open most explicitly. Indeed, such strategies attempt to maneuver the reader into the dynamic of seeking continuity and order through the assumption of an explicitly masculine approach, and it is the significance of the choices made by the reader that informs the next part of my discussion. *Winesburg, Ohio* seems to perpetually promise a level of significance and ultimate meaning behind a veneer of metaphor and symbol, and it is a particular feature of the short story cycle form that it both generates and frustrates desire for totalizing meaning. These features account for much of the formal novelty of *Winesburg, Ohio,* yet they were a product of the gender anxieties that I have been describing, anxieties that exerted considerable pressure on existing representational models.

"THE READER AS VOYEUR": "COMPLICITOUS" READINGS OF *WINESBURG, OHIO*

Through its repeated use of metaphor and cryptic narratorial direct address, *Winesburg, Ohio* rhetorically presents to readers a specific set of loci in which they are invited to participate in the creation of meaning. For example, Wing Biddlebaum's story is a "story of hands" (10), Enoch Robinson's story is "the story of a room almost more than it is the story of a man" (92), and the "paper pills" Doctor Reefy collects in his coat pockets with "odds and ends of thoughts" (16) scribbled on them have their significance emphasized by the title of the story and their recurrence in its final sentence. By the use of such methods, significance is very obviously announced but not explained; as Weinstein comments, this provides a discourse where the "polished surface is maddeningly significant" (97). The suggested reading strategy provided by such a style is to accept the hermeneutic challenge set by the narrator, but the very rhetorical nature of this symbolism serves to alert the reader's consciousness to the interpretative act they are performing.

Even more "challenging" than the use of symbolism are the statements by the narrator about the significance of certain events but without any indication of what that significance might be. For example, in "Mother," Elizabeth Willard watches a conflict between Abner Groff, the baker, and a cat in the alleyway outside her room window:

> Once when she was alone, and after watching a prolonged and ineffectual outburst on the part of the baker, Elizabeth Willard put her head down on her long white hands and wept. After that she did not look at the alleyway any more, but tried to forget the contest between the bearded man and the cat. It seemed like a rehearsal of her own life, terrible in its vividness. (17)

The seeming incongruity between this scene and Elizabeth's situation as a frustrated and imaginative woman in an unhappy marriage, suffering from poor health, makes the final sentence in the above quotation a particularly enticing one for the interpretative exercise, and failure to offer a credible interpretation has sometimes produced a tone of indignant hostility towards Anderson from his critics. In his review of *Winesburg, Ohio* in the *New York Tribune* (reprinted in the Norton Critical Edition of the book), Heywood Broun commented, "Oftentimes we are not with Anderson" (160), and in response to the last sentence in the quotation from "Mother" given above, "We never knew quite why" (161). However, perhaps the statement of this kind that has attracted most attention has been the one that occurs at the end of "Sophistication." This statement is heavily coded as "significant" in several ways. One is its structural position, as Rigsbee has noted, in that it occurs at the end of the penultimate story, the last story before the short and rather formulaic "Departure," which focuses on George leaving Winesburg (186). It also gains emphasis from the fact that it deals with the thematic core of George's meeting with Helen White, the woman long identified as the main object of male desire within the text, and also from the tone of the story, which suggests that this is the most significant interpersonal encounter in all of the stories in *Winesburg, Ohio*. The passage runs as follows:

> For some reason they could not have explained they had both got from their silent evening together the thing needed. Man or boy, woman or girl, they had for a moment taken hold of the thing that makes the mature life of men and women in the modern world possible (136).

As Rigsbee notes, "The tone and placement of this passage make it clearly a key thematic statement; yet, there is very little clarity in the passage itself or even in the story about exactly what the 'thing' is that Helen and George have experienced" (186). Several critics have proffered explanations: Glen E. Love finds it exemplifies Anderson's credo that true communication is achievable not in language but "in the feelings, in a common bond of human sympathy" ("Silence" 54). White believes that "there is no closer bonding possible than this quiet acceptance and trust between George and Helen, between two people who silently recognize each other's individuality and integrity. This is true maturity, true sophistication . . ." (*Winesburg* 49). Edwin Fussell sees the "thing" as "the realization that loneliness is a universal condition and not a uniquely personal catastrophe; love is essentially the shared acceptance by two people of the irreducible fact, in the nature of things, of their final separateness" (113). For Ralph Ciancio it is the reconciliation of "the despair that comes from learning that man is a finite and grotesque creature" with "knowledge of 'the sweetness of the twisted apples,' a more genuine and elevating kind of sophistication that both presupposes and negates the first" (1005). For Rigsbee, it is "a product of their mutual treasuring of those tender, vital feelings that Anderson associates with the feminine" (186).

The plurality of interpretations indicated here—and there are others—not only shows the ambiguity of the statement. It also denotes its self-referentiality as a statement of importance that *requires* interpretation and thus creates a definite place for the reader within the text. Umberto Eco's concept of the model reader is relevant here; the model reader is the reader envisioned by the author, one who shares the same codes and assumptions as the author and is thus "supposedly able to deal interpretatively with the expressions in the same way as the author deals generatively with them" (7). What this implies, as Kay Boardman notes in her discussion of Robert Allen, is that the model reader is "a textual place and therefore a property of the text, rather than a truly hypothetical reader" (201). However, if we as readers accept this "place" by making an interpretation of these particular textual features, we become what Boardman defines as a "colluding" reader, or what Colquitt calls a "complicitious" one: a reader who accepts the most obvious or enticing reading strategy or "place" and by doing so accepts certain ideological assumptions which that place involves. In this case, the place of the "model reader" is gendered and masculine, as the project of interpretation, "making sense," and the unification of semantic subunits that this offered place involves is defined as masculine throughout the text, as I have discussed. This offer of a collusive reading strategy that entails a masculine gendering of order and unity is perhaps most obvious in the earlier story "Nobody Knows."

In that story, what most critics have supposed to be the sexual encounter between George and Louise is marked by an ellipsis, a jump from George and Louise sitting on a pile of boards by Will Overton's berry field to George getting back on to Main Street much later that night.[17] Of course, narrative always functions through the interplay between elision and selection, but every ellipsis requires an effort on the part of the reader to fill the gap; as Eco comments, this means "the reader collaborates in the course of the fabula, making forecasts about the coming state of affairs" (32). In fact, there is no textual evidence that a sexual encounter does occur; Louise's note to George, "I'm yours if you want me" (28), is ambiguous at best. At the end of the story, George "laughed nervously. 'She hasn't got anything on me. Nobody knows,' he muttered doggedly . . ." (29), which is no more definite. The irony is that nobody *does* know; in possibility, anything may have happened.

The construction of meaning here is entirely dependent on what Eco describes as "inferential walks," namely intertextual reference to "already recorded narrative situations . . . analogous 'topoi,' themes, or motives" (32). The "inferential walk" that has often been made by critics in this situation—that is, their inference that a sexual encounter took place—is one that treats a depersonalized, aggressive masculine sexuality as an acceptable norm, something to "be expected" in this particular narrative situation. In consequence, if the supposition that a sexual encounter did occur is made without reflection, then the reader becomes complicit with an attitude of male aggression, of the reduction of woman to the status of sexual object, or as Colquitt phrased it in her fine analysis of the reading dynamics of Anderson's "Death in the Woods," with the "'vast calamity' of masculinist convention . . ." ("Reader as Voyeur," 190). The text gestures toward its silence; nobody knows, but "we" can guess "what happened"; but by examining "our" guess "we" encounter not just the ideology of the text in its construction of such a space but a reminder of "our" own ideological conditioning.[18]

The masculinization of interpretation that the text offers here is inseparable from an aesthetic of the organic whole, and the nascent writer George's activities of making legible, unifying, and writing are closely linked. When the text has been discussed as a "unified" collection of stories, it is usually discussed within the tradition of the *Bildungsroman* or *Kunstlerroman,* with the ability to "unify" attributed to George's role as a writer, both of fiction and journalism.[19] To Elmer Cowley, George's role as the newspaper reporter means that he "belonged to the town, typified the town, represented in his person the spirit of the town" (107). Doctor Parcival tells George, "If something happens perhaps you will be able to write the book that I may never get written" (27). The masculinization of narrative, obvious in George's experiences in "An Awakening," is also reflected in "Departure." When he leaves Winesburg, he perceives of it as a "background on which to paint the dreams of his manhood" (138), an aestheticization of experience that again allows for the creation of an artistic whole. Reflecting the argument that all notions of unified identity or aesthetics are inherently phallocentric, an idea most famously advanced by Hélène Cixous and Luce Irigaray, George's problem of aesthetically unifying both Winesburg and his own conception of self is predicated on the essentialized difference of Helen White. In their encounter in "Sophistication," "what he felt was reflected in her" (134), and the elemental feature of their mutual experience is that "I have come to this lonely place and here is this other" (135). It is her essential "otherness," the binary polarization between masculine and feminine reinforced by this encounter, which "renewed and refreshed him" (135).

This "renewal" is of the masculine identity George has been struggling to achieve throughout the collection, and it is completed through a revitalizing reflection of difference. Anderson's image of reflection here evokes the tradition of feminist thought on the necessity of "femininity" for the definition of boundaries of "masculinity," a tradition that has often used the mirror as its figure for this operation. One thinks, for example, of Virginia Woolf's observation that women have "served all these centuries as looking-glasses possessing the magic and delicious power of reflecting the figure of the man at twice its natural size" (45) or Irigaray's description of masculine specularization, which makes women "waste or excess in the little margins of a dominant ideology, this mirror entrusted by the masculine 'subject' with the task of reflecting and redoubling himself" (104). George's legitimation within the world of art and the correspondent "refreshing" of a unitary masculinity necessitates the mirroring function of Helen: the only seemingly readable female body in the entire text therefore becomes an exercise in narcissism. With this epistemology, George totalizes Winesburg and essentializes gender.[20] Yet if this is a precarious state of totality and security with which to end the text, it is all the more so as we are told that Winesburg is a painted background; once again (as with Belle Carpenter and Kate Swift) Anderson cannot invoke his conception of female subjectivity without drawing attention to the framing structures of representation within which these subjectivities exist.

The imperative of a totalizing knowledge and a practice of representation that are tacitly masculine is therefore implicit in both George's growth into manhood and the reading dynamic toward which the text gestures the reader. Moreover, this collusion of the reader in engaging in a masculinized practice of interpretation is implicit not only in the hermeneutic "challenges" I have been discussing but also in the generic structure of the text. As a short story cycle, *Winesburg, Ohio*'s combination of separate text units invites the reader to make connections, to engage in a process of finding similarities. J. Gerald Kennedy has argued that "lacking a continuous narratorial presence, the [short story] sequence—like the decentered modernist novel—places the reader in a strategic position to draw parallels, to discern whatever totalizing meanings may inhere in the composite scheme" and that this process "enhances the pleasure of the text" ("Winesburg" 196). This may go some way to explaining why the task of establishing the unity of *Winesburg, Ohio* has always attracted critics, especially those grounded in "the holistic assumptions of New Criticism" (Kennedy, "Winesburg" 195). Unifying features have been seen to include George as the *Bildungsroman* protagonist, the universal application of the theory of Grotesquerie established in "The Book of the Grotesque" (Ciancio 994; Cowley, "Introduction" 14; and Arcana 66), the myth of androgyny (Bidney), the structural pattern of the Dance of Death (Stouck, "Dance of Death" 526), or the importance of "feminine" qualities (Rigsbee).

However, I think it is fair to these critics to state that none of their explanations of unity can be applied consistently across all the twenty-one stories that make up *Winesburg, Ohio,* just as my own arguments have gravitated towards certain stories and not mentioned others. Discussions that focus on George Willard often have no place for analysis of "Tandy" or "The Untold Lie"; those that analyze the category of grotesquerie often omit discussion of Joe Welling in "A Man of Ideas" or Tom Foster in "Drink." It is therefore a feature of *Winesburg, Ohio* that although it invites interpretation, and even very obviously encodes a textual place for a model reader to engage in interpretation, it ultimately frustrates such an exercise across the entire text through the diversity of its individual text units. Thus the structure of the text seems to problematize its own logic, namely the ability of narrative under masculine control to provide continuity and order.

Winesburg, Ohio thus engages directly with what Luscher feels to be the "quest for coherence" implicit in reading all short story cycles (156). However, although the text does seem to endorse George's search for knowledge and control, it focuses on his frustrations and self-aggrandizement more than on his successes. This pattern can also be replicated by the reader who, attracted by the text's invitations, attempts to impose a totalizing meaning onto the text. Luscher's comment that "our desire for unity and coherence is so great that we often use our literary competencies to integrate apparently unrelated material . . ." (155) seems particularly apt for the mode of reading suggested by the textual strategies of *Winesburg, Ohio,* strategies that invite totalization but simultaneously frustrate it—and thus draw the reader's attention to the problematics of their reading endeavor. Such a strategy can only function by exclusion and a willful blindness to contradiction and plurality.[21]

The next book Anderson wrote after *Winesburg, Ohio, Poor White* (1920), is notable by its contrast to these reading dynamics, as indeed was Anderson's previous novel, *Marching Men* (1917), which I shall discuss in the following section. *Poor White* provides a historically sweeping story of the coming of industrialism to the Midwest, with the inevitable dystopic conclusion, under the auspices of a confident and controlling narrative voice. Indeed, it features none of the fragmentation, disjunction, or reluctance to endorse totalizing concepts that are found in *Winesburg, Ohio.* It also takes a grandly mythopoetic approach to historicism, seeing a national "mood" or character as determining social and economic change, rather than giving a more strictly materialist explanation; it is a linear narrative animated by the spirit that there is a teleology to these changes, a national "destiny." Yet this did not compromise what was taken to be its veracity as a social document; indeed, Anderson boasted in 1934 that it was "a source to which practically all of the historians of the period go. It is already used in most of our colleges and universities to tell the story to the present generation of American youth" (*Selected Letters* 177). Once again, *Poor White* is attracted to the theme of the formation of masculinity, of boys growing into men (particularly through their encounters with women): this was a fascination that extended for much of Anderson's career, and he rarely depicted it as anything other than a complex, clumsy, fraught, and contested experience. Yet the narrative dynamics of *Winesburg, Ohio*—and the degree to which, as I have suggested, this was implicated in an embattled attempt to cement a patriarchal masculinity through a politics of representation—was something Anderson was not to repeat. In consequence, suggesting reasons for these texts' very different perspectives on narrative, gender, and knowledge requires a historical perspective.

"A TIME OF TOO MUCH GREATNESS": ANDERSON, *WINESBURG,* AND THE GREAT WAR

For much of his writing life, Sherwood Anderson was fascinated by history. In his letters, autobiographical writings, and fiction, he often produced accounts of the coming of industrialism, the Civil War, or the expansion of the frontier. Omitting most reference to dates, statistics, contemporary source material, and individual accounts, he tended to present American history as a grand narrative that implicated all American subjects: he took little account of cultural diversity and emphasized the role of those he felt to be representative Americans, such as Lincoln and Grant. He even considered writing a biography of Grant in collaboration with Gertrude Stein; he also discussed writing a history of the Mississippi. This interest was most clear in shaping his thoughts on national identity and Americanness, but it was also central to his ideas of gender identity.

As Anderson predicated masculinity on agency and action, then "history" as a narrative of change and development becomes inevitably gendered as masculine in his work. In *Winesburg, Ohio,* George's progress into manhood is reliant on developing a historical sense:

> There is a time in the life of every boy when he for the first time takes a backward view of life. Perhaps that is the moment when he crosses the line into manhood. . . . If he be an imaginative boy a door is torn open and for the first time he looks out upon the world, seeing, as though they marched in procession before him, the countless figures of men who before his time have come out of nothingness into the world, lived their lives and again disappeared into nothingness. (131)

The "backward view," the survey of a "procession" of men, and the placing of the self in relation to such a procession to a degree determine "manhood." Moreover, this implies that for Anderson, what separates "nothingness" from meaning, or (put differently) oblivion from history, is a set of fundamentally aesthetic criteria—a system of order. This was outlined most clearly in Anderson's important prewar novel *Marching Men,* in which the relation between masculinity and what becomes constituted as history was couched in remarkably aggressive and militaristic terms. Indeed, the extent of Anderson's proto-Fascist politics in the novel suggests the virtual inevitability of his reassessment of them as the war unfolded. Composed at some point between 1906 and 1913, *Marching Men* discusses military discipline as the way of creating both an organic society and establishing the coordinates of history; this relationship is evident in the following passage, which is worth quoting at length:[22]

> In the heart of all men lies sleeping the love of order. How to achieve order out of our strange jumble of forms, out of democracies and monarchies, dreams and endeavors is the riddle of the Universe and the thing that in the artist is called the passion for form and for which he will also laugh in the face of death is in all men. By grasping that fact Caesar, Alexander, Napoleon and our own Grant have made heroes out of the dullest clods that walk. . . . The long march, the burning of the throat and the stinging of dust in the nostrils, the touch of shoulder against shoulder, the quick bond of a common,

> unquestioned, instinctive passion that bursts in the orgasm of battle, the forgetting of words and the doing of the thing, be it winning battles or destroying ugliness, the passionate massing of men for accomplishment—these are the signs, if they ever awake in our land, by which you may know you have come to the days of the making of men. (48)

The imposition of order by masculine force, the links between this epistemology and the act of writing, the analogy between military conquest, creativity, and phallic sexual gratification—all these features that are problematized in *Winesburg, Ohio* are put forward with a deeply disturbing sincerity in this passage.[23] Indeed, Anderson's misogyny and stress on war as restorative rather than destructive—as what Filippo Tommaso Marinetti called the "world's only hygiene"—recalls the manifestos of the Italian Futurists which became central to Fascist aesthetics after World War One, and which also interested D. H. Lawrence and Wyndham Lewis ("Manifesto" 147).[24] As David Forgacs has noted, "the discourse of Fascism is full of imagined acts of violence which heal and restore order where there had been a perceived state of disease and disorder," and commonly the source of disease and disorder was represented as a woman (5). The kind of imaginary violence in which Anderson indulges here celebrates the fullness of a masculinity established through the wounding of an unnamed and objectified other, a passive victim of a violent assault. The "Marching Men" of the novel's title, established in a homosocial system that crucially obliterates all difference between them (their leader, Beaut McGregor, boasts that they have "cease[d] to be individuals" and are instead "a moving all-powerful mass") become an undifferentiated, absolute aesthetic correlate to a passive other, a distinctly feminized antagonist (183). It is this dynamic, the novel suggests, that produces history.

However, as Forgacs goes on to discuss, imaginations of violence are very different from the actualities of warfare, and during the First World War a sense of this discordance led several Futurists to retract their prewar positions of militaristic misogyny.[25] It is no surprise that the war presented a challenge to Anderson's teleological historiography of masculine power, to the totalizing narrative made possible by the "love of order" that he was naturally inclined to believe formed the most significant moments of historical reality. Yet rather than a radical change in his faith in this historical model, he oscillated in his opinions about the value and meaning of the war, opinions undoubtedly affected by his own memories of military service during the Spanish-American War. As he was later to remark, after seeing the carnage of 1914–18, he had "picked the right war" in which to be a soldier.

During his service in 1898–99 he was most affected by the imaginary of violence rather than actual combat; he trained extensively in the South before sailing to Cuba four weeks after the armistice and consequently never saw action. Indeed, his nostalgic recollections of marching and drilling resemble the passage quoted from *Marching Men* above; as he remembered wistfully, "one's individuality became lost and one became part of something wholly physical, vast, strong, capable of being fine and heroic, capable of being brutal and cruel" (*Storyteller* 272). It also became a fond memory for the possibilities of male homosociality, one in which the tempering regulation of "homosexual panic" never seemed to intrude:[26]

> Suppose a man spend certain months not thinking consciously, letting himself be swept along by other men, with other men, feeling the weariness of a thousand other men's legs in his own legs, desiring with others, fearing with the others, being brave sometimes with the others. By such experience can one gain knowledge of the others and of oneself too?
>
> Comrades loved! (*Story Teller* 274)

Moreover, this aesthetic (and tacitly erotic) relation to militaristic violence was compounded in Anderson's positive memories of military service by the fact that his enlistment got him out of a dead-end period of manual work in Chicago, when he was too tired to absorb any of the lessons in the evening classes he was attending (Townsend 36–37). These experiences colored his perspective of the First World War, at times leading him to see it as a glorious opportunity for young men to escape the hollow and basely materialistic experience of working life in America. He wrote to his friend Marietta Finley in November 1916:

> In some of my books I have worked it out. I made a picture of trains coming in at the railroad stations in Chicago, and bearing young men from the cornfields, strong bright eyed young men, thousands of them, walking over the bridges and into the loop district and to spiritual death. The bodies live but the thing that made them bright eyed and eager dies. I should prefer my sons to die in the war and terror of a Verdun. . . . Boys, you know, are right when they are thrilled by the tales of war and are not thrilled by the tales of the stock-exchange. (*Letters to Bab* 14–15)

In many ways this is similar to the adventure-seeking attitude of war as a thrilling and potentially noble opportunity that sidestepped the grubby materialism of American life—an attitude held by many of the early American volunteers, according to ex-servicemen such as John Dos Passos and Malcolm Cowley. Indeed, a martial ideal of male civic virtue, the opportunities the armed services gave for escaping what Michael C. C. Adams has called "civic claustrophobia," and the persistence of a romance of chivalry around the military figure, made war attractive to many men in the United States.[27] Moreover, as Adams and T. J. Jackson Lears have remarked, it offered an alternative not just to the expanding culture of the bureaucratic, corporate state but also to a bourgeois domesticity often perceived as effeminate.

These were all factors that provided a strong attraction toward a romanticized martial ideal for Anderson, especially during the initial phases of the war. Counterbalancing this, however, were the experiences and opinions of the intellectual circles with which he was becoming involved and indeed relying upon for publication. This was most obvious in his dealings with the *Seven Arts,* a magazine that had published several of his Winesburg stories and had championed him as displaying—in Waldo Frank's words—"emerging greatness."[28] The magazine would eventually collapse owing to a withdrawal of funds; its financial backer balked at its controversial antiwar stance, particularly evident in the essays of Randolph Bourne—a stance that also caused it to be placed under surveillance by U.S. intelligence services. Waldo Frank was then the assistant editor of the *Seven Arts* and had glowingly praised the "Promise of Sherwood Anderson" in its first number. Held at the Newberry Library, Frank's correspondence with Anderson during the war continually refers to his own fear of imprisonment for his conscientious objection and criticism of the herdlike mentality that he felt was preventing varied debate on the war. Anderson was sympathetic toward Frank and also worried when, in 1918, his friend and colleague Paul Rosenfeld was drafted and agreed to serve. These concerns crystallized in another letter to Marietta Finley, one markedly different in tone and feeling to the one previously quoted:

> I had some dreams when the war began. I saw in fancy men marching shoulder to shoulder and doing big deeds. Instead, as you know men have gone into the ground and there is only the horrible, mechanical guns and the deafness and the stench of decaying bodies.
>
> Well, I won't go on! Thinking of it has driven me near to madness. (*Letters to Bab* 64)

In place of an escape from the mechanized modes of production of industrial capitalism, the soldiers now find themselves at the mercy of its military counterpart; in the same letter Anderson called the war "industrialism gone mad." Instead of stressing the integrity and impenetrability of the clean, healthy male body, it is a war in which they decay in death. And rather than masculinity being buttressed and reinforced through the bonds of martial homosociality, men are engulfed by the feminized, womb-like trenches of passivity and death.

It was between these two positions that Anderson oscillated throughout the war. He wrote to Waldo Frank on December 7, 1917, that "[a]s an antidote to the war I now read history. Histories of Poland, Russia, Austria, Italy, France. One gets the sense of the long line of events. The present sinks into nothingness" (*Letters* 27). He also advised Finley to read history as an "antidote"; surely this reflects his hope that the narrative continuity of these histories, and their chronicles of individual accomplishment and brilliance, would sustain his faith in a male subjectivity that relied heavily on those foundations. On the other hand was the "madness" of the opposite position, as quoted above; in another letter he remarked of the war: "In me always . . . there has been the sense of a persistent outcry of little distracting voices. Now it is as though they have begun to shout madly and meaninglessly" (*Letters* 15). As is the case in "An Awakening" and also in "The Teacher," when George believes "the town had gone mad" (91), "madness" for Anderson seems to denote aberrant sexuality, perverse desire, or the failure to conform to a certain set of parameters within which he believed male subjectivity to exist. If the war could not be made to bear meaning, therefore, it represented a crisis for Anderson's teleological view of history. At a more profound level, it also shook his reliance on the masculinized politics of narrative that underpinned his view of gender identity.

In addition to the trauma of assessing military experience as meaningless slaughter rather than a utopian environment of homosocial and patriarchal community, Anderson was also troubled by the effect on language of wartime experience. As mentioned, Lears has discussed the significance of the categories of authentic and inauthentic writing for Anderson's sense of gender identity, especially Anderson's tendency to view advertising writing as both inauthentic and linked to homosexuality. Throughout his career, Anderson protested against the vacuous or inane usage of language—usage he often associated with empty political rhetoric, advertising writing, and popular magazine fiction. Anderson saw just such a degradation of political discourse and popular journalism during the war; as he wrote to Finley just before the American declaration of war, "in the days to come . . . we are all to be swung here and there by the winds of terrible words" (*Letters to Bab* 63). He later wrote to Waldo Frank in September 1917 that "I still believe that this Middle West has not let itself be led into the spirit of hatred the newspapers are trying so hard to build up" (*Letters* 16).

However, this "spirit of hatred" and jingoistic rhetoric exhibited by the press was more troubling for Anderson than the inauthenticity of advertising writing, as the propaganda relied precisely on the same grand narratives of American history that he had shown such fondness for. Indeed, his reappraisal of the value of unity and order as the staple for a patriarchal masculinity may have been influenced by seeing teleological history's sense of destiny and the unified national identity this implies, used rhetorically by Wilson's administration to motivate American citizens for mobilization and conflict. Moreover, this rhetoric was also used to effect draconian laws such as the June 1917 Espionage Act, which made speaking, writing, or organizing against war an offence with a maximum penalty of ten years' imprisonment or a $10,000 fine. George Creel, head of the Committee on Public Information (CPI)—the body established by Wilson in April 1917 to conduct propaganda in the USA—stated that his aim was to weld Americans into "one white hot mass . . with fraternity, devotion, courage, and deathless determination" (Schaffer, 5). Wilson himself, a few weeks after American entry into the war on April 6, 1917, declared that "some day historians will remember these momentous years as the years which made a single people out of the great body of those who call themselves Americans" (Schaffer, 7). And perhaps the most (in)famous "meaning" by which the war was inscribed a place within a purposeful history in American rhetoric is here given by the then secretary of state, Robert Lansing, in a statement that also relies on the utopian conception of unity:

> Were every people on earth able to express their will, there would be no wars of aggression, and, if there were no wars of aggression, then there would be no wars, and lasting peace would come to this earth. The only way that a people can express their will is through democratic institutions. Therefore, when the world is made safe for democracy . . . universal peace will be an accomplished fact. (Schaffer, 10).

And yet the disillusionment felt about this vision of history can be seen in American writing about the war from the next generation of artists and intellectuals; Dos Passos, who served as an ambulance man in France, decried such speeches as Lansing's as the "gradual lulling to sleep of people's humanity and sense by the phrases, the phrases. . . . America, as you know, is ruled by the press" (159). And for him as for Anderson, the war disrupts the progressive narrative sequence of masculine history, the long line of men:

> The woods all about him were a vast rubbish-heap; the jagged, splintered bodies of leafless trees rose in every direction from heaps of brass shell-cases, of tin cans, of bits of uniform and equipment. The wind came in puffs laden

> with an odour as of dead rats in an attic. And this was what all the centuries of civilization had struggled for. For this had generations worn away their lives in mines and factories and forges, in fields and work-shops, toiling, screwing higher and higher the tension of their minds and muscles, polishing brighter and brighter the mirror of their intelligence. For this! (146–47)

The disillusionment with this vision of nationhood and history was therefore doubly felt. It was felt by those facing the terrifying battlefield conditions in Europe, who saw the end point of "civilization" as the rubble and carnage of the Western Front. Yet it was also palpable on the home front, as the rhetoric of national unity, purpose, and mission was increasingly used to legitimate the destruction of civil liberties, apologize for the huge increase in vigilante extralegal persecution of ethnic and racial minorities and the American left, and foster a xenophobic and intolerant political culture of "100 percent Americanism." Such a climate forced the closure of periodicals like the *Seven Arts* and reduced the American left from its relatively strong prewar position to a marginal influence throughout the Republican 1920s.[29]

The connections between Anderson's responses to the events of the war and the narrative strategies and formation of gender subjectivities in *Winesburg, Ohio* should now seem obvious. As Edward W. Said has stated, "Appeals to the past are among the commonest of strategies in interpretations of the present," and although *Winesburg, Ohio* has often been discussed in the context of its narrative present, the 1890s, little mention has been made of the context of its time of composition (3).[30] According to William L. Phillips, Sherwood Anderson wrote the stories of *Winesburg, Ohio* one after the other between late 1915 and early 1916, yet they were not collected for publication until 1919 (24). Therefore, the stories—and crucially the principles that governed their collection and organization—were in development precisely at the time when Anderson's thought about the relation between narrative and gender was undergoing this interrogation, a process he found confusing and even traumatic. Kaja Silverman has discussed the relation of historical trauma to male subjectivity, arguing that history is a "force [that] disrupts the equilibrium of the dominant fiction, generating temporary irregularities and even radical change within textual practice" (118). This "dominant fiction" is inseparable from the operations of patriarchal culture; it is "the mechanism by which a society 'tries to institute itself as such on the basis of closure, of the fixation of meaning . . .'" (115), and as a result it is "merely within a culture's dominant representational and narrative reservoir that the paternal signifier 'grows' into an organ, and becomes available to the male subject as his *imago*" (110).

History, for Silverman, is defined in terms diametrically opposed to those Anderson would have used; she sees history not as a form of continuity, or as a narrative, but as a force of rude intrusion, one that by definition troubles the representational practices of the "dominant fiction."[31] It is precisely this quality of disturbance that troubles the narrative and semiotic practices of *Winesburg, Ohio,* as I have been discussing. It is a text that carefully lays out the mutually constitutive nature of patriarchal masculinity, narrative, and social order, only to consistently remark on the fragile and precarious nature of this process. Later, in his recollection of the war, Anderson stated, "It was a time of too much 'greatness.'. . . It was a flood. It was to me terrible, unbearable. . . . I wanted passionately now not to think of great soldiers, statesmen, writers, but of being first of all little" (*Memoirs* 448). The fragmentation of experience that *Winesburg, Ohio* depicts can, therefore, be read as a questioning of the value of narrative continuity, the aesthetic of unification, and the possibility of masculine narrative control prompted by the seemingly meaningless slaughter of the war.

If Anderson's type of thinking about history had been identified by Creel as one of the most effective ways to mobilize Americans for the war effort, it surely prompted Anderson to a realization of Walter Benjamin's maxim that "all efforts to render politics aesthetic result in one thing: war. War and war only can set a goal for mass movements on the largest scale while respecting the traditional property system" ("Mechanical Reproduction" 234). Indeed, Anderson was later to repudiate the proto-Fascistic activities of the marching laborers in *Marching Men* on precisely these grounds: paramilitary activity and the homosocial camaraderie and mass sentiment fostered in such political groupings was, he felt, the "strength of fascism," an "impulse" that was "too easily perverted" (*Memoirs* 185, 187). Yet Anderson was unable to theorize masculinity in any alternative sense; politics-as-aesthetic may lead to war, but he could never conceive of an ideal of masculinity as other than primarily aesthetic, as existing outside categories of beauty, order, and an organic model of working practice. The wartime story cycle of *Winesburg, Ohio* shows the strain and insecurities of this model of masculinity as George grows into manhood; yet it does not end, as Simolke suggests, with George able to both "transcend the dominant social ideology of gender roles" and "transcend gender" (64–65). Rather, it shows George's dogged adherence to a set of aesthetic and representational systems of order and narration to mediate his experiences and identification in relation to women and homosexuals. The inconsistency, inadequacy, and narcissistic nature of these systems are foregrounded again and again, but George's only alternative is the marginalization of a Wing Biddlebaum or the "half insanity" brought about by being rejected by Belle Carpenter. It is this tension that brings about the fragmented narratives of *Winesburg, Ohio,* and also the lure of totalizing reading strategies that the text holds open but simultaneously works to frustrate. This was a particular product of the time; neither before nor since did Anderson's work reflect such tensions between narrative and gender role nor identify the huge investment masculinity had in representation.

Floyd Dell, Anderson's first significant literary contact in Chicago, remarked in 1961 that the "non-heroic" mood of *Winesburg, Ohio* "turned out to be the post-war mood of many critics and writers" (320). This view that Anderson's text exhibited a profound reaction to the war is an assessment that has been lost in much subsequent criticism. This is despite the fact that two of Anderson's admirers in the 1920s, Ernest Hemingway and William Faulkner, would use the short story cycle as a form for questioning many of the romantic and patriarchal myths that surround war in *In Our Time* (1925) and *The Unvanquished* (1933) respectively. Anderson would continue to try to buttress patriarchal masculinity throughout the 1920s, yet crucially this always needed a third term to mediate and articulate a masculinity/femininity binary; if homosexuality was the predominant term in *Winesburg, Ohio,* Anderson's trips to Alabama and Louisiana in the early-to-mid-1920s increasingly led him to involve a discourse of blackness in this articulation. If Anderson was implicated in a "matricidal" impulse of modernism, he was also implicated in its fascination with the "primitive" and the racial "other." It is to this that I turn next.

CHAPTER 2

SHERWOOD ANDERSON AND PRIMITIVISM

After his return to Chicago following his trip to Mobile and Fairhope in February 1920, Sherwood Anderson wrote to Jerome and Lucile Blum that "I'm going back to Alabama this winter to paint and write. If necessary, I'll be an unfaithful husband to Tennessee [Mitchell, Anderson's second wife] and run off into the woods with a black wench. I'm going after the American Nigger. He's got something absolutely lovely that's never been touched."[1] This letter is revealing in its exemplification of how African Americans became an imaginative, symbolic, and erotic touchstone for Anderson, permeating and conditioning much of his experience of the South both in Alabama and, later, in his two periods of extended residency in New Orleans. It connects African Americans—and importantly in this example African American women—with the characteristics of sexual availability, sexual desirability, and an essential, premodern version of purity that form part of the "basic grammar and vocabulary" of what Marianna

Torgovnick has termed primitivistic discourse (8). It was through this discourse, applied to the African Americans Anderson encountered in the South, that he articulated many of his own fears and desires on the subject of race and gender, sometimes challenging and sometimes confirming the racial politics of the dominant white culture of his era. Indeed, his blend of radicalism and conservatism in these representations, his mix of progressive hopes and reactionary stereotype, can be seen as a characteristic example of American primitivism in the 1920s.

The extent of that fascination and its recurrence in much of Anderson's writing about the South have often been ignored, simplified, or treated as an embarrassing but ultimately inconsequential part of his career by Anderson's critics. Yet such a move obscures the crucial role that race played in Anderson's nostalgia for preindustrial forms of labor and community in the United States and also tends to dismiss his fantastical portrayals of African Americans as simply naïve when in fact they dovetailed very neatly with the "Young American" critique of the contemporary industrial, corporate separation of culture and labor. It is easy to see why previous Anderson critics have reacted in this way; his representations of African Americans are almost invariably offensive and draw on crude stereotype, facts that his African American readers of the 1920s did not fail to note. He also had no interest in African American political agency, no commitment to African American civil rights other than an abhorrence of lynching, or much interest in engaging African Americans as individuals. Yet his views on African Americans underpinned his thinking about gender, region, sexuality, and whiteness throughout the 1920s and beyond. At least for the reason that it gives a more full and accurate account of Sherwood Anderson's intellectual and imaginative practice, then, a serious consideration of his views on race is called for.

However, the question does arise as to whether this legitimates a lengthy discussion of such pernicious views. Certainly it would seem to engage the same problems as are found within specific strands of whiteness theory. As Richard Dyer cautions, analyzing how images of nonwhite people construct white identity runs the risk of "reproducing the relegation of non-white people to the function of enabling me to understand myself" and doing "analytically what the texts themselves do" (13). The dangers of such a structural replication of certain of Anderson's imaginative uses of African Americans are commingled with the danger of rehabilitating the racist tropes, images, and stereotypes that inform his writing, a rehabilitation operative at least by keeping such tropes in view if not by endorsing them. These dangers are hard to completely resolve or refute; they will always make this type of work in some ways uneasy. Yet scholarship in the past fifteen years has demonstrated the rewards of such work, despite this unease. In labor history, important studies have been done on the centrality of cultural configurations of African Americans to white working-class formation, the way in which—to quote David Roediger, writing on minstrelsy—they "achieved a common symbolic language—a unity—that could not be realized by racist crowds, by political parties or by labor unions. Blackface whiteness meant respectable rowdiness and safe rebellion. It powerfully addressed the broadest tensions generated by the creation of the first American working class" (127). Other studies have identified the centrality of slavery and the presence of the black unfree to notions of exceptionalist ideas of individualism and freedom that underpin many U.S. mythologies of national identity. The *locus classicus* for literary studies in this field remains Toni Morrison's *Playing in the Dark*, and her closing remarks there remain convincing on the validity of this kind of approach:

> Studies of African Americanism, in my view, should be investigations of the ways in which a nonwhite, Africanist presence and personae have been constructed—invented—in the United States, and of the literary uses this fabricated presence has served. . . . Ernest Hemingway, who wrote so compellingly about what it was to be white male American, could not help folding into his enterprise of American fiction its Africanist properties. But it would be a pity if the criticism of that literature continued to shellac those texts, immobilizing their complexities and power and luminations just below its tight, reflecting surface. All of us, readers and writers, are bereft when criticism remains too polite or too fearful to notice a disrupting darkness before its eyes. (90–91)

Work on whiteness, or on deeply problematic representations of African Americans in the work of white writers, inevitably carries the shadow of a reactionary literary criticism that gives white voices a priority. Yet, as Morrison's work makes clear, the task of examining the functionally enabling role of Africanist personae in such writers' work is an indispensable one, just as is examining the fulcrum of blackness that articulations of U.S. cultural nationalism frequently turned upon in their most significant moments—of which the 1920s is surely one.

For Anderson, such personae enabled considerations of national and class identity, reflections on how languages and imaginations of race were becoming annexed into consumer discourse and advertising strategies, and the significance of sexuality to community formation. African American men in particular seemed to him to be engaged in older, more communal, and craft-based models of working practice and to have a virility and sexual dominance missing from white working-class men. Of course, this fits into the familiar contours of modernist primitivism. Yet studies of the conflation of African Americans with "the primitive" in the U.S. culture of the 1920s have often represented it as simply a Freudian faddishness, or seen it as a form of cultural critique steeped in antimodernism and nostalgia. Both of these categories have applicability to Anderson's thought, yet in the past both have been used to wholly contain his representations of African Americans. This omits—or oversimplifies—much of the sociopolitical and cultural significance of "blackness" in Anderson's work. As well as overlooking the significance of African Americans to Anderson's gender politics, such a view downgrades the way in which African Americans acted as a counterpoint to theories of Puritan racial degeneration, the significance of "blackness" to Anderson's view of cultural nationalism, Anderson's growing awareness of the commodification of race, and the spatialization of racial identity. These factors undoubtedly require greater investigation within Anderson studies, and they also deserve consideration within assessments of the cultural criticism of the left in the 1910s (which proved highly influential to Anderson), assessments that have often been silent on the racial politics of key figures such as Van Wyck Brooks or Waldo Frank.[2] Moreover, they elucidate significant discourses surrounding race that Jean Toomer would respond to as he wrote *Cane*.

As David Theo Goldberg states in his criticism of the book by Torgovnick cited above, "any use of the term 'primitive' in a straightforward referential sense carries value" (*Racist Culture,* 162). Goldberg is surely right in this assertion, and I hope to treat "the primitive" as a discursive practice and nothing else in the following chapter. However, as Goldberg makes clear in his discussion, if "the primitive" is deeply problematic as a referential category, its use in the history of racialization and Western conceptualizations of the "Other" is both long and important. Moreover, and unlike both the majority of the examples that Torgovnick draws on and the cultures that Post-Impressionist to Surrealist European artists used as their source of the primitive, the issue becomes even more complex when discussing two groups with such a geographically and economically contiguous history as white and black America. In applying such a discourse to African Americans, Anderson unavoidably invokes a set of issues geographically, economically, and thus emotionally closer to white America than primitivism inspired by or responding to pan-global colonialism. The long history and complexity of sexual, economic, and cultural exploitation (and to a lesser extent exchange) between the two groups make this a special case in the history of the discourse of primitivism, especially in a decade when there was such an obvious clash in racial discourses contesting political legitimation. Anderson was aware of these high stakes if nothing else; in the decade of such various racial discourses as the passing of eugenic science-inspired laws on segregation in the South, the Harlem Renaissance, Garveyism, immigration restriction, and the huge rise in both the membership and the political aspiration of the Ku Klux Klan, he stated, "If I could really get inside the niggers and write about them with some intelligence, I'd be willing to be hanged later and perhaps would be."[3]

The questions to ask about this statement are several. By 1920 Anderson was established as perhaps the preeminent fictional interpreter of several features of contemporary America: small-town white masculinity in the United States, the effects of the growth of corporate industry on America's rural hinterlands, and a denuded cultural sphere that left most Americans inarticulate and atomized in the face of the emotional turbulence of life. Why then in his 1920s novels, story collections, and essays did he so regularly turn to portrayals of rural African Americans? Why are his descriptions of watching African American laborers—often from concealed positions—so infused with anxiety, envy, and celebration? And why did this contribute to the sudden downturn in his critical fortunes after 1925? The answers demonstrate much about the place of race in the "Young American" critical project and about their anxieties over the white working class. Anderson's attempt to "really get inside the niggers" must be approached with caution, but it has much to tell.

PRELIMINARIES: THE CONTOURS OF PRIMITIVISM IN AMERICAN MODERNISM

The traditional critical response to the discourse of primitivism employed by white writers in the modern period, including America, is that it was an ideological strategy intent on staging a rupture with the preceding generation of white literary culture rather than any genuine desire to reassess interracial relationships or racial identity (Chip Rhodes 170–71). Indeed, this oedipal structure to primitivism, as Sieglinde Lemke has termed it, was not unique to the modern period of America (16). In discussing writers as diverse as Rousseau, Melville, and D. H. Lawrence, Michael Bell finds that "primitivism denotes, or arises from, a sense of crisis in civilisation . . . [it] is born of the interplay between the civilised self and the desire to reject or transform it" (80). Writing in 1922, the white supremacist Lothrop Stoddard, in his chapter "The Lure of the Primitive," seemed to share that view, identifying the artistic "glorification of the primitive" as the first stage in the movement of society towards violent revolution, citing Rousseau and Tolstoy as his case studies. He then accused the arts movement of his age as having a similar objective; criticizing primarily the move away from nonrepresentational art, he found it represented "a fierce revolt against things as they exist, and a disintegrative, degenerative reaction towards primitive chaos" (127).

Such outrage from the extreme wing of reactionary politics illustrates the attractiveness of primitivism as an available discourse for writers of the period to adopt in their pursuit of what Raymond Chandler called "Terrible Honesty." Such "honesty" was intended as a radical challenge to what was often perceived as the dominant puritanical and sentimental culture, which Ann Douglas in particular has identified as characterizing the previous generation. The need for "reality," precision, and "truth" was frequently expressed in the era; Malcolm Cowley identified the moderns as wanting "their work to be true—that was a word they used over and over—and they wanted its effect to be measured in depth, not in square miles of surface" (*Exile* 298).[4] Sherwood Anderson commented in a letter of 1935 to Miriam Philips that "if you do at all good art, in any art, you begin to disturb people. Closeness to life always hurts" (*Selected Letters* 193), and as Douglas comments, "Opposing every form of "sentimentality," they prided themselves on facing facts, the harder the better" (*Terrible Honesty* 33).

This struggle for a tone of authentic objectivity as a way of challenging the culture of the previous generation necessitated the creation of positions or discourses with the semblance of objectivity, from which "reality" could be truthfully reflected. These "mirrors" on the culture have been frequently discussed—the alienated and expatriate artist, formal experimentation, and the huge cultural interest in psychoanalysis, for example. The discourse of primitivism functioned in this way; by observing what were classed as "primitive" societies, the "reality" of modern American civilization could be revealed in all its imperfection. Within America, this reflective function of the "primitive other" was consolidated by two developing academic fields, anthropology and psychology—a fact usually considered in accounts of modernist primitivism.[5]

The view of culture as relative, and of American culture as comparable with non-Western cultures without teleological notions of progress being invoked, was largely informed by developments in anthropology—especially the work of Franz Boas (Handler, "Boasian Anthropology" 252). His theories challenged previously dominant ideas of the evolutionary nature of cultures, ideas that had presupposed that various cultures and societies represented stages in human development. This in turn involved the notion of hierarchy, with Anglo-American or European culture invariably placed at the apex of human achievement. Boas's more relative and supposedly non-hierarchical approach to various cultures inevitably helped to dissolve the "invisibility" of American culture and present American cultural conditioning as an object of inquiry.

However, to make American culture "visible," all points of inquiry about American life had to be related to a different culture to debunk their status as "normal" or "universal."[6] As Margaret Mead, perhaps the most famous student of Boas, stated in her influential book *Coming of Age in Samoa* (1928), "[I]f we would appreciate our own civilization, this elaborate pattern of life which we have made for ourselves as a people and which we are at such pains to pass on to our children, we must set our civilization over against other very different ones" (17). Noting the increasingly problematic period of adolescence for the American teenager and the high incidence of neuroses, Mead goes on to use the "mirror" of Samoa to argue for a more liberal attitude to sex and education within American society and an alternative adolescent ethos to that of rivalry and competition. As Marcus and Fischer note, the "ethnographic paradigm" developed within anthropology in the 1920s "entailed a submerged, unrelenting critique of Western civilization as capitalism," a critique that suggested that "we can learn basic moral and practical lessons from ethnographic representations" (129). Indeed, so much was this so that poststructuralist critiques of ethnography from this period see it as far more revealing about the constitution of Western subjectivity than it is about the details of non-Western identities and cultures.[7] As I shall discuss in chapter 3 on Toomer's, Frank's, and Anderson's writings on the South, the use of this "ethnographic paradigm" as a tool of cultural criticism was very much *en l'air* among a wide range of intellectuals and cultural producers in the early 1920s.

Anthropology was not the only discipline of the time using "the primitive" for the purposes of cultural criticism: psychology, with its interest in the violent, selfish, and sexual desires of the unconscious, saw an anthropological analogue to the id in supposedly "savage" peoples. As Lemke rightly notes, this involves a metaphoric use of the "primitive," rather than the metonymic sense in which it was utilized in anthropology, and these two senses necessitate very different approaches (14). Yet both were highly significant to the broad cultural construction of the "primitive" in the 1920s, and in practice this distinction often collapsed. Freud, who kept a variety of paintings and statues of mythological subjects in his study, aligned himself with the views of much nineteenth-century anthropology through his evolutionary categorization of "savages" as representing an early stage of the "civilized" mind, the position Boas and his followers rejected (Torgovnick 194). As a result Freud, in *Totem and Taboo: Resemblances Between the Psychic Lives of Savages and Neurotics,* relied on the parallel between "primitives" and children, another recurrent trope in the history of primitivism. This employed analyses of the psychosexuality of the social formations of Australian aboriginal and Polynesian cultures as a mode of comparison with his central subject, the psychological development of the Western infant.

That Freud's anthropological research was deeply flawed—as the anthropologist A. L. Kroeber (who had trained under Boas) quipped, *Totem and Taboo* has as much relation to primitive societies as Kipling's *Just So* stories—is an indication that his primary interest was not in non-Western cultures but in the possibility of constructing from them a myth of primal origin that could be applied to both Western individuals and Western society.[8] He begins *Totem and Taboo* with the assertion that "savage and semi-savage" races assume "a particular interest for us, for we can recognize in their psychic life a well-preserved, early stage of our own development" (1). He then goes on, through an analysis of "primitive" ritual, to postulate the oedipal foundation of "religion, ethics, society and art" (260) which paves the way toward his radical oedipal reading of Christianity. And, tellingly for my subsequent analysis of Anderson, Freud's project of writing *Totem and Taboo* was involved with the same sense of personal release that Anderson felt in writing of supposed "primitives"; during its composition Freud confessed to feeling "all omnipotence, all savage" (Douglas, *Terrible Honesty* 229). Both psychology and anthropology—despite their very different configurations of "the primitive"—therefore adopted the notion of the primitive as a privileged locus from which to discuss Western subjectivity, particularly its processes of gender formation. This gave "the primitive" a functional role that, as postcolonial critics have often pointed out, carried less concern with observing the complexities and details of non-Western societies than with using them as a vehicle for discussing Western societies.

These are the usual institutional contexts within which American modernist primitivism is discussed. In addition, Western artists such as Paul Gauguin, Pablo Picasso, Emil Nolde, and Paul Klee—to name but a few—became interested in non-Western subjects and forms in the period before the

First World War. In America (and influenced by these artists) Mabel Dodge moved to the Tiwa Native American Pueblo at Taos and established an artists' community there that was to attract writers such as D. H. Lawrence and Witter Brynner and painters such as Marsden Hartley, Georgia O'Keeffe, and John Marin (Watson 341). Probably of more significance was the primitivist attitude to black popular music; as V. F. Calverton opined in Nancy Cunard's anthology *Negro* (1933), "[T]he Negro has retained unquestionably in his art a certain primitivism that is wonderfully refreshing in contrast to the more stilted affectations of the more cultured styles and conceptions" (80). Many authors (both black and white) referred to jazz in terms of freedom, wild abandon, and sexuality; in a scene at a Harlem cabaret, the heroine of Nella Larsen's *Quicksand*, Helga Crane, feels "drugged, lifted, sustained by the extraordinary music, blown out, ripped out, beaten out, by the joyous, wild, murky orchestra." When the music ends, she feels "that not only had she been in the jungle, but that she had enjoyed it" (59).[9]

It is important to note that both of the academic disciplines mentioned above had a central concern with Western sexuality and the formation of gender identity, concerns that were fundamental to Anderson. Both Freudian psychoanalysis and the Boasian tradition made strong critiques of the types of sexuality produced by Western industrial capitalism. And yet, as Douglas's comments on Freud given above and Torgovnick's discussion of the anthropologist Bronislaw Malinowski's diaries reveal, the personal and psychological investment of the individuals engaged in writing non-Western cultures into academic discourse is a factor that cannot be ignored. As I hope to go on to show, rhetoric about presenting the "truth" often functioned as a morally imbued justification for talking about desire, yet it was a "truth" that in Anderson's work was linked to a reasonably cohesive set of criticisms about the economic structures of modern America. Primitivism, then, sits at the center of his preoccupations of economic change, gender identity, and sexuality and in a fashion more complex than has previously been acknowledged.[10]

The critical reaction to Anderson's representation of the African American communities he observed in Mobile and New Orleans, and to his brief but illuminating exchange of correspondence with Jean Toomer, has been mixed according to the project of the critic in question. Critics of the Harlem Renaissance have identified Anderson as a "Negrotarian," Zora Neale Hurston's term for a white person engaged with the increase in African American cultural production at the time. In attempting to provide a broad categorization of these "Negrotarians," David Levering Lewis identifies "genuinely humanitarian" Negrotarians such as Heywood Broun, Ruth Hale, Pearl Buck, and T. S. Stribling; "salon Negrotarians" such as Carl van Vechten; and the "Dollars and cents" Negrotarians of the publishing industry such as Albert Barnes, Otto Khan, Horace Liveright, and Florenz Ziegfeld. Anderson falls into a group for whom "the new religion of Freudianism with its sexual trapdoor under the ordered mind, transformed the African American's perceived lack of cultural integration from a liability into a state of grace" (99). Sterling Brown too saw Anderson's novel *Dark Laughter* as utilizing African Americans as essentially a handy psychoanalytic tool; it "used 'the negro way of life of levee loungers' to beat such whipping boys and girls as American neuroticism and acquisitiveness" ("A Century of Negro Portraiture" 574). Nathan Huggins, who produced one of the earliest comprehensive accounts of the Harlem Renaissance, also classified Anderson as involved in a racial/psychological "game of masks" in his representation of African Americans. Such games of racial masquerade, Huggins contends, have characterized much American cultural production either by or about African Americans and typify "[t]he way that the Negro has been used by whites, and the way he has permitted himself to be used" (84).

Similarly, Ann Douglas uses Anderson's interest in African American experience as illustrative of the 1920s' appetite for psychological interpretations of "the primitive," drawn partly from Freud's "equation of modern neurosis with the 'savage' and the 'primitive mind'" (*Terrible Honesty* 49). In an extension of Levering Lewis's argument, however, she also identifies a spiritual as well as a self-consciously psychoanalytic motive for the interest of Anderson and other contemporary white writers such as Hart Crane and Waldo Frank in the African American community. What they "hoped to get from their friendship with black moderns like Toomer," she argues, was "the Negro genius for religious feeling, the saving expressiveness that American Calvinism had in their view conspicuously lacked" (*Terrible Honesty* 94). Douglas also contends that the cult of the primitive was an effective way of rejecting what she calls the feminized culture of the previous age, a method of killing the "Victorian Matriarch" represented by writers such as Harriet Beecher Stowe and political figures such as Frances E. Willard, leader of the Women's Christian Temperance Union.

In contrast, critics of Anderson have tended to gloss over his thematic engagement with racial discourse or to ignore it altogether, perceiving it as one of the many failed projects or errors of judgment that Anderson indulged in during his career and an issue that bears little relation to his most discussed work, *Winesburg, Ohio*. Such a shunting of race to the periphery of Anderson's career occludes its obvious centrality to his writing about class, labor, and gender, topics that almost all Anderson's critics have seen as preoccupations in his career. James Schevill, his earliest biographer, discusses *Dark Laughter* as a "complete failure"; his criticism is that it is "mostly a pastiche. James Joyce's *Ulysses,* the 'European mood,' and New Orleans Jazz are the main influences" (209). Of more recent critics, Glen A. Love's article "Horses or Men: Primitive and Pastoral Elements in Sherwood Anderson" seeks to locate Anderson's engagement with racial discourse as a version of pastoral rather than primitivism. Love sees the tradition of pastoral as an attempt to resolve conflicts between rural simplicity and the complexities of modern urban life, rather than what he sees as the purely escapist fantasy of primitivism. This reading is applied to Anderson's so-called racetrack stories, among the most famous of his work aside from *Winesburg, Ohio,* and their portrayal (in every case from the perspective of a young, white, male first-person narrator) of a world of childhood innocence among the uninhibited and heavily physicalized racehorses and "negro swipes."[11]

Although Love concedes that Anderson's presentation of African Americans is "unacceptable" and "reflects a popularly-held primitivistic stereotype of the Negro in the 1920s," his essay is grounded in the holistic critical endeavor of New Criticism (247). Thus he attempts to contain Anderson's inscription of fundamental racial difference within what he terms the "critical question" in Anderson's career; "what are the possibilities for meaningful individual life in an urbanized industrial America" (237). Walter B. Rideout's biography of Anderson's stay in New Orleans, "'The Most Cultural Town in America': Sherwood Anderson and New Orleans," dismisses Anderson's approach to African Americans as "romantic self-deception" and finds that in *Dark Laughter* "the Negro would not be a personality but a symbol of what whites now lacked" (82). But beyond that there is little discussion. Similarly, Anderson's most thorough biographer, Kim Townsend, has a fuller discussion but tends to ignore the primitivistic attitude of works such as "Out of Nowhere into Nothing" (1921), *Horses and Men* (1923), and *Sherwood Anderson's Notebook* (1926). Instead, he focuses on *Dark Laughter,* an "astonishingly bad book" (223) that employs "all the clichés" of African Americans, exemplifying Anderson's attempt to become "inward with the ways of blacks" in the midst of the "fashionable" status of black culture (225–26).

Perhaps most startling and troubling in its positioning of Anderson's primitivism is the most recent collection of Anderson's writings, *Southern Odyssey: Selected Writings by Sherwood Anderson,* an interesting attempt to reposition Anderson within southern studies rather than the midwestern context in which he is normally discussed. Yet in the introduction to one of Anderson's most problematic primitivist representations—his article "Negro Singing: Hampton Quartette Entertains Large Crowd"—the editorial gloss seems to replicate some of Anderson's assumptions; it remarks that Anderson "had a particular preference for this music in its most primitive, untrained form—for instance, the kind sung by the chorus of servants on a southern plantation" (103–4). In another gloss, this time on Anderson's views on African American writing, the comment is made that "Anderson cautions that this [authentic black literary] voice must not become tainted by whiteness, nor should it exaggerate its inherent blackness in a self-conscious way" (196). This is perhaps the most glaring example of the need in Anderson studies for a more theoretically rigorous, and critical, approach to his representations of black Americans.

Both approaches have their failings. As I have already suggested, there is a tendency to either oversimplify Anderson's engagement with racial discourse, or to downplay its importance—or even its incidence. I would argue that African Americans were central to Anderson's perception of the South, of sexuality, and of American economics for the majority of his writing career. Although evident beforehand, this takes on a central significance after his trip to Mobile and Fairhope in 1920. During this trip Anderson's letters are full of his sense of delight and discovery, of thinly veiled desire and a penetrative sense of curiosity, over the black communities he observed. As he wrote to Hart Crane in 1920, "The negroes are the living wonder of this country. What a tale if someone could penetrate into the life and house of the southern negro and not treat it in the ordinary superficial way."[12] He later referred to Alabama as the "land of the negro"; his third wife, Elizabeth Prall Anderson, commenting on their decision to move to a residence near the wharves in New Orleans in 1924, noted that Sherwood Anderson "said he wanted to live near the wharves so he could fully enjoy the 'ships and darkies.'"[13]

Following this trip, Anderson's correspondence (especially during his periods of residence in the Deep South, in Alabama from February to May in 1920, and then in New Orleans from January 1922 to August 1922 and July 1924 to late spring 1926) refers to his imaginative fascination with African Americans with great regularity. The black gardener in "Out of Nowhere into Nothing" (1921) provides an example of a black man who "by educating himself had cut himself off from his own people"; a supposedly tragic figure, his professional life in Chicago is ruined by false accusations of the murder of a white woman (*Triumph of the Egg* 227). The "Negro swipes" of the racetrack stories of *Horses and Men* (1923) provide an integral element to the atmosphere of innocence, physicality, and freedom associated with the racetrack environment. *Many Marriages* (1923) features, in the "fanciful world" of the Andersonian representative John Webster, a voyeuristic fantasy focused on the body of a young black woman (10–12). Chapter 10 of *Dark Laughter* focuses almost exclusively on the influence of African Americans on the community of New Orleans, giving an atmosphere of "[s]ong in the air, a slow dance" (76). Throughout the novel the black domestic servants of Fred Grey (a materially successful—but sexually repressed—white northern businessman) provide a primitivistic and uninhibited counterpoint to the neuroses fostered on him by modern industrial civilization. Indeed, the title refers to the uninhibited "Dark Laughter" of the servants, and on the final page the contrast between the races is pointedly made:

> Why couldn't Fred laugh? He kept trying but failed. In the road before the house one of the negro women now laughed. There was a shuffling sound. The older woman tried to quiet the other, blacker woman, but she kept laughing the high shrill laughter of the negress. . . . the high shrill laughter ran through the garden and into the room where Fred sat upright and rigid in bed. (319; my ellipsis)

In *Sherwood Anderson's Notebook* (1926) he includes a number of "[s]ketches out of a Man's life" dealing with his experiences in New Orleans, which include reflections on race, his love of black work song, and a condemnation of white racist violence. Later essays, including "Look Out, Brown Man," "The South," and "Negro Singing," as well as reviews of Langston Hughes's short fiction and an article protesting lynching, continue to attest to his interest in black-white relations. Anderson's 1932 novel *Beyond Desire* reflects his growing awareness of labor conditions in the industrial South, as well as how these conditions were differentiated according to race. Yet despite his awareness that African Americans were often given the worst and most dangerous jobs in the textile industry, he continued to believe in a core of primitive identity among African Americans that resisted the spiritual and sexual degradation he connected with the white industrial working class. The continuation of comments on race in his correspondence throughout the 1930s, and in several sections of his posthumously published *Memoirs* (1942; critical ed. 1969), identify this as a persistent area of interest for Anderson that has been neglected in critical study.

Yet this interest had no commitment to racial equality in social or economic terms, as Anderson himself freely admitted. In his essay "The South,"

Anderson gives perhaps his most succinct comment about his racial politics and his perception of the relationship between the white northern artist and the African American southern laborer:

> I got the nigger craze. All northern men of the artist class who go south get it.
>
> Well, for those of us who tell tales, sing songs, work in colors, in stone, the negroes have something—something physical—rhythm—something we want to get into ourselves—our work.
>
> I had not gone the length of wanting the negro to replace the white. I hadn't even gone with Abe Lincoln who said "Just because I want to see justice done the black is no sign I want to sleep with him." I wasn't thinking of justice. (57)

Such a bald statement of racism, in its facile acceptance of the utility of African Americans in economic and imaginative terms but its flat denial of the possibility of their political advancement, is implicit in much primitivist discourse. Anderson argued with Jean Toomer over the need for black literary magazines, seeing them as being too self-conscious; in an analogous comment, he argued against education for African Americans, seeing it as destructive of some precultural essence.[14] His primitivism, too, expressed multiple contradictions (which Sander Gilman has found to be constitutive of the phenomena of the stereotype); African Americans were sexually desirable yet unapproachable, sexually potent yet childlike, organically related to the land yet "alien" to American identity, possessing an enviable sense of community but no individual consciousness, culturally rich yet with an identity founded solely in the body.[15] Yet, as I have argued, many of the most notable features of Anderson's writing which have been remarked upon again and again—his connections with the Young Americans' project of cultural nationalism, his critique of industrial patterns of labor, his concern with the formation of masculinity—are incomplete without reference to his constructions of race.

PRIMITIVISM AND THE NATION: YOUNG AMERICA, BLACK AMERICA

As Casey Nelson Blake notes, the cultural criticism of the Young Americans has been well represented in surveys of American thought at the beginning of the century and is regularly remarked upon by cultural historians investigating the transition between the Victorian and modernist periods (1). Yet they are often omitted from assessments of American literature of the time and from discussions of American literary modernism in both its Anglo American and African American aspects. Moreover, the racial nature of their cultural critique has often been overlooked. It is this racial component that forms an essential link between their brand of cultural nationalism and the primitivistic writing of Sherwood Anderson; indeed, his conceptualization of race and gender would be difficult to explain without reference to this element of their cultural criticism.

Many of the commentators already cited have made a connection between Anderson's treatment of sexuality in his work and his interest in African American subjects. Yet in contrast to most of these commentators, I will argue that this is most accurately considered in terms of a Whitmanian, rather than a Freudian, tradition. The tradition of celebrating sexuality and the sexual body that derives from Whitman has a close association to his strand of cultural nationalism. This forms a key difference to the crude escapism that often characterized the popular, Americanized version of Freud gaining prominence in the mid-to-late 1910s, which stressed the psychological benefits of an expressive attitude to sex. Whitman was one of the central figures for the cultural criticism of the Young Americans, and it is around the juncture of sexuality, cultural nationalism, and race that Anderson's interest in African Americans takes on its most polemical shape. This is in contrast to the frequent ascription of this interest to lightweight, fashionably Freudian erotic fantasy (although he was, of course, frequently guilty on this score).

Moreover, Anderson adapted theories advanced by Van Wyck Brooks, and especially Waldo Frank, which pathologized "the Puritan" in racial terms. (This aspect of their cultural criticism was also significant to the thought of Jean Toomer). Anderson's fascination with "blackness" was also integral to one of his main projects throughout his career, namely how to redress what he perceived as the degradation of working class white masculinity within the industrial economy. Although confused and pernicious in any form of practical application, Anderson's thought illustrates well that for those on the left in the aftermath of World War I and the Russian revolution who were unwilling to countenance a political alternative to industrial capitalism in America, a 'historical' alternative was often very appealing.[16]

From the very beginning, Sherwood Anderson's critical reception has focused on sex. As F. Scott Fitzgerald remarked in his comical chronicle of the progression of sexual liberalism in literature throughout the twenties, the publication of *Winesburg, Ohio* in 1919 marked the stage when "we learn there's a lot of sex around if only we knew it" ("Jazz Age" 13). Anderson was dubbed "The phallic Chekov" by his friend Paul Rosenfeld ("Sherwood Anderson"

186), and on *Winesburg, Ohio*'s publication in England in 1922 the *Evening Standard* found him to be "obsessed by sex" and that the "monotony of the subject is completely unbearable."[17] Anderson himself rather enjoyed this and liked to refer to himself as a "primitive" or a "pagan," seeing himself as a champion of the rejection of restrictive sexual morality and oppressive bourgeois convention.[18] His rhetoric of sexual liberation has often been linked to Freud, yet—as Frederick J. Hoffmann has argued—Anderson was only ever aware of Freud at second hand and frequently denied any interest in psychoanalysis.[19] Hoffman's thesis has its weaknesses—particularly with regard to Anderson's story "Seeds," included in his 1921 collection *The Triumph of the Egg*. The story fictionalizes Anderson's experiences of conversation with the Freudian psychoanalyst Trigant Burrow at Lake Chateaugay in 1916 and 1917 and intimates that Anderson did have more awareness of Freudian theory than he was ever willing to let on.[20] Yet far more important to Anderson's thinking about the politics of sex was the view of the sexual body as a key site for a national renewal of social relations, rather than any narrowly psychological vision—a tradition inherited from Walt Whitman.[21] Rather than working within a Freudian framework, this genealogy of his interest in sexuality aligns him more centrally with the cultural criticism of "The Young Americans," a group that coalesced around the *Seven Arts* magazine—the first magazine to print stories from *Winesburg, Ohio*. Anderson's primitivism, often considered as an offshoot of a "vulgar" Freudianism concerned only with a more liberated sexuality, can therefore be seen to have a wide relevance within his political and cultural thinking.[22]

Whitman was a key figure to Van Wyck Brooks and Waldo Frank, the Young American critics who were the most important intellectual peers to Anderson in the early part of his career. Central to both Brooks's and Frank's understanding of Whitman was what they felt to be his primal authenticity; they claimed him as the original American version of what Brooks was to call the "national genius." Brooks's *America's Coming of Age* (1915) had found Whitman to be a poet in "the most radical and primitive sense of the word," one who "first gives to a nation a certain focal centre in the consciousness of its own character," and Waldo Frank articulated similar ideas (131). Both critics felt the need for a similar "radical and primitive" figure within the present day, a "focal center" for national cultural regeneration. Frank saw Anderson as possessing this potential; in his review of Anderson's first novel, *Windy MacPherson's Son,* he heralded him as "a signal for a native culture" and drew parallels between Anderson and Whitman ("Emerging Greatness" 21). The Young Americans' view of Whitman—as America's preeminent poet of organic inclusiveness, who appealed to a "primitive" common national denominator and encouraged the spiritualization of desire—was crucial to Anderson's attraction to cultures he felt to be "primitive." As Anderson was to say later in an introduction to an edition of *Leaves of Grass,* "Who was it said only the negroes had brought real song into America? Hail, all hail, negro workmen, river hands, plantation hands, makers of songs, but hail also Whitman, white American lustful one. . ." (vi).

If Whitman-as-primitive involved a metaphoric introduction of racial "Othering" into the cultural criticism of the Young Americans, however, even more significant was their engagement with certain popular ideas of racial science, particularly their designation of "the Puritan" as a racial identity. As has often been noted, a central point for Brooks and Frank's assault on American economic, social and cultural formations was to link what they felt to be deeply flawed contemporary phenomena to a "Puritan" tradition. Brooks felt that such a tradition had divided American cultural and social life into a disastrously bifurcated situation of "highbrow" and "lowbrow," divorcing culture (he used the word with a morally beneficial sense which he inherited from Arnold) from the pragmatic commercialism of everyday American life.[23] Such a severance of cultural production from social actuality "conventionalized [for his parents' generation] the spiritual experience of humanity, pigeon-holing it, as it were, and leaving them fancy-free to live 'for practical purposes'" ("Industrialism" 197). Brooks saw the most unfortunate outcome of this situation as a separation of economics and working practice from cultural production; Frank saw a similar bifurcation but typically shifted the emphasis of its failure. This was the Puritan attenuation of an organic, socially inclusive spirituality; as a result, "for three hundred years, [the Puritan] has wilfully slain life for power. And from the material of his race, mastery has sprung. But also, from the material of his race, life has been drained away" (*Our America* 149). Anderson was impressed; as he wrote to Brooks in May 1918, "[Y]ours is the first, the only, note in American criticism that I have ever thought worth a damn" (*Letters* 36–38).

Moreover, and as the quote from Frank suggests, he and Brooks did not theorize the detrimental effect of a Puritan heritage upon America within terms of culture, or religion, alone. Instead, it was linked to a narrative of racial degeneration, a practice that drew heavily on the discourse of Social Darwinism and its most visible practical discipline, eugenics. A keen student of H. G. Wells, Brooks was familiar with Fabian Socialism's Progressive commitment to eugenics, and the mid-1910s was a period in which eugenics was rapidly becoming both institutionalized and popularized.[24] Indeed, as

Susan Hegeman has noted, Brooks's bifurcation between "highbrow" and "lowbrow" represents his most famous use of phrenological and racialized language to describe social difference (67). Implicated in much of the discourse produced by eugenic scientists and organizations was the view that culture was biologically determined (a view that would become challenged by Boasian anthropology to a much greater degree in the 1920s). This linkage meant that cultural critique was often associated with the pathologization of race and a characterization of certain racial groups as "degenerate" or "defective." If culture was causally linked to race, then cultural degradation or inadequacy must be linked to a narrative of biologized racial decline, which of course was the line taken by hard-line, conservative eugenecists like Stoddard in his invective against the "degenerate" racial stock that was producing the literary and visual products of modernism.[25]

By contrast, Frank and Brooks argued that Puritan "stock" was responsible for contemporary American degradation, a view that was at odds with those of conservative intellectuals and many others involved with scientific Progressivism. This included most hard-line eugenicists, who saw this Puritan "stock" as being among America's most precious; as the Yale geographer Ellsworth Huntington wrote in *The Character of Races* (1924), Puritans were "highly endowed with physical vigor, initiative, and courage" (304).[26] Yet Waldo Frank saw their hereditary products quite differently:

> Their jaws are rigid. Their eyes are as lead, they have so long denied the beauties of the world. Their complexions are like greasy ash. On the brow of the young man is the bland complacency of the feeble mind, and the shoulders of the girl twitch with the energy which she dares not utter. These people are descendants of Puritan New England. (*Our America* 100)

"Feeblemindedness" was one of the key terms eugenicists used to justify their programs of selective sterilization or segregation: Frank, therefore, took the epitome of the white, Anglo-Saxon Protestant body as his example of degeneracy, a heredity that had produced a "drooping generation" (149). At the end of *Our America,* he introduces his archetypal figure of national regeneration, a young soldier just returned from France:

> Everywhere, is the impotence of senility. He slaps his thigh and finds that only he is sound. And who is he? That also he begins to understand. He is what America has immemorially denied: the dreamer, the lover. He is the failure. And he alone stands healthy above the crumble of words. (230)

The soldier is a figure of health and virility, pitted against a civilization crumbling from its inherited deficiencies. The epistemological foundation of the male healthy body therefore underpins Frank's countercultural program, just as it did for the conservatism of the hard-line eugenicists, and in their search for healthy bodies Frank and especially Anderson found the African American body particularly attractive. Frank noted of a trip to the South, "The farther away from town, the more complete the Negro plasm, the more free the sweetness of the people" (*Memoirs* 105). Here he uses the term "germ plasm," which both geneticists and eugenicists argued was the substance responsible for the almost complete role of heredity in determining the characteristics of any given organism. For Anderson and Frank, this acted as a "source"—finite and material—for the racial regeneration of the country or at least a convenient trope for such a program. Such beliefs accounted for much of Frank's interest in African American culture and his interest in Jean Toomer, as I shall explore in chapter 3. As George Hutchinson has discussed, key figures in the Harlem Renaissance saw African American culture as capable of filling "the void Whitman's white descendents continually decried in their fulminations against the emotionally desiccated, spiritless America of the puritan and the pioneer, against the yawning chasm between the highbrow and the low" ("Whitman" 212). Yet as the quotations above suggest, Frank had also identified African Americans—although crucially here the African American body rather than African American culture—as capable of filling that 'void,' albeit in a very different fashion to that envisaged by Alain Locke and others.

This turn to African American bodies by writers such as Frank and Anderson represented the development of an idea of Van Wyck Brooks's, but one that Brooks himself was unwilling to develop. This idea had suggested that national cultural renewal must come from an "organic" and primitive common denominator. As several critics—and indeed Anderson himself—have argued, Brooks was unable to formulate an effective possibility of redress or reintegration for the bifurcated society he had described; this led to his later work being accused of excessive pessimism and cynicism.[27] Yet Brooks had claimed in his essay "The Culture of Industrialism" that

> it is the real work of criticism in this country to begin low. . . . the only strictly organic literature of which this country is capable is a literature which is being produced by certain minds which seem, artistically speaking, scarcely to have emerged from the protozoa. . . . Not that we are Hottentots, or even peasants, although our arrested development somewhat resembles that of peasants. No, we are simply at the beginning of our true national existence. . . . (201–2)

The "organicism" Brooks refers to is the reintegration of working practice with cultural production, ending the schism he felt had been brought about by Puritanism, and in calling for protozoan minds, he probably was thinking of writers like Anderson. Brooks would later praise Anderson's "fresh healthy mind and his true Whitmanian feeling for comradeship . . . and the 'proud conscious innocence' of his nature," features that had led to Anderson being championed by the *Seven Arts* between 1916 and 1917 (qtd. in Townsend 146). Yet Brooks was unwilling to look outside an Anglo-American ethnicity for models for this organic reintegration, as his haughty dismissal of "Hottentots" suggests. However, other critics—such as Frank, Randolph Bourne, and Anderson—were less racially exclusive in their search for "protozoan" sources of culture.[28] Anderson demonstrated that he had taken Brooks's pathologization of "Puritan" racial identity to heart when he wrote to him in December 1918 that "I have been reading The Education of Henry Adams. . . . New England can scarcely go further than that. . . . We do, I am sure, both live and die rather better in the Middle West. Nothing about us is as yet so completely and racially tired" (*Letters* 43).[29] Accordingly, in his 1921 short story collection *The Triumph of the Egg*, the "racial tiredness" of New England is exemplified in the character of Elsie Leander in "The New Englander": she is thin, taciturn, and sexually repressed.

However, in contrast to Brooks's reluctance to engage with non-Anglo-American culture as a way of resolving America's highbrow/lowbrow bifurcation, Anderson was drawn to African American life as a way of doing exactly that. One of the central aims of Brooks's critique, in Casey Nelson Blake's words, was to provoke "the recovery of a common civic life dependent on the reintegration of art and labor in new forms of creative work," and it is noteworthy that most of Anderson's depictions of African American men portray them at work (302). In many of these depictions, work song and labor coexist in a fashion which disallows the possibility of alienation from either coworkers or from the products of labor; as Thomas Yingling has noted, such representations celebrated a "preindustrial site of cultural collectivity where the body could not be reduced to the sum of its labour" (108). What Anderson bemoaned as the loss of "completion of self in work" that he felt was feminizing white male workers in assembly-line factories could be regained through such work song (*Memoirs* 387). In one essay he discusses observing African Americans cutting logs in Arkansas and singing; it was "the most real, the most tender, the most significant singing I have ever heard on American soil. . . . I have wanted this unity of things, this song, this earth, this sky, this brotherhood."[30]

In many ways this is analogous to Walter Benjamin's theory of the significance of storytelling in preindustrial culture; he argued that an oral culture guaranteed a method of bonding a community in a way in which literary culture (with its focus on the individual experience of reading) does not. Moreover, he claimed (in a statement that has also been accused of romanticism) that stories were archetypally told during work, in a way that integrated culture, working practice, and product. In his account, the rhythm of "weaving and spinning" determined the form, the audience, and the memorization of the story ("Storyteller" 91). He described storytelling as follows:

> [It] is an artisan form of communication. . . . It does not aim to convey the pure essence of the thing, like information or a report. It sinks the thing into the life of the storyteller, in order to bring it out of him again. Thus traces of the storyteller cling to the story the way the handprints of a potter cling to the clay vessel. (91)

Preindustrial, artisanal craft labor, Benjamin continues, was the "nature of the web in which the gift of storytelling is cradled" ("Storyteller" 91). It was something analogous to this nexus of community formed through teller, audience and repetition, integrally related to working practice, which Anderson romantically imagined as a refuge from the alienation and erosion of community he perceived in Fordist industrial production.[31]

Anderson went further in his celebration of African American culture than either Frank or Brooks, and this was arguably because gender politics and concern over contemporary white working-class masculinity were much more central to his cultural criticism. His views prompt recollection of Hazel Carby's point that "white fascination with primitivism" was often explicable as a series of "cultural excavations to recover and claim an essence of masculinity, often believed to have been lost in the modern industrializing world" (*Race Men* 46).[32] Indeed, African American life was significant to Anderson as a vision of community founded on a laboring practice that, through integrating labor and cultural production, could guarantee the hegemony of a patriarchal masculinity. Anderson believed that effective forms of community were heavily reliant on the potential of an economic system to continue to structure patriarchal hegemony, and much of his writing career involved an exploration of how this had been undermined or at the least made problematic by industrial capitalism.[33] To a large degree Anderson's exploration drew on Brooks's Morrisite critique of the alienation of the laborer from the products of his labor under industrial capitalism, while adding in his own thoughts about the detrimental effect this was having on white masculinity. Like Brooks and Morris, Anderson saw a possible escape from this situation in a return to craft.[34] He made the link between craft and patriarchy most schematically in *Perhaps Women,* produced at the depths of the Great Depression:

> The machine has taken away from us the work of our hands. Work kept men healthy and strong. It was good to feel things done by our hands. The ability to do things to materials with our hands and our heads gave us a certain power over women which is being lost. . . .
>
> [Man] has no definite connection with the things with which he is surrounded, no relations with the clothes he wears, the house he lives in. He lives in a house but he did not build it. He sits in a chair but he did not make it. . . . (41–42)

This privileging of gender power relations over class power relations illustrates, I think, that despite his repeated criticisms of the American middle class, Anderson's primary interest was less in challenging the economic infrastructure than in maintaining patriarchal hegemony within a period of rapidly changing economic circumstances. The coating of certain types of manual labor with the romantic gloss of "utopian possibility"—provided Anderson felt it reinforced patriarchy—is evident in much of Anderson's writing about the rural and dockyard labor he saw African Americans performing in the South. Therefore, and contrary to what W. E. B. Du Bois identified as the stereotype of the "shiftless" African American, lazy and undisciplined, Anderson's representations often focused on African Americans as *the* laboring class in the Deep South; as he wrote to Marietta Finley in 1920, "I am writing in the dark. The niggers are singing. The white male swears but they sing on and on. They haven't stopped singing and dancing for days although they've moved unbelievable quantities of freight and have worked day and night. They make me feel small" (*Letters to Bab* 121).

Although Anderson recognized that the dockworkers he saw were economically exploited, he believed they possessed an autonomy that came from the cultural production that accompanied their labor; the work song he loved listening to was "full of strangeness, sadness, race feeling," rooted in "something come out of Africa, something in the blood."[35] As this quotation suggests, this autonomy—and thus resistance to the degradation of industrial labor—was rooted in a biologically inherited culture. For him, culture was race, and it is interesting that one of the few moments to shatter an idyll of black community in his essay "Sugar Making" is when he sees "a young Negro woman, almost white. She had a slender lithe figure. Her face was ugly and degenerate. She had sullen eyes" (*Southern Odyssey* 175). Her ugliness is linked to her whiteness, and this racial "mixture" constitutes a biological degeneracy. This exemplifies Anderson's belief that the only way to erode black essentialized integrity, with its seemingly inbuilt resistance to degrading labor conditions, was through miscegenation. This idea, which attempts to link cultural decline with a loss of racial "integrity," plots a narrative of a degenerating racial future in much the same way as eugenicists did, and is an issue I shall discuss with reference to Anderson later in the chapter.

Representing black men as positively constitutive of masculinity, then, rather than relying on the polarities of bestial savagery or unmanly effeminacy that the white press often utilized, was undoubtedly part of Anderson's critique of industrial capitalism.[36] Indeed, in an essay reviewing Langston Hughes's *The Ways of White Folks,* he noted, "If you go modern you go so far as to recognize that the Negro man can be manly and the Negro woman beautiful. It is difficult to do even that without at least appearing to be patronizing" ("Paying for Old Sins," *Southern Odyssey* 198). Anderson's sense of his own "modernity," then, lay partly in his ability to represent African American men as "manly." It is worth remembering here Gail Bederman's point about the distinction between "manliness" and "masculinity": looking at dictionary definitions from the 1890s, Bederman finds the word "manly" presented as "the word into which have been gathered the highest conceptions of what is worthy of . . . manhood" (qtd. on 18). In contrast, "masculine" "was used to refer to any characteristics, good or bad, that all men had" (18).

Anderson's use of the word "manly" in connection with black male identity therefore carries a sense of moral or social value, rather than a more reductively essentialist conceptualization of black men somehow exhibiting or containing what is considered to be male.[37] He may not go as far as to argue for black men becoming role models for the white working class, but he suggests that the black male identity of the laborers he watched so avidly in Mobile and New Orleans presented desirable characteristics for social cohesion—characteristics that provide the moral positivity to their gender identity ascribed by the word "manly." In his most detailed definition of his own "modernity," Anderson drew on Brooks expressly to claim that one of the most important aspects of being part of the "modern movement" was that it had shown that "the force of the New England culture is pretty well spent" (*Modern Writer* 34). "Modernity" for Anderson was inherently racialized, for if what he felt to be a Puritan cultural hegemony was racially founded, then challenging that hegemony required an "other" race upon which he could draw not just symbolic but biological currency. And, as many critics have noted, the long history of racial evaluation within a system of comparative value—why one race is considered better than another—has inevitably been conducted in terms of gender; one of the main criticisms Anderson made of the "tired . . . New England atmosphere" was its "feminine force" (*Letters* 43).

It was this sense of black masculinity as "manly," exhibitive of a potent but spiritualized sexuality that was closely related to working environment (in *Dark Laughter* he even referred to the black dock workers as having "bodies like gods") that underpinned his idealization of African American communities (77). This is in contrast to how Clare Colquitt has described Winesburg; she has termed it a "small Midwestern town . . . devoid of rituals commemorating the essential harmony—and connectedness—of its inhabitants" ("Motherlove" 83). Anderson's representations of wandering around black sections of Mobile, or the following, which is his description of staying at a sugar plantation near New Orleans, are notable in contrast to what Colquitt describes:

> In the Negro quarters on the big sugar plantation the tired old Negro men and women sit on the steps before the cabins and smoke their pipes. There are fat middleaged wives there too. They come out of cabins and walk away toward the levee, their big hips rolling.
>
> There are beautiful young Negro men, tall lean ones. They go in the evening to the levee too. The young Negro bucks and the wenches walk with a rolling swagger. Life gathers up through them warmly. There are cries from the darkness up there on the levee. A high-pitched feminine voice cries, "Now you quit that, nigger. Now you quit that." (*Southern Odyssey* 175)

This suggests various things: a kind of easy mobility between public and private spaces, and between residential and "natural" space; an absence of the generational conflict that several cultural critics of the time identified as a feature of white American modernism; and a thinly veiled desire for the "beautiful young Negro men" whose exhibitionistic (but "authentic") virile sexuality acts as a point of social cohesion for the community, as "life gathers up through them."

However, these idealizations of African American communities in the service of a broader cultural critique involved a painful ambivalence for Anderson. It was an ambivalence that also indicates the severest of limitations to the efficacy of utilizing the cultural forms of minority racial groups in the service of critiquing dominant cultural practice, especially when tied to an essentialized view of race. As Anderson had followed Brooks in seeing race and culture as largely coextensive, he could celebrate African American communities and cultures but never participate in them. Accordingly, his representations are often marked by a sense of his own distance from the communities he observes. As I shall discuss in the chapter on the South and ethnography, Anderson felt uneasy about how to observe these scenes, about the extent to which his own visibility would destroy this atmosphere of idyllic community. For example, at the time of his description of the scene quoted above, he was "standing in the warm darkness, unseen at the edge of the quarter," and confesses "I am a Jack the Peeper" (*Southern Odyssey* 175–76). It was this double sense of "blackness" as explicable as a form of community, but also a social grouping which was hermetically sealed and from which he was excluded, which he expounded in a once-reserved letter to his friend Paul Rosenfeld dated August 19, 1922, now on open access at the Newberry Library. In this letter race becomes a way of belonging, a way of escaping and even resisting the alienation that Anderson connected with white Anglo-American industrial culture. It is worth extensive quotation:

> In New Orleans I found the negro and was happy living near him. My house in New Orleans was in a section occupied almost entirely by Italians. In the evening I walked about and was happy.
>
> . . . .
>
> Didn't just this race feeling have a certain value of its own, and is it not, partly at least, what I have been after? Are not all Americans, the mixed-bloods, after the same thing? Could it not be, in itself, something of the mother thing one seeks. Are not we mixed-blood Americans like people who walk along a street seeing houses lighted and having no houses of our own. Perhaps we quite overvalue the matter of having such a house but there might be, nevertheless, a hunger unsatisfied. . . . "if one lived here, were a member of this race, he would belong to something."
>
> I give you this reaction of my own at whatever value you may think it has. I keep wondering if the whole assertiveness of the Americans is not after all due to something of this sort. It would add some strength to Van Wyck's claim, wouldn't it?[38] [My ellipses]

Anderson's comment that his observations may validate Van Wyck Brooks's central thesis implies that the Puritan failure to provide socially effective forms of culture and community is a *racial* failure. Moreover, in this letter, race—except for whites who fell into the category of "mixed-blood Americans"—was conceived as a type of belonging, indeed an explicitly familial belonging. By being outside of any family structure or hermetic blood relationship, this description depicts Anderson's Anglo-Saxon whiteness as a type of racial heterogeneity, conceptualized as a mixture rather than as purity, as a lack rather than a tangible quality, and consequently, it becomes almost a non-identity. For the time, this type of description was extremely unusual. As Walter Benn Michaels has shown, family was becoming a more prevalent conceptual model at this time for nativist writers who were arguing for the continuation of racial segregation and immigration restriction. In discussing Charles W. Gould's *America: A Family Matter* (1923), Michaels argues that a new technology of racial exclusion developing in the 1920s was to imagine white Anglo-Saxon America as a *family.* In doing so, nativist writers aimed "to transform American identity from the sort of thing that could be acquired (through naturalization) into the sort of thing that could be inherited (from one's parents). Insofar as the family becomes the site of national identity, nationality becomes an effect of racial identity" (8). Despite their often shared assumptions and structural similarities, then, primitivism and this type of eugenic nativism could diverge on the trope of race as a hermetic family structure. This is significant because it demonstrates that primitivism is not merely a reconceptualization of the more outspokenly exclusionist racial policies of nativist writers like Gould, Lothrop Stoddard, or Madison Grant.

As well as prompting these observations, this letter illustrates that Anderson's sense of his own racial identity was interrogated by his experiences with those he deemed as "others." This is a standard point of theory for any poststructuralist analysis of race, but complicated here by Anderson's own awareness that this was the case. The feeling of being outside of any cultural collectivity is undoubtedly due in part to Anglo-American whiteness's ideological advantage in appearing "natural" and hence to a degree invisible, as Richard Dyer has discussed. However, in the letter quoted above, Anderson seems to sense—albeit dimly—that his own whiteness was something only formed in relation to "other" races and that it was a much less stable entity than others in the 1920s were suggesting. If American whiteness was not conceptualizable as a family, then what was it? If his whiteness became problematically visible in situations like this, why not explore it further? And if whiteness is motherless—as he seems to suggest—what does this suggest about the connections, and mutual constitutionality, involved between race and gender? The fact that this letter was reserved until recently—and there is no obvious explanation why—put alongside the unusually hesitant and self-questioning tone of the letter, suggest that these questions would remain at the margins of Anderson's ability or willingness to think about race. Yet they also represent a fascinating logical end point of his primitivism, in that the poverty of whiteness as lacking positive definition, as constituting what Goldberg has called a "leftover identity," is revealed (*Racial Subjects* 9). Moreover, it suggests that the myth of (a tacitly white) American individualism (which Morrison finds was so persistently defined against an Africanist presence) can easily turn to anxious feelings of isolation and solitude.[39]

Representations of African Americans, therefore, helped Anderson's critique of laboring practice in an industrialized America and shaped his ideas about effective forms of community and gender identity. Yet my discussion so far has been largely silent over the extremely problematic nature of Anderson's project, which was in many ways a one-way cultural extraction: indeed, Anderson frequently reified blackness as something to be "got," attained, or appropriated.[40] His was a project analogous to the phrase "love and theft," which Eric Lott uses to describe minstrelsy, or to what Langston Hughes felt "was mostly what [white people] wanted out of Negroes—work and fun—without paying for it."[41] The frequently disturbing political ramifications of Anderson's position, as well as the ways this contrasted to much of the cultural energies originating from the African American community at the time, is the subject that I turn to next.

Sherwood Anderson in Central Park, 1939. Photograph by Carl Van Vechten. (Courtesy of the Library of Congress, Prints & Photographs Division, Carl Van Vechten Collection, LOT 12735, no. 51.)

RACE AND SUBJECTIVITY: ANDERSON'S PRIMITIVISM AND THE NEW NEGRO RENAISSANCE

> ". . . no-one has told you, Brother, that at times you have tom-toms beating in your voice?"
>
> "My god," I laughed, "I thought that was the beat of profound ideas."
>
> **—RALPH ELLISON, *INVISIBLE MAN* 357**

Ellison's famous quotation about primitivism, of course, effectively represents it as a failure of dialogue, and this seems an appropriate way to introduce this section on Anderson. Although Anderson was not feted by the new generation of African American authors who helped constitute what has become known as the New Negro Renaissance, he was admired by them and was invited on more than one occasion to assist in promoting African American letters. Yet, with the notable exception of Jean Toomer, he assiduously maintained his distance from the personalities and institutions that characterized the movement. He was invited to contribute to *The New Negro,* an offer he declined; Jean Toomer asked for his help in establishing a new little magazine for African American writing, a request he refused (Helbling, "Sherwood Anderson"112). Anderson later commented that the "second-rate negro poet or artist" was "always getting twice the credit of an equally able white man. That's northern sentimentality," and criticized Langston Hughes's *The Ways of White Folks* for holding a "deep-seated resentment" towards whites.[42] Facts such as these—also evident from the deterioration of his epistolary friendship with Jean Toomer that I shall examine later—begin to suggest that Anderson's literary use of African Americans was not only indifferent toward, but was actively in opposition to, the direction that African American intellectual and literary culture was taking in the 1920s. Although cultural historians such as Ann Douglas, George Hutchinson, and Seiglinde Lemke have recently argued convincingly that the contours of the New Negro Renaissance owed much to dialogue across racial demarcations, Anderson demonstrates that African Americans could be symbolically and imaginatively central to varieties of white modernism without any such dialogue taking place and arguably *because* no such dialogue took place.[43]

The most useful way of initiating this discussion is perhaps to examine one of Anderson's typical representations of African Americans, one that exhibits the coexistence of "authentic" cultural production, a dignified labor, and effective masculine roles, and then to consider how this conflicts with some of the strategies being adopted by black intellectuals aiming for greater social inclusion for African Americans. This example derives from his "Notes Out of a Man's Life," published in his *Notebook* in 1926. It came as he sat in a concealed vantage point watching stevedores on a boat landing at Baton Rouge:

> Soft swaying bodies, dancing, dancing, dancing. In the night the great bugs, that came out of the darkness to the light, also danced about the heads of the negro stevedores.
>
> . . .
>
> Then it began. Generations of load bearers in the bodies of these men, the blacks. Did something whisper to them out of the silent river?
>
> First the soft beginning of laughter—out of the bowels of the ship. The laughter ran up the gangplank.
>
> A cry. Oh, ah ho, ah ho, ah ho. Las' sack now. Soon de las' sack. Oh, ah ha, ah ha.
>
> A dance in the bodies now. Swaying bodies going empty handed, dancing down a gang-plank.
>
> . . .
>
> But keep the song, black man, don't lose the song.
> When you lose that, we've got you, we whites.
> We'll get you in the end, of course.
> That's what makes the song sweet to hear while it lasts.
>
> ("Notes out of a Man's Life," *Notebook*, 132–35. My ellipses)

The stevedores share a sense of community in this portrayal, as the work song affirms their membership in a social community; in addition, work song establishes a relation between culture and labor (even if who owns the boat, and the conditions of employment, are left deliberately obscure). They are alienated neither from each other nor from their labor; furthermore, they seem to be inheritors of a common laboring ancestry, seamlessly continuing an unchanging practice of work on the river. This participation in a double community, both ancestral and interpersonal, is what Anderson felt was denied to white Americans and is an essential part of his "desire for the primitive," what Colin Rhodes describes as "a Utopian dream of a 'return' to some previous state of grace" so common to all versions of primitivism (20). However, such a strategy comes at a price. It is obvious that this seemingly timeless ancestral heritage of boat loading actually removes the stevedores from history rather than locates them in it: the only possibility of change within their existence is an end to their cultural "otherness" through integration into white society, rather than any attempt on Anderson's part to equip them with a specific and temporally precise history. Torgovnick explains this strategy:

> The primitive's magical ability to dissolve differences depends on an illusion of time and sense in which the primitive is both eternally past and eternally

> present. For the charm to work, the primitive must represent a common past—our past, a Euro-American past so long gone that we can find no traces of it in Western spaces. But the primitive must be eternally present in other spaces—the spaces of primitive peoples. Otherwise we cannot get to it, cannot find the magical spot where differences dissolve and harmony and rest prevail. (186–87)

Any precise past erects rather than dissolves differences; hence the mythical trope of "generations of load bearers" is sufficiently generalized to suggest a "common past." It is also apparent that the foundation for this "magical ability to dissolve differences" and establish community was centrally concerned with the body. A kind of racial *essence*—as Anderson, said, "something come out of Africa, something in the blood"—is involved here, an essentialization that is central to the operation of primitivism.[44] Moreover, the essence that Anderson associates with "blackness" is displayed, performed, and embodied rather than being in any way an essence that is in some way contained—and thus at odds with—the body. This idea of a racial essence that was separable from the body—and of the body as a container for this essence that the essence could ultimately transcend—is one of the constitutive factors Richard Dyer has identified with the construction of whiteness.[45] As he says, a discourse has existed within biological determinations of whiteness that has "stressed that which cannot be scrutinized, that little something more that makes whites different"—a quality he terms "spirit," which makes whiteness to a degree founded on an invisibility (23). The opposite to this is evident in Anderson's representation above; these bodies are racialized through a temporal and visual immanence that effectively removes them from history. This leads to a conception of black culture as static, a result of his erasure of any differentiation between culture and biology: as he is watching a *performance* of "blackness," it is a static model that can only ever be reproduced.[46]

This contrasted with much of the work of the writers of the New Negro Renaissance towards greater cultural and political recognition for African Americans. For example, Arthur A. Schomburg, the black historian, stated in "The Negro Digs up his Past," an essay in Alain Locke's seminal anthology of 1925 *The New Negro,* that "[h]istory must restore what slavery took away, for it is the social damage of slavery that the present generations must repair and offset" (231). Schomburg, whose large collection of African and African American historical materials was bought by the New York Public Library in 1926 and which still forms a world center for African and African American scholarship, felt that black America needed to respond to "the very pressure of the moment to become the most enthusiastic antiquarian of them all" (231). One of the main ideological strategies of racist discourse in America had been to label "[t]he Negro . . . a man without a history," as Hegel had done; to posit a race as without history is to identify it as analogous to nature (237). Only if a culture is viewed as static can it be naturalized in this way, and this was at least a part of the reason that historians such as Schomburg—and later cultural anthropologists such as Zora Neale Hurston—placed dynamism at the center of their conception of black history and culture.[47] Indeed, changing definitions of the word "culture" in the 1920s—largely based on the methodology of Boasian anthropology—assisted this project.[48]

Also at odds with primitivistic representation was the insistence by some members of the New Negro Renaissance on an absolute separation between culture and biological heredity. At its extreme this took the form of arguing for the cultural sameness of black and white America; George S. Schuyler opined that the "Aframerican is merely a lampblacked Anglo-Saxon," and Melville Herskovits asserted in *The New Negro* that Harlem (in comparison to the rest of New York) represented "the same pattern, only a different shade!"[49] This turning away from the body as the locus of racial identity was also evident in several works of the New Negro Renaissance. It is interesting to note that in Winold Reiss's portraits in *The New Negro*—including those of W. E. B. Du Bois, Countee Cullen, Elise J. McDougald, Paul Robeson, Mary McCloud Bethune, and Robert Russa Moton, for example—the faces and hands are painted in great representational detail, but their torsos and clothing are sketched in simple, brief pencil lines that do not accentuate the form of the body (or, in the case of Cullen's portrait, omit it totally). This attempt to shift the discourse of blackness away from the corporeal and onto the cerebral, rational, and therefore historical was in complete opposition to Anderson's focus on the body as the mainstay of his primitivistic representations. As Torgovnick has noted, conceptualizations of primitivism are rarely separable from those of nature and physicality, and as she remarks, the appeal of "going primitive" has usually been synonymous with "getting physical" in the twentieth century (228).

As I have suggested, Anderson saw "blackness" as performative both in its citationality and his conception of it as an act of display—ways of racialization that whiteness did not share. This is evident in his two favored representational frameworks for the black body: the body as dance and the body as painting. The motif of the "dancing" body was one Anderson used again and again in his writing about African Americans (for example, he wrote to

Alfred Stieglitz in 1924 on the subject of New Orleans that "I get here what I have always got—the slow, lazy laugh of niggers, the niggers' bodies in a slow dance, at work, walking") and reflects the popular interest in African American forms of dance at the time (*Letters* 129).[50] What Anderson seemed to conceptualize as the "essence" of blackness was performed in dance, but, to his continual frustration, it proved highly resistant to any further explication.[51] Yet this intangibility, indefinability, of a racialized "essence"—and crucially also its tendency to be configured as excess—is precisely what gives it its symbolic, psychological, and social power, as critics such as Slavoj Žižek have discussed.[52] As Eric Lott has noted, a type of excessive physicality attributed to African Americans was consolidated in minstrelsy, and any discussion of the white reception of African American dance is incomplete without reference to this tradition. As he observes about patterns of blackface in the 1840s, "the shows . . . were ingenious in coming up with ways to fetishize the body in a spectacle that worked against the forward motion of the show, interrupting the flow of action with uproarious spectacles for erotic consumption," and as a result, "'Black' figures were there to be looked at, shaped to the demands of desire" (140). Dancing provided just this spectacular space and the trope of excessive enjoyment, an enjoyment that was reliant on an embodied, intangible, racialized essence.

These paradigms of "blackness" were also obvious in Anderson's views on painting, and in his comments to Jean Toomer in their brief correspondence. As he wrote to Toomer in early 1924:

> A man like yourself can escape. You have a direct and glowing genius that is, I am sure, a part of your body, a part of the way you walk, look at things, make love, sleep and eat. Such a man goes rather directly from feeling to expression.
>
> [He then talks about his own trips south.]
>
> . . . .
>
> The negro life was outside me, had to remain outside me. That may have been why I wanted to paint. There was less mind, more feeling. I could approach the brown men and women through a quite impersonal love of color in skins, through the same kind of love of line as expressed in lazy sprawling bodies. (My ellipsis; Turner, "Intersection" 107)

Chip Rhodes declares that "[t]here are few purer expressions of the vogue of the Negro in the twenties" than this letter, in its claim that Toomer's genius was purely physical (182). In going "directly from feeling to expression," Anderson implies that Toomer's artistic production was not only continuous with his body and its desires but indistinguishable from them;

in consequence, the "ideal" African American cultural production he saw Toomer as epitomizing was little more than the metonymic extension of the black body. In effect, this is the *reductio ad absurdum* of the theory that biology is culture, in that it makes the black body an object of culture and all black culture an extension of the black body. This effortless immediacy of creation echoes other constructions of the primitive at the time; Stallabrass notes that in British anthropology and art history "primitive" art was seen to be "unconscious because the relationship between vision and representation is direct" (100). Yet this immediacy—or immanence, as I have previously termed it—is also closely connected to visual representation.

As the long quotation above exemplifies, the way Anderson felt he could best represent African Americans was through painting. During his first trip to Alabama, Anderson took up painting with incredible zeal; in the previous few years he had not shown any interest in practicing the visual arts himself, but the presence of African Americans in Mobile impelled him to take it up. In fact, one of his paintings of an African American survives at the Newberry Library. In part this was because of his correspondence with Jerome Blum, who was at that time living in Tahiti and trying to paint the indigenous population in the manner of Gauguin; Anderson responded to his letters, and to W. Somerset Maugham's fictionalization of Gauguin's life in *The Moon and Sixpence* (1919), with great enthusiasm.[53] Indeed, Anderson was a lifelong fan of Gauguin and even considered writing a biography of him at one time; Townsend even suggests that Anderson's "escape" from Chicago to Mobile in 1920 was self-consciously modeled on Gauguin's flight to the South Seas (161). Anderson confided to Waldo Frank that he would like to go to Fairhope for "about six months . . . not to write, but to paint" and, in another letter, expressed the hope that "[t]ogether we will stop at cabin doors and talk to sweet souled niggers. You will see the greens, the blues, the golden yellows, the living red of their tawny skins and the soft eyes, the eyes that know failure but no defeat."[54]

This "quite impersonal love of color in skins" attests to the temporal immanence he felt associated with blackness: this immanence was only *truly* representable through the spatial nature of visual media, in contrast to the inherent temporality of language. This immanence becomes attached to the trope of color, as can be seen in the quotations above; as Stallabrass notes, the obsession with color in representations of "the primitive" shows that "to concentrate on color was to concentrate on the surface and on the subjective: surface becomes essence" (110). Indeed, the focus on color is a recognition of an externalized "essence" and its need to be visible (in contrast to the "spirit" of whiteness). Yet also, in Anderson's description of the multiplicity of color in "black" skin, there is perhaps an admission of the sheer polyvalency of the black body within his thinking. In allowing this diversity of color into his description of bodies—and attesting that *this* is the reason that he wishes to be near them—he gestures toward his investment in these bodies as sites that he can load (as we have seen) with multiple and often contradictory meanings.

Moreover, this multiplicity again illustrates how "blackness" enabled Anderson's construction of his whiteness. Dyer suggests that whiteness as a hue has often been involved in conceptual slippage with white as a skin color, and notes that the charge of moral and aesthetic superiority associated with whiteness has an "emphasis on purity, cleanliness, virginity, in short, absence, [which] inflects whiteness . . . towards non-particularity, only this time in the sense of non-existence" (70). If whiteness as a racial identity and as a color (or non-color) is intimately involved with absence, then "other" colors become invested with all things that whiteness lacks. Anderson's investment of black bodies with multiple color therefore attests to the impoverishing nature of whiteness as absence, his inability to define it in positive terms (as seen in the letter about whiteness being somehow outside of the family). However, it also attests to its epistemological strength—as Dyer points out, if it is nothing it also functions as everything, as universal, and as endless in its possibility. The black bodies Anderson so admired had multiple semantic possibilities but not endless ones—unlike whiteness.

This leads on to perhaps the most obvious—and pernicious—aspect of Anderson's thinking about race. His main concern for Toomer in their correspondence was that he would "let the intense white man get him. They are going to color his style, spoil him" (Turner, "Intersection" 106). The threat that Anderson perceived to Toomer's quality of "genius" which was "a part of [the] body," the "impersonal" quality of a physicalized mode of artistic production, was consciousness—or individuality. The African American community that he constructed as an escape from the isolating experience of modern white society was founded on the premise of black nonindividuation, a racial technology that Felipe Smith has identified as significant in white America's imagination of the United States as a racially segregated nation.[55] Accordingly, Anderson showed little desire to converse or even approach individual African Americans during his stay in the South: "Try down there to associate with the negro; sit with him, eat with him, talk with him. You would learn nothing. A white man of the right sort will tell you everything—more clearly" ("The South" 58). Much more conducive to him was the construction of African American community from a discreet anthropological distance, a distance that allowed the willful negation of personality or individuality. This of course precluded the development of any friendships with African Americans, as Jean Toomer soon found out. Despite the complexity of Toomer's racial heritage and despite the fact that even as *Cane* was published Toomer was disavowing the entire concept of an essentialist racial heritage, Anderson saw him purely on his own terms and brushed aside Toomer's attempts at self-definition. As Toomer complained in a letter to Waldo Frank, "He limits me to Negro" (*Letters* 113).[56]

In defining African American subjectivity as nonindividuated, self-awareness and economic awareness among African Americans were not merely something Anderson was uninterested in but something he argued against. In the same letter to Jerome and Lucile Blum already quoted above, he commented, "The Negro race in America is something. The reformers are trying to make them race conscious, fight for their rights and all that. It's silly" (*Letters* 68). Moreover, his refusal to countenance African Americans as anything other than a communal entity was also at odds with his commitment to a republican individualism common to the Young American critics. This was obvious from his admiration for individuals who clashed with the dominant principles of the time, such as Theodore Dreiser, or political leaders such as Lincoln or Grant whom he felt had contributed to a tradition of personal liberty. (He considered writing biographies of both Grant and Lincoln, neither of which he completed.) It also partially explained why he refused to join the Communist Party in the 1930s, despite his increased involvement with leftist politics. Yet this tradition of republican individualism had from its inception been racialized and gendered, extending suffrage and the definition of autonomous subjectivity according to those criteria. As Morrison has noted, the centrality of individualism to imaginations of American identity is inconceivable without an Africanist presence; "individualism" is a translation of the concept of freedom, a concept that emerged from being measured against a "bound and unfree, rebellious but serviceable, black population . . ." (44). If Anderson shared what Blake has characterized as the broad aim of the Young American critics—that is, the cultivation of "the good life of personality lived in the environment of the Beloved Community"—he also believed that although African Americans could offer resources to this project, they could not fully participate in it.[57] As a result, Anderson's primitivism encoded the structures of previous racist discourse which primitivism had so enraged, and both held a commitment to the denial of any political or economic advancement for African Americans.

CONSUMING THE BODY: ANDERSON AND *DARK LAUGHTER*

These types of representation attendant on Anderson's use of primitivism as a form of cultural critique are glaringly ugly for contemporary readers, and it would be disingenuous to pretend otherwise. Yet there were other significant limitations to this project, ones which are revealing in what they exemplify about the different discursive spheres in which race was operative in the 1920s—and indeed the way in which race was coming to mean new and different things within a rapidly expanding consumer economy. These limitations were most evident in the book that marked the turning point in Anderson's reputation. This was his most infamous contribution to primitivist literature, *Dark Laughter*, which was written during his residency in New Orleans in 1924 and published in 1925. One of the central inconsistencies of *Dark Laughter* is that the staple motifs of primitivism it employs, such as voyeurism, erotic fantasy, and a celebration of sensual pleasure, were all motifs that were being used to promote consumer desire within an economy experiencing a transition toward a primarily consumerist base. The discourse of primitivism, therefore, which Anderson intended to be a powerful critique of industrial capitalism, was simultaneously operative as an effective marketing and advertising tactic within that very system of industrial capitalism. What I hope to show are the ways in which Anderson's text engages with both these deployments of primitivism and therefore becomes fundamentally complicit with new technologies of consumer formation and market expansion. I examine to what extent this accounts for *Dark Laughter*'s positioning within the literary marketplace, and to what degree Anderson was both aware of and concerned about the wider economic implications of the "vogue of the Negro," of which *Dark Laughter* became a part.

As already suggested, the discourse of radicalism that surrounded primitivism was in many ways unfounded. Yet as the 1920s progressed, the economic critique of industrial capitalism that Anderson intended to buttress with primitivistic representations began to be less and less sharply distinguishable from the strategies of an economy increasingly based on consumerism. As I have mentioned, primitivism was often connected to both modernism and modernity, and this figuration of primitivism as "modern" often overlapped with the incessant demand for ever-changing tropes of "the modern" within the rapidly expanding commodity market, of novelty and fashionability that rendered earlier consumer durables obsolete. Moreover, the discourse of primitivism was also annexed into the inducement of consumer desire within 1920s mass culture to encourage subjectivities that would consume more. Chip Rhodes notes that

> the mass cultural imperative to produce consumer desire dovetailed nicely with what David Levering Lewis has called the "vogue of the Negro," the white fetishization of blacks as "primitives" that emphasized their capacity and appetite for pleasure. Mass culture induced consumer demand for new products by locating the desires and needs these new goods spoke to with an authentic, ahistorical subjectivity at odds with the Puritan, savings-oriented culture that advocated discipline and deferred pleasure. (171)

As Goldberg has noted of whiteness in America in the past fifteen years, "Self-defined for many years as the residue of all the identities it took itself not to be, all those it excluded as abject, whiteness is now revealed as a left-over identity. And leftovers no longer sell in an economy of throwaways" (*Racial Subjects* 9). This also applies (albeit in a more limited fashion) to the 1920s, and this meant, as Rhodes notes, that discourses of "blackness" became important in "the construction of consumers to enable the boom in consumer durables" (176).[58] This process was also encouraged and manipulated by the publishing industry. *Dark Laughter* was Anderson's biggest financial success; he claimed later that 1925 was "the one year of money making I ever had, the year of *Dark Laughter*"—money that enabled him to buy the farm in Virginia where he lived for the rest of his life.[59] Indeed, he later boasted that the book made him "suddenly 'nigger-rich.' Lord, how the money rolled in."[60] In a letter to his publisher, Horace Liveright, before *Dark Laughter* was published, he wrote, "Bet on this book, Horace, it is going to be there with a bang. . . . The book won't be exactly mild, my dear Horace, and it may stir up the dry bones some, but I do not believe there is anything in it that is suppressible. It is the kind of book that just now ought to arouse a lot of interest" (*Letters* 142–43). As Glen Love dryly remarks of this letter, "Anderson seemed to believe that the book's primitive currency would carry it" (*Horses or Men* 243–44).

The thematic concern with "blackness" implied by the title was also present as part of the advertising blurb on the original dust jacket. This consideration of the public reception of his work, and even the implied notion in this letter of writing to the demands of his readership, is a highly uncharacteristic statement on the part of Anderson. His concern with public reception may have been motivated by an anxiety to reassure Liveright, his new publisher, that he could deliver the goods; Liveright had offered Anderson a lucrative financial package to entice him away from Ben Huebsch for the publication of *Dark Laughter*. In addition, Liveright's superior distribution and advertising organization undoubtedly helped *Dark Laughter*'s popular success. I also would not suggest that Anderson perceived *Dark Laughter* as being less radical or experimental than his other work, or that he calculatingly catered to public taste. However, he was clearly aware of a public demand, a demand that Hart Crane had defined in the *Double Dealer:* "I would like to see Anderson handle the negro in fiction. So far it has not been done without sentimentality or cruelty, but the directness of his vision would produce something new and deep in this direction" ("Sherwood Anderson" 212).

Primitivism, then, clearly occupied more than the single role of providing a mirror for white writers seeking to challenge conventional thinking. Indeed, at this point it is worth noting that the umbrella term "primitivist discourse" tends to obscure wide variations within the politics of the various writers who utilized some of the tropes I have been discussing. Claude McKay's *Banjo,* for example, attempts to articulate a version of resistant black solidarity across the diaspora through primitivism. His confrontational vision outlines a Pan-African primitivism involving intellectual leadership, a rejection of Christian and Cartesian dualism, and a militancy that comes from a history of shared oppression.[61] Similarly, African American artists whose work contained some of the tropes hitherto mentioned, often in attempts to explore African American oral or folk culture, found this aspect of their work appropriated by white patrons in ways they found disturbing.[62] Primitivism, then, was not stable, unidirectional, or consistent, and I would argue that critics such as Chip Rhodes who argue that "[McKay, Toomer, and Hughes] uncritically employed the discourse of blackness as they made their way through the social hierarchy and ideological institutions of the period" are overly reductive in their treatment of it (180). Nevertheless, because primitivism was so concerned with usually vague links between vast but emotive ideas such as freedom, the body, sexuality, and a kind of primal integrity, it was a discourse that was as flexible as it was attractive. This, of course, made it an ideal discourse for mass consumerism and popular fiction, as W. E. B. Du Bois noted about DuBose Heyward's *Porgy.* White writers, he felt,

> . . . cry for freedom in dealing with Negroes because they have so little freedom in dealing with whites. DuBose Heyward writes "Porgy" and writes beautifully of the black Charleston underworld. But why does he do this? Because he cannot do a similar thing for the white people of Charleston, or they would drum him out of town. The only chance he had to tell the truth of pitiful human degradation was to tell it of colored people. . . . In other words, the white public demands of its artists, literary and pictorial, racial

> pre-judgement which deliberately distorts truth and justice, as far as colored races are concerned, and it will pay for no other. ("Criteria" 103–4)

In other words, primitivism allowed the possibility of wish fulfilment, usually of an erotic nature, within a space exempt from the moral codes and restrictions that publishers attended to white characterization—and promised a sizeable readership in doing so. Although it is unlikely that Anderson tailored aspects of *Dark Laughter* to the mass market, it is true that *Dark Laughter*—containing the most extreme of his primitivistic representations—consistently engages with the circulation of readerly desire and fantasy around objectified black bodies and considers the economic significance of such objectification. Chapter 10, set entirely in New Orleans, stands as the structural center of the book; the protagonist, Bruce Dudley, works his way down the Mississippi to New Orleans and then back to Ohio following his flight from his wife and job in Chicago, an escape brought on by the imaginative and spiritual stagnation he felt there. It is evidently a narrative of quest to an altogether more mythological and spiritual "other" space, in a river journey that suggests obvious parallels with both *Huckleberry Finn* and *Heart of Darkness*. In a text that Kim Townsend wryly decides "must have set some kind of record for the number of questions in a novel" (224), the narrator wonders, "[H]ad Bruce fled from his own city, Chicago, hoping to find, in the soft nights of a river town, something to cure him?" (*Dark Laughter* 122). To find his "cure" Bruce must make a literal journey to the margin of American society; Anderson once referred to New Orleans as "on the lip of America," a punning phrase that indicates his belief in the correspondence between marginality and truthful expression ("New Orleans" 289). Once in New Orleans, primarily through observing the African American community, Bruce gains the self-awareness and liberty to both recognize and attain the true object of his desire, which later becomes realized as Aline Grey, the wife of his boss. However, rather than a specific narrative experience that Bruce lives through in New Orleans, his time there is figured as a succession of unconnected images. This example comes as Bruce looks across the street at a "nigger girl of twenty": "sometimes [she] sleeps alone but sometimes a brown man sleeps with her." She also "knows Bruce is looking" (79):

> Bruce lay lazy in bed. The brown girl's body was like the thick waving leaf of a young banana plant. If you were a painter now, you could paint that, maybe. Paint a brown nigger girl in a broad leaf waving and send it up North. Why not sell it to a society woman of New Orleans? Get some money

> to loaf a while longer on. She wouldn't know, would never guess. Paint a brown laborer's narrow suave flanks onto the trunk of a tree. Send it to the Art institute of Chicago. (80)

This quotation exemplifies several features of how Anderson's primitivism were obvious expressions—and generative strategies—of white male desire. In addition to the penetrative nature of the male gaze, there is the representation of the black body and the black woman as erotic object. Her status is thus remarkably similar to black women under slavery, sexually available to their masters (due to the great danger involved in refusing them) and defined purely by their corporeal properties of sexuality and capacity for labor. As a result Anderson's portrayal is, again, continuous with earlier racist strategies and representations.

Perhaps a more complex issue raised by this presentation, however, is the transformation of the eroticized black female body into a pictorial image, the painting, a transformation with the primary purpose of commodification. As I have noted, Anderson's fascination with African Americans was deeply connected with his love of painting, and this desire to use the spatial medium of painting in his representation of African Americans rather than the temporal medium of narrative could be seen as just another way of dehistoricizing black subjectivity. However, in a subtler formulation, a painting also has greater exchange value than narrative in its status as an original image and thus becomes a better symbol of a commodity within consumer capitalism. The painting is an image that can be taken out of its original sociohistorical context, invested with the desires of a white audience and sold back to them as literally a product of those desires. In this nexus, the complicity of consumerism, racial discourse, and white desire is revealed in a similar fashion to Chip Rhodes's comments about the use of black racial identity as a stimulant to white consumer desire. It also suggests a correlation between this practice and the mechanics of colonialist representation, which, as Janmohammed has argued, has the principle of psychological "exchange value" between self and other at its heart, just as colonial material practice had exchange value as its primary motivation (21).

This section of *Dark Laughter* therefore expresses Anderson's cynicism about the motives of white representation of African Americans, or white patronage of black artists in the twenties. Indeed, exactly what white artists and patrons had invested—in every sense—in black bodies presents a constant sense of unease in Anderson's primitivism. This was evinced in his discussion of the difficulty he found in representing African Americans in his review of Langston Hughes's *The Ways of White Folks*, his disparaging comments about northern artists getting the "nigger craze," and his suspicion about the motives behind the critical acclaim forwarded to some writers of the New Negro Renaissance. Anderson had worked for many years as a successful advertising copywriter and clearly understood the relationship between the organization of desire and a consumerist economy. In a lecture of 1925 he discussed the "standardization of taste and material desires" that had become necessary with the new industrial technology of mass commodity production, and the function of mass market magazines to "create through advertising, a nation-wide demand for certain commodities" (*Modern Writer* 14).

Such awareness of the processes underpinning consumer formation is evident in the quotation from *Dark Laughter* given above, as Anderson depicts the ease by which the multiplicity of desires around "blackness" and the feminine can be diverted into desire for material goods. The figuration of these desires, in the object of the painting, can be exported to the North and carefully denuded of all the complex social actualities—and atrocities—of interracial relations in the South to make it more saleable. This "purification" was economic expediency, which Anderson saw going on all around him in 1925, and it was this that must have reminded him of the strategies for ensuring the mobility of desire that he had used as an advertising writer. This unease about his own complicity in replicating the structures of a mass consumer economy he railed so persistently against is evident in his writing about African Americans, and the above example is as close as he got to admitting the inadequacies of his own representations.

Objectification, of course, involves the negation of agency, and this was criticized by William H. Baldwin, who reviewed *Dark Laughter* in *Opportunity*, Black Harlem's leading monthly magazine for the arts. His comment that in the novel "Negroes flash into the story and fade out again—as aimlessly as the fireflies of a summer evening" (137) employs not only the metaphor of the gaze-attracting "flash" of black representation but also the "aimless" depiction of characters without agency, invested only with available, eroticized bodies. In contrast, having gained what he wanted from New Orleans, and having cast his gaze across many black promiscuous women, Bruce is free to leave and goes on to determine the narrative course of the novel. The black characters, however, remain spatially rather than narratively determined: with no lives but erotic ones, they remain biographically and historically obscure and are thus defined purely by their function of bearing the projection of white desire from either character or reader.

Such erotic titillation doubtlessly accounted at least in part for the market popularity of *Dark Laughter* and also explains the reason it marked the beginning of a steep decline in Anderson's critical reputation, not least among the next generation of American writers. Writing to Maxwell Perkins in December 1925, F. Scott Fitzgerald stated that Anderson's last two books (the other was *A Story Teller's Story*) had "let everybody down who had believed in him" and were "cheap, faked, obscurantic and awful" (*Letters* 214). In Hemingway's brilliant parody of Sherwood Anderson, *The Torrents of Spring* (published in direct response to *Dark Laughter*) a naked Native American "squaw" walks into the beanery where Scripps O'Neill, the character based on Bruce Dudley, is eating. "Scripps O'Neill was feeling faint and shaken. Something had stirred inside him, some vague primordial feeling, as the squaw had walked into the room" (94). Indeed, *The Torrents of Spring* was subtitled "A Romantic Novel in Honor of the Passing of a Great Race," a title that both gestured toward the white supremacist and eugenic popularizer Madison Grant's 1916 book *The Passing of the Great Race* and the "passing" of Sherwood Anderson's (and to a lesser extent Gertrude Stein's) status as significant figures for the avant-garde.

In linking Anderson to a kind of decaying and monolithic whiteness in this way, Hemingway attempts exactly what Anderson had done in his representation of African Americans: to effect a schism from the previous literary generation through a claim to understand authentic "blackness." As Anderson had found, polemical affiliations with marginalized racial groups presented an appealing way to challenge aesthetic and social orthodoxy. Yet this move could be endlessly repeated whenever the avant-garde were perceived as forming a new orthodoxy, which many writers believed to be true of Anderson by 1925.[63] Eventually, then, Anderson's pursuit of "Terrible Honesty" led to his use of representational strategies involved in the subject formation of consumers within a commodity-driven economy he professed to despise. Not only that, but he also found himself on the receiving end of an aesthetic schism enacted on the grounds of race by which a younger generation of authors sought to consign him to irrelevance, a strategy he had performed five years earlier. Small wonder that 1925 was often considered the nadir of Anderson's career.

THE STORIES AND SPACES OF PRIMITIVISM: RACIAL ERASURE AND RACIAL INVASION

As should be obvious by now, Anderson had a considerable investment in his imaginative use of African Americans; it helped to constitute his definitions of gender identity, national identity, erotic fantasy, and his own whiteness. Yet at points in his work the sheer symbolic power with which Anderson loaded these bodies can become a disturbing excess, can threaten to overwhelm his white protagonists. This applies particularly to those African Americans who are seemingly "out of place," who have migrated north, a fact that suggests the interdependence of race and geography and the extent to which region determined racial identities. This was an interdependence that had considerable bearing on both Anderson's and Toomer's representations of the South, and it was a relationship that Toomer would brilliantly critique in his consideration of American racial politics in *Cane*. The reasons for the threatening potential of certain African American bodies in Anderson's work (and the desperate measures by which Anderson attempted to contain these threats) is the subject of this final section, which will go on to examine how Anderson used narrative in an attempt to plot a teleology onto "blackness" and thereby gain a degree of imaginative control over its threatening potential. This translated into fantasies of African American extinction, mirroring fantasies of racial extinction in eugenic and anthropological texts of the period.

As the earlier chapter on *Winesburg, Ohio* makes clear, Anderson was deeply committed to story as a way of making sense of the world and as a method of exerting control over it. This passage from *A Story Teller's Story* illustrates this well:

> One has been walking in a street and has been much alive. What stories the faces in the street tell! How significant the faces of the houses! The walls of the houses are brushed away by the force of the imagination and one sees and feels all of the life within. What a universal giving away of secrets! Everything is felt, everything known. Physical life within one's own body comes to an end of consciousness. (290)

Feminist critics have argued that it is Anderson's denial of agency to his women characters that represents the severest fault in his conception of gender; as Marilyn Judith Atlas comments, in *Winesburg, Ohio* Anderson "does not, even when the possibility naturally presents itself, create a female character who wants, and is able, to form her own life" (264). This also applies to his African American characters; as evinced in *Dark Laughter*, they are often simply without stories, "better" represented by descriptions that tend toward a spatialized immediacy rather than temporal, gradual disclosure—a focus on color, surface, and readerly projection. Yet these descriptions are of separate figures contained within a race that can be acted *upon* by whites engaged in making the story of industrialization. In his *Notebook*, Anderson declared (in a statement he repeated elsewhere) that it was the threat of the immanent demise of a preindustrial, essential "authenticity" among African Americans in the face of the consolidating forces of industrial capitalism that made their song "sweet to hear while it lasts" (*Notebook* 134). As Fanon noted, the yoking of certain racial groups to historical grand narratives over which they have no control—a sense of history happening *to* people, not *because* of them—was perhaps the most damaging restriction upon black attempts to develop a belief in the possibility of their own agency. This underpinned his criticism of Sartre's inscription of racial identities within a larger historical dialectic, as this narrative positioning means "it is not I who make a meaning for myself, but it is the meaning that was already there, pre-existing, waiting for me" (134). Yet for Anderson, this ascription of a lack of agency—a historical passivity—to a racial group allowed him to mediate some of the psychosexual fears of African Americans that are evident in his primitivistic representations.

To explore how and the degree to which fantasies of racial extinction had currency and potency at the time, it is necessary to undertake a more detailed narratological explanation of how narratives of race functioned in the 1920s. It was a feature of eugenic racial discourse, earlier versions of Progressive Era racism, and many incarnations of primitivism that they all employed a narrativization of race. The combination of social Darwinism and nineteenth-century anthropology provided this new technology, as both saw race as an unending process of conflict, progress, conquest, and the stratification of hierarchy. This annexed traditional narrative devices, and traditional narrative pleasures, such as tragedy, progress, reversal, and success, into the construction of racial identity: all these functions had been identified as central to narrative as far back as Aristotle. Indeed, Claude Bremond, in his formulation of a narrative grammar, indicates that the base structure of all narrative is a sequence of interactions between amelioration or degradation, perhaps indicating that the popularity of eugenic rhetoric tapped into very elemental desires that narrative structures evoke.

At the very least it is obvious that the strategies of writers such as Lothrop Stoddard are heavily reliant on narrative. For racist discourse, a narrativization of race implies a teleological end, one that carries the "promise" of eliminating all the chimeras of race, its disturbing liminalities, changing boundaries, and psychological complexities. In Stoddard's *The Revolt Against Civilization: The Menace of the Under-Man* (1922), this closure of race is implicit in his view of the end point of history:

> The eugenic ideal is . . . *an ever-perfecting super race.* Not the "superman" of Nietzsche, that brilliant yet baleful vision of a master *caste,* blooming like a gorgeous but parasitic orchid on a rotting trunk of servile degradation; but a super *race,* cleansing itself *throughout* by the elimination of its defects, and raising itself *throughout* by the cultivation of its qualities. (242–43; italics in original)

However, before this end point is reached he has carved out a sweeping historical narrative:

> Man's march athwart the ages has been, not a steady advance, but rather a slow wandering, now breasting sunlit heights, yet anon plunging into dank swamps and gloomy valleys. Of the countless tribes of men, many have perished utterly while others have stopped by the wayside, apparently incapable of going forward, and have either vegetated or sunk into decadence. Man's trail is littered with the wrecks of dead civilizations and dotted with the graves of promising peoples stricken by an untimely end. (3–4)

The specter of the end is central to the rhetorical strategy of Stoddard's polemic. Throughout the text he raises the prospect of the "false end," that which does not accord with the reader's expectations. These "false" (or, perhaps more appropriately, dead) ends are a variant of the obstacles that prevent the movement of what A. J. Greimas calls the "actant-subject" toward the "actant-object" in all narratives—they carry the *possibility* of terminating the narrative prematurely, yet the logic of narrative does not permit this.[64] In Stoddard's text Western civilization is figured as the hero, assailed by the possibility of the "false end"; for example, "Racial impoverishment is the plague of civilization. This insidious disease, with its twin symptoms the extirpation of superior strains and the multiplication of inferiors, has ravaged humanity like a consuming fire, reducing the proudest species to charred and squalid ruin" (82). Stoddard's narrative of how the destruction of great civilizations will finally be countermanded by the "eugenic ideal" of the "ever perfecting super race" represents a basic narrative paradigm which Bremond calls an enclave—namely, a process of degradation followed by a reversal into a process of amelioration. Yet this "amelioration" is an enactment of the fantasy of racial death; Madison Grant believed that the most desirable end result of a eugenics program would be the elimination of "worthless race types" (51).

Primitivism too had its fantasies of racial extinction. The notion of racial death being the result of contact between non-Western, often tribal, communities with white, Western populations was widespread in anthropology, notably in famous anthropological texts of the decade such as Bronislaw

Malinowski's *The Argonauts of the Western Pacific* (1922) or Margaret Mead's *Coming of Age in Samoa* (1928). Indeed, such predictions formed one of the central rationalizations for conducting anthropological studies in the first place. As James Clifford notes, this trope of what is often termed "immanent demise" offers us the promise of "treasures saved from a destructive history, relics of a vanishing world" (*Predicament* 201).[65] In addition to the anthropology of the twenties, which has often been accused of primitivistic reductionism in its treatment of non-Western subjects, African American writers such as Jean Toomer, Zora Neale Hurston, and George S. Schuyler—all for very different reasons and in different generic forms—imagined a future without African Americans, or without African American culture.[66] In contrast to the eugenicists, these writers saw non-white populations as fragile, and liable to be destroyed by European-American technology, disease, culture, and economic rapacity. Anderson connected this to racial dilution and absorption, seeing white hegemony asserting itself at a biological as well as a cultural level:

> You're a nigger down South and you get some white blood in you. A little more, and a little more. Northern travellers help, they say.
>
> . . . .
>
> A little more white, a little more white, graying white, muddy white, thick lips—staying sometimes. Over we go!
>
> Something lost too. The dance of bodies, a slow dance. (My ellipsis; *Dark Laughter*, 80–81)[67]

Michael North has written on the use of the figure of the "vanishing Negro" in the early twenties; this was disseminated in short magazine fiction through the revitalization of the "dialect craze" made popular several decades earlier by such plantation nostalgics as Joel Chandler Harris and Thomas Nelson Page. Noting that the figure of the "vanishing Negro" introduced by Harris and Page "continued to disappear for at least the next thirty years," North continues:

> [T]he "disappearing Negro" was serviceable on several levels. It functioned as wish fulfilment, revealing the barely submerged hope that the freed slaves would simply die off. It served as a metaphor of the temporal reversal of the Post-reconstruction period, taking readers imaginatively back in time as the South was being taken politically back in time. And it fed nostalgia for a time when racial relationships had been simple and happy, at least for whites, suggesting they might be simple and happy again if southern whites were simply left alone to resolve things themselves. (*Dialect* 22–23)

Anderson's use of this trope can perhaps be explained through his unease over the great African American migration to the North, which peaked during the First World War. Anderson lived in Chicago between 1913 and 1920, years in which the African American population of the city increased enormously.[68] Yet in his Chicago stories, letters, and memoirs there is little mention of this phenomenon, a remarkable fact given his keen interest in politics and patterns of social change. In addition to this omission, there are several representations of northern African Americans that take a quite different tone to those of the southern African American laborers already discussed; these figures are threatening, predatory, and invasive, and this is dramatized through the threat of male rape. In many ways this threat represents the opposite side to the admiration he had expressed over southern African American laborers; if they indeed made him "feel small," then black men occupying the midwestern space Anderson had always delineated as white could enact a forced feminization of white men.

In the story "The Thinker" in his 1919 collection *Winesburg, Ohio,* Anderson introduces a young white man, Seth Richmond, who has run away from home on a boyish adventure and jumps a freight train with some friends. In his explanation to his mother about why he did it, Seth explains that "I knew . . . that if I didn't go on I would be ashamed of myself. I went through with the thing for my own good. It was uncomfortable, sleeping on wet straw, and two drunken negroes came and slept with us" (70–71). Similarly, his story "The Man Who Became a Woman," originally included in his collection *Horses and Men* (1923), deals with a young white racetrack worker in a Pennsylvania town who feels sexually threatened by two African Americans. Having just returned from the town, the boy narrator goes to sleep in a hayloft above one of the stables, only to be disturbed by "two big buck niggers" who mistake him for a girl. He finds himself unable to speak to let them know his identity:

> . . . I was scared.
>
> Because the two big black faces were leaning right over me now, and I could feel their liquored-up breaths on my cheeks, and their eyes were shining in the dim light from that smoky lantern, and right in the center of their eyes was that dancing flickering light [you see] in the eyes of wild animals. (*The Egg and Other Stories* 86)

In both stories the threat is of an African American invasion of white male space, figured as the rape of the white male body—and in "The Man who Became a Woman," a white male body that has become perceived as female. That spatial transgression is perhaps analogous to the migration to the North of thousands of African Americans, dissolving the primitivistic combination of distance and perpetual availability that Anderson was attracted to in the South. Indeed, he once defined his position as "[l]iking negroes—wanting them about—not wanting them too close" (*South* 55). That Anderson explicitly linked "The Man who Became a Woman" to a fear of black sexuality was revealed in a letter to Alfred Stieglitz, in which Anderson warns him that Georgia O'Keeffe may not enjoy the story as "I remember once she told me she was afraid of 'niggers.'"[69] The threat of the violation of the white male body—the black body getting 'too close'—transforms the African Americans' supposedly liberated sexuality into bestial urges and changes what Anderson admiringly called an "unmoral" quality in African Americans into a threatening licentiousness. Both of these were key tropes used to justify what Felipe Smith has called "lynching discourse," in which reasons for committing lynching such as black attempts at economic independence, self-assertion, or crimes against property would become subsumed under the heading of the "one crime" of rape.[70] Moreover, it dramatizes the fact that if Anderson chose to glorify black masculinity, the very power he invested in it could feminize the white masculinity he spent much of his career trying to reimagine.

Anderson's anxiety over northern African Americans not only resulted in this willingness to use the most virulently racist representations available; it also relates to the "wish fulfilment" of racial extinction and Anderson's use of the trope of the "vanishing Negro." By fantasizing the racial erasure of southern African Americans, especially through the gendered representation of the implicitly male "northern traveler" having children with African American women, Anderson reverses the terms of the spatial transgression. Imagining a future without blacks through narrative became a way of negotiating what was to him the threatening racial diversification of the northern population. In effect this is an attempt to preserve a space of racial exclusivity, a need for a mental geography of America with areas that are not multiracial. As Felipe Smith has noted, one of the crucial factors in the imagination of separate, white spaces in America was through "the imagining of America as parallel racial space-times, one progressive, the other static to regressive, [which] sought to exclude black Americans from the intellectual and creative production of modernity, the time-space of the nation" (37). Indeed, as Jean Toomer cannily observed, Anderson could not see African Americans as urban or engaged in any kind of dynamic ethnogenesis; in black areas of Washington, he felt that "a wholly new life confronts me. A life, I'm afraid, that Sherwood Anderson would not get his beauty from. For it is jazzed, strident, modern" (*Toomer Reader* 25). Anderson even admitted that he was perplexed by the appeal of jazz. Clearly the symbolic function of African Americans for him required an ethnic and spatial fixity, and when this began to slip in his confrontations with urbanized, rapidly developing black culture, it found its way into his writing as a form of bodily threat. In this, as in other things, Anderson's primitivism and eugenics shared a similar outlook, and not least in their fantasies of black racial extinction as the eventual resolution of this demographic change.

The discussion of Anderson's representations of African Americans causes a real problem of legitimacy. His work in this area reinscribes tropes of blackness that were—and in some cases continue to be—used in the restriction of full subjectivity to African Americans, in their exclusion from many spaces, opportunities, institutions, and stories. Ideas such as black nonindividuation, cultural stasis, and the threat of rape from black men were all significant in the oppression and exploitation of African Americans during the 1920s, an oppression Anderson was fully aware of, including the violent extremes that formed part of its operation.[71] Yet what such study reveals—and its justification lies therein—is the extent to which race was a constituent factor in the construction of other categories of identity from which it has traditionally been regarded as separate. Anderson's depiction of African American working practice, within the parameters of the cultural critique laid down by Brooks and Frank, purported to offer an alternative to the industrial and Fordist labor conditions he saw as degrading both culture and patriarchal masculinity. Yet in describing this alternative, his own whiteness became more visible and therefore seemingly more complex, rootless, and nondescript in a way that only intensified his search for a racial "essence" he believed existed in African Americans. Not only that, but his conceptualization of gender was interpolated with race in his admiration of what he perceived to be a black masculinity, but this existed alongside the concomitant fear that it would invade and feminize both the white male body and the "white space" of the northern city.

In many ways his investment in African America is revealed in his search for an adequate medium within which to represent it: the painting, the dance, the narrative. It had to be one that would allow both identification and differentiation, devoid of content to the degree that authorial or spectatorly desire had a screen blank enough for projection. However, Anderson was to discover that representations of an exotic "other" that encouraged readerly desire, yet were typified by vague political content, could all too easily be annexed into the service of a consumer-based economy. Yet perhaps the best reason why Anderson's representations of African Americans are worthy of study, in contrast to the scientific texts or Madison Avenue advertising campaigns of the 1920s, is suggested by one of the initial reviewers of *Dark Laughter*, who commented that Anderson "is not a deep thinker" but a poet at his best when describing a "soft, vague reverie" of "those who are born like himself to drift gently through life." This is "symbolized by that mellow, careless laughter with which the Negroes, the perfect vagabonds, greet the situations over which those of another race puzzle their heads and search their hearts" (Krutch 627). It is perhaps because of the imprecision inherent within Anderson's refusal (or inability) to adopt a scientific register when discussing race, and the self-contradiction this often leads to, that his writing on the topic of racial difference gains value for study. For surely the imaginative register represents the clearest example of the polyvalency and potency of "blackness," its symbolic and economic currency, its mediational and constitutional function for the white self and community at this juncture in history—all elements that scientific discourse has persistently tried to mask, a masking that is a condition of its own production. It was this mobility and polyvalency that Jean Toomer would explore and interrogate much more incisively, including the possibilities it offered for African American self-determination and resistance.

DOUBLE DEALING IN THE SOUTH

WALDO FRANK, SHERWOOD ANDERSON, JEAN TOOMER, AND THE ETHNOGRAPHY OF REGION

> The South needs consciousness. And pruning. And the courage to break through New England to itself. Abundance, there is.
>
> —JEAN TOOMER TO LOLA RIDGE, 20 AUGUST 1922 (*LETTERS* 72)

As the preceding chapter suggests, for Sherwood Anderson the nature of racial identity was significantly determined by spatial factors. Yet this was far from unique: his evident fear of African American communities in northern cities, when counterbalanced against the frequently jocular and voyeuristic primitivism with which he treated southern African Americans, is just one example illustrating the significance that region and location have on racial identities within the United States. Indeed, Anderson's stark differentiation between northern and southern African Americans prompts recollection of David Theo Goldberg's point that racial identity is inconceivable without recourse to spatial considerations; he notes that "racisms become institutionally normalized in and through spatial configuration, just as social space is made to seem natural, a given, by being conceived and defined in racial terms" (*Racist Culture* 185). Given the seemingly intimate relations between "race" and "space," therefore, it is hardly surprising that others in the 1920s were also interested in the relation between race and region. This was certainly true of cultural criticism from the left, criticism which (in contrast to the main thrust of Anderson's writing about race) was increasingly tending to discuss cultural difference not through resorting to the reductive *temporal* polarizations of civilized and primitive, but through the primarily *spatial* differentiation implied by cultural relativism. This was true of the cultural criticism of Waldo Frank, work that drew upon anthropological critiques of U.S. corporate capitalism and that consequently assisted the popularization of the new anthropology in the American liberal and arts press. Such activity on Frank's part helped shape a spatialized and anthropologized view of cultural nationalism that would be influential throughout the 1920s and provided Jean Toomer with many of the starting points for the extraordinarily sophisticated and astute analysis of American racial politics he produced during the period of *Cane.*

This is the thematic focus of this chapter, which examines the emerging framework of conceptuaizing region (and its relation to racial identity) in the work of Frank and Anderson—and suggests the ways in which this provided a discourse that Toomer would engage with and in many ways reject as he wrote *Cane.* Strongly influenced by the new temporal relations between cultures being established by innovative anthropological theories, as well as their methods of managing cross-cultural observation, Frank's program of cultural criticism was interested in what he called the "buried cultures" of ethnic minority groups in the United States, regionally located cultures he believed might function as sources capable of promoting a cultural renewal of America. It was this theory that stimulated his interest in the African American heritage of Jean Toomer and that underpinned their fascinating trip to South Carolina together in 1922. This project of cultural excavation is just the best-known example of the significance of ethnographic paradigms to the way in which all three writers thought about what has been called the "culture concept," and indeed Anderson was receptive to the popular ethnographic writings of his day, which appeared in the same little magazines as his fiction. Certain schools of contemporary ethnography were crucial in informing Frank's, Anderson's, and Toomer's literary excursions to the South, and significant parallels exist between the literary criticism of the Boasian anthropologist Edward Sapir and the evolving thought of Jean Toomer. However, the perpetual ethnographic dilemma of the disturbing presence of the observer was acutely felt by Frank and Anderson, as evinced by the strategies of racial masquerade that both believed were necessary for them to understand African America; this was partly responsible for Toomer's eventual break with Frank. The dilemmas circulating around the dynamics of authorial power, identity, and temporality that recent critics have shown as inherent to the project of ethnography are visible in the writing of these three authors, at the very moment when—as James Clifford has shown—the "new genre" of the ethnography was emerging. Among the most pressing of these dilemmas included determining the relation between race and culture, how to observe and how to textualize culture (especially when the notion of "culture" was itself undergoing rapid change), how to constitute themselves as authoritative figures capable of undertaking this exercise, and how to determine exactly what separated an "authentic" culture—or representation of a culture—from an "inauthentic" one.

Late in his writing career Anderson adopted a tongue-in-cheek tone about the complexities of this project, tacitly acknowledging the futility of a pursuit of the "real" South. After living in either Louisiana or Virginia for ten years, he wryly remembered a conversation he had held in Savannah:

> . . . the southern woman who sits beside you at dinner says, "But how can one of you Yanks ever know the South?"
>
> You ask her, "But have you ever been in a North Carolina Cotton Mill town, in a cypress lumber camp down in the swamp country, in the hut of a tenant farmer in Alabama?"
>
> "But those places are not the South. This is the South.
>
> "In New Orleans . . . this is the real South.
>
> In Natchez, Birmingham, Charlotte . . . this is the Real South." ("This Southland" 189)

Yet earlier, identifying the "authentic"—in both racial and regional terms—was as much a fascination for Anderson as it was for Waldo Frank. This fascination with the region has much to do with the virtual nature of "the South": as Richard Gray has noted, it is not so much a location as "a set of structural possibilities, frames for composing and articulating experience" (xii). For Anderson, Frank, and Toomer, these structural possibilities were both attractive and exasperating, and why this was so gives an important insight into the way that both white American and African American culture were being imagined in the American modernisms following the war. Moreover, Toomer's decision to withdraw from representations of southern, rural

African Americans—the much remarked "swan-song" for the "folk" that *Cane* represents—can perhaps be best understood by his growing awareness that the representational strategies available to him were incompatible with his own racial politics. Yet working through these strategies gave *Cane* much of its complexity, its internal tensions, and the material for narrative. Examining some of the parameters for theorizing and representing cultural and racial otherness in the early 1920s is therefore essential for understanding Toomer's dilemmas over class, race, and region, and how this affected his cultural production. It is also important for recognizing the newly anthropological cast of the cultural nationalisms of postwar American modernism, and how some of those paradigms were resisted or reformulated by racial minorities keen to stake a place in the U.S. cultural terrain that was not "buried" and ripe for a white intellectual unearthing.

OUR AMERICA: BURIED CULTURES, MISSING CULTURES

In the cultural criticism of the Young Americans that came to the fore around the First World War, there was an imperative sense that a source for a national cultural renewal needed to be located. As I have discussed, for all the main critics—Van Wyck Brooks, Randolph Bourne, and Waldo Frank—the impediment was the "Puritan," the figure that Brooks and Frank believed had delivered a hopelessly bifurcated industrial culture split between the grubby pragmatics of money-making and an etherealized, often merely decorative attitude toward cultural production. As mentioned in the previous chapter, these critics often took the contemporary language of eugenics to present this "failure" of Puritanism as a pathology of race, seeing the source of a national renewal as residing within the valuable "germ plasm" of other groups. Significant as this may be, it was also concurrent with a regionalization of "Puritanism." This tended to see New England and Puritanism as coextensive and suggested that this one region had exerted its cultural hegemony over the rest of the country. As Susan Hegeman has argued, within the Young American critics it was in the work of Waldo Frank that this spatialization-of-the-culture concept became fully established; his *Our America* (1919) "offered up a schema of spatial sites, both real and hypothetical, for imagining the transformation of American culture—from one of alienation and incompleteness to something approximating completion and organic integrity" (104). Frank's discussion of what he called "buried cultures," specifically Native American and Mexican-American, identified them as possible models for an organic culture that could counteract the alienations and fractured social relations of industrialized, capitalist America. *Our America*—which also included a rapturous appraisal of Sherwood Anderson—was the best-received and most influential text of his long career; recollecting this book in particular, his friend and fellow "Young American" Gorham Munson later remarked that Frank "probably did more than any other writer of the avant-garde to reveal the opportunity for a new turning of our culture" in the postwar period (*Awakening* 54). That "turn"—part of which was the conceptualization of a series of spatial sites as locations for cultural rejuvenation, as Hegeman has argued—would be widely influential, and nowhere more so than in Toomer's thinking as he wrote *Cane*. An account of the racial and cultural agenda of *Our America* is therefore useful for understanding the nature of the new cultural politics of regionalism in the 1920s.

Our America's contribution to cultural geography was to envision the United States as a spatial range of coexistent, differentiated cultures, which offered a range of possibilities for synthesizing a counter-hegemonic national identity. As Hegeman has shown, this diverged from Brooks's evolutionary and temporal explanation of American culture in its suggestion that "little geographic pockets of real, organic culture emerged from under, or perhaps in spite of, the burdens of American history" (106). Indeed, in describing "cultures as spatially arrayed possibilities, so thus did *Our America* diverge from Brooks's historicism, to describe the coexistence of Puritans, Pioneers, and still others, as physically existing in specific geographical regions" (106). Frank's vision, then, was one where spatial discovery and artistic synthesis would combine to produce a national identity; as he prophesied in the foreword, "We go forth all to seek America. And in the seeking we create her. In the quality of our search shall be the nature of the America we create" (10).[1]

At this juncture it is worthwhile to consider the usage of the terms "space" and "place," as they are important concepts for both Frank's social criticism and for my assessment of his work and its relation to the work of Jean Toomer. Cultural geographers have been keen to separate the two terms; Mike Crang opines that "places provide an anchor of shared experiences between people and community over time. Spaces become places as they become 'time thickened.' They have a past and a future that binds people together round them" (103). Erica Carter, James Donald, and Judith Squires agree; they see space becoming place as "the flows of power and negotiation are rendered in the concrete form of architecture; and also, of course, by rendering the symbolic and imaginary investments of a population. Place is space to which meaning is ascribed" (xii). These definitions are useful in suggesting that "place" exists as a dialectic between a physical location and the processes of culture that interact with that location. This usage is certainly close to Frank's sense of "place," and his accounts of the organicity of this dialectic in America's "buried cultures" were central to his celebration of these cultures. I would like to preserve elements of this definition of "place," but the major problem with it is the suggestion that "space" is essentially precultural, inert, and merely awaiting the imprint of human activity to transform it into "place." As later discussions of the intimate relations between race and space will show, and as the cultural geographer Doreen Massey points out, not only are social relations enacted spatially, but spatial conceptualizations are inescapably a social product. Therefore, space cannot be viewed as "a 'flat' surface . . . because the social relations which create it are themselves dynamic by their very nature" (156). Space is a more abstract and generic concept than place, but this does not make it an inert, undynamic, or natural category—and it is with these provisos that I shall use the term.

The function of Frank's exploration of America, in common with the cultural criticism of Van Wyck Brooks on which Frank drew so extensively, was to provide alternatives to what Frank called the "hegemony of New England," the "practical convergence of Puritan and pioneer" (*Our America* 75). Frank reasoned that in contrast to the "incubus" of English culture, it was an "ethnic chaos from which a new world must be gathered" (*Our America* 164). Particularly relevant to Frank's program of gathering a "new world" from "ethnic chaos," as Hegeman suggests, were the "buried cultures" of Mexican-American and Native American peoples. Indeed, Frank remarked of the Pueblo Native American of the American Southwest that "in his spirit, his works, his physiognomy to-day—after centuries of violence, centuries of brutal contact with cultures he was helpless to forefend—we may read the answer to our ignorance" (*Our America* 109–10).

Frank's treatment of these "buried cultures" in chapter 4 of *Our America,* and more broadly their role in his cultural criticism, involved several things. As the term "buried cultures" indicates, his discussion relied upon the metaphors of excavation and salvage (both of these cultures had almost been erased by "Caucasian floods," according to Frank) (*Our America* 107). Moreover, Frank's ability to identify and interpret these cultures involved a claim to an authoritative and scientific knowledge, a knowledge that was able to reconfigure these "buried cultures" as a functional component within a wider program of American cultural criticism. This process of the "salvage" and observation of cultures that exhibited significant differences to European-American society, and the subsequent use of such observations within cultural criticism, was similar to the methodology of anthropology in the early 1920s. Moreover, Frank's two examples of "buried cultures" were drawn from the terrain of the American Southwest: this area had long been a favorite of American anthropologists, and in the 1920s it would be the site of some of the most famous fieldwork case studies in the history of American anthropology.[2] These similarities indicate, as Stocking has noted, that "in the 1920s, the mapping of the 'geography of culture' of cultural criticism overlapped that of cultural anthropology to an extent that we may not appreciate today, when the boundaries between academic anthropology and the outside world are more sharply imagined" ("Ethnographic Sensibility" 220).

I shall discuss later the precise methodology by which Frank went about the problematic process of observing and writing cultural difference. For the moment, however, it is significant to note that among the "buried cultures" that he felt required excavation and interpretation was the culture of "the African on the American continent" (*Our America* 97). Yet Frank admitted he had "no space and no knowledge" to undertake this project. However, it was one that continued to fascinate him; in 1920, and following Sherwood Anderson's rapturous letters to him about African American culture in Fairhope, Alabama, Frank wrote to him asking for "whatever 'dope' you have" on the South.[3] Frank followed Anderson's suggestion to go to Mobile and Fairhope, even staying in the same hotels as Anderson had done, yet it was not *local* enough for him; he complained to Anderson that "although the place is physically lovely beyond words and the negroes of course, as everywhere in the South [*sic*], the atmosphere of 'intellectualism,' the lack of any really indigenous population, makes the place somewhat unfriendly to my mood."[4] This irritation about failing to find any "indigenous population" indicates that Frank believed "indigenous" to be coextensive with culturally unique, and therefore that place was a primary determinant in cultural difference. Moreover, the tone of the letter suggests that it is the fault of Mobile, rather than his own methodology, that location alone had not yielded a pocket of organic culture capable of resisting Puritan hegemony. Yet experiences such as this undoubtedly contributed to Frank's feeling that African Americans were the "true" repository of "indigenous" southern culture, particularly as the social and legal barriers of Jim Crow kept him at such a remove from African American culture that his fantasies as to what it might contain rarely had any chance to be disproved or modified. As he wrote earlier in the year to Alfred Stieglitz from Richmond, Virginia, "The negroes move me deeply . . . their inaccessibility is a constant sorrow to me. They naturally look upon me as just a White. If only they knew how close I am to them in spirit! But I can never tell them."[5]

This was the context within which Jean Toomer met Waldo Frank. After having met briefly in New York in 1920 at a party held by Lola Ridge, Toomer asked Frank in 1922 to read some of the material that would form *Cane.* Frank and Toomer's relationship has received considerable critical attention of late, yet the discursive parameters within which they both engaged the black South—and how they addressed the vexed concept of "authentic" blackness—needs to be discussed in greater depth.[6] Toomer renewed contact with Frank in March 1922, in what was one of his first attempts to establish relations with a leading figure in white modernism. He had read *Our America* in 1920 and noted to Frank that "[i]n your *Our America* I missed your not including the Negro" before going on to explain how "my life has been about equally divided between the two racial groups." He also reminded Frank that "no picture of a southern person is complete without its bit of Negro-determined psychology" (*Letters* 31). Frank, obviously impressed with the work Toomer sent him, replied in late April with a two-page, single-spaced letter offering careful and considered criticism, and their friendship—so vital for the production of *Cane*—was properly underway.

Toomer would later remember this time in two different ways. On the one hand, he was attracted to the broad outlines of Frank's theory—when considered in the abstract. He later remarked:

> The activities of men whose social criticism appeared between the years 1915–1920 turned up many national realities, notably the reality of the Puritan, but for all that America is still a nation to be explored. And from this extended exploration will come, I think, a balance and an inclusion hitherto lacking in cultural thinking.[7]

Yet when he considered this program in terms of his personal relationship with Frank, he recalled this period as one where he was exploited; he noted that "[t]he material of "Cane" was mostly negro [*sic*]. Frank, I knew, was bent on having the various peoples and locales of America become articulate. Would he be able to understand, and, if he understood, would he value my position? I didn't know."[8] Toomer's fear foreshadows a criticism made by several recent commentators about the model of cultural pluralism that was developed as a social paradigm for multiethnicity in the 1920s by Horace Kallen and others, a theory that has many similarities to Frank's model of culture. With its stress on the value of preserving the autonomy and self-sufficiency of cultural groups within a nation state, recent critics have argued that cultural pluralism could rely on the same racial essentialisms as that of a rabidly white supremacist Progressive Era racism.[9] Toomer was clearly concerned that his stress on his hybrid identity, what he called "a synthesis in mind and spirit analogous, perhaps, to the actual fact of at least five or six blood minglings," was lost within Frank's federalist view of cultural interaction (*Letters* 31). Yet, at the time, he was clearly willing to stress his knowledge and involvement with African American life to further his friendship with Frank (and the rewards this could offer his literary career). Moreover, he was impressed by Frank's lofty tone of Whitmanian prophecy, and his ambitions to promote a more ethnically and racially diverse version of American culture. Given this—and Frank's frustration at the "inaccessibility" of African American culture—it was almost inevitable that Frank would see Toomer as an ideal opportunity to "know" the black South.

SHERWOOD ANDERSON AND NEW ORLEANS: "THE MOST CULTURAL TOWN IN AMERICA"

As well as the "buried cultures" of African America, Mexican America, and Native America, Frank's geography of culture had also located Chicago as a potential source of national renewal. In his chapter on Chicago in *Our America*, he discussed the major figures of the Chicago Renaissance as examples that "men may still meet their city and their prairie, and have life of them," a life capable of creating "values out of the American chaos" (147). Chicago, he felt, had to a degree resisted the spiritually and socially disadvantageous effects of industrialism, which was in his estimation the inevitable result of the Puritan tradition. Primary among the figures Frank admired in this chapter was his friend and literary associate Sherwood Anderson, a man who had produced a "Prophecy for the American world" (141).

However, as my previous chapter began to discuss, in the mid-1920s Anderson undertook a dramatic shift in regional allegiance, ceasing to live in the Midwest that had always been his home and moving first to New Orleans and then to rural Virginia. Moreover, after 1925 his fiction dealt predominantly with the South. His move is indicative of the interest that cultural producers at the time were feeling about what H. L. Mencken called the "Sahara of the Bozart," and also of the exhaustion of the Chicago Renaissance. Yet his move also exemplifies the way in which the "culture concept" was changing and how the South could be perceived as a refuge from the hegemony of industrial capitalism and what was often termed "standardization." Anderson's nostalgic turn of mind, belief in "organic" cultures, and faith in racial essentialism were all significant in his attraction toward the region, and as these factors were also strongly implicated in Frank and Toomer's relation to the South, Anderson's apostasy from Chicago provides a useful counterpoint for considering their interrelation of race, region, and culture.

As Bernard Duffey has examined, the central "prophecy" in both Anderson's early work and the Chicago Renaissance more generally was a mood of liberation—a belief in freedom of expression, sexual and imaginative liberty, and a dislike of forces tending towards "standardization." Yet as the 1920s progressed, the vital and radical tone of the writers of the Chicago Renaissance became outmoded and increasingly irrelevant to a younger literary generation, who to a certain degree took these values for granted. Accordingly, Chicago began to be superseded as a literary center, and many of the key figures began to disperse—Floyd Dell and Edgar Lee Masters to New York, Ben Hecht to Hollywood, and Carl Sandburg and Vachel Lindsay moving elsewhere.[10] In the 1910s Anderson had flourished in the bohemian intellectual circles of the Chicago Renaissance, nourished by Floyd Dell's encouragement and assistance in helping him place his first novel with John Lane, Margery Curry's literary evenings, and the "little children of the arts" who gathered around him at the rooming house at 735 Cass Street where he wrote *Winesburg, Ohio*. Yet by 1922 he had moved from Chicago and was spending more and more time in the South, especially New Orleans.

Relations between Chicago and New Orleans have often been complex, competitive, and productive, particularly in the 1910s and 1920s, and Anderson's affinities with both were no different. Anderson's major engagement with the cultural life of the city was with the *Double Dealer*, a New Orleans–based little magazine that ran from 1921 to 1926. Indeed, Julius Friend, one of the editors, remarked that of all the "outside" figures involved in the history of the *Double Dealer*, Sherwood Anderson was the most important. Anderson lived in New Orleans in 1922, and then from 1924 to 1926; he was already a national literary figure, having just won the *Dial*'s prize for literary achievement of $2,000 in 1921, which in subsequent years went to T. S. Eliot, William Carlos Williams, and Ezra Pound (Townsend, 184). Accordingly, he was welcomed by the editors of the little magazine struggling for national recognition and financial stability. In return he found them "as pleasant a crowd of young blades as ever drunk bad whiskey," and although he never submitted his best work to them—his stories were selling at this time for up to $750 each—he did donate an article written after he had attended the Mardi Gras festival of 1921 (Rideout, "Cultural Town" 81).[11]

This exchange was valuable to both parties. The *Double Dealer* had begun to follow an editorial policy of promoting a specifically regional modernism, one that could bring about "the restoration of a venerable city to its former standing as a cultural city second to none in America," in order to promote "a protest, a rising up against the intellectual tyranny of New York, New England, and the Middle West" (DD 1.4, 126). This editorial is couched in a programmatic language that partly accepts and partly reacts to H. L. Mencken's famous slur on the South as "the Sahara of the Bozart," what he described as "a vast plain of mediocrity, stupidity, lethargy, almost of dead silence" (326). Indeed, Mencken is the bête noire of the *Double Dealer* in its early issues, roundly abused yet repeatedly mentioned. The *Double Dealer* was keen to effect this "protest" through a reformation of what it perceived to be a hackneyed and stereotyped set of southern motifs within literature; as one 1921 editorial remarked, "The old Southern pot-boiler must go out—the lynching-bee, Little Eva, Kentucky Colonel, beautiful Quadroon stuff—a surer, saner, more virile, less sentimental literature must come in" (DD 1.6, 215). Rather than a modernism centrally concerned with formal radicalism or experimentation, it encouraged a reassessment of how representations of southern regionality could be turned aside from both stereotype and the superficial titillations of "local color," a way in which—as Eudora Welty was later to say—"place can focus the gigantic, voracious eye of genius and bring its gaze to point" (123).

It was desire for a regional aesthetic that fuelled their enthusiasm for Anderson; high among their hopes was that "some Southern Sherwood Anderson, some less tedious Sinclair Lewis, lurks even now in our midst" (DD 1.6, 215). Both Anderson and Chicago stood as a benchmark for what a regionalist aesthetic could achieve; the *Double Dealer* had appointed Vincent Starrett as its Chicago correspondent in a (rather begrudging) acknowledgment of Chicago as "the literary capital of the United States" (DD 1.1, 28). It praised Sherwood Anderson as "our premier novelist," and the editors often asked him for advice and assistance. If culture was to be linked more explicitly to geography, then having America's "premier novelist" turn apostate from America's "literary capital" to endorse New Orleans was an important gesture in both pushing towards a regionalist aesthetic, and in reorganizing the geography of America's cultural field. Anderson obliged by submitting to the *Double Dealer*—as well as some of his least successful prose-poem "Testaments"—an article entitled "New Orleans, the *Double Dealer* and the Modern Movement."

In the article, Anderson explained how industrialism, standardization, and the mass media had restricted cultural outlets for individual expression in the North, and particularly Chicago. In opposition to this was the "Modern

Movement," which was "an effort to re-open the channels of individual expression" (283). New Orleans represented an ideal location for this movement, as it was what he called "the most cultural town in America." Indeed, this phrase may have been chosen as a tacit response to H. L. Mencken's dubbing of Chicago as "the most civilized town in America" in 1917 (qtd. in K. Williams 41). Anderson takes special care to define the word "cultural," detaching it from its Arnoldian sense of "the best that has been thought and said," and indeed its common application in the early 1920s as being synonymous with high culture. Instead, he engages a rapidly evolving sense of "culture"; he asks, "[D]oes not a real culture in any people consist first of all in the acceptance of life, life of the flesh, mind and spirit? That, and a realization of the inter-dependence of all these things in making a full and flowering life" (288). Anderson described his delight at visiting an oyster-shucking contest, watching African American dockworkers at work, taking a streetcar through the *Vieux Carré,* and watching a prizefight all in the same day in New Orleans—and that this constituted the culture to which he was attracted.

Anderson's definition of culture here is very similar to the ideas of Boasian anthropologists at the time; indeed, it recollects the definition produced by Edward Sapir in his essay "Culture, Genuine and Spurious," which appeared in the *Dial* in 1919, a publication Anderson was very familiar with. Sapir's essay proposed a definition of culture that "aims to embrace in a single term those general attitudes, views of life, and specific manifestations of civilization that give a particular people its distinctive place in the world" ("Culture" 311). Yet Sapir's definition of culture proposed that it was more than just the sum of what he called "tradition" and "social inheritance"; indeed, Susan Hegeman has described it as "poised between . . . the absolute binary of the ethnographic and the aesthetic, the staunchly nonevaluative and the rigidly hierarchical" (88). This combination of culture as social inheritance, which suggests a purely relativistic, nonjudgmental approach, and a view of some cultures functioning better than others, led to his distinction between "genuine" and "spurious" cultures. The "genuine" culture, he explained, was genuine primarily on aesthetic grounds; it "is not of necessity either high or low; it is merely inherently harmonious, balanced, self satisfactory . . . a culture in which nothing is spiritually meaningless" ("Culture" 314–15). Moreover, Sapir believed that social space was central to the incidence of genuine cultures; they were only possible, he believed, in "relatively small social and . . . minor political units, units that are not too large to incorporate the individuality that is the very breath of life" ("Culture" 330).

This stress on individuality was a crucial part of Sapir's theory of the "genuine" culture, as he was concerned to avoid presenting such culture as a monolithic, deterministic force. Indeed, he had been careful to balance the "individuality that is the very breath of life" with the culture that nourished and supported this individuality. This view proposed a dialectic, with individuals capable of shaping and developing the "genuine" culture, just as that culture worked to shape the tastes, views, and aesthetics of individuals. As Hegeman has argued, critics such as Frank were attracted to Sapir's concept of "genuine" culture and its concomitant view of a spatialization of culture, where these resources of renewal could be geographically located and used. Yet Frank's and Anderson's focus on the deterministic nature of place, their attraction to "locally distinct cultures . . . as alternatives to the homogenizing influence of . . . consumer society" was "predicated on ignoring the complex dynamic relationship of individual and collective suggested by Sapir, in favor of a more basic view that the individual psyche is a storehouse of cultural memory, and (reciprocally) that cultures are 'personalities writ large'" (Hegeman 92).

Frank's view of the relation between culture and the individual therefore tended to treat culture as essentially a resource rather than a process, a view which, in comparison to Sapir's theory, significantly reduced the agency and the relevance of the individual in cultural production. Even in the late 1920s Frank would still be referring to culture as product rather than process, a view that tended to describe culture in the terms of material substance; in one book review he would note, "The country to our south has greater treasures for us than its oil and its gold. It is a land immeasurably rich in human spirit . . ." ("Mexican Invasion" 275). This was a view shared by Anderson, as evident in his assessment of the South as a storehouse of culture for the revitalization of the nation. With this approach to southern culture, Anderson demonstrated a similar motivation to Frank's attraction to southern "blackness"; it had virtue as something "indigenous," finite, localized, and capable of providing potent myths and images for criticism of hegemonic trends in national culture. Yet both Anderson and Frank faced related problems with this essentially static, and firmly delimited, view of culture. One was cultural contact: how a "genuine" culture could preserve its integrity when penetrated by an outsider, or how it could engage in dialogue with other cultures without losing the "authenticity" of its own voice. The second was determining exactly what, or who, was "authentic," and what criteria went into that judgment. In encountering these issues both Anderson and Frank were engaging with the evolving problems of American anthropology, and in several cases came up with similar answers.

THE AUTHORITY OF THE ETHNOGRAPHER: KNOWING THE SOUTH

> "What is it? Something you live and breathe in like air? A kind of vacuum filled with wraithlike and indomitable anger and pride and glory at and in happenings that occurred and ceased fifty years ago? A kind of entailed birthright father and son and father and son of never forgiving General Sherman, so that forever more as long as your children's children produce children you wont be anything but a descendent of a long line of colonels killed in Pickett's charge at Manassas?"
>
> "Gettysburg," Quentin said. "You cant understand it. You would have to be born there."
>
> "Would I then?" Quentin did not answer. "Do you understand it?"
>
> "I don't know," Quentin said.
>
> **—WILLIAM FAULKNER, *ABSALOM, ABSALOM!* (289)**

> . . . all the critics are jumping on me for not knowing the South, and you are the one man who knows I do, who was in a position to state so with some authority.
>
> **—WALDO FRANK TO JEAN TOOMER, SEPTEMBER 29TH, 1923.**[12]

If cross-cultural contact and representations were increasingly drawing on discourses of anthropology in the 1920s, this was partly due to anthropology's ever more public face. This was the decade of several of the "classics" of modern ethnography, such as Bronislaw Malinowski's *Argonauts of the Western Pacific* (1922) and Margaret Mead's *Coming of Age in Samoa* (1928); scholars such as Robert Redfield and Ruth Benedict began their fieldwork in Mexican and Native American communities in this decade, and Elsie Clews Parsons published her collection of African American folklore collected from the South Carolina islands in 1923. New ideas in anthropology were not only *en l'air,* but they were particularly current in the little magazines and intellectual circles that Frank, Toomer, and Anderson frequented. Of particular salience was how new ethnographic paradigms impacted upon Frank and Toomer's trip to South Carolina in 1922 and also how the trip led Toomer to distance himself from some of the precepts of contemporary ethnography that proved incompatible with his racial politics.

Most significant among the various schools of anthropology at the time was the methodology of Franz Boas, which gradually came to prominence over the early years of the century, until by 1926 every anthropology department in U.S. universities had a Boas student as its head (Krupat 84). It is notable that well before the most celebrated case of American literary and anthropological cross-fertilization, namely Zora Neale Hurston's fieldwork in the black communities of rural Florida under the direction of Boas, the little magazines that published the likes of Frank, Toomer, and Anderson were also regularly publishing anthropological articles. In addition, New Negro Renaissance figures such as Alain Locke, Jean Toomer, and W. E. B. Du Bois were all familiar with Boasian ethnographic ideas, particularly his challenges to the racist theories of anthropology that had dominated the previous generation. H. L. Mencken, in the "Sahara of the Bozart," had called for a survey of the population by "competent ethnologists and anthropologists . . . the older stocks of the south, and particularly the emancipated and dominant poor white trash, have never been investigated scientifically, and most of the current generalizations about them are probably wrong" (327).

The affiliation between literature and anthropology also took place at the level of metaphor. An article on Sherwood Anderson, written by N. Bryllion Fagin and entitled "Sherwood Anderson and Our Anthropological Age," appeared in the *Double Dealer* and cast him as an "explorer in the anthropological consciousness of America" (99).[13] Later in his writing career, Toomer would remark of the black body that "Artists and Anthropologists have been drawn to it," presumably seeing a correlation between the physical anthropology of Boas students such as Melville Herskovits, who had gathered anthropometric data from black communities in Harlem and Washington, and the focus on the black body of primitivistic writing of the time ("Negro Emergent" 51). The exchange worked the other way too; studies examining the textuality of ethnography have often noted that Boas-educated anthropologists such as Edward Sapir and Ruth Benedict were keen poets. Indeed, in the first edition of the *Double Dealer* in which Jean Toomer appeared, there was also poetry by Sapir. And in 1922 the Boas student Elsie Clews Parsons edited a collection titled "American Indian Life," consisting of twenty-seven fictional pieces by professional ethnologists on cultures about which they had published scientific papers; Boas, in what Krupat believes was his only venture into fiction, contributed the last story (70).[14]

As already noted, the view of cultures as spatially concurrent—and not existing primarily within an evolutionary framework—was significant to Frank and Anderson, although the primitivism of both complicates this issue. It was this spatialization of culture that is perhaps Boas's most famous legacy to the imagination of cultural difference, and which provoked many of the changes in the discipline of anthropology in the early twentieth century. Moreover, the growth in Boas's influence was concurrent with the increasing professionalization and institutionalization of anthropology. As well as facilitating this new "spatialization" of culture, the rise to prominence of Boas's students also involved new methodologies of collecting and textualizing anthropological data. The principal new methodology linked to professionalization was that of participant observation, and this produced a new (and literary) genre, the ethnography. As the historian of anthropology James Clifford notes:

> [I]n the 1920s the new fieldworker-theorist brought to completion a powerful new scientific and literary genre, the ethnography. . . . [a] new style of representation [which] depended on institutional and methodological innovations circumventing the obstacles to rapid knowledge of other cultures. (*Predicament* 30)

Clifford describes this style, with its methodological basis for quickly coming to terms with other cultures (a speed of assessment necessary because the duration of fieldwork projects for professional ethnographers, due to tight budgets, was often limited), as "a synthetic cultural description based on participant observation" (30). The ethnography arising from participant observation relied upon living in close proximity to the subjects, emphasized trained powers of observation, and involved an essentially synchronic approach, and it was conceived in contrast to the more leisurely writing of the colonial functionaries who had conducted the previous generation of anthropology. The synchronic temporality of ethnography meant the final text was largely ahistorical and did not take into account the effect of historical events upon contemporary daily practices; in consequence it gave a picture of what has been called the "ethnographic present."[15] Frank showed his familiarity with this discourse as one that allowed writers to write (as Foucault called it) "*dans le vrai*" in validating his source of knowledge of the Native American cultures he discussed in *Our America*. In praising the work of Dr. Edgar Lee Hewett, director of the School of American Research of the Archaeological Society of America, Frank remarked that he was "a remarkable friend of the . . . Indian. His spirit is strangely akin to theirs. He lives near them, he speaks their tongue, he knows their needs" (116). This was in marked contrast to the "colonists of artists" that had developed in Taos or Santa Fe; they "do not understand or absorb. Like all painters of the 'picturesque,' they are mere truants from reality" (116).

Participant observation, then, drew much of its "ethnographic authority" (to borrow Clifford's phrase) from the ability to identify with and "naturalize" oneself into an alien population, while simultaneously giving a supposedly objective rendering of pre-extant phenomena.[16] In describing this, it is interesting to note the politics of vision. Clifford has noted the recent reaction against a scopocentric history of ethnography in which a primary relevance was given to *things observed* (*Writing Culture* 11–12). Ethnographies encouraged a kind of panoptic vision, whereby the ethnographer was supposed to see everything and yet remain a subject who was not observed, who did not disturb the social interactions or patterns of the culture under study. Accordingly, ethnographers frequently use the trope of invisibility. For example, Malinowski, often seen as the figure who centralized the methodology of participant observation, noted in his influential text *The Argonauts of the Western Pacific* that "as the natives saw me constantly every day, they ceased to be interested or alarmed, or made self-conscious by my presence, and I ceased to be a disturbing element in the tribal life which I was to study . . ." (7).

Finally, the stress on the "ethnographic present," a representation that did not require detailed historicization on the part of the ethnographer, came to have a particular bearing on the subjects under observation. Such a mode of representation was particularly inflexible in describing and theorizing cultural change, and this often led to a kind of absolutism and a lack of fluidity in categorizing which cultural traits in an observed population were "authentic" and which were not. This meant that ethnographies tended to reify their subjects as "authentic," an authenticity conferred by their display of a fixed, unchangeable, and dehistoricized set of traits. Such a move is often dismissed as "salvage ethnography," which Clifford describes as a situation where "the historical contacts and impurities that are part of ethnographic work—and that may signal the life, not the death, of societies—are systematically excluded" and in which the presentation of a "vanishing tribal world [is] rescued, made valuable and meaningful, either as ethnographic culture or as primitive/modern 'art'" (*Predicament* 201–2). This situation often militated against considerations of cultural dynamism and specifically cultural interaction. A certain set of cultural practices came to confer "authenticity," therefore, and ethnographies tended towards the reification of authentic "native object[s]."[17]

I have sketched these parameters as a way of introducing the discursive framework within which Toomer and Frank undertook their trip to South Carolina in September 1922. Frank had urged Toomer toward this for months; he wished to complete a chapter on the Negro for his revision of *Our America* and was working on a novel about race relations in the South, *Holiday*. Indeed, what Frank wanted out of this trip—his shopping list of culture, as it were—was the factor that determined their choice of location.

Frank wrote to Toomer about what he required, after Toomer had first suggested visiting Harpers Ferry and then Kentucky.[18]

> Here is my need, Jean, as regards town. . . . [*Holiday*] is simply the story of a lynching. The picture of the drab hideous unpainted town of the whites, the niggertown next-door, possibly in a marshy pinewood. . . . Now what I want, just incidentally, is to be once again in such a town . . . where there are such white persons, and such black ones. Is Kentucky the place? Is it sufficiently *south*? What about one of the Carolinas? . . . You understand of course that what I want is not to photograph in my book the town we choose: I have that town clear already and it is not a factual town. But I wish to soak once more in the color and atmosphere that first inspired my idea. That is why I wish an ethnic similarity and an economic and cultural as well to that first inspirer.[19] [Frank's emphasis; my ellipses]

Frank was completely open about the fact that it was an imaginative South that would determine his geographical South, that a reified set of characteristics of what he felt constituted "southernness" was more significant to him than the local particularities and social dynamics of Harpers Ferry and Kentucky that Toomer had carefully detailed in their correspondence. This evinced a shortcoming Sapir was considering in the *Dial* of that year, in an essay that essentially set down guidelines for what would now be called "ethnographic fiction." In "A Symposium of the Exotic," he tentatively mapped out a set of aesthetic criteria considering whether "the conscious knowledge of the ethnologist [can] be fused with the intuitions of the artist" (570). The problem, he felt, was that

> Few artists possess so impassioned an indifference to the external forms of conduct as to absorb an exotic *milieu* only to dim its high visibility and to make room for those tracks of the individual consciousness which are the only true concern of literary art. It is precisely because the exotic is easily mistaken for subject, where it should be worked as texture, that much agreeable writing on glamorous quarters of the globe so readily surfeits a reader who possesses not merely an eye, but what used to be called a soul. (570)

Mistaking "the exotic" for subject, or turning your characters into mere representatives of a set of cultural characteristics, tended to lead to writing that was "sentimental and unelemental" (570). Far better was the dialectic between individual and culture Sapir had outlined in "Cultures, Genuine and Spurious," both on the grounds of ethnological accuracy and aesthetic quality. Culture did not have a completely deterministic relation to an "authentic" subjectivity in this view, which in common with Toomer's opinions placed a premium on individual agency. There could be, Sapir commented, "no genuine communal culture without the transforming personal energies of personalities at once robust and saturated with the cultural values of their time and place" ("Culture" 322).[20] Yet keeping a barrier between the subject and the exotic did not figure in Frank's geography of the South, and accordingly, Toomer wrote to Jesse Moorland, a friend, advising him that he wanted the "bite and crudity of pure Negro-white southern life" to "give my work an immediacy and vigor which could come to it in no other way," and therefore asked him if he knew of a town in the Carolinas which would be "representative of its kind."[21] Yet, interestingly, Toomer had suggested Harpers Ferry to Frank at least partly because "transition and intercourse between the races is neither difficult nor hazardous," and in his letter to Moorland, Toomer requested contact with any people in the town who could "receive me without undue attention being given that fact."[22] If Frank's South was fixed, it was also objectified into being undynamic; it was not conceptualized in terms of social interaction or process, and consequently was not a culture he felt could—or would—respond to him. In contrast, Toomer was much more circumspect. As *Cane* would make clear, he saw the observer as intimately involved in the dynamics of culture, and representation as an act deeply implicated in violence—both as a potential instigator of violence, or an act inviting retribution. Toomer had misgivings about Frank's attitude towards the trip, and about Frank's possible lack of comprehension of Toomer's subtle theories of racial identity, but as he would recall in his autobiography, "I argued myself out of the suspicion by reminding myself that Waldo Frank was the author of *Our America*" (*Wayward* 125). It seems that *Our America*'s headlining, triumphal endorsement of multiculturalism was enough, at that moment, to quell Toomer's suspicions over exactly how multiple cultures were expected to relate and interact with one another within the details of Frank's theory.

These were issues that were to seriously trouble Frank and Toomer's relationship later. Yet on the trip, Frank decided on a course that would enact the technique of "invisibility" encouraged by participant observation in a particular way—by "passing." Toomer had written him that, as it was September and he had been out in the sun all summer, he would have to be "known as Negro" but also because "only by experiencing white pressure can the venture bear its fullest fruit for me" (*Letters* 63). Frank decided that he would "pass" as well; he described how "[a]n old Ford with three of Toomer's friends bounced us along dirt roads into the dark world. . . . I was asked questions: What do you do for a living? In what city do you live? What is your church? Never: Are you a Negro?" (*Memoirs* 105). Frank needed to erase the visibility of his whiteness, which had, indeed, only become visible through contact with a racialized "other." As he was discovering, the ethnographic practice of observation—reliant as it was on situations of interracial contact—caused whiteness to become materialized in ways that were quite new and surprising to him (especially as a New York Jew whose own "whiteness" was precariously situated in the racial taxonomies of the 1920s).[23] Situations of interracial contact therefore caused not only a polarity of racialization but simultaneously prompted an impulse in Frank to erase that polarity in order to fully become a "participant observer" of black culture.

Toomer understood well the kind of strain that "passing" involved; as he wrote later, it involved "great psychic strain and a constant feeling of insecurity," motivated by a "fear lest [one] be found out" ("Crock" 57). Yet this was the method Frank believed would allow him access to "authentic blackness," sensing that African American culture had long evolved subtle and manifold strategies for indirection, ambiguity, or codification in situations of interracial contact, as Lawrence Levine has shown.[24] Nor was this effacement and embrace of "invisibility" confined to Frank's trip to South Carolina; in a remarkably consistent application of the ethnographic paradigm, Anderson, too, found self-effacement the only way to achieve an "objective" view of black society:

> There was a thing I felt, that the negroes, when they were grouped, no whites about, were one thing but when a white man appeared I believed a change took place. I wanted to prove this to myself and so on several mornings I went, very early, and concealed myself in some piles of lumber near where a group of negroes would be, I knew, at work.
>
> I felt the thing I had anticipated did take place. When the negroes were away from the whites at their work there was a tone of sadness. . . . (*Memoirs* 481)

Indeed, on several other occasions, Anderson concealed himself on the edge of lumber camps, or in the shadows of black residential areas, to observe without his presence being known.

Moreover, as well as Frank's and Anderson's anxious interplay between the visibility of their whiteness and their strategies to efface it, their writings about these experiences draw heavily on the terminology of location and suggest the significance of spatial differentiation in establishing racial identities. It is in this aspect of both men's attempt at masking their whiteness—whether through "passing" or through hiding—that they most closely approached the dilemmas over the relationship between "authoritative" texts and the spatial position of the observer that were preoccupying the innovators of ethnography. For example, Frank enthused in his memoirs that

Toomer had offered him "a chance to see and feel the Negro from within the inside angle of the Negro" (*Memoirs* 104), and Anderson wrote to Toomer that he wanted to write "[n]ot of the Negro, but out of him. Well I wasn't one. The thing I felt couldn't truly be done" (Turner, "Intersection" 99). It is noteworthy that, as a function of a spatialized view of culture, all these conceptualizations of race are spatialized; Frank felt himself "within the inside angle" of blackness, Anderson wished to write "out of" the Negro. Blackness becomes identified with a separately locatable space—and authority rests on the ability to occupy this space.

Passing, of course, was a social practice virtually defined by transgressive movements in racialized space. Toomer's comments on "passing" quoted above, which deal with the fear of being found out, were based on his understanding of "passing" as primarily a practice undergone to improve socioeconomic opportunities—which was the major reason that he "passed" as white (in a legal sense if nothing else) for much of his life.[25] This account does not make allowance for whites passing as black, which was a tradition with long historical connections to minstrelsy and blackface and also to a very different psychological dynamic to the types of "passing" Toomer describes. Chief among this is the fear not of being found out but of over-identification—a fear not of being punished for transgressing into monoracial space but of being unable to escape it. Upon reaching the South, Frank reported that his "place on earth had frighteningly shifted" (*Memoirs* 105). Later, "Lying in dark sleep I would dream I was a Negro, would spring from sleep reaching for my clothes on the chair beside the bed, to finger them, to smell them . . . in proof I was white and myself" (*Memoirs* 105).

Frank's anxiety prompts a recollection of Ellison's comment that "when the white man steps behind the mask of the trickster his freedom is circumscribed by the fear that he is not simply miming a personification of his disorder and chaos but that he will become in fact that which he intends only to symbolize . . ." ("Change the Joke" 1545).[26] Moreover, this location of blackness in the realm of fantasy, the dream, gestured to Frank's ambivalence; it may be a space of unbridled desire but it was also chaotic and threatening. These observations suggest that, as Homi Bhabha stated about a different set of mimic-relations but which are pertinent here, "the *menace* of mimicry is its *double* vision which in disclosing the ambivalence of colonial discourse also disrupts its authority" ("Mimicry" 237). It was through such racial mimicry that Anderson and Frank's relation to "blackness"—as well as their authority to represent it—became a miasma of ambivalence, invested with desire and disgust, fantasy and hopes for objectivity.[27]

Becoming "invisible," then, made visible the social, psychological and often the sexual structures of interracial relations that drew so much effectiveness from being generally *unseen* or naturalized. Yet the reason why Frank embarked upon this, the reason most significant to my overall argument, bears most centrally on the relation between race and space. With his construction of "southernness," Frank had, to an extensive degree, collapsed the boundaries between race, culture, and region, seeing "blackness" as the primary source of southern culture. This made "blackness" something to get "inside" of, but also a territory with a periphery and a "heart." This is revealed in both Anderson's and Frank's use of the metaphor of the interior, the almost literal "heart of darkness" where an essentialized blackness was to be found. As Torgovnick has observed, this trope is a familiar one within primitivistic discourse, often used to geographize explorations of an "Africa [that] is "dark" and dangerous; its core, center or heart counts most . . ." (10). Thus Frank noted that "the farther away from town, the more complete the Negro plasm, the more free the sweetness of the people. . . . all the troubles dimmed in the deep dark country lands Toomer and I visited together"—and the central interracial encounter of the memoirs, his speech on science to a congregation of rural African Americans, took place in "the church deep in the pines" (*Memoirs* 105–6). Anderson too had described the black crew working on the Mississippi riverboat as "country bred negroes" from "the back country" (*Memoirs* 483). As a result, blackness becomes spatialized as both the heart and the margin, an original essence *and* a cultural other. It is here that the evolutionist formulation that Hegeman argued Frank had dismissed in his adaptation of Brooks's theory of culture returns in the guise of primitivism. The spatialization of cultures as temporally coexistent gives way almost completely to a theory of evolutionary difference between cultures, a theory in which blackness represents an earlier phase of development and therefore identifies it as a site for nostalgic return.

As both heart and margin, however, blackness becomes a difficult location from which to make a representation. As poststructuralist and postcolonial critiques of the ethnology of the twenties have noted, "objectivity" was maintained as a separate entity to the day-to-day experiences of fieldwork; it resided in an authoritative language that excluded otherness even as it described it. As Malinowski noted of his own fieldwork, "the distance is often enormous between the brute material of information, as it is presented to the student in his own observations, in native statement, in the kaleidoscope of tribal life—and the final authoritative presentation of the results" (*Argonauts* 3–4). Thus, the objectivity upon which their ethnographic authority rested was defined by the retreat to a white space of order and structure capable of organizing the "kaleidoscope" of difference through linguistic form.

A similar pattern can be found in Frank's trip to South Carolina. His project of cultural criticism relied on the figure of the centered, omniscient artist assembling disparate ethnic and racial elements into a new national culture; he suggested that it was the task of the artist to transfigure what he called the "American chaos." In 1925 he claimed in his article "The Artist in Our Jungle" that "America . . . is a multi-verse craving to become One; it both challenges and invites the purpose of the religious artist" (152). Frank felt he could empathize with the blacks of rural Georgia, but to describe them he needed to return to the position of the omniscient, "religious artist"; in other words, he needed to be "white and myself." Both he and Anderson flirted with interracial identification, but Anderson too found it impossible to "write out of the Negro." This was a point Frank counseled Toomer on; the thing necessary for "the creating of literature" was to find an authorial stance divorced from race, where race ceases to be a factor; of course, this was the tacit stance of a whiteness that gains so much of its political and social power through being normalized and "taken for granted." It was for these reasons that Frank advised Toomer to "take your race or races naturally, as a white man takes his" (*Cane* 161).

The close relation between space and racial identity and the suggestion that the "omniscient artist" is necessarily white inevitably put strain on Frank's relationship with Toomer. Frank's belief that blackness was to a considerable degree spatially determined caused two problems, both in his friendship with Toomer and with his obvious desire to reject the bigoted and often brutal racism that he saw in the South. The first—as Sherwood Anderson had already found—was that southern African Americans who did not "know their place" and who migrated to the North in droves could be disconcerting and threatening; consequently, the racial language of both men is never more aggressive and bald than when discussing African Americans living in the North.[28] The second problem was that by seeing "other" racial identities as spatially—and therefore conceptually—limited, Frank blithely ignored the implication that the man he later described as "the great promise among Negro writers" did *not* in fact have the freedom to take things "naturally," to enjoy the discursive and geographical mobility that Frank felt whiteness allowed (*Memoirs* 102). This became clear when Toomer's cultural capital as possessing the "authority" of blackness (and thus southernness) became important to protect Frank from the critical ridicule *Holiday* was receiving.

At this point, Toomer taking his race "naturally" was the last thing Frank desired. Indeed, Frank later criticized Toomer for his "need to forget he was a Negro," perhaps because in "forgetting" Toomer also abandoned the racial identity that could best endorse both Frank's novel and his cultural criticism (*Memoirs* 107). Frank received some very stern criticism about his pretensions to knowing the South—for example, John McClure in the *Double Dealer* chortled that "Frank . . . knows no more about the South than he knows about Afghanistan," and in his 1925 mauling of Frank's fiction Paul Rosenfeld remarked that *Holiday* might have been a "brilliant fantasy" but was "expressive of no reality outward or inward, and [is] unthinkable in any sense as a representation of the South" (DD 6.32, 27; *Men Seen* 103–4). Frank felt that Toomer had not done enough to endorse the authenticity of his representation of the South, as the epigraph to this section reveals, for he believed Toomer was the "the one man who knows I [know the South], who was in a position to state so with some authority." Toomer's "authority" came from his identity as Negro—an identity that was decidedly *not* the carefully nuanced, American racial identity Toomer had explained to Frank.

It was this kind of essentialism—where culture and regional identity slipped gradually back to a racial basis upon which their authenticity was grounded—that formed one of the main reasons why Toomer and Frank's friendship cooled.[29] Moreover, it reinforced to Toomer that ethnographical methodology was problematic; as he wrote in his 1924 essay "The Negro Emergent," anthropologists may have been "drawn" to the black body, but the real point of significance for positive social change was that "the Negro is finding it for his own experience" (90). It is arguably no coincidence that Toomer wrote "Theater" and "Box Seat"—the two stories in *Cane* that disavow most pointedly the ability of observers to remain unimplicated in the spectacles they observe—after he returned from Spartanburg. Similarly, he undertook a thoroughgoing revision of Kabnis in the fall of 1922, a story that—as my next chapter demonstrates—represents his clearest statement about the limitations of "participant observation." Initially, Toomer had been drawn to Frank's position in the debates around the representation of the rural black "folk" and the idea that this folk embodied an "authentic" and privileged black subjectivity. He was inspired by the notion in *Our America* that "buried cultures" could help promote an American cultural renaissance, and by Frank's program of multiculturalism. Indeed, Toomer responded with enthusiasm to Frank's need for what J. Martin Favor has called "geographies of blackness" to act as a cultural and spiritual resource for America, a response that culminated in his guiding Frank around the

African American community in Spartanburg, South Carolina. Yet Toomer had growing doubts about both the ramifications of Frank's version of cultural pluralism and his use of ethnographic methodologies to stress the importance of "buried cultures." These doubts crystallized his suspicions about discussing southern, rural African Americans as embodying some type of racial essence and also led him to conceive of "ethnographic authority" as a more problematic authorial position than writers such as Frank were suggesting. The attractions—and pitfalls—of reifying "Southern culture" and identifying certain individuals as embodying it are seen even more clearly in Sherwood Anderson's writing. The fact that he and Frank ignored the dialectic between individual and culture that formed such an important part of models such as Edward Sapir's led to extraordinary strategies of masquerade, concealed observation, and fantasy in their attempts to "write out of the Negro," to place themselves firmly within a "geography of blackness."

Ultimately, the importance of that dialectic led Toomer to consider other models of observing rural black culture in the writing of *Cane*, particularly the tradition of the Northern, urban black pedagogue "reconnecting" with the rural South—a discourse with great significance for the New Negro Renaissance and African American cultural nationalism. The traces of anthropological "geographies of blackness" still reside in his writing, yet Toomer could see that its claims for representational authority, and for a professionalized, objective language free from the complications of history, was not an adequate medium for textualizing rural Georgia. He would turn to a much more complex range of representational strategies for writing the South, to a series of interlocking forms and languages that say as much about the limitations and failings of these mediums as they do about the morphological and cultural landscape he took as his subject. How these different forms and languages jostle against one another, and how this architectonic addresses the representational dilemmas of *Cane*, is the subject of the next chapter.

"THINGS ARE SO IMMEDIATE IN GEORGIA"

ARTICULATING THE SOUTH IN *CANE*

WHAT TO DO WITH THE FOLK: *CANE* AND THE AFRICAN AMERICAN TRADITION

White anthropologists and white authors drawing on anthropological methodology were not the only people demonstrating an increased interest in southern African American culture during the 1920s. In the early years of the century the experience of a "return" South on the part of northern-based African Americans was documented several times; W. E. B. Du Bois's trips to teach in a Tennessee school and his time at Atlanta, Zora Neale Hurston's return to Eatonville, and Toomer's trip to Sparta, Georgia, are just three examples. The idea of Toomer "returning" to an area he had never visited before—a phrase used by several commentators and present in *Cane* itself—was due to the way in which cultural and sectional identity formation often relied on race as the predominant criterion for determining who "belonged." This chapter begins by examining Toomer's engagement with

African American strategies of representing southernness in the 1920s and how, ultimately, he rejected notions of a racialized basis to culture—a view that conflicted with the desire of many critics of the New Negro Renaissance to celebrate him as what William Stanley Braithwaite called "the very first artist of the race" (83). This rejection was inextricable from Toomer's inclination to anchor his ideas concerning social differentiation around class, and his privileging of those who possessed what he termed "aristocracy" irrespective of racial determination. In many ways *Cane* charts this process, and it functioned as a testing ground for Toomer to balance and assess various strategies of representing rural, working class African American subjectivity. These included strategies taken from "Young America" and the African American autobiographical tradition—and ultimately he dealt with many of the most vexing issues inherent in those strategies through his representation of African American voice and dialect.

Part of the ambivalence that makes *Cane* such a fascinating text is that the problems and issues Frank and Anderson faced in their trips to the black South—of observation, of identification, of reification, of the racialization of "authoritative" language—were ones Toomer also faced, yet equipped not only with the anthropological framework of *Our America* but also with a quite different tradition. This was a tradition established since the Civil War within what Joel Williamson has called the "mulatto elite." Toomer was a member of this elite, having grown up in the exclusive "four hundred" of Washington's mulatto community in the house of his grandfather, an active Republican politician who had been governor of Louisiana during Reconstruction.[1] The tradition was that of the urban intellectual mulatto teaching in one of the "black belt" areas of the Lower South to the children of poor, rural black families. As Williamson describes, after the Civil War and during Reconstruction, many members of this elite traveled from urban centers in both the North and the South to rural areas to educate the newly emancipated slaves, and this tradition was continued by the intellectual leadership of several key figures of the New Negro Renaissance.

Such teaching experience was crucial to W. E. B. Du Bois's *The Souls of Black Folk* (1903), a text with which Toomer was undoubtedly familiar; it includes the chapter "Of the Meaning of Progress," which detailed Du Bois's time spent teaching in a country Tennessee school. The chapter recounts the spirit, industriousness, and desire to learn and "progress" among the community but also how this spirit is ground down over a long course of years by racist systems of sharecropping, economic exploitation, and limited opportunity. Yet by 1933, when James Weldon Johnson wrote about his experiences teaching in Georgia undertaken in the early 1890s, the tone was notably different. Johnson shared Du Bois's anger and frustration at the rigidity of America's racial politics in denying equal access to social, financial, and professional opportunities and facilities. Yet his account of teaching in the South placed greater significance on both an ethnic similarity between himself and his students and on the importance of folk culture.[2] He included his realization that "I felt myself studying them all with a sympathetic objectivity, as though they were something apart; but in an instant's reflection I could realize that they were me, and I was they; for a force stronger than blood made us one" (*Along* 51–52). He later continued:

> I gained a realization of their best qualities that has made any temptation for me to stand on a little, individualized peak of snobbish pride seem absurd. I saw them hedged for centuries by prejudice, intolerance, and brutality; hobbled by their own ignorance, poverty, and helplessness; yet, notwithstanding, still brave and unvanquished. I discerned that the forces which lie behind the slow but persistent movement forward lie in them; that when the vanguard of that movement must fall back, it must fall back on them. The situation in which they were might have seemed hopeless, but they themselves were not without hope. The patent proof of this was their ability to sing and to laugh. (*Along* 52)

This change exemplifies an important political and aesthetic shift that occurred during the New Negro Renaissance. Williamson has defined this as the result of an increasing bifurcation in America's racial politics, which at this period was increasingly recognizing only two categories around peoples of European and/or African ethnicity—white and black. This tended to dissolve the category of "mulatto" into black—the result of the infamous "one drop rule"—and led to a different conception of the cultural role of the mulatto community. This was to change "the mission of the mulatto elite from one of carrying white culture to the Negro mass to one of picking up black culture within the Negro world and marrying it smoothly to the white culture that they knew so well" (Williamson 151–52). Or, as Alain Locke put it, "Where formerly [Negroes] spoke to others and tried to interpret, they now speak to their own and try to express" ("Negro Youth" 48). Inevitably, this altered role within the African American social elite pushed to the forefront the question Henry Louis Gates Jr. has found to be perhaps the most pressing for African American aesthetics during the Harlem Renaissance—"what to do with the folk" (*Signifying* 179). In consequence, during the Renaissance, as J. Martin Favor has discussed, some versions of black subjectivity became viewed as more authentic than others, and increasingly "authentic blackness" became linked to a southern, rural, and working-class subjectivity.[3]

Toomer famously undertook a journey to the South that engaged these issues and was also (according to all his accounts) a very moving and stimulating experience. In significant ways *Cane* is the product of two trips south and two methodologies of recounting those journeys: his trip to South Carolina with Frank in 1922 and his trip to Georgia in 1921 to teach at a school in Sparta. It was the former trip that followed the precedent of members of the northern mulatto elite traveling south both to educate and to forge bonds of cultural affinity with southern African Americans. So affected was he by this earlier trip that he wrote about it in a fashion different from almost all his other pronouncements about race and in ways that have been central to his critical reception from the 1920s onwards. His recollections are framed in language that charts an epiphany of "discovery" similar to Johnson's; it is a response he outlined in various autobiographical texts but also in letters to Waldo Frank, Sherwood Anderson, and, here, to the *Liberator:*

> Within the last two or three years . . . my growing need for artistic expression has pulled me deeper and deeper into the Negro group. And as my powers of receptivity increased, I found myself loving it in a way that I could never love the other. It has stimulated and fertilized whatever creative talent I may have within me. A visit to Georgia last fall was the starting point of almost everything of worth that I have done. I heard folk-songs come from the lips of Negro peasants. I saw the rich dusk beauty that I had heard many false accents about, and of which, till then, I was somewhat skeptical. And a deep part of my nature, a part that I had repressed, sprang suddenly to life and responded to them. Now, I cannot conceive of myself as aloof and separated.[4]

Tapping these "deep" resources embodied in the "Negro peasants"—resources of history, memory and ancestry—became a staple of the aesthetics of the New Negro Renaissance. Indeed, the fact that this was so illustrates that there were many continuities between the cultural criticism of the Young Americans and that of the New Negro Renaissance, both in terms of an interest in Boas's ideas and in the presentation of a critique of the prevailing social order from marginalized pockets of cultures constructed as authentic. It is noteworthy that one of Harlem's most perceptive critics, Alain Locke, saw a renewed African American interest in folk culture as being in many ways similar to Frank's pluralistic and spatialized investigation of culture as integral to a politics of national renewal. He remarked, "It is a curious thing—it is also a fortunate thing—that the movement of Negro art towards racialism has been so similar to American art at large in search of its national soul" ("Beauty" 24). In 1928 the drama critic Rowena Woodham Jelliffe stated this even more clearly, noting, "White America, becoming pressed for spiritual elbow room and weary of its mechanical way of life, has turned with genuine appreciation to the drama of the folk level. That the Negro happens most admirably to supply that need, both as source material and interpreter, is a fortunate happenstance for the Negro race . . ."—a happenstance likely to provide a "new social appraisal" of African Americans (214).

Indeed, the pluralistic cultural field delimited in part by the Young Americans, the new little magazines, and the young generation of mainly Jewish New York publishers who had published authors such as Anderson and Frank, were more interested than most in publishing work that challenged the racial as well as the regional hegemony of New England. Accordingly, it was firms like Boni and Liveright and Alfred Knopf, or magazines such as the *Nation* and the *Liberator*, that published many of the new generation of African American authors.[5] Yet there was a crucial difference between the appraisals of "folk art" by African American intellectuals and by these sections of the white avant-garde. Frank's program tacitly relied on the external observer, the artist who could synthesize these ethnic materials and differences, who was capable of transfiguring the "American chaos" into a coherent aesthetic and cultural whole. Yet within the African American tradition the author was encouraged to demonstrate an affiliation with that racial group alone, and in *Cane*'s contemporary reception this is how it was often received.

This reception tended towards a celebration of what was perceived as Toomer's process of discovery, return to, and affiliation with a homogenous and culturally rich "folk," embodied in the women of part 1 and anchored in an organic relationship to the earth and soil of both Africa and the rural South. Critics were often moved to lyrical rapture in the presence of such a "folk spirit"; Matthew Josephson found that "Toomer is close to the soil, his book is dripping of the Negro South . . ." (179). Montgomery Gregory, reviewing *Cane* for the black journal *Opportunity*, noted that Toomer had "sprung from the tangy soil of the South" (*Cane* 165) and went on to stress the organic connection between folk, soil, and text even further: "Cane is not OF the South, it is not OF the Negro; it IS the South, it IS the Negro . . ." (*Cane* 166). Unsurprisingly, he favored part 1, in which "the matchless beauty of the folk-life of the southern Negro is presented with intriguing charm" (166). In addition, Scruggs and VanDemarr note the selective anthologization of *Cane* in *The New Negro* in 1925; poems were selected that "made it possible for [Alain] Locke and other black critics to celebrate a unified folk spirit and an ennobling past recaptured by the modern artist" (221).

Such an "authentication" of Toomer was widespread, yet was clearly a response that ignored the subtleties of Toomer's racial self-definition. In one of the most significant African American assessments of Toomer at the time, by William Stanley Braithwaite in *The New Negro,* he was described as "the very first artist of the race . . . a bright morning star of the race in literature" (83–84). Such a view saw Toomer as a prodigal son, the artist returning to a heritage made "true" by the black members of his extremely diverse—and largely "white"—ancestry (Kerman and Eldridge 26–27). This type of criticism exemplified well the view of journals like *Opportunity* (under the editorship of Charles S. Johnson and closely linked to the ideas of Alain Locke) that there was a pressing need for the excavation and development of an African American cultural tradition to augment and give historical cohesion to a growing sense of organized, racial community. Given this, it is perhaps no surprise that "Song of the Son" may be the most frequently quoted section of *Cane* in criticism of the time—"O land and soil, red soil and sweet-gum tree . . . Now just before an epoch's sun declines / Thy son, in time, I have returned to thee . . ." (14)—or that it was the only section of *Cane* to be published in the *Crisis,* the journal then edited by W. E. B. Du Bois.[6] Indeed, Jessie Redmon Fauset, the literary editor of the *Crisis,* praised the poem lavishly for its evocation of a beautiful folk heritage in her correspondence with Toomer and warned him against the "modern tendency" toward "inmeshing the kernel of thought in envelopes of words."[7]

Toomer was surprised and disconcerted by these reactions, both in their suggestion that formal experimentalism was inadvisable in optimizing the political effect of his writing and the extent to which he was identified with the African American literary community. At the time he seemed not to realize two aspects of the racial politics within which his schoolteaching trip to Georgia was conducted. The first was that, in identifying black belt Georgia as part of his ancestry, as just one of the several cultures from which his family came, that this culture would come to have a primacy over all the others. In Walter Benn Michaels's words, he discovered that at this point in history (and, Michaels argues, now as well) "racial identity remained an essential component of cultural identity," that is, "his" culture was in fact determined by his race (139). He also failed to recognize that writing about the teaching trip to the South was a rhetorical gesture with historic precedents, one that stressed racial affiliation and above all racial commitment at the expense of class-based loyalties. In stating that his trip had "stimulated and fertilized whatever creative talent I may have within me," he misjudged the fact that this imaginative commitment would be taken as a political and racial commitment, a commitment he would spend much of his life after *Cane* in trying to disavow, as has been well documented.[8]

Ultimately, then, despite Toomer's obvious feelings of affinity with the black working class and his dislike of bourgeois conventions and pretensions, J. Martin Favor's observation that he "rejected a color-based racial essence in favor of a class-based, transracial similarity" must be heeded (57). As Barbara Foley has noted, in one of his autobiographies Toomer confessed that one of his greatest fears in being labeled a "Negro" was that "my aristocracy might be invaded; I might be called into question by louts, white, black, or any other color" (*Wayward* 93). Foley is right to identify that Toomer was interested in and supportive of socialism and that in the tradition of the "aristocracy" of the "Washington Four Hundred" Toomer was politically active and engaged with the politics of African American advancement. Yet Toomer's belief in the primacy of "individualism" in public and social life led him to a distrust of collectivism, a distrust that has so often been linked to a bourgeois politics. As he was to say in 1935, he was "not a collectivist in so far as this term means regimentation and rule by herd psychology," believing instead in "freedom—and by this I mean the opportunity to function constructively to the utmost possible development of the individual, to the utmost possible contribution on the part of the individual to the group and the group to the individual." This ethic, he claimed, underpinned "my personal efforts [that] have allowed me to attain a position beyond class limitations."[9] At the last, Toomer's political affinities were with other such "aristocrats" and "individuals," irrespective of race, and despite his protests to the contrary, it was clear that these "individuals" would be drawn predominantly from the middle class.

Yet if the political implications of Toomer's aesthetic commitment to African American life became painfully obvious to Toomer after *Cane,* the conflicts this commitment raised with his own racial position—what he defined as being the "first American"—are implicit in the text itself. As Favor has commented, *Cane* "begins to question the adequacy of any discourse of black identity at all, at least in its geographical component" (79). I would agree that *Cane* offers an interrogation of "authentic" black subjectivity rather than a celebration of it and also—a feature I shall explore in the next chapter—that it considers some of the forces and discourses that could be brought to bear to effect a transformation of racial subjectivity. The interrogation of "authentic" black subjectivity in *Cane,* almost by necessity, involves a critique of the two strategies of representation of southern rural African Americans I have discussed thus far. Moreover, it is a critique that bears directly on the issue of the representation of speech. The concepts of voice and authenticity have a long history of interrelation, and it is through this relation that Toomer made some of his most subtle points about ethnographic method, the construction of "folk" culture, and the racial essentialism that often underpinned both.

"FALSE ACCENTS": AUTHENTICITY AND SPEECH IN CANE

> If we are to believe the majority of writers of Negro dialect and the burnt-cork artists, Negro speech is a weird thing, full of "ams" and "Ises." Fortunately we don't have to believe them. We may go directly to the Negro and let him speak for himself.
>
> **—ZORA NEALE HURSTON, "CHARACTERISTICS OF NEGRO EXPRESSION" (1031)**

It is significant to note that the two models of engaging with geographic and cultural "otherness" already discussed—the participant observer and the "artist of the race"—are both considered, and critiqued, in *Cane*. It is equally noteworthy that this critique is most evident in the area of dialect and the representation of black speech. As previously mentioned, Gates sees the Harlem Renaissance as perplexed by "what to do with the folk." Yet this was a dilemma that closely related to what Gates describes as one of the two central issues for black writing after the Civil War, issues that extended through the Harlem Renaissance—namely, "the precise register which an 'authentic' black voice would, or could, assume" (*Signifying* 171).[10] *Cane* is a text that deals with cross-cultural contact and the implications and viability of an essentialized racial "authenticity" through its choices over the representation of black speech. Accordingly, I shall trace some of the issues around the representation of black speech as a prelude to an examination of how Toomer goes about it in *Cane*.

The relation between Black English and Standard English in cultural representation has been much discussed, recently as well as in the New Negro Renaissance.[11] As Tommy Lott has shown, the assessment of the "authenticity" of how black dialect was represented involved and must still involve the criteria of the writer's political intentions and affiliations, a factor invariably invoked due to the long tradition of denigration and debasement of African Americans through the medium of dialect in the minstrel tradition. When the black subject spoke in literature during the New Negro Renaissance, the form of what was spoken was of greater significance than what was said, and the reasons why the author had adopted that form were most significant of all. If it was on grounds of entertainment or condescension, it was minstrelsy; if it was conducted to restore "pride and cultural self-respect" for the purpose of "reawakening an oppressed people," as Alain Locke stated, it was "authentic" folk-art (qtd. in T. Lott 93). Other African American critics in the 1920s, such as James Weldon Johnson, believed that even dialect literature produced with favorable political and social intention toward the African American community was inappropriate, considering the demeaning heritage of black dialect literature. In his preface to *The Book of American Negro Poetry,* Johnson expressed himself as holding "no indictment against dialect as dialect" but found himself "against the mold of convention in which dialect in the United States has been set" (xli). Dismissing the aesthetic or cultural value of black dialect in literature virtually out of hand, he argued that "[the colored poet] needs a form that is freer and larger than dialect, but which will still hold the racial flavor," seeing dialect literature as hopelessly limited to "two full stops, humor and pathos" (xl–xli).[12]

This hostility toward dialect on the part of some African American writers was compounded by the fact that as well as the ingrained tradition of minstrelsy in popular culture, black dialect played a role in the rhetorical strategies of white modernism. As Michael North has discussed, several white modernists used representations of African American dialect in their published work, or in their correspondence, as a provocative gesture that was intended to assert the radicalism of their aesthetics. Yet North argues that this was a strategy that frequently caused consternation among African American authors, as "linguistic imitation and racial masquerade" can stand "for a most intimate invasion whereby the dominant actually attempts to create the thoughts of the subordinate by providing it speech" (*Dialect* 11).[13]

The relationship between voice, authenticity, intentionality, and cultural capital was not merely restricted to imaginative literature. Franz Boas, in an influential essay of 1899, "On Alternating Sounds," commented on the ethnographer's tendency towards "sound blindness" (72) that is a result of the fact that "a new sensation is apperceived by means of similar sensations that form part of our knowledge" (74). Therefore, observers of a different culture are prone to reduce unfamiliar phonetic constructions into the structures of their own language, providing a barrier to "objective" translation and transcription.[14] Edward Sapir also emphasized the value of direct transcription in ethnographic fiction; he remarked that "the accent of authentic documents always reveals a significant, if intangible, something about native mentality that is over and above their content" ("Symposium" 571).

In addition to professional ethnographers, the necessity of overcoming "sound blindness" as a prerequisite of authority was an issue confronting writers of fiction who found their material in the South. Indeed, the dialect tradition of African American folktales from the South, which included such writers as white southerners Joel Chandler Harris and Thomas Nelson Page, but also involved African Americans such as Paul Lawrence Dunbar and Charles W. Chesnutt, laid heavy emphasis on the importance of "authenticity" in represented speech (Gavin Jones, 44). Nor was this an exhausted trend by the 1920s—North remarks that the dialect "craze" that had swamped the literary magazines with dialect stories in the 1880s was experiencing a resurgence in 1919 (*Dialect* 24). The dialect tradition was extremely formalized in its conventions of what constituted "authentic" representations of dialect, so much so that Zora Neale Hurston remarked that "I run the risk of being damned as an infidel for declaring that nowhere can be found the Negro who asks 'am it?' nor yet his brother who answers 'Ise uh gwinter'" ("Expression" 1031). Her comments illustrate that for all writers in America of the time dealing with the South, this tradition of the high aesthetic value of "authenticity" in represented speech was one that had to be confronted. In consequence, certain uses of language became both a marker of race and a prerequisite for authority.

These cultural contexts were very significant for Toomer as he considered the politics of representing black speech within *Cane*. He was interested in the relations between knowledge, language, and race throughout his career, and what types of racial status or knowledge conferred "authority" to speak of African America became a pressing issue for him as he attempted to place *Cane* with magazine editors and publishing firms. Some of the most intriguing connections he made between these three forces were achieved at the level of metaphor, and of specific interest is Toomer's use of the metaphor of the veil as a margin, which once lifted gives entry into a distinct area of experience or discourse. This metaphor was given an intrinsically racial cast in W. E. B. Du Bois's *The Souls of Black Folk*, in which the veil, representing the color line separating the lives and experiences of black and white Americans, is the organizing motif.

In Toomer's autobiography, however, he uses this metaphor to describe learning to read. A slow learner, while looking at his peers he wondered

> by what miracle they, when they were my age and had been confronted by just this baffling task, had been transported past the barriers into this magic land. . . . The teacher had threatened severe punishment for all the dullards or lazy fellows who persisted in remaining stupid after a certain day. . . . Before judgement day arrived I had rent the veil. (*Wayward* 45–46)

During the period when he was composing *Cane*, however, Toomer used the metaphor of the veil differently—this time in its Du Boisian sense—that is, as a metaphor of a racial barrier. This occurred in a letter written in response to Claude Barnett of the Associated Negro Press. Barnett had asked Toomer to define his racial identity to settle an argument over whether Toomer was "Negroid"—an argument in which Barnett's "literary men" friends had contended that Toomer's "style and finish are not negroid."[15] Toomer responded that the answer to this question "involves a realistic and accurate knowledge of racial mixture, of nationality as formed by the interaction of tradition, culture, and environment, of the artistic relation to the racial or the social group, etc" but that, notwithstanding this important qualification, "I am the grandson of the late P B S Pinchback. From this fact it is clear that your contention is sustained. I have 'peeped behind the veil.'" And behind this veil were "the old folk songs, syncopated rhythms, the rich sweet taste of dark skinned life" (*Letters* 159–60). These two uses of the same metaphor indicate that Toomer saw the veil as not only the boundary of racial segregation, demarcating distinct social and cultural structures, but a barrier between literacy and illiteracy. The veil, then, is language itself, the point at which transformation, translation, understanding, and segregation occur—necessary for any form of conceptualization, yet often put to racially divisive use. This was obvious in Toomer's later writing about language and race; in "Race Problems and Modern Society," he noted of people—like himself—who, in choosing not to define themselves according to race, "have been so compelled, and are now so accustomed, to use the dominant, which is to them an alien, language, that they can find no words for even talking to themselves, much less to others" (187). If language came to be demarcated in the same metaphor as the barriers between black and white Americans, then language was deeply implicated in the structural relations between the races that Toomer found so problematic.

This became obvious in the politics of speech in *Cane*.[16] Toomer was scrupulous about wishing to represent black southern, rural speech accurately; while in Georgia he kept a notebook in which he recorded examples of southern dialect, and in discussing the spirituals, he observed how local black residents of nearby towns objected to them. "They called them 'shouting.' They had victrolas and player-pianos," he noted, accusing them of exactly the "sound blindness" he was anxious to avoid (*Wayward* 123). Similarly, in a letter to the *Liberator*, the socialist periodical, he was keen to assert his own authority by describing his firsthand experience of southern "rich dusk beauty that I had heard many false accents about" (*Letters* 71).

This concern with represented speech was partly due to its significance for anthropological discourses of authority, but also due to the centrality of voice in Waldo Frank's cultural criticism. Frank had always seen the individual speech-act as a political force, the way of establishing national, gender, and cultural identity; in *Our America* the trope of the voiceless giant is used several times, and he claimed of America, "To bound it is to stifle it, to give it a definite character is to emasculate it, to offer it a specific voice is to strike it dumb" (8). However, despite this egalitarian and democratic ideal of polyphony outlined in *Our America,* Frank's recollection of his trip to Spartanburg with Toomer casts a different light on his politics of voice. In his memoirs Frank recalled speaking to a congregation of several hundred members in a black church near Spartanburg on his trip south with Toomer. His talk was based on the subject of science allowing for new ways towards religion, rather than acting as a replacement for it, and drew applause from the crowd. Afterwards, Frank asked Toomer if he thought the crowd had liked it; Toomer averred but eventually responded, "[T]hese people . . . don't know what the word *science* means" (106). Frank's monologism here illustrates well the concern Toomer began to have about his cultural program—that the differentiation of people due to race or region would lead to a reification of their characteristics that would preclude any possibility of an autonomous voice. Sounding like a variation on Sapir's caution that culture should not override the agency of individuals, Toomer later remarked in an essay titled "The Individual in America": "In truth, as long as [a person] puts stock in race he is, by this very circumstance, more a part of the herd than he recognizes, and it will be difficult for him to become individualized. Also, he is impeded from grasping the true nature of another individual. Example: Waldo and myself."[17]

Toomer's worry about Frank's tendency to discount individual variations within a culture, a leveling-off that made an aesthetically unified model of American culture easier to achieve, was also revealed in Toomer's review of *Holiday.* Toomer noted "breaks in texture, of the dialogue . . ." and while abstaining from overtly criticizing Frank's use of dialect, he observed a "too obvious duality of origin which suspends one between the desire to accept Cloud [the protagonist of Holiday] as a Southern Negro, and the desire to accept him as a character created by Frank for the specific purposes of his design" ("Waldo Frank's *Holiday*" 10). This was despite the fact that Toomer had advised Frank on how to revise some of the dialect in *Holiday* to be more credible. Ultimately—and in similar fashion to the main criterion Lott has found for the assessment of "authenticity" in speech—it was

Frank's inadequate intentions for using dialect that led Toomer to make this criticism. *Holiday,* he felt, was a "subjective design," one that had "utilized certain elements of the South because these seemed most suited to its purposes" ("Waldo Frank's *Holiday*" 7). Far from Toomer's or Sapir's ideal of a dialectic between the individual and a wider, inherited culture, Frank's unashamedly aesthetic view of a totalized and organic American culture would select only those traits, individuals, and locations that could function together in aesthetic accord. It is notable that Toomer identified Frank's use of represented speech as one of the points where this was most obvious. As Bakhtin has suggested, the representation of a character's speech in fiction is the most visible site of conflict between authorial ideology and what he called the possibility of a character who operates as a "fully valid, autonomous carrier of his own individual world" (*Poetics* 5). If the authorial intention is not geared toward producing the autonomy of a character, Toomer suggests, then the speech itself is degraded and inauthentic.[18]

All of this—Toomer's recognition of the implication of language within racial politics, the two conflicting models he had for geographical and ethnic investigation and textualization, the failure of Frank's dialogue in *Holiday,* and its implications for his broader cultural program—inevitably brings an enormous pressure to bear upon the representation of speech in the characters of *Cane.* Furthermore, as Favor has noted, the representation of the "folk" by the urban intellectual involves class tensions, as the observer strives to negotiate a racial affiliation while aware of the class differences between himself and the rural working class.[19] In *Cane* this is particularly acute in the two sections dealing with an urban observer or intellectual traveling to the rural South. In "Fern" the narrator, who is "from the North," believes he may be able to "bring [Fern] something," which the men of Georgia have been unable to do (17–18). Fern's mesmerizing nature as someone who has an intangible and inscrutable attractiveness presents this northern narrator with a challenge in both communication and representation. These were the two tasks, of course, that also faced the ethnographer, and throughout the story he struggles to speak both to her and for her. He asks himself "What could I do for her? Talk, of course," believing that he will be able to—in a sense—vocalize Fern; he seems to suggest that through a performative speech act he will bring her total subjectivity into being and eliminate the aura of mystery surrounding her, an alluring enigma for many years. Yet when he walks with her in the canefield he admits that he "must have done something—what, I don't know," which prompts Fern to run off and begin "swaying, swaying. Her body was tortured with something it could not let out" (19). The vagueness of "something" and the admission that he did not know or could not recall what he did to alarm Fern indicates that he cannot even narrate his own actions, and Fern's lack of voice becomes exacerbated into a "torture." Eventually she produces a "broken song," but at the end of the story—with the narrator on the train returning North—it is his regret over the "fine, unnamed thing" that he was unable to do for her which persists.

As many observers have commented, this problem of how to articulate becomes even more acute in "Kabnis."[20] It is fitting that Toomer's presentation of expressive paralysis occurs in the cellar of Halsey's workshop, which is known as "the Hole." The underground is a space Melvin Dixon finds to be one of three archetypal locations in African American literature; in modern texts it represents "a stage for self-creating performances and for contact with black culture" (4).[21] He cites *Cane* and Claude McKay's *Banjo,* but other examples include the "hole" of Ellison's invisible man, the Dalton's basement in Wright's *Native Son,* or—if the trope is shifted to a more generic image of "down"—Janie Starks's experiences "Down on the muck" in Hurston's *Their Eyes Were Watching God.*[22] Halsey's cellar is determined as the "blackest" of holes by the fact that Father John, a mute ex-slave, presides over the space like a "bust in black walnut" (*Cane* 106), and this subterranean encounter with slavery has led Houston Baker to describe "The Hole" as representing "the collective unconscious of black America" (*Singers* 77).

It is at this moment of intense self-examination and awareness of the historical trauma of slavery, provoked by his encounter with Father John, that Kabnis is exposed to three versions of spoken language, each with their own politics of racial representation.[23] The first is that of Lewis, the other northern mulatto in Sempter who has been dubbed a "participant observer" by Lindberg (58). His is the language of fact-finding, of gathering information, of clinically attempting to discover the secrets and injustices endured in this community. Indeed, it has been suggested that he is modeled on NAACP investigators such as Walter White, who traveled to the South in the 1920s to investigate the details of lynchings.[24] Layman complains that he is always "pokin round and notin something," including an account of a brutal lynching that "weren't fer notin down" (91). It is this lack of empathy, the emotional contact sacrificed for the aim of objectivity, that ultimately makes Lewis's representational strategy inadequate for "knowing the South." As he approaches Carrie Kate, who rejects his advances, his eyelids "settle down" like "the glowing white ash of burned paper" (103). The inability to make emotional contact with Carrie—and by extension African American southern women—means that his understanding, and consequently his ability to fill the paper ready to admit his representation of the South, goes up in metaphorical smoke. Later, as the others sit in "the Hole" and drink corn whiskey, Lewis watches them:

> Lewis finds himself completely cut out. The glowing within him subsides. It is followed by a dead chill. Kabnis, Carrie, Stella, Halsey, Cora, the old man, the cellar, and the work-shop, the southern town descend on him. Their pain is too intense. He cannot stand it. He bolts from the table. Leaps up the stairs. Plunges through the work-shop and out into the night. (112)

When Layman asks Lewis if he is "getting t like our town," he replies that "I'm afraid it's on a different basis" (100). By severing any emotional response to the town, however, Lewis crucially refuses to comprehend the emotional tenor of the community, which has been formed to a considerable degree by a history of oppression and sexual exploitation but also by a history of resistance and resilience. As a result his reportage—and representation—is locked into recording the "ethnographic present," a dehistoricized account of brutalities and injustices divorced from an empathy that is sensitive to the wider social and personal implications of these acts. The "pain" is "too intense" for such a representational strategy and language, and therefore the participant-observer and the geography of "the Hole" cannot long remain in contact. In consequence, Lewis leaves in defeat, a tacit admission that an ethnography of the South is both inadequate and ultimately untenable.

The second type of voice to which Kabnis is exposed that might adequately represent the African American community is rural, southern African American dialect. Kabnis is described as "suspended a few feet above the soil whose touch would resurrect him," enfeebled by not being able to embrace the culture of the African American South (*Cane* 98). Yet earlier in the story, he had considered doing just that by adopting the face, and the voice, of the South; his deliberations continue as he questions whether such a strategy would reveal to him the essence of a racial "soul." His train of thought runs as follows:

> If I could feel that I came to the South to face it. If I, the dream (not what is weak and afraid in me) could become the face of the South. How my lips would sing for it, my songs being the lips of its soul. Soul. Soul hell. There aint no such thing. (84–85)

If there is no such thing as an essentialized regional or racial "soul," then there is no such thing as an "authentic" dialect or language with which it can be represented. Gates has discussed this treatment of dialect in *Cane:*

> Toomer employs the black oral voice in his text both as a counterpoint to that standard English voice of his succession of narrators but also as evidence of the modernist claim that there had existed no privileged, romantic movement of unified consciousness, especially or not even in the cane fields of . . . rural Georgia. . . . Existence, in the world of *Cane*, is bifurcated, fundamentally opposed. . . . (*Signifying* 178)

This bifurcation of existence, Gates goes on to argue, involves not only a binaristic separation between the standard English voice of the narrator and the spoken dialect of his other characters but comes to structurally reinforce other binaries in the text—divisions of region, gender, and race. Indeed, in "Kabnis" this division is at its most extreme, due to its nature as a semidramatic piece, with much of it in the format of dramatic dialogue. In consequence, the division between the narrator's commentary, or "stage direction," and characters' voices is often absolute, effecting a crippling linguistic stalemate that Gates contends would be mediated and resolved within the African American tradition only by Zora Neale Hurston's formulation of the "speakerly" text. Yet I think the situation is more complex than Gates suggests with reference to "Kabnis." The key to this is the speech of Kabnis to Halsey about language, art, and labor:

> An as f you, youre all right f choppin things from blocks of wood. I was good at that th day I ducked th cradle. An since then, I've been shaping words after a design that branded here. Know whats here? M soul. Ever heard o that? Th hell y have. Been shaping words to fit m soul. . . . I'll tell y. I've been shaping words; ah, but sometimes theyre beautiful an golden an have a taste that makes them fine t roll over with y tongue. Your tongue aint fit f nothing but t roll and lick hog meat. (111)

What Kabnis disdains here is the link between labor and black oral culture; Halsey's absorption in his craft of "choppin things from blocks of wood" makes his "tongue" fit only for rolling cigarettes and eating. Kabnis is uninterested in a mode of expression that will reveal its origins in a history of economic exploitation and manual labor, which was something he has avoided since he "ducked the cradle." Just as he finds facing "Father John" and the history of slavery difficult, as well as the "face of the South," so he seeks craft as a *metaphor* for forging a mode of expression, but not as an *actuality.* What this does is to ignore the long history of the relation between black oral culture and labor, as evident in the rich tradition of African American work songs and humor that has been so well documented by Lawrence Levine.[25] What such a decision does is move Kabnis into a kind of aestheticism, a program to develop a language divorced from practicality and made "beautiful an golden." Instead, he finds that the "form thats burned int my soul. . . . lives on words," but they are "[m]isshapen, split-gut, tortured, twisted words" (111). The pressures that Kabnis places on a "folk language"—his wish for it to be divorced from practical activity and a degrading history (as he complains, "things are so immediate in Georgia") compounded with his contradictory wish for it to retain the beauty of the folk songs that he hears at night—functions to warp the dialect he wishes to create. As Hutchinson notes, Kabnis "longs to achieve an identity by means of verbal expression and is frustrated by his inability to shape the right words, to *name* his reality adequately" ("Racial Discourse" 240).

The final language from which Kabnis recoils is what Bakhtin has called the "Unitary language," a language that is primarily used to maintain and enforce hegemonic power. In this case it is the language of religion and the Bible. The key figure in Kabnis's consideration of this form of language is Father John, who is described as a "Black man who saw Jesus in the ricefields, and began preaching to his people. Moses- and Christ-words used for songs. Dead-blind father of a muted folk who feel their way upward to a life that crushes or absorbs them" (106). Father John's muteness comes to play a vital role in "Kabnis," especially as he is an ex-preacher and, as Kabnis taunts him, has seen the "hell" of slavery. John's comment at the end of the section—"th sin th white folks 'mitted when they made the Bible lie"—forms the dramatic climax to the piece and offers the reason for his muteness (117).

As Goldberg has stated, "language (like radio and television) is a technology of governmentality, a means of domesticating the influence of the colonial occupier/master. The occupier's language . . . orders the anarchy, the lack of form, supposedly afoot in the preoccupied country or space" (*Racial Subjects* 97). If Father John's words are "Moses-and-Christ" words, which have been used as a "technology of governmentality" by white slaveholders, then he is placed in a situation of either using the language that maintained his enslavement or remaining silent. Moreover, Kabnis brushes aside the possibility that African American adaptations of Christianity in slavery could produce either a beautiful and original folk culture or a discourse that could enunciate the desire for liberation and even insurrection. He challenges John: "When you had eyes, did you ever see th beauty of th world? Tell me that. Th hell you did" (114–15). Christianity is portrayed as false consciousness and nothing else, an opiate with a unidirectionally oppressive effect. As Houston Baker has noted, when John condemns white religion, he can do it only in the terms of that religion—hence Kabnis's furious commands for him to shut up (78). Therefore, another expressive register, or a framework for knowing and speaking the folk, is removed.

Such a reading would seem to present *Cane* as a profoundly stagnated text, one that faced the complex politics surrounding the overdetermination of the black voice with a mixture of rage and withdrawal. Indeed, many critics have seen Kabnis's failure to "reconnect" with rural, African American folk culture in these terms.[26] Yet this view of *Cane* as essentially cynical and pessimistic underestimates the importance of the text's intense enthusiasm for formal experiment. If Toomer was not willing to give a determined indication of "the precise register which an 'authentic' black voice would, or could, assume," he surely saw the *form* of *Cane* as a new and powerful utterance. Perhaps the epigraph to *Cane*—"Oracular. / Redolent of fermenting syrup. / Purple of the dusk, / deep-rooted cane" (iii)—refers to the oracular status of the text of *Cane,* rather than to the sugar plant that provides one of its recurrent images, as most critics assume. Such an emphasis on the formal structure that contains these African American voices, rather than the voices themselves, alleviates what might otherwise be a paralyzing singularity of focus on the overdetermination of the black voice in the culture of the 1920s. Certain characters in *Cane,* such as the narrator of "Fern," have a concern that the African American voice can never be fully apprehended, and Kabnis is troubled by his realization that language is heavily implicated in racially oppressive social structures. Yet these characters appear in only one text piece each, out of the thirty individual text pieces of an incredibly innovative short story cycle; it is a cycle whose diversity and novelty overshadows the philological dead ends of any one of its many characters. Therefore, reading the epigraph as suggesting that it is *Cane,* rather than cane, which is oracular, indicates that it is the very *form* of *Cane* that enunciates, as Ellison said of *Invisible Man:*

> The final act of *Invisible Man* is not that of a concealment of darkness in the Anglo Saxon connotation of the word, but of that of a voice issuing its little wisdom out of the substance of its own wilderness. . . . He gets his restless mobility not so much from the blues or from sociology but from the circumstance that he appears in a literary form which has time and social change as its special province. ("Change the Joke" 1548)

Toomer's obsession with the subject of form, revealed through his correspondence during the writing of *Cane,* illustrates his desire to open new parameters for expression around issues of racial identity that are not reliant on the representation of voice. Indeed, Toomer was aware of the need for innovative formal and philological strategies in writing in order to circumvent the racially Manichean tendencies of many of the models that were available to him at the time. This illustrates one of the ways in which Toomer anticipated key issues in postcolonial studies—namely how to establish an effective dialogue between racialized and cultural identities without falling back into modes of exchange that would just reinscribe those same, reductive identities. As quoted earlier, he complained that those who did not wish to use America's normative terminology of race "can find no words for even talking to themselves, much less to others"; he later stated that "words are the original germ carriers of the majority of our prejudices" ("Germ Carriers" 82).

These complaints, of course, are similar to Henry Louis Gates Jr.'s famous question: "[H]ow can the black subject posit a full and sufficient self in a language in which blackness is a sign of absence?" ("'Race,' writing and difference" 12). It has been Toomer's interest in transforming conceptualizations of race through transforming the ways in which it can be represented that has helped boost his recent critical fortunes; as Ross Posnock has stated, Toomer's resistance to the "dogmatism of identity logic" (207) has led (in some quarters) to a celebration of him as "a visionary prophet of a 'trans-racial American identity'" (30). Indeed, Toomer's wish to transcend what he called the "entire machinery of verbal hypnotism" of racial categories continues to plague contemporary critics facing the challenging task of providing an adequate deracialized discourse within which to discuss Toomer's ideas of transracialism. As Hutchinson claims, it presents the critic with an "ethical challenge" in *Cane*'s revelation of "the significant silences of our own deeply racialized social text, the gaps and absences which critics, in turn, have failed to make speak" ("Racial Discourse" 244).

Ultimately, Toomer's decision not to provide an answer to the question of "the precise register which an 'authentic' black voice would, or could, assume" is an indication that he was more interested in theorizing revisions to the black subject, rather than exploring how a supposedly preexistent subject could find access to voice. *Cane* therefore presents what may be considered a tactical circumvention of the question of how the black subject can speak, a shift in emphasis towards the formal structures within which race was articulated. In consequence, Toomer's most famous text is more a prelude to an investigation of how racial subjectivity can be reimagined within modernity than a fatalistic throwing up of hands.

Part of that circumvention, however, is *Cane*'s awareness of the centrality of speech to the dominant models for textualizing regional and racial difference available in the 1920s—a centrality Toomer ultimately suggests is misplaced. *Cane* ruminated on the spatialized view of "buried cultures" expressed in Frank's *Our America,* a view that dovetailed with Sapir's notion of the "organic" culture of harmonious internal relation, which could act as a compelling alternative to standardized, corporate America. Yet such a view tended—in Frank's version at least—on the one hand to obliterate the possibility of the creative individual and on the other to enforce an "ethnographic present" completely inadequate to address the saturation of history that Toomer felt in Georgia. *Cane* was also influenced by the African American, mulatto tradition of "reconnecting" with the folk, a tradition that proclaimed an obliteration of differences of class, region, or education in favor of a racially based identity. This "reconnecting" also served to celebrate a cultural heritage based on race. Both Frank's ideas and "reconnecting" with the folk, however, had the capacity to perceive a limited range of characteristics and traits as representing "authentic" blackness, an authenticity that often resided for the purposes of representation in oral culture and specifically speech. If Toomer finally cannot create "authentic" black speech, cannot provide a definitive dialect that enunciates an essentialized identity, it is because he chooses not to endorse the possibility of such an identity.

In consequence, Toomer came to the conclusion that notions of an authentic black subjectivity rooted in a rural folk would have to be killed off before any radical politics of changing America's racial discourse could take effect, before what he called the "Negro emergent" could be possible. Indeed, his own self-conception as somebody who was of a new race, "an American, neither white nor black," necessitated the allocation of this rural folk a historical rather than transhistorical identity (*Wayward* 92). As Favor has noted, in *Cane* "the South becomes a locus of history and the past rather than an indicator of the present," thus ceasing to be "a primary, immediate, and always-lived marker of identity" (63). By contrast, in a letter to Waldo Frank, Toomer praised the "jazzed, strident, modern" culture of Washington's Seventh Street, the main thoroughfare of Black Washington, but remarked, "Negro? Only in the *boldness* of its expression. In its healthy freedom. American" (*Letters* 116). For Toomer, then, black cultural forms evolving into modernity would become divorced from any essentialistic tie; he mocked those who believed "that the thing we call Negro beauty will always be attributable to a clearly defined physical source" (*Toomer Reader* 24). In an early poem he described himself as "The First American," and thus his own modernity was predicated on the "disappearing Negro" of which he wrote in *Cane*. In effect, the "pure Negro" had to be in the process of disappearing for his conception of himself to exist. If *Cane* was, as he stated, a "swan song" for the rural folk, it was also the welcome call for new visions of race in modernity. As he wrote to Lola Ridge, "I think my own contribution will curiously blend the rhythm of peasanty [*sic*] with the rhythm of machines. A syncopation, a slow jazz, a sharp intense motion, subtilized, fused to a terse lyricism" (*Toomer Reader* 17). *Cane* may not provide an authentic black voice, but it does begin to examine forces that could destabilize and radically reform racial politics in the United States.

CHAPTER 5

CANE, BODY TECHNOLOGIES, AND GENEALOGY

In *Cane,* Jean Toomer was ultimately less interested in celebrating an "authentic" African American subjectivity than he was in investigating the processes of racialization in the United States from a "Negro" perspective. As the last two chapters have indicated, Toomer was well aware that perspective was a crucial condition of any discourse on race, and consequently it is one of the key thematic and structural concerns of *Cane.* As many critics have noted, the dynamics of looking are central to the text, whether it be the "spectatorial artist" looking at rural black southerners, Paul looking through the "dark pane" of his Chicago window toward his past in rural Georgia in "Bona and Paul," or audiences looking at performers (and vice versa) in "Theater" and "Box Seat."[1] Always at play in such gazes are what Linda Martín Alcoff has described as a "mediation through the visible, working on both the inside and the outside, both on the ways we read ourselves and the way others read us," which forms "what is unique to racialized identities as against ethnic and cultural identities" (278). *Cane* demonstrates an awareness of how that "mediation" produces raced identities, an awareness drawn primarily from the experiences of an African American community whose "perceptual practices" were finely attuned to "reading" interracial and intraracial difference (Alcoff 275). Equally, Toomer was interested in social factors that could disturb this process of racialization, an interest stimulated by his long-held ideal of a racially integrated society. Sensitive to the ways in which bodies become racially marked, he considered how programs of disciplining and training the body might disrupt such inscription; aware of the transformations that technology was having on perceptions of materiality, he wondered how it might affect perceptions of the racialized body.

Accordingly, Toomer turned at least in part from the hesitations and reservations that more organicist writers such as Anderson and Frank had about the "machine" toward a more European attitude, one that perceived the machine as offering the potential for a (sometimes violent) liberation from past aesthetic and social formations. Technology's potential to transform both subjectivities and the social relations of the cityscape worked its way into some of the most utopian moments of *Cane,* particularly in its second section. Similar glimpses of the faultlines of racialist thinking are also offered in Toomer's examinations of genealogy, mainly through those people who are somehow marked as "illegitimate" and especially through the figure of the bastard. Bastards in *Cane* often lay bare the frameworks of "legitimacy" from which they are excluded and carry the potential to trouble or even obliterate the spatial differentiation of races that determined the American social landscape. This interest in both technology and genealogy offered Toomer the mechanisms for investigating the material basis (or otherwise) of race, and to suggest it may not be as deterministic or as immutable as many at the time suggested.

Many of the ways in which *Cane* points to the constructedness of race, and suggests alternatives to the normative processes of racialization in the United States of the early twentieth century, are a product of Toomer's consistent belief that identity was more about design than determination. In his late 1920s autobiography "Earth Being," he attested that "I would far rather form a man than form a book" (*Wayward* 19).[2] For much of his life he was interested in the possibilities of developing his sense of self, something that almost all biographical portraits of him have noted. This took various forms and was usually under the aegis of a particular philosophical, technical, or spiritual system; it applied to his intense involvement with the regimen of physical culture exercises he undertook in the early 1910s, his ambition to be first a musician and then a writer during the early 1920s, his involvement with Gurdjieffian philosophy from 1924 onwards, his social experiment in communal living at Portage in 1931, and his interest in the Alexander technique in the 1940s. Each of these was initially characterized by Toomer's extreme enthusiasm and remarkably energetic application, an enthusiasm akin to what he jokingly later referred to as a "neophyte on the threshold of a new world."[3] These various "neophytisms" illustrate Toomer's belief in a capacity to reshape and reform his subjectivity, a view that takes subjectivity as a version of aesthetic formalism, something to be shaped and revised in relation to an ideal; as he said, "My whole being is devoted to making my small area of existence a work of art" (*Wayward* 19). Such statements attest to the strength of Toomer's belief that a process of continual self-creation, which he termed "individualization," was the most significant personal, social, or political concept imaginable. Toomer's consistent engagement with processes of "individualization" led him to see all categories of identity as discourses to be probed and questioned, rather than as "natural" and immutable. In many ways *Cane* represents an attempt on Toomer's part to explore the nature of racial categories: how they function through genealogies, how sign systems mark a body as raced, how bodies can resist or elide such operations, and how what he termed the "field of force" within which subjectivities are enscripted exists as a complex terrain of race, class, and gender (*Wayward* 20).

Despite the degree to which Toomer pushed his interrogation of "race," it is true that he never fully articulated a position where he denied a biological foundation to race. Nor should *Cane* be read as an attempt to dismantle the possibility of "racial identity," a premise that would have seemed ludicrous to its contemporary reviewers. Instead, it should be seen as a text that brings changing forces in the construction of other areas of subjectivity, particularly those circulating around the production of gender, into confrontation with the processes of racialization. It is this confrontation that establishes *Cane* as a profound meditation on the future of race in modernity. Some of these changes—in conceptions of masculinity, in aesthetic programs that draw extensively on machinery as a source of formal inspiration, in the demographies of the audience for American modernism in the early 1920s—are brought into fruitful contact with ideas around race in *Cane,* and specifically African Americanism. In many ways these changes are responsible for the destabilization and interrogation of racial essentialism that many recent commentators have seen as being one of the most fascinating features of *Cane:* as George Hutchinson puts it, "it is precisely the ambiguity—and mobility—of Toomer's "identity" in a society obsessed with clarity on this score that motivated the restless searching through which *Cane* came about, through which Toomer left it behind, and without which there could be no book like it" ("Identity" 54). The forces that create much of this ambiguity and mobility of identity are very similar to the ones Sherwood Anderson brought to his representations of African Americans. Like Anderson, Toomer was concerned about the impact of Fordism on African American life, with its twin attributes of the increasing mechanization of the workplace and the increasing standardization of material production—yet he was also enthused by the novelty, dynamism, and modernity of that process. Like Anderson, he was interested in changing definitions of masculinity, yet was reluctant to see those changes as leading inevitably towards "feminization." And like Anderson he was fascinated by the great migration, yet saw the new black communities of the North as exciting developments in cultural interaction rather than as a racial invasion. If Anderson saw these forces of industrialization, migration, and gender change as threats to subjectivities that he wished to preserve, with all the problems of primitivism which that entails, Toomer begins to view them as appealing technologies for articulating a new vision of racialism in modernity.

MASCULINITY AND PHYSICAL CULTURE: "THE HUMAN FIGURE AS NATURE'S MOST AMAZING WORK OF ART"

As many critics have identified, Toomer was well aware of the fact that gender and race have a mutually constitutive effect within the development of subjectivities.[4] In consequence, changing conceptions of masculinity within the early twentieth century were significant to his consideration of the future of racial identities within the United States. Moreover, the late nineteenth and early twentieth centuries represent a period in America when masculine subjectivities were undergoing rapid change. Gail Bederman talks about an "obsession" with manliness during the period, an obsession which was a response to changing social and economic factors that made it increasingly difficult for men to define themselves *as men* in the way that the preceding generation had done. For the middle class into which Toomer was born, much of this difficulty was because opportunities for autonomy in the business sphere, such as self-employment and small-scale, competitive capitalism, were being severely eroded (Bederman 12). Instead, they were increasingly employed in new corporate, bureaucratic, and service jobs.

In such an environment, "feminine" qualities such as communication skills, teamwork, and flexibility began to be demanded in place of the aggression, competitiveness, independence, and self-denial that typified what

Michael Kimmel has termed the "self-made marketplace man" ("Consuming Manhood" 21). The self-made, marketplace man, he argues, had been the dominant figure for middle-class masculine identity in the mid-nineteenth century, but as the gap between this model and workplace actuality widened, men had to find other areas outside the workplace where they could develop a sense of "manliness." Various strategies of how men attempted this have been much discussed. These include the cult of the frontier and the explosion in the number of "dude ranches," praised and frequented by men such as Theodore Roosevelt, and its correlative, the upsurge in American militarism and praise of the martial ideal that culminated in the Spanish-American War in 1898—and contributed to subsequent imperialist adventures. Others include the increasing popularity of fraternal orders during the period, with as many as one in four American men being members in 1897, a total of 5.5 million (Kimmel, *Manhood* 171). The rise in racism and lynchings, which made the 1890s such a horrific decade for race relations, has also been attributed to men's obsession with their gender. The increasing visibility of feminist activism and a swelling immigrant population also exerted additional pressure on white middle-class men to delineate subjectivities capable of continuing their hegemonic authority. Yet perhaps the response that has most significance for representation, and which attracted a young Jean Toomer, was the cult of the body and the rise in popularity of sports.[5]

The physical culture craze that swept across Europe and America in the latter years of the nineteenth century, making millionaires and celebrities of figures like Bernarr MacFadden and Eugene Sandow, helped to install sport as the leisure activity of the modern age. The precursor to modern bodybuilding, the physical culture movement made millions of dollars by publishing techniques for developing muscular physiques in magazines such as MacFadden's *Physical Culture*—a magazine that prescribed health in terms of a disciplined attitude to diet, exercise, work, and leisure. The craze was to a large degree dependent on representations of idealized physiques, which were becoming more important to social ideals of gender identity. As Kimmel notes, "The ideal of the Self-Made Man gradually assumed physical connotations so that by the 1870s the idea of 'inner strength' was replaced by a doctrine of physicality and the body" (*Manhood* 120). In crude terms, the site of "self-making" shifted from the marketplace to the gym, a shift that of course gave a more material basis for definitions of masculinity than the previous generation had experienced. As Kimmel goes on to discuss, this more materialized, externalized locus for gender identity required constant performance to differentiate itself from femininity:

> While "manhood" had historically been contrasted with "childhood," to suggest that manhood meant being fully adult, responsible, and autonomous, the new opposite of "masculinity" was "femininity," traits and attitudes associated with women, not children. Manhood was an expression of inner character; masculinity was in constant need of validation, of demonstration, of proof. ("Consuming Manhood" 21)

This change represented a fundamental shift in the way that masculinity was produced; as Kimmel argues, it introduced a new value to materiality, where "[t]he body did not *contain* the man, expressing the man within; now, that body *was* the man" (*Manhood* 120).

This development provided the basis for the economic success of the discourse of physical culture, which operated in several ways. It generated a consumer desire in the space between a consumer's self-perception and the presentation of idealized physiques and practices—the space between the real and representations that claimed the authority of an "ideal." Yet it also delivered the promise of closing that gap, if not eliminating it, through its commodified disciplinary knowledge and products. It promised the ever-alluring paradox of both conformity to a peer group and individual agency, the double attraction of a fixed formal ideal and the ability for self-determination that typified the "scare" advertising and marketing that was such a feature of the 1920s (Douglas, *Terrible Honesty* 34–35). It was this paradox that attracted Jean Toomer to the movement, and specifically to the work of Bernarr Macfadden.

Bernarr Macfadden was a significant figure in what Toomer called his "first neophytism," his first enthusiastic burst of self-reformation and consideration of identity politics. MacFadden had built up a personal fortune of $30 million by 1930; he published *Physical Culture* magazine, wrote a five-volume *Encyclopedia of Physical Culture* (which Toomer bought), and published several other books. Much of this output was devoted to "descriptions" of a normative masculinity, achievable through a code of discipline and with a firm emphasis on aesthetics—as MacFadden said, "for health to be known, it must be seen" (Mullins 28). MacFadden's 1916 book *Manhood and Marriage* is a fairly typical example of how the physical culture movement discussed masculinity, and how central anxiety was to its commercial success. The opening chapter—"The Importance of Virility"—asks readers to pose themselves the question "Am I a complete man?" And it continues, "[W]hen this query cannot be answered satisfactorily, when you feel that there is a doubt as to the possession of the qualities essential to true manhood, then indeed is your position difficult" (9). Yet this "true manhood" can be obtained and retained through an adherence to the "laws that govern the retention of manly powers," laws that he spends the remainder of the book outlining (1).

Moreover, as Foucault has discussed, the proliferation of sexual discourse and sexualities within modernity (without which texts such as MacFadden's would have been impossible) involved the production of extensive discourse about sexual "deviation." By naming and categorizing certain sexual practices as "aberrations," legal and medical discourses developed a whole series of regulatory mechanisms facilitating the encroachment of power over people's bodies and pleasures. This was evident in MacFadden's demographic ideal, which was a "race of normal, sound, healthy and vigorous individuals," which, of course, means he spends much of his attention defining deviations from this "normality" (*Encyclopedia* 2416). Perhaps the most pernicious threat to normative masculinity, according to MacFadden, was masturbation, which Foucault identifies as one of the key discourses by which "power advanced, [and] multiplied its relays and effects" over children's bodies (*Sexuality* 42).[6]

MacFadden cited evidence that the practice of masturbation was almost "universal" in male youth and opined that it is the most likely cause of a boy's emasculation (the transfiguration into the "feminine" that Kimmel sees as the new antithesis for models of masculinity). So disturbing is it that by far the longest chapter in *Manhood and Marriage* is entitled "The Truth About Masturbation" (*Manhood* 151). Emasculation or feminization thus becomes the ultimate "scare" tactic underlying MacFadden's exhortations against "deviation": "to be a male and not a man, to wear the clothes indicative of the male sex and realize that you are masquerading—a hypocrite, a pretender—is indeed a torturous experience" (*Manhood* 8). Indeed, masturbation entails an emasculation that is both a degeneration and a destruction of the normal male body; comparing it to castration, MacFadden claimed it resulted in the "slow undermining of manhood and all that goes with it" (*Manhood* 160). Only a strict regimen of physical discipline, Macfadden suggests, including exercises, diet, and willpower techniques, could counteract this degeneration, which MacFadden also linked to spots, memory loss, a pale complexion, and a "lagging gait" (*Manhood* 162).

This was the context in which Toomer encountered MacFadden's journal *Physical Culture*. As an adolescent he had entered a period of what he called "sex indulgences," which he described as "the most desperate struggles of my life." Due to the medical discourse surrounding masturbation, he believed it had been the cause of a long and unpleasant childhood illness and saw it as a "practice which more than any other bleeds away the body and soul . . ." (*Wayward* 50–51). As a recourse from what he felt to be a debilitating habit, he entered a program of physical discipline:

> I went in for physical training. I regularly took exercises at home. I took several correspondence courses in muscle-building and health promotion. Dumb-bells, wrestling. Finally, I began heavy weight lifting. . . .
>
> I tried dieting and nature cure. I ran across the *Physical Culture* magazine and was thus introduced to Bernarr MacFadden. I bought his encyclopedia, and, in addition to following his prescriptions, I began talking and arguing his ideas with everyone.
>
> And then came another spell of sex which reduced me so low I feared I was going into decline. In a desperate condition I began breathing exercises, lived more carefully than ever, and, by sheer force of will pulled myself out. . . .
>
> No-one knew the fight I was making. But, in time, everyone saw the results. They came to regard me as an exceptionally strong and healthy young man. (*Wayward* 89–90).

During this period he observed the dietary restrictions advised by the journal, installed gym apparatus along the walls of his room, and bought a set of lung-testing equipment, which he "blew into . . . until [his] lung capacity became the marvel of experts." He took the "Farmer Burns correspondence course in wrestling" and "got some fellows to come to my room to work on."[7] He also kept scrapbooks containing pictures of Greek statues and men in body-building poses, and this developed in him a sense of the aesthetics of the human body; through these activities and images he grew "to respond to the human figure as nature's most amazing work of art."[8] This was the first instance of many in Toomer's life where formalized training of the body offered the promise of a radical change in identity. It promised to eradicate both abnormalities and indiscipline, bringing Toomer in line with the "normality" of white, middle class American male values that MacFadden both interpreted so astutely and helped to form.[9] Yet equally significantly (and this is similar to Jay Gatsby's involvement with physical culture in *The Great Gatsby*), it seemed to offer an identity that was in many ways devoid of history, the chance of a reformation into a "strong and healthy young man" and the banishment of a history of weakness and "indulgences." Indeed, re-creating the body as a method of re-creating identity continued to appeal to Toomer. During one of his later brief periods of study at various colleges in the mid-1910s, Toomer posed for a photograph in a manner reminiscent of the poses found in magazines like *Physical Culture* (reproduced on page 179). One of these college sojourns involved him studying as a gym instructor at the American College of Physical Training in Chicago (attracted partly by the fact that it used to be directed by MacFadden). Later in life he dabbled with the Alexander technique (which advocates specific muscular training and "conscious control" of involuntary muscular activity as a method toward holistic health), and became deeply involved with the ideas of G. I. Gurdjieff after seeing a program of dance at his exhibition in New York. Toomer was moved by these dances, feeling that they "seemed to take hold of the body and literally recreate it. . . . They involved the whole man, I felt sure, and were means in the service of an essentially religious aim" ("Gurdjieff" 107).[10]

Such was Toomer's early involvement with the discourse of physical culture and its promise of corporeal transformability, an involvement so significant

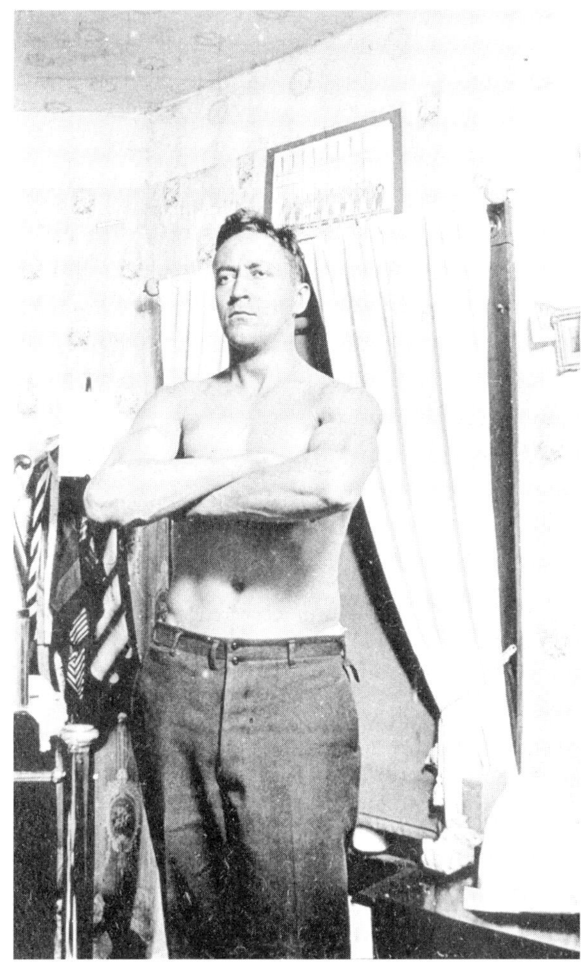

Jean Toomer at college, 1916. Photographer unknown. (Courtesy of the Jean Toomer Papers, James Weldon Johnson Collection, Beinecke Rare Book and Manuscript Library, Box 65, Folder 1491.)

that he played out his enthusiasm for it in various but similar body disciplines throughout his life. Yet there was another element to this discourse to which Toomer's "first neophytism" did not make reference, yet which was evident a few years later in society at large, and which he would bring to bear on the writing of *Cane*. As already mentioned, physical culture's linkage of masculinity with agency—one could *choose* whether to be a man or not—and the strand of it that promises a liberation from inherited physical limitations is a function of changing definitions of maleness, in which masculinity has to be repeatedly *proved*. Yet the correlative of a system of masculinity that required continual proof was that an identity based more on display did not require a narrative of origins to validate it; indeed, the nature of the posed, well-built body was that the pose itself came to define the body, a representational phenomenon that banished the history and the specificity of the body inhabiting the pose. Roland Barthes has written of this in his discussions of photography:

> I lend myself to the social game, I pose, I know I am posing, I want you to know I am posing, but (to square the circle) this additional message must in no way alter the precious essence of my individuality: what I am, apart from any effigy. What I want, in short, is that my (mobile) image, buffeted along with a thousand shifting photographs, altering with situation and age, should always coincide with my "profound" self; but it is the contrary that must be said: "myself" never coincides with my image, for it is the image which is heavy, motionless, stubborn (which is why society sustains it), and "myself" which is light, divided, dispersed. . . . (*Camera* 13)

Barthes, here, sees the pose as a cumbersome and inflexible representational imposition on his "profound" self, but for marginalized racial groups who lived with such cumbersome and inflexible associations applied to them by white American society, adopting the "poses" of idealized masculinity could have precisely the opposite effect. Ideas taken from the physical culture movement (aimed at a white, male, middle-class readership) take on a very different status when appropriated by racial groups whose bodies had been overdetermined by white racist discourse, and this applied especially to African Americans. In this respect it is interesting to look at the photograph of Toomer at college (possibly in Chicago) and posed in a manner reminiscent of many of the photographs in *Physical Culture*. Stripped to the waist to reveal his built physique, Toomer's arms are crossed in a pose to show off the size and the resolution of his biceps and shoulders; he is shot from below to emphasize his height and authority, factors also enhanced by the small window frame behind him. In looking to the left of the camera and avoiding the lens he stresses his autonomy, self-reliance, and even arrogance. As Richard Dyer has noted of the connections between "whiteness" and bodybuilding, the appearance of the built body has connotations that have often been central to white male identity, and which white masculinities have often hoarded for themselves. These include the display of a hard, taut body surface that provides "a sense of separation and boundedness," one that reinforces the impossibility of being "merged" with racial or gendered others; it also represents "the literal triumph of mind over matter, imagination over flesh" (152–53). As he goes on, "the point after all is that it is built, a product of the application of thought and planning, and achievement. It is the sense of the mind at work behind the production of this body that most defines its whiteness" (164). Yet in the photo of Toomer we see the proud affirmation of autonomy and "separateness," and the confidence borne of flesh that has been subjugated to the imagination. If these ideas, as Dyer suggests, are inherently racialized, then challenging effects are generated from their appropriation by a man who, in the census definitions of the time, would have been classed a Negro.

Toomer's emerging view contradicted the neo-Darwinian opinion that race and identity were inseparably linked, an opinion that frequently shaded into the white supremacist belief in "hard" heredity held by many in the eugenics movement. Toomer's view also avoided easy dualisms between body and spirit characteristic of the nineteenth-century constructions of masculinity that Kimmel has discussed. In 1924 Toomer commented that "[c]oncern with race is one of the main factors causing American materialism, interest solely in the physical aspects of existence. Our materialism, on the other hand, is one of the main factors causing concern with race. For both of these conditions emphasize the body—falsely—and false body values."[11] In his view, the body's materiality was largely contingent upon the discursive frameworks within which it was produced; it was material capable of being changed—and changing in return the very nature of individual subjectivity of which it formed a part. What was needed was a dynamic process in order to effect this change, which Toomer had sought in physical culture, the Alexander technique, and Gurdjieffian systematics of the body. It was this that Toomer hoped would be one of the features of the New Negro Renaissance; in his essay "The Negro Emergent" he exulted that "the Negro" was now "discovering his body" and putting it into the service of "his own experience" (90).[12] Toomer's thought here anticipates Judith Butler's recent examination of the ways in which the material body comes into cognitive being; she notes that

> psychic projection confers boundaries and, hence, unity on the body, so that the very contours of the body are sites that vacillate between the psychic and the material. Bodily contours and morphology are not merely implicated in an irreducible tension between the psychic and the material but *are* that tension. (66)

Toomer had exulted following his involvement with physical culture that "I had built up a certain strength of will over my body. I could *make* it do things. The bodies of the other boys simply moved of themselves."[13] Making and "making it do" come to be identical in this conception of the body, and the dynamic, disciplinary process of physical culture comes to shift the point of tension Butler describes above to allow for new parameters of the morphological imaginary. It would be wrong to claim that Toomer had no faith in a materiality that existed outside language and outside discourse, a proposition at the center of Butler's argument; yet he was aware of the way in which discursive practices, in interaction with the material, produced bodily morphologies. In *Cane* Toomer examined several dynamic processes that offered reimaginations of the body, in an effort to examine the "materiality" of race.

JEAN TOOMER AND TECHNOLOGY

Soon after becoming involved with the New York literati through the influence of his friend and mentor Waldo Frank, Toomer discovered a dynamic process that seemed to offer just such a reimagination. This was, as he put it, the "aesthetic-machine-beauty program as sponsored by [Gorham] Munson in *Secession* and [Matthew] Josephson in *Broom*."[14]

In many avant-garde European art movements—Futurism, Dadaism, Cubism—what intellectuals and cultural producers frequently described as "the machine" had already effected many changes to the morphological imaginary of bodies. In New York, such ideas had seized the imagination of many of the new generation of American writers and critics such as Munson, Josephson, and Malcolm Cowley, many of whom were shuttling between the United States and Europe during this time. This section examines how Toomer, often informed by this intellectual circle, applied this emergent set of aesthetics to racially marked bodies and to racial politics, and goes on to show how this underpins many of the most belligerent antiracist statements within *Cane*.

In using the term "technology," I hope to preserve the features implied when writers of the time talked about "the machine." This term was often deliberately vague, but its usage tended to denote instruments and innovations in the mechanical and physical sciences with tangible practical applications, particularly in three areas. The first was machinery's role within industrial production, particularly within the manufacturing industry, a role that was rapidly increasing in the era; indeed, Theodore Kornweibel has estimated that machines displaced 3,272,000 workers within the manufacturing industry between 1920 and 1929 (313). The second area was the electricity industry; many writers were particularly fascinated by the transformative function of powerhouses and dynamos. The third involved developments in communication, particularly the motor car and the camera, and new forms of electric communication such as wireless telegraphy, the telephone, and the radio. Most uses of the term saw technology as a potent and powerful force that needed to be accommodated or harnessed, but which also identified "the machine" as possessing a more abstract type of power that resided in its capacity for radical novelty and innovation.

Toomer's engagement with the aesthetics of "the machine" really began with his correspondence with Gorham B. Munson. He first wrote to Munson (who was also a close friend of Frank) in the autumn of 1922 and soon praised (with reservations) the announcement of a "mechanics for a literary secession" that Munson made in the November 1922 issue of *S4N*. Munson's programmatic statement included the rejection of a duality between "machinery and the values of life," and claimed that "the glory of the French dadaists . . . rests principally on their endeavor to put Machinery into positive equilibrium with man and nature" ("Mechanics"). Munson's statement was in effect a manifesto for the little magazine *Secession,* then in its third issue, which he edited along with Matthew Josephson and Kenneth Burke. It was in Toomer's exchange of letters with Munson, and his contributions to *S4N,* that his thought about machinery and mechanics was most fully developed.[15]

Unlike other writers in his circle such as Waldo Frank or Sherwood Anderson, Toomer absorbed Munson's argument that establishing a duality between "machinery and the values of life" was not only simplistic and untenable but also disregarded an aesthetic resource of great importance. These ideas became clarified in Toomer's review in *S4N* of Gorham Munson's book-length *Waldo Frank: A Study,* published in 1923. Munson's book, while generally flattering in its appraisal of Frank's work, had criticized Frank's views on industrialism and the potential of machines. Munson felt that in Frank's *Our America* (1919), the machine had been portrayed as a "necessary evil" that required "anti-bodies to offset its ravages" (*Waldo Frank*

23). An alternative, Munson mused, was the position of the leader of the Italian Futurist movement, Tomasso Filippo Marinetti. He felt Marinetti's ideas offered a recognition that "culture must now work out a harmony between three factors, man, nature, and machinery," and went on to suggest that "we must . . . bring the machine within the scope of the human spirit" (24). Indeed, in a paragraph that now seems remarkably prescient, Munson sees contemporary technology and popular culture as a cause for aesthetic, cultural, and national celebration. He notes that *Our America*

> underestimates certain phenomena of American civilization that may seem most significant and healthy later on, such phenomena as our skyscrapers, bridges, motion pictures, jazz music, vaudeville, electric light displays, advertising. It may have missed completely the peculiar genius of the American people thrusting into a new age. (*Waldo Frank* 25)

Toomer's review enthused over Munson's vision of spiritualizing machinery and stressed the personal appeal this had for his own aesthetics. Elsewhere in *S4N* he elaborated on his formal attraction to machines, praising as "the only art attitude" the decision to use "modern forms, and not the hurt caused by them, as the basis of the national literature" ("Open Letter" 19–20). These "modern forms" were analogous to new mechanical technology, indeed sometimes were identical with them; he enthused that "I neglected the 'poetry of the people' for such things as motorcycle motors, dynamos and generators. . . . There is not a statue in Washington with the living beauty and line of certain Pierce-Arrow cars" ("Open Letter" 20). Indeed, this was a statement that echoed Marinetti's famous aphorism in "The Foundation and Manifesto of Futurism" of 1909 that "a roaring motor car which seems to run on grapeshot is more beautiful than the *Victory of Samothrace*" (147). Moreover, this statement had been repeated by Enrico Prampolini in his article "The Aesthetic of the Machine and the Mechanical Introspection in Art," which had appeared in the October issue of *Broom* and which Toomer may well have read there. Yet despite the hollow formalism of some of Toomer's statements, which were little more than avant-garde posturing, he was quick to appreciate Munson's caution that duality was a limitation in thinking about human relations to machinery. This anticipates a point made by the contemporary critic Hal Foster, who has talked about the "double logic of the prosthesis" in modernist assimilations of machinery into its aesthetics. Foster contends that this double logic established a crippling polarity between the human body and the machine, as "so opposed, the two could only conjoin, ecstatically or torturously, and technology could only be a "magnificent" extension of the body or a "troubled" constriction of it." This led to a situation in which "one could only *resist* technology in the name of a natural body or *accelerate* it in the search for a postnatural body on its other side" (5–6).

Toomer realized this "double logic" would lead to a system of either technophobic rejection of mechanical technology or slavish admiration of its formal principles. After Munson had sent him an edition of *Secession* in September 1922, Toomer wrote to Waldo Frank that the authors in that issue (many of whom were heavily influenced by French Dada at the time) were "too comfortable, too sure, within their forms. . . . There is no overflow into mystery. . . . Already they have measured their horizons" (*Letters* 78). As Munson became closer to Frank and Toomer, he began to diverge from the position of Josephson for the same reason, noting in a letter to Malcolm Cowley that Josephson's recent article on American billboards "goes no deeper than the romantic's thrill upon finding strange materials to exploit. I am sympathetic with the recognitions and exploitation achieved by the skyscraper primitives, but I detest their superficial justifications."[16] Indeed, this became the central point of criticism against those in America who adopted most rigorously the precepts of Dada.[17]

Instead, Toomer began to consider models for effacing a dualism between mechanism and organism. He toyed with notions of either "spiritualizing" or "fecundating" the machine, but this was rather a lazy attempt at imagining the industrialized landscape within an organicist/Romantic perspective that was already an anachronism. As he later wrote, "'Back to nature,' even if desirable, was no longer possible, because industry had taken nature unto itself. . . . whether we wished to or not, we *had to go on*" (*Wayward* 129). Ultimately he envisaged the production, circulation, and transformation of energy by machinery as an important figure for art in two respects. One was its suitability for conceptualizing the streamlining of the circulation of desire within cultural production, irrespective of racial or political barriers. Second, it would serve as an analogue to the transformative energy that underpinned all artistic creativity. This was evident in his plans for a (never completed) novel to follow *Cane* in 1924, when he conceptualized his main character in the terms of a machine. Toomer imagined him to be

> (1) A generator, making his own qualitative energy.
> (2) A transformer, turning the crude energy of his material world into stuff of higher, rarer potency.
>
> Spiritual, as well as physical or economic determinism: there is no chaos.

> As a first and inevitable step in the racial unification of America: negatively, the lack of racial consciousness and self-consciousness; positively, a prescription which includes spiritual, intellectual, emotional states as well as the pleasant (or repulsive) variants of color or feature. . . .
>
> Hitherto, this consciousness, and hence the art of this country have been sectional. The consciousness from which this work springs is an inclusive one. Hence nothing less than a related and inclusive art-form will satisfy it. American, extra-American, European. Universal? I hope so.[18]

This reflects Cecelia Tichi's notion that "the dominant Romantic view of a holistic, spiritual world of vegetative and bodily being" was being replaced at this moment in American history by "a conception of the human being as a machine for the consumption and production of energy" (xii). Yet Toomer's conception takes this further; his artist-protagonist is a transformer of *materiality* as well as energy. The specific form of materiality to be transformed is the view of race as an essentialized materiality; this transformative mechanism is one that takes "race consciousness" and converts it into a "related and inclusive art form." This metaphor of the artist-as-machine designates him as both a generator and a transformer. This double role was a perfect metaphor for artists such as Toomer, who were committed to the view of the artist as having the capacity of transforming the world in an era when industrial production and mass culture had in many ways heightened their sense of irrelevance to society at large.[19] It also provided a way of negotiating the problem of how an artist was to have a controlling agency over the environment, to be an agent for social change, which reflected an awareness of the sensibility engendered by new, mechanized modes of production. In designating the artist/protagonist as a machine, therefore, Toomer moves beyond formal appreciation of machinery to an incorporation of its functional and economic capacities within his aesthetic program. Accordingly, he brings artistic activity into the language of industrial material production, yet without the sacrifice of the social idealism (in this case, a reassessment of America's racial politics) that writers such as Frank feared would be obliterated by industrialization. Frank may have wished for "anti-bodies" to offset the "ravages" of industrialization, but for Toomer an attractive "anti-body" to American racial politics was "the machine" itself.

Although this was not fully theorized until later, the relation between race, materiality, and aesthetics had been occupying Toomer's mind while he was composing *Cane,* and during that period he began to discuss it as his "duty" to transform the relation between race and normative standards of beauty. In a letter of 1922 he wrote about what he called the "tyranny of the Anglo-Saxon ideal":

> The ideal itself may be stated as follows: white skin is the most beautiful and desirable in the world; the minds of white races are superior to those of any other race; the souls of white folk are the chosen of God. . . . Paradoxical as it may seem, we who have Negro blood in our veins, who are culturally and emotionally the most removed from Puritan tradition, are its most tenacious supporters. . . . We are suspicious and often ashamed of our emotions. We hold their expression sinful. . . . Such wholesale substitution (I might even say perversion) of ideal must not continue. A beauty that is their own must be revealed to these people. (It is not necessary that white beauty be denied). Their eyes must open to the charm of soft full lines. Of dusk faces. Of crisp curly hair. . . . To do these things is to create a living ideal of one's own.
>
> It is my privilege and duty . . . to aid, perhaps in a large measure, to crystallize this ideal. (*Letters* 61–62; my ellipses)

In *Cane* Toomer showed he was well aware of the ramifications of a system of aesthetics that debased the black body. In "Kabnis," the final section of *Cane,* the effects of such aesthetic and racial "tyranny" are exemplified by the ex-slave, Father John. Father John lives in the cellar, where "they used t stow away th worn-out, no-count niggers in th days of slavery" (114); it is called "The Hole," symbolically becoming the hold of slave ships, the slave "underground," and the buried past—but also the structural support—of Halsey's Washingtonesque workshop above. This "black" hole centers around Father John; the architectural space is determined by the space of the body, as the hole's symbolic and economic function was literally constructed around the enslaved labor of the black body. Toomer saw the importance of aesthetics to this body-determination; Father John is described as on a chair "on a low platform," "like a bust in black walnut" (106); Kabnis taunts that "you sit there like a black hound spiked to an ivory pedestal" (114).

Such descriptions draw attention to the aesthetic constructedness of the body, as it is sculpted, a "bust," rather than "natural"—a designation that again demonstrates Toomer's unwillingness to take bodily materiality as a kind of precultural *tabula rasa.* Moreover, the fact that John is a "bust" on an "ivory pedestal" recalls the thesis of Peter Stallybrass and Allon White in *The Politics and Poetics of Transgression* about the significance of aesthetics of the body to social hierarchies of power. They argue that all hierarchies depend on differentiated bodies, marked at the extremes by what they call the "classical" and the "grotesque" body; indeed, they argue that "the vertical extremities" of any hierarchy "frame all further discursive elaborations" (3). Drawing on Bakhtin, they explain the basis of the classical body, which developed from classical statuary in the Renaissance:

> The classical statue has no openings or orifices whereas grotesque costume and masks emphasize the gaping mouth, the protuberant belly and buttocks, the feet and the genitals. In this way the grotesque body stands in opposition to the bourgeois individualist conception of the body, which finds its image and legitimation in the classical. The grotesque body is emphasised as a mobile, split, multiple self, a subject of pleasure in a process of exchange; and it is never closed off from either its social or ecosystemic context. The classical body on the other hand keeps its distance. (21–22)

The pedestalized, elevated classical body "structured, from the inside as it were, the characteristically 'high' discourses of philosophy, statecraft, theology and law, as well as literature, as they emerged from the Renaissance. In the classical discursive body were encoded these regulated systems which were closed, regulated, homogenous, monumental, cenetred and symmetrical" (22). Yet although the classical body was essential for the operation of social and aesthetic hierarchy, it is the "vertical extremities" of any hierarchy that "frame all further discursive elaborations," meaning that the grotesque body is as essential to the structures of power as is the classical body (3). This means that John's place on the ivory pedestal in "Kabnis" is a piece of ironic reversal on Kabnis's part, showing his understanding that hierarchies cannot function without both "vertical extremities" and that indeed the classical body is enabled and constructed by what is grotesque. Accordingly, the low or the grotesque, that which "is *socially* peripheral[,] is so frequently *symbolically* central"—hence John's place on the pedestal (5).

However, it is crucial to note that John is "spiked" to the ivory pedestal, a phrase that recalls the lynching earlier of Mame Lamkins's unborn child earlier in "Kabnis"; after ripping Lamkins's belly open, the lynchers saw "It was living; but a nigger baby aint supposed t live. So he jabbed his knife in it an stuck it to a tree" (*Cane* 92). The black body's position as grotesque, then, which participated in the maintenance of a social, economic, and political hierarchy of race with blacks occupying the position of the "low," was fastened in place by violence. Accordingly, the use of the term "spiked" to describe John's pedestalization provides a reminder of the ritualized violence of lynching conducted on the basis of race. Yet perhaps more significantly, it suggests that the "grotesqueness" of Father John is reliant on being brutally "spiked" into a system where antiblack violence serves to continually debase black bodies, and thus legitimate further violence and oppression against them because they have been so debased. Indeed, as several commentators have observed, Toomer was aware that this ritual helped to produce the racial categories of both whiteness and blackness; the white woman in "Portrait in Georgia" is "white as the ash / Of black flesh after flame" (29). As Walter Benn Michaels notes, "black flesh is burned in order to make a white body. What begins as a narrative of the attempt to preserve racial difference turns out to be a narrative of the origins of racial difference . . ." (62).[20]

Technology, as Toomer saw it, offered a way out of this closed circuit of aesthetics, oppression, and violence within the rural South. Toomer speculated on how technology's twin attributes of power and radical novelty might be useful in reconceptualizing the increasingly inflexible categorization of race within the United States, and in *Cane* this is perhaps best illustrated by his poem "Her Lips Are Copper Wire." Toomer sent this poem to Norman Fitts, the editor of *S4N,* in early 1923; this was the magazine, as I have suggested, in which Toomer had his most sustained involvement with the question of the relation between machinery and aesthetics. Fitts responded so enthusiastically to the poem that he translated it into Italian and sent it to Marinetti, telling him that it represented "one of the first attempts to write machinery poetry" in the United States.[21] It was published in the May–August number of *S4N,* along with Fitts's translation of Marinetti's "Futurism," one of his many manifestoes of the movement. The manifesto praised dynamism, speed and electricity, and found that there was "Nothing . . . more beautiful than a great humming powerhouse," which is one of the key images in Toomer's poem ("Futurism").[22]

Toomer's suggestion in the poem is that electrical power is a way of re-imagining forms of communication within the social experience of modernity.[23] As Armstrong has noted, many modernist texts are "permeated by electricity, generating a world pulsating with energy. It offers a model for communication. . . . Modernist texts are electrical, plugging into a scientific rhetoric which channels flows of energy and information" (19). Notably, the only moment of mutually rewarding sexual communion and communication in *Cane*—in contrast to the failures of such stories as "Karintha," "Esther," "Fern," "Avey," "Theater," and "Bona and Paul"—comes in the poem. Using the metaphor of electricity to suggest sexual passion, the black body becomes lightbulb and electrical wire, stripped of its insulation: "with your tongue remove the tape / and press your lips to mine / till they are incandescent" (57). Metaphorically transformed into this new technology, the black body gains a freedom that the "black hound spiked to an ivory pedestal," the southern, rural body of the ex-slave Father John in "Kabnis," could never have; it becomes powerful, capable of communication ("telephone the power house / that the main wires are insulate") and "incandescent" (114). It achieves the liberatory transcendence of interpersonal communion and freedom from white discursive structures of the black body through the raw energy of technology.[24] It is also worthwhile to note that the critic Stephen Kern has identified the telephone as the piece of technology that prompted the most dramatic alteration in perceptions of time and space within the late modern era, largely because it enabled the experience of being in two places at once. In "Her Lips Are Copper Wire," this idea of the telephone enabling the simultaneity of two different locations helps to break down the spatial determinations of race that had proved so oppressive in the rural South, and which I discussed in the previous two chapters. Accordingly, this poem is perhaps Toomer's most successful attempt to dissolve boundaries between organic and mechanical as a method of challenging other entrenched binaries of class and race.[25] As Toomer's friend Hart Crane would later write, "new verities" were offered by such ideas, and "Power's script,—wound, bobbin-bound, refined" was now "stropped to the slap of belts on booming spools . . ." ("Cape" 79).

One of the main symbolic attributes of "the machine" was its association with power, as Crane's phrase suggests, and it was just such power that Toomer saw as capable of destroying oppressive racial structures. Power was crucial to both machinery and imaginative creation; as he wrote to Munson, "a weak machine is ready for the scrap heap. . . . What to a poem, sketch or novel that lacks power . . . that can do no work?" ("Open Letter" 19). If that power was conducted by the electric wire and telephone cable in "Her Lips Are Copper Wire," in "Box Seat" the power of modern technology is presented as challenging racial hierarchies in a more violent and aggressive way. The protagonist, Dan Moore, is fascinated by the possibility that new technologies could smash old strictures of class and race that determined the production of the black body. Much of this violence is directed against the buildings of black, middle-class Washington. Throughout the story, the spatial organization of housing and architecture according to class and race is metonymically linked to bodies, a link that applies particularly to the segregated housing of Washington's middle-class black neighborhoods and the middle-class Lincoln Theatre. This metonymic link is emphasized by the houses having "eyes" and being described as "virginal," as "shy girls whose eyes shine reticently upon the dusk body of the street" (59).

The architectural space in this story is therefore rigidly controlled and determined by class and racial hierarchy, but this is founded on a differentiation of bodies: without a discourse of bodies sorted according to race and class, the segregated principles of housing would lose their point of anchorage. Accordingly, we are told that the architecture of the street is anchored by Muriel's seat: "The house, the rows of houses locked about her chair" (63). This is reinforced later when bodies are "bolted" into seats: "The seats are bolted houses" (64). In response to these incarcerating structures (and in a gesture similar to that of the Futurists), Dan sees violence against architecture but also against the body as necessary to articulate new possibilities of identity. Moreover, this violence is accomplished through the new technologies of the age; as he says of the houses:

> Break in. Get an ax and smash in. Smash in their faces. I'll show em. Break into an engine-house, steal a thousand horse power fire truck. Smash in with the truck. I'll show em. Grab an ax and brain em. Cut em up. (59)

Technology, violence, and dismemberment combine in Dan's fantasy of assaulting black, bourgeois Washington, which in the above quotation is imagined as incorporated in both a system of bodily aesthetics and in the bricks and mortar of Washington's residential spaces. This metonymy between bodies and architecture—and the necessity of destroying them both—is later taken a stage further in Dan's Samsonian fantasy of destroying the black-only, bourgeois Lincoln Theatre:

> I am going to reach up and grab the girders of this building and pull them down. The crash will be a signal. Hid by the smoke and the dust Dan Moore will arise. In his right hand will be a dynamo. In his left, a god's face that will flash white light from ebony. (68)

Dan's assault is against both the building, which is an architectural expression of class and racial hierarchy, and against the overdetermination of the black body by white racist discourse. Here, he fashions a black god, ebony-faced; throughout *Cane* there are several representations that aim to draw attention to the race of religious icons, often with the purpose of making visible the "invisible" whiteness of Christian figures. This also occurs in "Esther," for example, when a "portrait of a black madonna" is drawn "on the courthouse wall" (23).[26] In "Box Seat," Toomer's ebony-faced god assaults the aesthetic norms of his society, effecting a challenging black appropriation of deity that protests the "tyranny of the Anglo-Saxon ideal." Yet this appropriation is possible only with the energy of the dynamo, the machine for the efficient transformation of mechanical energy into electric power. Here, it is the transformative capacity of the dynamo that converts Dan's seething resentment against the black Washington bourgeoisie into the focused action of resistance. In doing so, technology provides a significant counterweight to what Nathan Grant has described as the "generalized inadequacy that speaks to not only sexlessness but also aimlessness" that characterizes the men in part 2 of *Cane* (52).

This resistance, which sees Dan leap to his feet during the performance and shout out to the audience, might be metaphorically powered by the dynamo but is initiated by Dan's seeing deity in the grotesque body of one of the Dwarves. After the onstage boxing match between the two dwarves in the theatre, Dan sees "Words form in the eyes of the Dwarf." The Dwarf, battered and bleeding, urges "do not be afraid of me . . . I too was made in his image" (69). The Dwarf—described as "gruesome," "[forehead] bulging like boxing gloves," and with a face of "thick hide"—thus claims the status of the Adamic, divinely sanctioned body (66–69). This departure from normative representations of Adam or Christ applies aspects of physicality to the portrayal of a divine body that, in the 1920s, would have typified what Bakhtin has called the "grotesque"—dwarfism, a protruding forehead, and blackness.

Moreover, as Richard Dyer has shown, such figures as Adam and Christ had been progressively "whitened" throughout the course of the eighteenth and nineteenth centuries in Western representation. Indeed, in his discussion of the potency and operation of "whiteness" through the categories of skin color, hue, and symbolism, he identifies the significance of the progressive whitening of images of Christ throughout the Renaissance until by the nineteenth century the "image of him as not just fair-skinned but blond and blue eyed was fully in place" (68). Accordingly, when the Dwarf likens his grotesque body to God's, and when Dan shouts "Jesus was once a leper!" in the theatre, it assaults the tradition of the closed, distant, and inviolable classical white body that structures class and racial hierarchies. Rather than besmirching the classical body of God and Jesus, therefore, these statements call into question the very legitimacy of the category of the classical itself. Just as Dan's Samsonian fantasy destroys the architectural expression of class and race hierarchy in Lincoln Theatre, so his outburst challenges the principles of hierarchical structuration encoded in the body. By making the body of Jesus black, then stunted and diseased, he makes visible the social implications involved when religious iconography normalizes certain types of bodies.

Such fantasies of destruction in order to create anew were common to several European art movements that shared Toomer's fascination with the machine: Dadaism and Futurism come to mind. Indeed, Dan's fantasy of destroying Lincoln Theatre is a moment similar to those Peter Nicholls has identified as typical of Italian Futurism, in that "the Futurists knew only those beginnings in which the self emerges new-born, without father, mother, past" (85–86). Yet it must be noted that Toomer's fantasies of regenerative destruction could move disturbingly close to the misogynistic and belligerent rhetoric for which Marinetti is infamous. This is implicit in Toomer's gendering of Dan's violent reaction to the status quo; a reason for Dan's fury is the inability of his sometime girlfriend, Muriel, to cast off bourgeois morality and taste. Similar to the Futurists, then, Dan's violence seems rooted in a belief that "the feminine denotes a particular psychological formation which is in some sense resistant to the new" and therefore serves as a significant limitation to the inclusiveness of Toomer's liberatory fantasies of technologically enabled protest (Nicholls 88).

A less obviously gendered aspect of Toomer's interest in how technology could help transform racial politics involved his conception of the transformation of social space within rapidly changing urban environments. New types of social relations formed through networks of modern communication technology was an idea that Toomer had also observed in Munson's *Waldo Frank: A Study,* particularly in Munson's comments on Waldo Frank's 1922 novel *City Block,* which focused on the concept of *unanimisme.* This was an idea developed by the French poet, novelist, and playwright Jules Romains: he saw modern urban life as an harmonious rhythmic system, in which the bodily rhythms of the population and the rhythms of the mechanized city became synchronized, melding the entire environment into what he called an holistic "*unanime*" (qtd. in Rosalind Williams 179). This epiphanic urban conglomeration reconfigured both the body and social space, as Romains explained:

> The period of abstractions is going to end. Society, categories, classes, "le monde," "le demimonde," "le peuple," abstractions; collective words that designate no collective being. Nothing of all that has concrete existence, and therefore nothing of it will last. . . . What exists, what is beginning to exist with a complete, bodily, conscious life, are groups; streets, city squares, meeting halls, theatres. These are the beings that have a future. (Qtd. in Rosalind Williams 193)

The rhythm of the *unanime* was largely determined by urban traffic patterns; Romains's first experience of a *unanime* came during rush hour, when the "wheel of the omnibus that gives sparks . . . [gave] a rhythm to my impersonal thought" (Rosalind Williams 190). Technology and urban space therefore provided the potential of liberation from social divisions and categorizations through the erasure of the boundary between organic and inorganic entities. In his work on Frank, Munson believed that *City Block* repeated this model of urban interaction within an American setting; he declared that "from the formal unity and matter-unity of *City Block* to *unanimisme* is only an inch" (53). Frank, a good friend of Romains's, was less sure about the applicability of the concept to *City Block,* noting to Malcolm Cowley that "I have always smiled sweetly when a very small group of men in Europe attached me to the Unanimist school. In order to do it, they have had to adumbrate their use of the word so that it might contain almost all of a certain dimension of art from Egyptian sculpture to El Greco. . . ."[27] Frank's wish to ally himself with a mystical-prophetic tradition including figures such as El Greco, Whitman, Spinoza, and Blake perhaps explained his reluctance to accept an inorganic model of social relations, but that did not stop others from seeing the possibilities of *unanimisme* in his work as one of its most interesting features. As well as Munson's study, a special Waldo Frank edition of *S4N* printed in January 1924 featured two articles assessing his relation to *unanimisme,* including an essay by the French critic Pierre Sayn, which found that Frank's adaptation of Romains's concept had "fashioned literary material and offers a total representation of the world which corresponds with the intellectual and scientific development of the twentieth century."[28]

Such ideas are evident in *Cane*'s second section, much of which Toomer wrote as he explored these concepts during his most intensive period of contact with Waldo Frank, and which he set in the urban environments of Washington and Chicago. Indeed, contemporary reviews made mention of his adoption of *unanimisme;* Matthew Josephson in *Broom* was uneasy about Toomer's attempt to apply "cerebral super-forms" to "the hysteria, the passion, the madness and the great sweetness of his Negroes," and urged him to forget "his lessons in psychoanalysis and *unanimisme*" (179–80). Yet it was these "cerebral super-forms," the networks of the transformative technologies of modernity, which suggested radical possibilities for African American organization, community, and subjectivities. In "Seventh Street," for example, the rhythm of the "Ballooned, zooming Cadillacs/Whizzing, whizzing down the streetcar tracks" provides the tempo for this vignette of the main street in the African American district of Washington (41).[29] The lines, part of a repeated stanza of verse, are repeated before and after the main prose-poetry section of the piece and represent a framing, organizational force for the community. Just as in Romains's initial *unanime,* the convergence of the rhythm of mechanized transport and the rhythm of thought suggests a symbiotic connection between poet, populace, and a technological, urban milieu. Moreover, the vitality of the *unanime* is specifically focused and directed, as the energies of African American modernity target the edifices of an outdated racial architecture; the "wedge" of the street will destroy the "whitewashed wood," the "stale soggy wood" of white hegemony in Washington (*Cane* 41). Indeed, it is telling that Toomer chose to begin *Cane*'s second section with this presentation of the energy and the aggressive, dynamic optimism of the culture of Washington's Seventh Street—which, as Scruggs and VanDemarr have pointed out, "literally *wedges* itself between the city's two most significant national buildings," the Capitol and the White House (165). It is instantly differentiated, in terms of color, speed, patterns of labor, and technological sophistication from the "goat path in Africa" that is Dixie Pike in the Sempter, Georgia, of part 1 and "Kabnis" (12). Moreover, in correspondence with fellow Washingtonian writer Mary Burrill, who had disliked "Seventh Street," Toomer insisted on the absolute novelty of 1920s Seventh Street, that its spirit of "dash and bravado" was quite different from the "Seventh Street of Yesterday." Part of this insistence was motivated by his belief that Seventh Street's novelty was due to the unprecedented rhythms and aesthetics of the urban landscape determined by new technologies; as he chided Burrill, "you would hardly contend that the few stray Fords of years back have anything in common with the lines of Cadillacs and Packards, other, of course, than they are all basically automobiles—which contention would obviously be beside the point" (*Letters* 108).

The aesthetics of the Futurists, Dadaists, and the Unanimists who followed Romains suggested ways in which technology could be a powerful symbol of formal novelty and rapid social change. To a large degree it was this view of "the machine" that made it such an attractive image for Toomer to apply to the transformation of both the morphological imaginary of bodies and the racial hierarchies that were enabled and reproduced through the organization of social space. Toomer also saw the importance of urban space for the future of African American communities, and heavily qualified any celebration of a rural "folk" identity as providing the essence of the race. This brings to mind Maria Balshaw's recent thesis that urban community and ideals of urbanity need to be seen as much more central to the project of the New Negro Renaissance than heretofore; she notes that for much 1920s African American writing, "the ideal of the rural past only makes sense in the new urban context, as a site of memory rather than a location one might actually return to" (5). Yet as well as offering exhilarating possibility through its streetcar tracks, Cadillacs, and its high-speed disregard for the law, Seventh Street gains much of its transgressive energy from being a "bastard of prohibition and the war" (41). This hints at the second important discourse of identity, and of the body, which Toomer engages with in *Cane*—genealogy.

CANE AND BASTARDY

As the previous section suggests, much of Toomer's energy in the second part of *Cane* (and in many subsequent essays and reflections) was expended on deconstructing the binary logic of American racial discourse. Indeed, as Hutchinson notes, "the great irony of Toomer's career is that modern American racial discourse—with an absolute polarity between 'white' and 'black' at its center—took its most definite shape precisely during the course of his life" ("Identity" 53). Along with the belligerent fantasies of liberation from this polarity that were powered by the metaphorical potency of "the machine," however, he was also interested in examining the instability of the boundaries between "black" and "white" and the types of figures who could disturb the facile application of racial categories. Accordingly, *Cane* has a fascination with the illegitimate in several senses: with "bastards," with miscegenation, and with the amount of questions, unease, and discomfort that figures embodying such "illegitimacy" seem to provoke.[30] As Hutchinson notes, the quantification of races and bodies was reaching unprecedented levels in the early 1920s: the draft for the Great War had provided physical and mental data on millions of American men, all of which had been recorded alongside their designated racial or ethnic category. Moreover, scientists committed to the view that race was the primary determining factor in character and intelligence had a significant role in drafting the 1924 Johnson-Reed Act. The act transformed America's "Open Door" immigration policy and imposed particularly stringent quotas on immigrants from southern and eastern Europe, and virtually eliminated immigration from the so-called "Asiatic barred zone." This heightened social concern with the "legitimacy" of bodies is a crucial context for examining the role of the bastard in *Cane,* a role that often unsettles and challenges the concepts of "hard" heredity and its deterministic view of genealogy that were becoming so widely accepted.[31]

Such deterministic views were infamously epitomized in the widely read text *The Passing of the Great Race* (1916), in which its white supremacist author, Madison Grant, presented a case for racial and ethnic segregation based on a belief in irreconcilable biological difference between races. He posited that racial purity was vital for national survival and warned that "the result of the mixture of two races, in the long run, gives us a race reverting to the more ancient, generalized and lower type" (18). To counter the threat of what was often called "race suicide" he proposed that "the laws against miscegenation must be greatly extended if the higher races are to be maintained" (60).[32] Of course, the social and political significance that this kind of discourse placed on race required a correspondingly exact taxonomy of races and a schema of how this taxonomy could be visually recognized. Accordingly, Grant pursues a somatic classification of race with a lengthy list of anthropomorphic criteria to differentiate races, including height, hair, and eye color, and the "cephalic index"—the correlation between the length and width of the skull (19). What this provides is an interpretative schema for reading the body:

> . . . every generation of human beings carries the blood of thousands of ancestors, stretching back through thousands of years. . . . the face and body of every living man offer an intricate mass of hieroglyphs that science will someday learn to read and interpret. (35)

Grant's dream of technology was that it would strengthen and perfect current racial categorizations, not transform them, as Toomer had hoped. Science was Grant's answer to what he perceived as the threat of the "passing of the great race"; he foresaw a eugenic science based on technologies that could "read and interpret" bodies, technologies that provided a code of racial legibility. This legibility would result in the easy application of the pragmatic component of his social policy, which aimed to "breed from the best" or "eliminate the worst by sterilization or segregation" (52). Within this social policy based on strict reproductive discipline, the figure of the bastard—outside the "laws" of reproduction laid down by Grant's program—becomes the epitome of the threat to white civilization. This trope is applied both racially and politically; racially he railed against "[populations] of race bastards in which the lower type ultimately preponderates" (77). Politically, he was committed to a patriarchal aristocracy as the ideal form of government and saw socialism as the "illegitimate offspring" of democracy, which would establish "the rule of the worst and put an end to progress" (72).[33]

The call of Grant, and others like him, for more legislation to prevent miscegenation would be heeded in the 1920s, as a host of new statutes to this effect entered state legislatures.[34] Toomer's call for racial amalgamation, the creation of what he called the "American race," and a more flexible approach to racial identity were consequently at odds with the overall trend of the racialization of America during this period. Yet it is interesting to note that the figure of the bastard is particularly significant to both Grant and Toomer. This is perhaps because both present the figure of the bastard not only as a deviation from an order that seeks to present itself as "natural" but also as a destabilizing presence to a rigidly hierarchical society. This representation has many precedents: as Alison Findley has noted, in English Renaissance drama the bastard became a figure threatening the existing patriarchal class hierarchy, and putting bastards center stage proved that "[t]he existing hierarchy was . . . not as natural as those who promoted it suggested. A gap opened up between the ideal and the real, between what was sanctioned and what was possible" (4). Both Toomer and Grant seem to see the bastard in these terms, the former excited by the bastard's ability to challenge and provoke the dominant discourses of identity politics, the latter deeply afraid of the prospect of this figure disturbing the "natural" status of both white and patriarchal hegemony. In *Cane,* Toomer interrogates the process of genealogy, questioning writing such as Grant's that sees it as providing a bulwark to coherent identity. *Cane* also plays with the idea of racial legibility, particularly in "Bona and Paul," when the trained black body becomes illegible and therefore profoundly threatening to an increasingly segregated society.

In the 1920s, the stigma of African Americans being a "bastard race" was a powerful one. The high incidence of illegitimate children in slavery—often caused by the rape of black women by white owners or overseers, or by the lack of concern shown by plantation owners in formalizing slave marriage—was a deeply traumatic heritage, which African American society still found troubling around sixty years after emancipation. Moreover, social studies of African American families at the beginning of the century—and extending memorably into the controversial Moynihan report in the mid-sixties—often identified "disorganized" patterns of family organization among African American families. These were patterns that accepted childbirth outside marriage and identified paternal absence as statistically more frequent than in white communities.[35] Responses to such studies and to this stigma were varied in the 1920s; they included a stress on paternalism as the bedrock of a stable racial and familial identity, the celebration of a heroic black matrilineage attributed to what Doyle has called the figure of the "race mother," or social science that attempted to dispel this stigma.

The latter course was taken by Melville Herskovits, a Franz Boas–trained anthropologist who contributed to Locke's *New Negro* in 1925. In 1926 he contributed an article to *Opportunity* titled "Does the Negro Know his Father?" which began by noting the stereotype that "Negroes simply don't know their ancestry" (306). This was a belief that—among other things—was used by insurance companies to justify higher premiums on life insurance policies for African Americans. Herskovits's study attempted to disprove this assumption, circulating a questionnaire among a selection of African Americans that asked for their own knowledge of their racial ancestry, which he then verified using anthropometric data to verify if their answers were correct. The answers he was given roughly correlated to the physical data he observed, allowing for a concluding—and robustly stated—refutation of the stereotype of the prevalence of illegitimacy in African American families. Most vociferous in dispelling this stigma were elements of the black intellectual middle class, who often resented any literary representations of black nonmarital sexual relationships or representations of interracial sex. This was evident in the response to Langston Hughes's poem "Red Silk Stockings," which was roundly condemned by much of the African American press in 1926 for its representation of nonmarital miscegenation (Hughes, *Big Sea* 266).

Toomer—always critical of black bourgeois morality—took a much more interrogative (and less dismissive) approach to the parameters of bastardy for black subjectivity. Although present in "Seventh Street," *Cane*'s most detailed exploration of the trope of bastardy comes in "Kabnis." This is introduced early on: "The earth my mother. God is a profligate red-nosed man about town. Bastardy; me. A bastard son has the right to curse his maker. God . . ." (85). A self-identification with bastardy makes Kabnis rude, cynical, and alienated. He feels disconnected from the North, which he has fled; the South, which he cannot settle in; the heritage of slavery epitomized by Father John; and a white community that fills him with a paralyzing fear. He identifies himself as the son of the black "earth mothers" of part 1 and a white "red-nosed" God prone to drunkenness and sexual adventurism, thus racializing this notion of bastardy and establishing a genealogy based on what is implied as the rape of black women by white men. Yet, as Maclean has noted, the "lack or refusal of a father's name is a form of social exclusion which can paradoxically be a form of social liberation, conferring a real or imagined freedom from the law of the Father" (97). Kabnis, in stating that "a bastard son has the right to curse his maker," appoints himself a position both outside and inside the established law and authority of his natural father, understanding its modes of operation, yet with sufficient autonomy to be freely critical. Indeed, Gutman notes that the phrase "outside child" was applied to illegitimate children in the South in the first half of the twentieth century (73). This kind of familiar alienation makes Kabnis capable of criticizing Hanby's self-righteous program of racial uplift, or of the veneration of the image of Father John.

By the end of *Cane*, Kabnis decries Father John as a bastard, the "white folks" as a "bastard race" and himself as an embodiment of sin. This descends into a torrent of abuse, confusion, and fever, a maelstrom that gestures to the unquantifiable origins of identity and that seems to condemn any notion of traceable ancestry as impossible. Indeed, this bastardy is described by Lewis as the unleashing of a torrent of energy that scrambles geographical, racial, class-based, and spiritual categorizations, a dissolution that is terrifying and yet allows for moments of remarkable poetic and imaginative intensity. This occurs when Kabnis is pushed by Lewis into retorting, "My ancestors were Southern blue-bloods" and that "there ain't much difference between blue an black"; Lewis replies, "Enough to draw a denial from you. Cant hold them, can you? Master; slave. Soil; and the overarching heavens. Dusk; dawn. They fight and bastardize you" (108–9). This energy results in Kabnis's anguish over his own identity but also his magnetic centrality to *Cane*'s final section. His anguish is personally excruciating but critically productive, and it is a position that Toomer attributed both to bastardy and, arguably, to his own racial situation. Indeed, without wishing to belabor biographical explanations for *Cane*, Toomer's comment to Waldo Frank that "Kabnis is me" (*Toomer Reader* 25) and his remark that *Cane*'s "easy flowing lyricism" was in fact "born in an agony of internal tightness, conflict and chaos" would seem to support comparisons on this point (*Cane* 156).

Despite the significance of bastardy to destabilizing racial essentialisms in *Cane,* however, these moments of poetic intensity also challenge the hegemonic social structure that is most troubled by bastardy—namely patriarchy. Social scientists have interpreted the stigma attached to children born out of marriage—that is, the pejorative categories of "illegitimacy" or "bastardy"—as due to the fact that "such persons are deemed a serious threat to the traditionally defined family which relies . . . upon institutionalized patriarchy—with its concepts and practices of monogamy, monandry, private property, heterosexuality, and legitimacy—for survival" (Zingo 15). This makes bastardy an issue about women's capacity for secrecy and unknowability, about women's ability—as Maclean has argued—to defy the authority of the patronymic and introduce different possibilities of naming, and thus subjectivity, into the social order. Yet this has often led, and continues to lead, to the social ostracism and punishment of women who have had children outside marriage—the fate suffered by the white Becky in *Cane,* who has two black sons and is ostracized from both black and white communities. As Maclean notes, within patriarchal culture "the decenteredness, the fluid potential of these women, is devalued as emptiness, as dissipation in all senses of the term, as an essential lack. They are condemned as harlots, as bad mothers, and of course as bad artists" (101).

Absorbing such arguments, Laura Doyle has proposed that *Cane* exhibits a tension between a patriarchal culture's need to romanticize and celebrate mother-figures and the problems inherent in establishing a racial-patriarchal order based on the figure of the "pure" black mother. This becomes most evident in Kabnis's search for a basis to an essentialized African American aesthetic; she argues that Kabnis discovers that the black male artist

> cannot succeed in the Romantic project of subsuming mother figures into their art: the black mother cannot neatly serve as the black man's basis for cultural reproduction because of her prior reproductive function for the white man's culture [in slavery] and the white man's concomitant monopoly over the cultural discourses that negatively mythologize black women. (104)

She goes on to contend that this situation makes both Toomer and Kabnis tortured artists, as "the mythology [Kabnis] needs tortures and cripples his art" (108); and in such a view *Cane* becomes the "Swan song for the race mother" (81). Such a view incorporates bastardy, seeing it as a category that destabilizes racial and patriarchal hierarchies, but Doyle sees this as a paralyzing rather than a liberating force within the text. This is because Kabnis "repulses the Romantic vision of a gendered, soil-soaked artistry" as "a black man's visionary art will only expose him as a usurped and un-named 'bastard son' . . ."—a repulsion that results in Kabnis's tortured silence and inability to create (107). Yet such a negative interpretation ignores notable moments in *Cane* when women obliterate the social space in which patriarchy establishes its field of operations, much as the figure of Dan Moore did to the architecture of black bourgeois Washington. Moreover, both occasions—in "Carma" and "Esther"—are founded on the women's ability to have children to men who are not their husbands. Doyle is right to note Toomer's reservations about the figure of the "race mother," yet is too restrictive in suggesting that "*Cane* perpetuates the Romantic gendering of materiality and remains caught in the reductive inscriptions of motherhood and embodiment which are deemed acceptable by racial patriarchy" (82). In contrast, I would argue that it is precisely through their capacity as mothers of illegitimate children that Carma and Esther challenge both patriarchal notions of social spaces and the materiality of race.

Critics have noted that Carma is doubly inscribed, both by the patriarchal laws that determine she should "not take others" while married and by the male narratorial voice that relates her tale as "the crudest melodrama" (13).[36] Yet when her husband, Bane, accuses her of adultery, she runs off into a canefield with a gun, and later a shot is heard. As the men search, we are told that "[t]ime and space have no meaning in a canefield": the interim between Bane's accusation and the repercussion of judgment sees a dissolution of patriarchal ordering of space and time (13). For a period, her body is literally lost to the searching men, causing a disturbing hiatus in the male control of the female body, one that invokes a solution of the wider spatial and temporal reference points of the social order. A similar occasion occurs in "Esther," a story that turns on Esther's fantasy about bearing a child to Barlo. The child in her dream is the quintessential "grotesque" body: "Black, singed, woolly, tobacco-juice baby—ugly as sin . . . its breath is sweet and its lips can nibble" (24). Its "grotesque" status is taken from both its blackness and its bastardy; at this point Esther cannot escape from the determination of white patriarchal discourse and its hierarchical classification of bodies. Hence, ugliness is the physical corollary of the "sin" that patriarchal morality labels bastardy. Nonetheless, she "loves it frantically," and this dream perhaps motivates her, years later, to go to Barlo and ask him for sex. As she leaves him in confusion after changing her mind, "There is no air, no street, and the town has completely disappeared" (27). Once again, her action of transgressing patriarchal codes in the wish for a bastard child obliterates the social space of the town, which has previously been described with the same scrupulous exactitude as Esther's limited opportunities and dwindling future. The topographical layout of the town—which in her walk to the brothel where Barlo is staying is relayed precisely—is dissolved in a fashion that again links racial and gendered hierarchy, social space and the body, and in establishing this Toomer proposes both their interdependence and the destabilizing pressure that the illegitimate body can exert.

In contrast to these liberatory moments are attempts to control and maintain a black patriarchy through genealogy, of which Fred Halsey in "Kabnis" forms the best example. His parlor is adorned with family photographs, dating back to his great-grandparents, and this reception room is how Halsey wants to be received: the product of an unbroken patrilineal line, the inheritor of a narrative of origins constructed by the images on the wall. The grandfather has eyes that are "daring. The nose, sharp and regular. The poise suggests a tendency to adventure checked by the necessities of absolute command. . . . His nature and features, modified by marriage and circumstances, have been transmitted to his great-grandson, Fred" (87). Yet his portrait is "that of an English gentleman who has retained much of his culture," and his great-grandmother has only a "Negro strain" (87). Such somatic readings illustrate that "race purity"—or even the notion of "race"—is fallacious, yet not in a society where, as Layman explains, "Nigger's a nigger down this way . . . An only two dividins: good and bad. An even they aint permanent categories" (89). In privileging this genealogy,

Halsey is engaged in what Toomer elsewhere called "play[ing] a game and agree[ing] not to see what we cannot help but see and know," namely that "all the main races are mixed races—and so mixed that no-one can unravel them in all their blended complexity" (*Wayward* 92). Halsey's proud display of his ancestors illustrates the frequent social function of the genealogical exercise, but also how this function is at odds with what a tracing of origins can reveal. As Foucault notes:

> Where the soul pretends unification or the self fabricates a coherent identity, the genealogist sets out to study the beginning—numberless beginnings, whose faint traces and hints of colour are readily seen by a historical eye. The analysis of descent permits the dissociation of the self, its recognition and displacement as an empty synthesis, in liberating a profusion of lost events. . . . The search for descent is not the erecting of foundations: on the contrary, it disturbs what was previously considered immobile; it fragments what was thought unified; it shows the heterogeneity of what was imagined consistent with itself. ("Nietzsche" 81–82)

The sought-after coherence of identity that inspires the genealogical impulse is therefore challenged by what such genealogy reveals, and this is obvious in Halsey's case but is also evident in the proprietary male gaze in *Cane*. As Scruggs and VanDemarr note, Carma's "yellow flower face" "is the product of miscegenation, and the 'flower' of miscegenation appears in "Kabnis" as a metaphor for rape" (147). Indeed, "Miscegenation is the thing in *Cane* not named but always there. . . . *Cane* depicts a world in which black men and women cannot escape their racial history. Black women had coerced sexual relations with white men under slavery and after Emancipation; because black men could not prevent this rape, a gap was created between the two sexes that misunderstanding, mistrust and violence might fill" (139). The control of the female body necessary for patriarchy requires that the female body be legible, inscribed with codes that make it accessible to discursive operations, just as the body must be racially encoded in societies that see race as a category of identity. As a result, and especially in part 1 of *Cane,* the male narrators give detailed description of the bodies of women while their own bodies are absent or not represented; as Brooks notes, "the male body is ostensibly deproblematized, decathected as an object of curiosity or of representation" in a patriarchal aesthetic (*Body Work* 15).

This description, particularly of the color of the women, invites a racial hermeneutic, as Scruggs and VanDemarr illustrate with their "reading" of Carma's face. Fern's face is described as follows: "soft cream foam . . . the creamy brown color of her upper lip . . . her nose was aquiline, Semitic"

(16). Esther has a "high-cheekboned chalk-white face . . . Esther looks like a little white girl" (22). Louisa's "skin was the color of oak leaves on young trees in fall," and Dorris has "[b]ushy, black hair bobbing about her lemon-colored face" (53). Each description opens a space for a racial interpretation of their features, an opportunity to "trace origins"; as Whyde notes, the "hermeneutical usurpation of [Carma's] body" means that she "disappears by being interpreted" (46). Doyle too notes that *Cane*'s first-person narrators show "an equivocal mixture of identification with women and a will to appropriate them for cultural—specifically textual—production" (95). Yet the interrogatory gaze so necessary for patriarchy to function, rather than revealing a genealogy of "purity" that will serve as the basis of a racial-patriarchal folk heritage in the women of *Cane*, instead reveals a history of miscegenation, violence, and rape. As Kutzinski notes:

> That [the women in *Cane*] are mysterious, elusive and sexually disturbing is not a function of their "nature" but of the male narrators' need to carefully filter out emotionally and ideologically troubling histories of sexual and economic abuse, along with obvious differences in social class, which would (and do) interfere with these figures' ability to represent cultural and spiritual purity and wholeness. (169)

That genealogy was a process that disturbs where it is supposed to support was understood well in the New Negro Renaissance. It formed the ironic climax to George S. Schuyler's *Black No More*, in which the Democratic Party launches a huge genealogical investigation of the entire population designed to disfranchise all people of "Negro or uncertain ancestry" (167)—but the investigation reveals that this runs to fifty million people, including all the Democrats' political leaders (196).[37] The novel therefore focused on a situation that was more disturbing to the American racial politics of the early twentieth century than what legible bodies revealed; namely, the possibility of *illegible* bodies. (Indeed, the imaginary electrical treatment in the novel, which makes African Americans "black-no-more," produces a wonderful send-up of southern anxieties over what the historian Joel Williamson has called the "invisible difference" of people with minimal African ancestry—the infamous "one drop.")[38] This racial illegibility corresponds closely both to incidents in Toomer's own life and to an experience he had in Sparta, Georgia, the town that forms the basis of Sempter in the southern sections of *Cane*. In one of his autobiographies, he notes seeing an "apparently white" girl on the streets of Sparta talking and laughing with a girl who was "obviously Negro." Surprised by this display of interracial familiarity, he asks one of the local residents for an explanation, only to be told that "that white girl's colored." He goes on:

> If a white girl is colored, who is white? . . . In any case it was quite apparent that the rigid barrier that is supposed to exist between the races at all points, and that does exist at some points, had been breached more than once to produce her. What an incredibly entangled situation the racial situation is in the United States. There are facts and events, plenty of them, that will never be told; or, if told, that would not fit into any familiar category. No book could possibly contain them.[39]

This body—unmarked by the "hieroglyphs" of race that Grant hoped would make all bodies instantly assignable to racial categories—cannot be "read" into the social text, a text that relies, as Stallybrass and White note, on somatic hierarchies of race, gender, and class. This kind of textual unrepresentability—no "book could possibly contain" her racial status within the racialized language of 1920s American culture—exemplifies the representational crisis triggered by "invisible difference." Consequently, the questions and conjecture that circulate around such bodies created a crisis for racist discourse, such as Grant's, which posited immutable difference between races. It also forces whiteness into becoming visible, necessitating its definition and its limitation. Toomer had firsthand experience of this; people attempted to read and interpret his membership of a single racial group in such a fashion for much of his life. Paul Beekman Taylor notes that during Toomer's residence in Bucks County, "when rumors began circulating that he was colored, people began to notice a color, took note of racial characteristics, and, in some cases, even invented them to fit conventional readings of racial stamp" (44). During Toomer's time at the University of Wisconsin, he received rough treatment on the football field because it was rumored that he was an Indian, and the story of Paul in "Bona and Paul" was based on his experiences in Chicago (*Wayward* 95).

In this story it is Paul's racial illegibility—a difference that is visible but unnameable—that makes him a center of both curiosity and desire. Art, his white Norwegian roommate, thinks, "Queer about him. I could stick up for him if he'd only come out, one way or the other, and tell a feller" (77); when they enter the Crimson Gardens cabaret, the other students there "leaned towards each other over ash-smeared tablecloths and highballs and whispered: What is he, a Spaniard, an Indian, an Italian, a Mexican, a Hindu, or a Japanese?" (76). The word "queer" is used again shortly afterwards as Paul considers the difference between himself and the southern, white Bona:

> From the South. What does that mean, precisely, except that you'll love or hate a nigger? Thats a lot. What does it mean except that in Chicago you'll have the courage to neither love or hate. A priori. But it would seem that you have. Queer words, arent these, for a man who wears blue pants on a gym floor in the daytime. (77–78)

Pertinent here is Judith Butler's discussion of the "queer" in Nella Larsen's *Passing* (1929). She notes that during the Harlem Renaissance,

> "queer" did not yet mean homosexual, but it did encompass an array of meanings associated with the deviation from normalcy which might well include the sexual. Its meanings include: of obscure origin, the state of feeling ill or bad, not straight, perverse, obscure, eccentric. As a verb-form, "to queer" has a history of meaning: to quiz or ridicule, but also to swindle and to cheat. . . . [And "queering" can be] what upsets and exposes passing; it is the act by which the racially and sexually repressive surface of conversation is exploded, by rage, by sexuality, by the insistence on color. (177)[40]

Paul's "queerness" involves many of these factors, which coalesce around the questions his body provokes but refuses to answer. He also represents a disturbing "deviation from normalcy," as his physical, and specifically sexual, presence seemingly coexists with his racial absence. As Siobhan Somerville has discussed in her chapter on the frequent use of the phrase "queer" in Toomer's writing, "the vocabulary of 'queer' emerged in Toomer's texts as a way to mark figures who disrupted or scrambled the boundary logics of race and gender, figures who indirectly included Toomer himself" (139–40).[41] Indeed, this disruption of racial boundaries is obvious in the substitution of geography for race illustrated in the quotation about the students given above. The students (unsuccessfully) engage in a geographical scramble to try and "place" Paul, an endeavor that again exemplifies how Toomer believed spatial and racial fixity to be coextensive. Such ambiguity allows Paul an access to all spaces; from the "unpainted cabins" of black Georgia to the Crimson Gardens cabaret of Chicago, a club that Barbara Foley has argued operates a policy of segregation and thus is representative of new segregative codes being instituted in public facilities at the time ("Washington" 308). Most challenging of all to white hegemony, however, is that his ambiguity allows him access to the space of Bona's body. Bona is attracted to this ambiguity, which does not carry the prohibition of definite knowledge and the accompanying social censure, yet retains the attractiveness of difference: "He is an autumn leaf. He is a nigger. Bona! But dont all the dorm girls say so? And dont you, when you are sane, say so? That's why I love—Oh, nonsense. You never loved a man who didn't first love you" (72). Paul's perversity—since he has no "place," he is always out of place—makes him the most disturbing figure to white racist discourse in *Cane*, not merely transgressing boundaries but interrogating the very efficacy of those boundaries, founded as they are on a belief in racially legible bodies.

Notably, it is his trained body, schooled in the physical education class that begins the story, which provides at least some of this ambiguity. As the story opens, Bona is watching the "young men and women . . . drilling" on the "school gymnasium floor," and "the dance of [Paul's] blue-trousered limbs thrills her" (*Cane* 72). It is precisely the formal structure of bodily movement of the dance or the drill, rather than the racial identity of Paul's body itself, which allows her this space of erotic fantasy. At this point it is worth returning to Linda Martín Alcoff's essay "Towards a Phenomenology of Racial Embodiment," which discusses the way in which racialization is a learned visual perceptual practice, one that becomes "organized, like bodily movements used to perform various operations, into integrated units that become habitual" (275). Alcoff argues that this "habitual" nature of racialized perceptual practice makes it very hard to analyze critically, and especially to change, but she does see this as possible; she continues that "perceptual practices are dynamic even when congealed into habit, and that dynamism can be activated by the existence of multiple forms of the gaze in various cultural productions and by the challenge of contradictory perceptions" (275). It is exactly the "contradictory perception" of the drilled and posed body of Paul that disturbs Bona's habitual perceptual practice of racialization and opens the space for her erotic fantasy.

This racial illegibility caused by the "contradictory perception" of Physical Culture is also something Paul himself ponders on. As he considers the nature of Bona's affection for him, he assesses the binary choice of normative American racial politics—that is, whether to "love or hate a nigger," as "Queer words . . . for a man who wears blue pants on a gym floor in the daytime" (77–78). Physical culture enables Paul to elide some of the either/or determinations of racial identity to be found in American society; the discipline promised a selective erasure of history and heredity, two of the factors that white discourse had used to assign black bodies a hierarchical place. The confusion this causes Bona is obvious. Calling Paul "cold," Bona thinks to herself "colored; cold. Wrong somewhere" (76); his calm, focused and laconic character—linked to his program of physical discipline—calls into question either the validity of racial markers such as exuberant emotion and shiftlessness that were connected to blackness, or Paul's racial status as black. Either way, Paul's body becomes somehow "wrong" and unsettling to Bona, but specifying—assigning Paul a geographical or hierarchical location—is not possible. Indeed,

Bona's vague allocation of "somewhere" illustrates the multiple, shifting, and indefinite nature of identity that is revealed under a close examination.

Later in the story, Art's girlfriend Helen thinks about Paul, "whom the whole dormitory calls a nigger," and decides that "men like him (Paul) can fascinate. One is not responsible for fascination" (78). To fascinate, of course, means to cast a spell over as well as to compel attention, and it is interesting in this regard to note that magic was described in terms of bastardy in the 1920s. This was true of perhaps the most influential anthropological writer of the period; in *The Golden Bough,* J. G. Frazer called magic a "bastard art," and in his preface to Bronislaw Malinowski's *Argonauts of the Western Pacific,* he described it as the "bastard sister" to the sciences (27, xii). This conflation is perhaps because both bastardy and magic exist outside the normative order of the patriarchal, progressivist, industrial societies of the West, and yet both have the potential to disturb and compel attention from that order.

Toomer's attraction to the figure of the bastard is clear in *Cane,* both for the ways in which such figures unsettle patriarchal orderings of social space and for the ways in which they lay bare some of the premises of racialization in the United States. Similarly, he was interested in the way bodies become racially marked and what happens when this process is disrupted—and what disciplines are capable of disrupting it. In claiming he is the bastard son of a God, Kabnis takes a position capable of launching a penetrating critique of the racial politics of the United States, just as Paul's "fascinating" nature reveals the fears and desires of those around him on the subject of race. Part 2 of *Cane* also explored how technology could disturb the racialization of social space. This could be through new communications technology—such as the telephone in "Her Lips Are Copper Wire"—or technophilic fantasies of destruction that promised to dynamite the architecture of racial and class hierarchy from within. Alternatively, as in the "unanimisme" of "Seventh Street," it suggested that the new mechanical rhythms of the black urban cityscape would help determine a new and potentially liberatory embodiment of blackness. Ultimately, however, it is the technology of bodily training and physical culture that holds most promise: the mobility inherent in Paul's explicitly "built" identity remains Toomer's most utopian statement about how racially deterministic "hieroglyphs" could be erased or rendered unintelligible. Moreover, Paul's identity—which eludes spatial and racial fixity and therefore enables his access to a multiplicity of people, locations, and traditions—indicates some of the broader ambitions of the text of *Cane.* These ambitions—for the racial composition of its readership, and how this is manifest in *Cane*'s formal structure—form the subject of the final chapter.

CHAPTER 6

CANE, AUDIENCE, AND FORM

If the allocation of a position to Paul provides the narrative drive of "Bona and Paul," this hints at an issue that was central to the conception, production, and reception of *Cane* as a whole—namely, the cultural positioning of a text structurally and thematically committed to hybridity. Toomer was acutely aware of how the cultural field of the American 1920s was determined by race, and the scope of his ambitions to avoid the categorization of literary production according to racial criteria is evident in the range of little magazines that eventually published text pieces of *Cane*. Moreover, Toomer's interest in theories of reader response being developed in the 1920s can be fruitfully read in conjunction with his attempts to craft a multiracial audience for *Cane*. This concern with reception is also manifest in the structure of *Cane*, particularly in the diversity of its text units and in the integrative reading strategy the text promotes, a strategy common in the short story cycle. It is these topics that form the focus of this final chapter.

CANE IN THE CULTURAL FIELD

In his essay "The Field of Cultural Production, or: The Economic World Reversed," which outlines a model of the dynamics of fields of cultural production, Pierre Bourdieu has discussed the tension between an artist's *disposition* and the available *positions* in the cultural field. It is this tension—between the agency of an individual and the structural possibilities that exist—that determines the dynamic of what he calls "position taking" in relation to the other works, authors, and cultural institutions in the field. This tension is particularly visible in *Cane,* where the discrepancy between the author's ideals and the actuality of available positions comes to have a complex and revealing relation to its formal and textual strategies. *Cane* exists at the center of debates about the nature of racial identity and what can be said about it, in the positions of the literary-cultural field in 1923; it also exhibits a significant degree of self-awareness of its own cultural positioning and cultural significance. This forms the final subject of this chapter on how Toomer imagined the future of race in modernity within *Cane;* for as I argued in chapter 4, *Cane*'s most strenuous attempts at transforming American racial politics occur at the level of literary form. Its formal strategies, and Toomer's virtually unique position within both avant-garde white New York and the New Negro Renaissance, provoke questions to an degree unparalleled in any other text of the time about the racialization of literary forms, the racialization of an implied readership, and how this could be negotiated in early 1920s America.

To a large degree, this situation was due to the zeal with which Toomer engaged with literary communities. He had become immersed in the New York avant-garde in the early 1920s and was particularly associated with the Young Americans. Toomer was on good terms with Frank, Hart Crane, and Alfred Stieglitz, and also with critics such as Paul Rosenfeld, Kenneth Burke, and Gorham Munson. The "transnational" cultural nationalism of this movement (to use Randolph Bourne's phrase) alerted Toomer to the impulse toward constructing an alternative, multiethnic, and above all native cultural tradition, one that specifically rejected an anglophilic approach. In addition, he was a friend to Alain Locke and sent him sections of *Cane* during his stay in Sparta, Georgia; he also attended literary salons in Washington along with people who would become important figures in the New Negro Renaissance such as Georgia Douglas Johnson, Edward Christopher Williams, and Mary Burrill (Hutchinson, "New Negroes"). His involvement in these cultural contexts means that before he began writing the majority of *Cane,* he would have been well aware of the issues surrounding the production, reception, and cultural function of African American texts.

Such a stress on reception is implicit in the formal structure of *Cane.* This fact reveals that at this specific juncture of literary history—the beginning of the New Negro Renaissance and an organized, centralized black literary community in Harlem, as well as the Young Americans' reconfiguration of American literary history and the nativization of the canon—any text perceived as African American would be subjected to an unprecedented overdetermination, irrespective of content. One example is "Karintha"; Karintha herself has often been seen as the epitome of Toomer's southern earth mothers: sexualized, "innocent," and primitive.[1] Yet the poem originally appeared in Toomer's (then unpublished) play "Natalie Mann," where it was recited by the Toomeresque poet Nathan Merilh to an avant-garde interracial gathering in his New York apartment. The piece that begins *Cane,* then, has the absent context of a very specific metropolitan audience. This context precludes any isolationist reading or a reductively formalist approach that merely celebrates its lyricism; it necessitates a consideration of its cultural function within the New York avant-garde. This deliberate intertextualization extends the context from the rural southern "folk" who "made a song" of how the "smoke is on the hills" to the northern, urban audience who are providing the access of this culture to print, who are facilitating its entry into what could be considered as American culture. This conception of the northern mixed-race audience as vital in the process of bringing southern rural black culture into literary forms runs throughout *Cane;* the narrator in "Fern" is from the north, as is the artist Kabnis, and this expands the contextualization of *Cane* beyond regional or racial locality in a way that has often been overlooked.[2] The poem "Conversion" also appeared elsewhere, in a short story where it was chanted by another Toomer-type figure, David Teyy in "The Withered Skin of Berries." Teyy chants this poem to Vera, an office worker in Washington who is "passing."

These scenarios—where literary production becomes the subject of the narrative, and where the internal audience is provided for us—is of course analogous to the sense of self-consciousness about writing race found in later works of the New Negro Renaissance, such as Claude McKay's *Home to Harlem* and especially Wallace Thurman's *Infants of the Spring.* Yet *Cane* seeks a self-consciousness that is not crippling but inclusive, a way of gesturing toward the wider audiences opening up for writers of color and writing about color. This sense of an audience carries an enthusiasm for new definitions of American identity being formed in urban radical circles, definitions that sought to include a wider range of experience and background than before. Yet this self-consciousness also draws attention to the diversity of audiences the text addresses, a diversity that, as I will discuss later, raises the extremely problematic issue of how to fashion a discourse that has the capability of addressing them all.

An awareness of this diversity undoubtedly raised Toomer's consciousness of the role of the reader in constructing the text, and a stress on reception was something he also learned from Waldo Frank. Frank was instrumental in editing *Cane* and getting it published with Horace Liveright; he was a sensitive literary critic, and his fiction influenced Toomer more than anyone's. His views—and those of other critics such as Gorham Munson—shared a formalistic approach; Frank saw literary form as the correlate to political and social forms of organization, which made the innovative artist a political and prophetic figure in the vein of Whitman. Indeed, artistic innovation was necessary to counter what he perceived as the current crisis in civilization:

> We live in fragmentary thoughts, desires, acts. Quite literally, the form of our lives is decomposing. And that means death. . . .
>
> The noblest function of Art is . . . not to subserve the intellectually accepted forms of life: but to conquer new forms of life and to bring them within the reach of the intellect. Art is the language which expresses vision of being that has not been conventionalized into simple words and concepts. ("Declaration" 21–26).

This conception of the social and political role of art meant that Frank's impulse was toward the formally cohesive. He saw formal unity as the province of the "religious artist" who would provide formal inspiration for models of social organization, a role well suited to America as "the life of America is a stupendous symbol of the human chaos which such an artist beholds in all life ere the transfiguring magic of his unitary vision has been worked upon it" (*Jungle* 152). This is another example of what I discussed in chapter 3, namely Frank's centralizing principle of authority—which saw the powers of social organization and the determination of a common aesthetic for public culture as the primary responsibility of the prophetic artist. As already mentioned, this principle made Toomer uneasy, especially when it began dealing with individual choices over racial identity. Moreover, a similar disregard for the significance of the public's role within cultural production characterized Frank's development of an aesthetic that privileged the unificatory powers of a "religious artist." Specifically, Frank was aware of, and disturbed by, the fact that formal cohesion within a text was as dependent on the reader as it was on him.

This was evinced by his foreword to *City Block*, the short story cycle located in a New York apartment block, which Toomer read on their trip south together in fall 1922. Frank instructed his readers that "CITY BLOCK is a single organism and . . . its parts should be read in order. . . ." (5), a dictatorial statement that he hoped would make his readers understand that "short stories in a sequence might accumulate a multidimensional reality that transcended the temporal, finite world they described" (Scruggs and VanDemarr, 114).

Frank's short story cycle—and, indeed, Frank's most obvious model, *Winesburg, Ohio*—proved very significant to Toomer's compilation of *Cane*. Toomer had written to Anderson that "Winesburg, Ohio and The Triumph of the Egg are elements of my growing. It is hard to think of myself as maturing without them," and he would later recall being struck by the "entirely new possibilities" that what Anderson called the "Winesburg form" offered.[3] The possibilities of a form that seemed to promote a highly integrative reading strategy, and yet which featured lacunae as a structurally central feature, appealed to him. Such lacunae, he felt, may be able to mediate both the "unspeakable" elements of American racial politics and the deep divisions in American society. Moreover, Toomer was much more comfortable than Frank about transferring some of the responsibility for cultural production from the artist to the reader. An indication of this was evident in his enthusiasm for the work of Gorham Munson on the process of reading. Munson was working on what he called an "aesthetic approach to reading" at the time, as was Kenneth Burke, who was Munson's friend and coeditor of *Secession*.[4] It was this approach that Munson applied to *City Block* in his *Waldo Frank: A Study* ("Comedy" 46). Accordingly, Munson wrote on the dynamics of the short story cycle with a perception and detail not to be repeated until Forrest L. Ingram applied both New Critical methods and a name to the genre in the 70s:

> *City Block* is composed of fourteen units, most of which truly leave sufficient independence for separate publication, but all of which try to cooperate in the creation of a larger form. They overlap, continue and relate to each other: their planes intersect: their arrangement and spacing help to create a unit greater than their sum as short stories. . . . [Frank is] intent on a spherical form. (*Waldo Frank* 49–50)

Toomer took note of Munson's implications about the role of the reader in the short story cycle. This is hinted at in the above quotation, which suggests that the layering, connection-making, and totalizing function of the reader is what the reader finds pleasurable in this form—a suggestion that is similar to how critics such as Robert M. Luscher have appraised the dynamics of short story cycles. Toomer extrapolated Munson's comments on the reading dynamics of *City Block,* noting that "[t]his book, in short, carries every potential of greatness. It but awaits complete realization in our own slow-moving minds" ("Critic" 27). At this point in his career Toomer was more interested in the possibility of ambiguity and its correlative, the process of readerly "realization," than in Frank's tendency to didacticism—as he wrote to Munson, "[m]ystery cannot help but accompany a deep, clear-cut image" (*Letters* 92).

Accordingly, *Cane* opened more spaces for the reader than both *City Block* and *Winesburg, Ohio.* It dispensed with the stable narrative voice of *City Block* and included fewer recurring characters; it involved a broader geographical span and more generic range. Indeed, Lola Ridge (the American editor of *Broom*) wrote to Toomer in 1920 that his poems gained their power through being "poems of concealment, rather than of revealment—a placing of flowers and ferns before closed shutters."[5] As James Nagel has recently discussed, the short story cycle has a particular applicability to representations of ethnic difference, conflict, and assimilation; he sees the nonsequential potential of the form, and its capacity for the relative autonomy of its constituent stories, as ideal for presenting "the process of immigration, acculturation, language acquisition, assimilation, identity formation, and the complexities of forming a sense of self that incorporates the old world and the new, the central traditions of the country of origin integrated into, or in conflict with, the values of the country of choice" (15). *Cane* is a salient early example of this and functions as much by ellipsis, silence, and rupture—all places for reader intervention—as it does by cohesion and narratorial authority. In doing so, it contributed to an aesthetic of writing about the South that was to be developed by Faulkner and Morrison. I do not mean to suggest that some texts have a "coherence" that the reader passively imbibes; obviously any semiotic statement is subjected to a whole series of cultural and historical contexts every time it is read, and would be unreadable otherwise. However, *Cane* contains a great number of occasions when the reader must make what Umberto Eco calls "inferential walks"—these "are not mere whimsical initiatives on the part of the reader, but are elicited by the discursive structures and foreseen by the whole textual strategy as indispensable components of the construction of the fabula" (32). Indeed, Scruggs and VanDemarr have discussed *Cane* as borrowing from the literary traditions of both the Gothic and the detective story, genres in which concealed knowledge is formally central:

> Toomer's narrators in the first part of *Cane* and in "Kabnis" can never quite say what they see nor, at times, make sense of what they see: there is always a disjunction between the characters' actions and the secret social terms by which they act. . . . Toomer's narrators want to look and want not to look, for what they see always draws them deeply into matters of "race" and American identity. Where the writing is at its most brilliant is where that tension between looking and not looking creates a tortured, imagistic text. (136)

As Pierre Macherey has identified, texts mark with silence those aspects of a dominant ideology that cannot be uttered; indeed, "it is in the significant silences of a text, in its gaps and absences, that the presence of ideology can be most positively felt" (Eagleton, *Marxism* 34–35). Just as Toomer wrote that "no book could possibly contain" the genealogy of the "white girl" he saw in Sparta, he went on to remark, "Even a fraction of those untold facts would reveal the situation to be more human, as well as more terrible, than the general public can possibly imagine."[6] It is this terror—what Scruggs and VanDemarr have called the "Terrors of American history"—that enforce many of the silences of *Cane*. For example, in stories such as "Karintha" the ellipsis assumes importance as a cursive figure that marks what cannot be represented. In that story, "A child fell out of [Karintha's] womb onto a bed of pine needles in the forest. Pine needles are smooth and sweet. They are elastic to the feet of rabbits. . . . A sawmill was nearby. Its pyramidal sawdust pile smoldered" (4). Many critics have filled this ellipsis with the assumption that Karintha killed her child and left it to burn in the sawdust pile, seeing the omission as representative of the silence over miscegenation and bastardy dictated by southern social mores.[7]

Just as Toomer expresses reluctance over endorsing the form of an "authentic" black voice, therefore, so he recognizes the significance of silence and taboo in societies scarred by a history of conflict and often brutal exploitation. The narrator in "Fern" wishes to do some "fine, unnamed thing" for Fern, and this sense of obligation, which is not communicable in language, forms the bond between them (19). Similarly, Lewis sees Father John as "A mute John the Baptist of a new religion—or the tongue-tied shadow of an old" (106). Some things, Layman observes, are not "fer notin down" (91), and such a strategy of silence necessitates an intervention by the reader, who *can* supply the hidden violence and "terrors" of the text of *Cane* and, in a wider sense, the social text. One effect of such a strategy is to make this reading process more engaged, self-aware, and even tactile; Toni Morrison has stated of her own language that it "has to have holes and spaces so the reader can come into it. He or she can feel something visceral, see something striking" (qtd. in Dixon 5). Such a process is as unsettling as it is intense, representing what Scruggs and VanDemarr have identified as a silence with political purpose—silences that draw attention to themselves and the prohibitive social codes which enforce them. Filling those silences removes any readerly distance that may exist, pushing the reader against the "tactile" surfaces of the lynched, abused, and murdered bodies that the text frequently omits to mention, and which form the social milieu of Georgia which is not "fer notin down."

Yet the question arises as to why Toomer uses this strategy of concealment in a text that reveals so much, that has such graphic depictions of violence in the lynching scenes of "Blood Burning Moon," "Portrait in Georgia," and "Kabnis." Critics such as Scruggs and VanDemarr and Kutzinski, as mentioned, see this silence as centering on the history of specifically *sexual* violence and abuse within the South that remained unspeakable. Yet rupture, division, and ellipsis are not used solely to cover the unspeakable terrors of American racial politics, although they function significantly in this way. It is also the fact that *Cane* attempts to take the position of what George Hutchinson has called a "biracial" text—a text that is both white and black, with a correspondingly "biracial" audience—that make its gaps and silences so much more pronounced, and so much more structurally central, than most other works produced in the period.[8] *Cane*'s lacunae emphasize the social divisions that American racial politics provoke, making visible the *presence* if not the content of secret knowledge—which some sections of the population will know, and which some will not. Moreover, in addition to the examples in individual texts that I have been discussing thus far, the diversity of the text units emphasizes the huge range of cultural references, across both African American and European American culture, which *Cane* employs. This diversity demands rapid changes in horizons of expectation (according to whether the piece is a sonnet, short story, or a prose poem constructed around a blues lyric, for example), thus emphasizing the social divisions underlying the profoundly racialized cultural field. Most obviously, social division is signified through the arcs that form the prefatory illustration to parts 1 and 2, and which are replicated to form the broken circle that appears immediately before "Kabnis."

This use of the gap and the silence, then, Toomer saw as a strategy with a double function. On the one hand, it was especially suited to a politically engaged African American writing that provided a sensitive formal response to the relationship between silence, taboo, and violence within American society. Such a strategy avoided the formulas of what Waldo Frank, in his foreword to *Cane*, called "'problem' fiction and moral melodrama," yet also outlined a coherent set of racial politics. Indeed, Toomer himself had little time for "problem" fiction or what James Baldwin would later call "protest novels"; he dismissed most other "books on the matter of race and the race problem," as they consisted largely of "strings of words expressive of personal prejudices and preferences" (*Wayward* 120). Instead, he hoped to provide a more flexible critical account of the lived experience of a racially divided society, one that would not exemplify Baldwin's later criticism that "the failure of the protest novel lies in its rejection of life, the human being, the denial of his beauty, dread, power, in its insistence that it is his categorization alone which is real and which cannot be transcended" (*Protest Novel* 28). The second function of this strategy was that *Cane* aimed not to determine a race to its implied reader, while still providing a forceful structural reminder to its readers about the divisions in American society that occurred on racial grounds.[9] Indeed, Toomer's awareness that the racialization of the cultural field was thoroughly coextensive with the racialization of readerships helps explain his desire to develop new audiences while he was writing *Cane*. He wrote to Frank in 1922, just before their trip to South Carolina, that

> I cannot think of myself as being separated from you in the dual task of creating an American literature, and of developing a public, large or small, capable of responding to our creations. . . . So far as the people here [the African American bourgeoisie in Washington] are concerned, the path to both of us is blocked somewhat by a rigid moral conventionalism (this, in reaction against the excesses of the slave regime, and found most acute in the otherwise most advanced minds). . . . But, underneath, the soil is good rich brown, and should yield splendidly to our plowing. (*Letters* 59)

Zora Neale Hurston too saw a kind of significant omission as an aesthetic associated with African American cultural production. In her essay "Characteristics of Negro Expression," for example, she characterizes African American dance as structured to provide "dynamic suggestion":

> That is the reason the spectator is held so rapt. He is participating in the performance himself—carrying out the suggestions of the performer.
>
> The difference in the two arts is: the white dancer attempts to express fully; the Negro is restrained, succeeds in gripping the beholder by forcing him to finish the action the performer suggests. (1023)

However, the "suggestions" that Hurston identifies here can be ignored or interpreted in a variety of ways, and in undertaking a similar strategy of frequent "dynamic suggestion," Toomer found that interpretations of

Cane varied enormously, often on the grounds of the race of the reviewer. Accordingly, *Cane*'s innovative attempt to address a multiracial readership was a shift that many of its contemporary reviewers found difficult to comprehend, as I shall discuss later.

Cane's modernist strategy of ellipsis and fragmentation therefore identifies some of its most perplexing internal tensions; how to ever be able to speak about forbidden subjects, how to defamiliarize a society's language of race within that same language, and who to include and who to exclude in its implied audience. In engaging with these issues, *Cane* preempted a debate that would occur in the later 1920s among the African American literary community about the politics of audience. This was most thoroughly dealt with in James Weldon Johnson's article "The Dilemma of the Negro Author," a dilemma similar to the "double consciousness" that Du Bois had famously proclaimed twenty-five years earlier.[10] Johnson explained that the Negro author faces

> a special problem which the plain American writer knows nothing about—the problem of the double audience. It is more than a double audience; it is a divided audience, an audience made up of two elements with different and often opposite and antagonistic points of view. His audience is always white America and black America. The moment a Negro writer takes up his pen or sits down to his typewriter he is immediately called upon to solve, consciously or unconsciously, this problem of the double audience. To whom shall he address himself, to his own black group or to white America? Many a Negro writer has fallen down, as it were, between these two stools. (477)

As Charles Scruggs notes, "nearly every black writer or critic in the 1920s complained of this dilemma" ("Dressed Up" 546). The choice—which Johnson felt was often depressingly absolute—involved in facing a racially bifurcated audience was between presenting a stereotyped, primitivistic, infantilized (or bestialized) image of African Americans for a white audience, or giving a presentation of morally impeccable, bourgeois, and affluent African Americans for a black audience. The danger of this situation is that "[t]he Negro author may please one audience and at the same time rouse the resentment of the other; or he may please the other and totally fail to rouse the interest of one" (Johnson 480). Moreover, any attempt to bridge this division can lead to a kind of schizophrenic authorial situation where "[i]f [the author] analyzes what he writes he will find that on one page black America is his whole or main audience, and on the very next page white America." The only possibility—and this is one Johnson sadly admits can only occur in the future—is for "a fusion. In time, I cannot say how much time, there will come a natural and gradual rapprochement of these two sections of the Negro author's audience" (Johnson 481).[11]

This idea of fusion approaches a much-cited comment made by Toomer in the *Liberator* in 1922, that "I am naturally and inevitably an American. I have striven for a spiritual fusion analogous to the fact of racial intermingling" (*Letters* 70). The word *fusion* for Toomer carried racial, psychological, and aesthetic connotations; indeed, it was an early frustration to him in writing *Cane* that Kabnis "has not reached its real fusion" (*Letters* 50). As Toomer's letter to Frank about audience exemplifies, the sense of *fusion* as both integrative and creative was something he had hoped to achieve for *Cane*'s audience; yet in other essays by African American authors such as Wallace Thurman, Sterling Brown, and Langston Hughes about the "dilemma of the Negro Author," all three cited *Cane* as a laudable experiment which did, in fact, fall between Johnson's "two stools." Thurman (one of African America's sternest critics of the editorial policies of the New Negro Renaissance's principal periodicals) noted that *Cane* "was of little interest to sentimental whites or to Negroes with an inferiority complex to camouflage. Both the personality of the author and the style of his book were above the heads of these groups."[12] Similarly, Langston Hughes noted that "[t]he colored people did not praise it. The white people did not buy it," despite it containing what he felt to be (along with the work of Du Bois) "the finest prose written by a Negro in America" ("Negro Artist" 1270).

However, Toomer's highly ambitious plan to negotiate these "two stools" of *Cane*'s audience—and occupy them both rather than falling between them—was evident from the moment he began sending out pieces to a wide variety of little magazines. The range of little magazines and other outlets to which he sent pieces of *Cane*—the African American periodical the *Crisis* and the Associated Negro Press; the socialist journal the *Liberator;* avant-garde magazines such as *Broom,* the *Little Review, S4N, Secession,* the *Modern Review,* and the *Dial;* and the *Double Dealer* (with its specifically regional, white southern editorial policy)—is evidence of the scope of the audience that Toomer felt he could address. Indeed, an admiring Norman Fitts wrote to Toomer in 1923 that "I seem to see copy by you in every periodical I pick up; congratulations!"[13] Yet this ambitious program was possible for two reasons. One was the diversity of the text units within *Cane,* which allowed him to select and match text units to the editorial policies of various magazines. There would have been little use in sending a Futuristic offering such as "Her Lips Are Copper Wire" to the *Crisis,* for example, given literary editor Jessie Fauset's caution to Toomer to avoid "inmeshing the kernel of thought in envelopes of words."[14] Similarly, Toomer would have met with refusal had he sent "Bona and Paul," with its inference of white female desire for the African American Paul, to the New Orleans–based *Double Dealer*, whose editor, Jack McClure, told Toomer in correspondence that both he and his clientele were firmly in favor of segregation. (Indeed, Toomer's pragmatism on the issue of placing his stories with little magazines is most evident in his relations with the *Double Dealer;* he retitled "Calling Jesus" as "Nora" to allow its appearance in the magazine, as McClure feared the reaction of his more evangelical subscribers to Toomer's earlier title). The second reason facilitating *Cane*'s diversity of audience was the degree to which Toomer omitted to supply contextual referents, those generic and linguistic markers for what Iser has called "horizons of expectation," which may have circumscribed and delimited his audience to an unwonted degree. These included a lack of a consistent narrative voice, a willingness to experiment with generic categories and expectations, and a reluctance to subscribe to very polarized traditions of black representation.

It can be argued, then, that *Cane* is so what Roland Barthes termed "writerly" precisely because it tries to surmount the problems of the implied reader being definitively racialized, so much so that some of its reviewers were confused by its combination of formal and ethnic points of reference. For example, several African American reviewers linked Toomer's aesthetic radicalism with *Cane*'s relatively open treatment of sex; both these traits drew extensively from the white, Greenwich Village literary milieu that Toomer frequented, and the reviewers disliked either one or both of these features. *Cane*'s most eminent reviewer, W. E. B. Du Bois, saw Toomer as "a writer who first desired to emancipate the colored world from the conventions of sex," but also felt "unduly irritated" by a work that contained "much that is difficult or even impossible to understand" (*Cane* 171). Roger Didier, reviewing for the Associated Negro Press, took issue with the phrase in "Fern" that "Fern's eyes said to them . . . that she was easy." He went on to remark that "Negro women are likely to protest at the insinuation in Mr. Toomer's fine picture of a Negro girl. . . . the question arises whether it is a good thing for the Negro race to take the lead in this sort of new and radical writing."[15] In contrast, Toomer's white avant-garde friend Gorham Munson misinterpreted some of the stories due to a lack of familiarity with African American dialect (North, *Dialect* 166), and, as I have noted, Matthew Josephson contended that Toomer's "cerebral super-forms" did not adequately represent the primitive spontaneity of his black subjects.[16] Robert Littell, praising the evasion of stereotypes in *Cane,* could only remark that

Toomer's alternative was "unfamiliar and bafflingly subterranean" (*Cane* 169). Even this brief survey indicates the problematics of *Cane*'s ambition to show allegiance to more than one cultural movement through its use of formal innovation, and the way in which its representation of a deeply codified and secretive society was perceived either as an annoying obfuscation or superfluous intellectualization. At a cruder level, it is also evident that divergence from certain "types" of representations of African Americans would draw censure from some critics. Moreover, that this issue was central to the whole nexus of production and racial discourse surrounding *Cane* is obvious from the way in which the relation of artists or performers to audiences populate *Cane*'s text.

THE INTERNAL AUDIENCES OF *CANE*

The sections dealing with the relation of performer to audience in *Cane* reveal the collaborative nature of this relationship and the potential it carries for the creation of communities, but also the frequent intervention of barriers of class, sex, or race. For example, in "Theater," Toomer presents dance as not only a liberatory practice, "the rhythmic means by which . . . characters release themselves from inhibiting forces," but, in a fashion similar to Hurston's theory, as a creative collaboration between dancer and audience (Turner, "Playwright" 378). During Dorris's dance, "The walls press in, singing. Flesh of a throbbing body, they press close to John and Dorris. They close them in. John's heart beats tensely against her dancing body. Walls press his mind within his heart" (55). Similarly, Dan in "Box Seat" dissolves divisions between audience and performer, as he responds to the stimulus of the performance of the dwarves by leaping to his feet and shouting. Barlo's performance in his incantatory sermon results in a magical response in the town of Sempter, as "hosts of angels and of demons paraded up and down the streets all night" and black madonnas are painted on courthouse walls (23). These "dynamic suggestions" that elicit response are of course similar to call and response, the antiphonal technique of many African American work songs or sermons, and critics have argued that this stress on audience in *Cane* is an assertion of a racial community formed through a communal response to the "call" of a leader.[17] Yet although *Cane* opens spaces for its internal audiences, which invite such a communal response to a clarion call, it also demonstrates that the "dynamic suggestions," the spaces in the performance where the "response" is expected, are moments where control must be relinquished by the dancer, preacher, or writer. In consequence, these spaces are areas where incomprehension, or a breakdown in communication, is as possible as communal affirmation or a celebratory "response."

At points in *Cane,* then, the "call" is answered, and at others it is denied. For example, the call of "eoho," first heard in the poem based on African American work song, "Cotton Song," is repeated and echoed throughout the text. The cry "eoho, eoho, roll away" is a version of a field holler, which is a call traditionally made by African American workers working alone in the fields—a practice that existed in slavery, but which Toomer may well have heard during his time in rural Georgia (*Cane* 11). Discussing these hollers, Lawrence Levine finds that they are typified as being either calls, which are antiphonal and anticipate a reply, or cries, which do not anticipate a response and are private attempts to vocalize feelings (*Black Culture* 219). It is this duality of the field holler that makes it such an appropriate form for Toomer to interpolate throughout his text, as it resides in such an ambiguous relation to both communication and expression. The field holler represents either an attempt at communication undertaken at great distance from its addressee, who may or may not answer, or an outburst made in full knowledge of the caller's complete isolation. This duality was one that Toomer was experiencing with *Cane,* as the letter to Frank about audience makes clear; he was unsure whether its innovative call would be heard, understood and reciprocated, or whether the lack of an audience would leave him isolated. Indeed, after going south with Waldo Frank—to whom he felt closer than any other writer in terms of common objectives in late 1922—he wrote to him "EOHO! EOHO! BROTHER! Things are moving . . ." (*Letters* 96).

The field holler appears again in "Calling Jesus," but its duality as both call and cry receives its fullest exploration in "Harvest Song," which is worth quoting at some length:

> My throat is dry. And should I call, a cracked grain like the oats . . . eoho—
>
> I fear to call. What should they hear me, and offer their grain, oats, or wheat, or corn? I have been in the fields all day. I fear I could not taste it. I fear knowledge of my hunger.
>
> My ears are caked with dust of oatfields at harvest-time.
> I am a deaf man who strains to hear the calls of other harvesters
> whose throats are also dry.
>
> It would be good to hear their songs . . reapers of the sweet stalk'd cane,
> cutters of the corn . . even though their throats cracked and the
> strangeness of their voices deafened me.

> I hunger. My throat is dry. Now that the sun has set and I am chilled, I fear to call. (Eoho, my brothers!) (*Cane* 71)

The fear of calling balanced against the desire to call, the setting of the call in parentheses balanced against the repeated hesitation over calling, and the deafening nature of the potential response balanced against the isolation of garnering no response produce the tone of ambivalent anxiety that dominates the poem. In one sense the field hollers of "Harvest Song" are left unheard, or even unuttered. Karen Jackson Ford, for example, claims that the "I" of the poem ends it "cold, blind, deaf, without capacity to taste" and "insensible to everything but memory" (116). Yet in another sense the field hollers of "Harvest Song" are antiphonal, responding across the barriers created by the separation of the text units to the exhortation of community voiced in "Cotton Song": "eoho, eoho, roll away! / We aint agwine t wait until th Judgement Day!" (11). The delicate ambivalence of "Harvest Song" forces the question of just what the "harvest" will be: the fruitful yield of oats, wheat, corn, and community, or the sterility and isolation of dust-caked ears. In many ways this poem mediates the author's anxiety about how *Cane* would take its place in the cultural field, how it would (or would not) cultivate what Toomer referred to as "the soil" of a new audience. Indeed, this perhaps explains both the centrality and the ambiguity Toomer accorded "Harvest Song" in a letter to Waldo Frank, describing it as both the end—and the pause—of *Cane*'s "spiritual phase" (*Letters* 101).

Breakdowns in communication between performer and audience occur elsewhere. In "Theater," for example, Dorris's dance becomes a "dead thing in the shadow" of John's dream, her call for union ignored by his "dictie" class arrogance. And Kabnis, although he rates Father John as a "good listener," is violently opposed to any kind of response: "Didnt I tell y to shut up?" he tells him, petrified of the history of slavery and violence he may reveal (116). These moments of failed community cause particular anguish to the male prophetic figures throughout *Cane;* Dan Moore, for example, sees a "portly Negress" at the Lincoln Theatre, whose "strong roots sink down and spread in the river and disappear in blood-lines that waver south" (65). This epiphany of ancestral consciousness is followed by a dream of community:

> Earth throbs. Dan's heart beats violently. He sees all the people in the house rush to the walls to listen to the rumble. A new-world Christ is coming up. Dan comes up. He is startled. The eyes of the woman don't belong to her. They look at him unpleasantly. From either side, bolted masses press in. He doesn't fit. (65)

As Kutzinski notes, Dan's "attempt at emotional and cultural revitalization/rebirth becomes monstrous in its exaggerated sentimentality" (167). Such moments directly counter Frank's position in *City Block*—that the narrator/author figure could lead the audience, or the reader, to new relations of community through the formal brilliance of his vision. Instead, Toomer was aware of the vagaries of response: Barlo may be preaching to the black community of Sempter, but also to whites who spit on him and to children playing in the background; the narrator in "Avey" talks "beautifully" but his audience falls asleep (48). Both Jules Romains's theory of *unanimisme* and Frank's aesthetic in *City Block* were based on the belief that the artist could provide artistic forms that would provide social models of coherence and unity, that the prophetic voice could harmonize a discontinuous environment. Toomer, in contrast, while being greatly attracted to this possibility (particularly as evinced by the *unanimisme* of "Seventh Street"), was much less confident about the possibility of a controlling consciousness, about the possibility of breaking down divisions in race, class, and gender through reintegrative formal rhetoric. The difficulty of producing an interpretative unity of author, text, and audience was central to this perspective, in what was both a more astute understanding of reading dynamics than Frank's and a sharper personal experience of the ways in which race affects reading. As mentioned, despite his ambitious attempts to get *Cane* published in a wide range of little magazines, the racialization of reading was emphasized to Toomer later in the huge variety of responses to *Cane*. This was seen in the difference between a southern journal stating he had a "fine tolerance," an African American critic finding him the "bright morning star of the race in literature," and his publisher selling *Cane* as "negro life whose rhythmic beat, like the primitive tom-tom of the African jungle, you can feel. . . ."[18] Toomer's subtle meditation on *Cane*'s potential audience, which goes on in the very pages of *Cane*, is therefore marked on the one hand by the ambitious optimism that a range of strategies might forge and hold a biracial audience, and on the other by an awareness of how precarious this attempt would be.

As Susan Blake notes, "the characters in Jean Toomer's *Cane* are struggling to impose form on a world of chaos," yet "their efforts to impose their idea of order on life only compound their fragmentation" (217). This gives *Cane* the quality of restless searching—for form and for an adequate response from its internal audiences—which is one quality that has led to its classification as a modernist text. As Bradbury and McFarlane note, modernist aesthetics often address "a problem in the making of structures, the employment of language, the uniting of form, finally in the social meaning of the artist himself . . . In this sense, modernism is less a style than a search for a style . . ." (29). *Cane*'s search is wide-ranging; it employs imagist-style poetry, symbolist, Dadaist, and Futurist ideas, iambic pentameters in the manner of Robert Frost, African American work song and spirituals, blues stanzas, prose-poems, short stories, melodrama, and Expressionist drama.[19] These often function as different modes of address seeking community or some basis of collectivity, a search that is both compulsive and continually frustrated. The modes of address—the "crystallization" of images toward which he was urged by Gorham Munson, the messianic sermons, the performances of Dorris and Kabnis, the "caroling" of "souls of slavery" (14), or the singing of Louisa and Fern—are not sustained or adequately answered. *Cane* displays an awareness that discontinuity—between either identity groups or text units—is something that invites the application of cohering principles and collective address. Yet such principles have to vocalize the silences between these units, provide common "roots"—yet these endeavors can result in the uncomprehending stare of the "portly Negress" in "Box Seat," as Dan does not "fit," or the effacement of Fern by the incomprehension of dusk as she sings "with a broken voice. A child's voice, uncertain, or an old man's" (19). What Arna Bontemps called *Cane*'s formal "Frappé," and its recurrent focus on audience, performance, and the dynamics of the spaces of performance, is really a search for an address in both senses of the word: a shared home and an inclusive mode of communication. Yet this search is at odds with the attitude of the audience at the Crimson Gardens, who see "not attractiveness in [Paul's] dark skin, but difference" (76). And it was both provoked and ultimately frustrated by the widely divergent, deeply racialized, "creative" readings applied to *Cane* from the first moment Toomer sent pieces of it into various literary communities.

At this point, Toomer's only way out of this impasse was grounded in the body and the possibility of literally re-creating it that he later saw in Gurdjieff's work. Society needed less a principle of organic integration than a Futurist conception of regenerative violence, recasting bodies outside of the reductive hierarchical discourses they occupied. Dan's destruction of the theatre is perhaps the main example of this vision, but the wedge of Seventh Street scything through the "whitewashed wood" of Washington is another, as is the fact that when Tom Burwell beats the white body of Bob Stone "each blow sounded as if it smashed into a precious, irreplaceable soft something"

(35). In his later phase as a visionary of a racially integrated America, he developed this idea, seeing that "there must be death before there can be new life" and that "the materials themselves need not die, but the forms in which they previously existed must be broken down before these materials can enter as new forms with new life" ("Americans" 107).[20] He goes on to formulate the nation as a stomach rather than a melting pot:

> Some foods, in relation to some eaters, do not noticeably resist dying and being eaten. . . . But certain foods, such for example as race-forms, through entering the stomach of a nation, do resist. This resistance both retards and stimulates the appetite, it both retards and stimulates digestion and assimilation. But the nation eats them. The race-forms die. ("Americans" 107)

Finally, then, race and the nation were bodies that needed refashioning, structures of materiality the dynamic modern age could alter. The processes by which this could be achieved were always vague—as many commentators have noted, Toomer was an idealist rather than a politician—but *Cane* strains toward the epistemological foundations of white patriarchal hegemony and produces tropes that unsettle those foundations. In doing so, and in attempting to forge a multiracial audience, *Cane* relies on the formal qualities of the short story cycle, particularly its ability to draw readers into integrative reading strategies and force them to encounter and explain often politically laden silences and absence. In addition, the trained black body, the engine or the electric lightbulb, and the bastard all interrogate and provoke, destroying and destabilizing social spaces and hierarchical structures. Without these challenges, audiences are consigned to being forever divided, confused, or unresponsive. As he wrote to Gorham Munson, "Stage folk are not respectable. Audiences are" (*Toomer Reader* 20).

CONCLUSION

Generally overlooked in accounts of 1922, the year of *Ulysses* and *The Waste Land* and arguably the *annus mirabilis* of modernism, is the brief exchange of letters that began late in that year between Sherwood Anderson and Jean Toomer. Yet this exchange reveals much about the racial politics of American modernism. It illustrates how developments in anthropology, cultural criticism, and the changing nature of the cultural field were impacting upon imaginative writing, and it touched upon many of the issues that related to Anderson's and Toomer's use of the short story cycle genre. The correspondence came at a crucial point in the careers of both men. Anderson's attachment to the Midwest and Chicago that had launched him to fame was waning, and he had just completed his first long period of residence in the South, a region soon to become his permanent home and one that would provoke a significant change in his literary style. Toomer was going over the final drafts of *Cane*, was immersed in the literary ferment of the New York avant-garde, and was attempting to raise his literary profile through publishing in a wide range of little magazines and entering into correspondence with many leading writers and intellectuals. In a sense, Toomer and Anderson needed each other. Toomer needed Anderson because he could bolster his career and help justify the tremendous energy he was expending on his literary "neophytism"; Anderson needed Toomer for his insights into "the Negro."

Yet as with much interracial cultural traffic in the period, this correspondence was marked by misunderstandings and differing demands. Anderson's formal radicalism in *Winesburg, Ohio* had been provoked by unease and uncertainty about the future of white masculinity in the United States; it was a text that anxiously considered how far narrative could go in underpinning the "dreams of manhood" of young men like George Willard. Anderson's search for reassurance through essentialisms and reified categories of identity was in complete contrast to Toomer, who was already realizing that Winesburg's formal innovations would be inadequate for his project of addressing a biracial, or even deracialized, audience. As was so often the case with Toomer's relationship to his literary peers, both Euro- and African American, the sticking point was the relation of race to culture: in one of the most telling exchanges of their correspondence, Anderson complained to him that "I did not want to write of the negro but out of him. Well I wasn't one. The thing I felt couldn't be truly done" (Turner, "Intersection" 102). Toomer replied as follows:

> As you say, you wanted to write not of the Negro but out of him. "Well I wasn't one. The thing is that it couldn't be truly done." I guess you're right. But this much is certain: an emotional element, a richness from him, from yourself, you have artistically woven into your own material. Notably, in Out of Nowhere into Nothing. Here your Negro, from the standpoint of superficial reality, of averages, of surface plausibility, is unreal. My friends who are interested in the "progress" of the Negro would take violent exception to such a statement as, "By educating himself he had cut himself off from his own people." And from a strictly social point of view, much of what they would say would be true enough. But in these pages you have evoked an emotion, a sense of beauty that is easily more Negro than almost anything I have seen. (*Letters* 105–6)

Toomer was keen to move away from the "strictly social point of view" and yet not let it drop out of the frame altogether. He knew that excessive attention to Du Bois's famous question of "how should the Negro be Portrayed" would lead to the Manichaean dilemmas over the portrayal of African Americans that would dominate much literary debate in the 1920s;

as Waldo Frank noted in the preface to *Cane,* "obsession" with "racial crisis" had so often in the past produced works of "exoticism, polemic, 'problem' fiction, and moral melodrama" (139). Yet whereas Anderson complained over his inability to access an embodied, "authentic" blackness, the shift that Toomer was beginning to make in this letter, and which became clarified later, is that toward formulating race as culture. If "Negro" was about emotion and a sense of beauty, and if a white writer could understand and communicate this as well as anyone, then cultural "belonging" and cultural authenticity are not necessarily linked to racial status. This democratization of culture—that "your" culture is not determined by the factor of race—was emphasized in a letter of Toomer's to Frank, in which he also criticized Anderson for differing "but little from the mass which must narrow and caricature if it is to grasp the thing at all." Yet he went on to note that

> the Negro is in solution, the process of solution. . . . the race is loosing [*sic*] its body. . . . One is even led to believe that the thing we call beauty will always be attributed to a clearly defined physical source. But the fact is, that if anything comes up now, pure Negro, it will be a swan-song. (*Letters* 115)

Toomer's ambition, so evident in part 2 of *Cane,* is to transform the relation between culture and the body, to disrupt the causal link between "beauty" and a "clearly defined physical source." He discusses how this is to be so at the end of this letter; it is evident in the "new life" that he found confronting him, a life "that Sherwood Anderson would not get his beauty from. For it is jazzed, strident, modern. Negro? Only in the *boldness* of its expression" (*Letters* 116). It is the forces of modernity that will effect this "solution" of the Negro; it is the dynamics of modern technology, urban spaces, and the rapidly changing cultural field that will transform how social discourse had been able to racially determine bodies, and to arrange those bodies into hierarchical relations. The word "solution" therefore comes to mean a process of dissolving and a process of solving. It comes to connote the dissolution of the racial determination of bodies, a dissolution that Toomer hoped would lead to America becoming a cultural melting pot, free from any racially essentialized rights of ownership; and it also suggests the means of a "solution" to the Negro "problem." Accordingly, Toomer was unimpressed by the ramifications of cultural pluralism, a celebration of African American "folk" heritage, or the status of a racial spokesperson. Instead, it was his exuberant enthusiasm for the new, for ideas about how formal principles of the corporeal might relate to language and identity, that brought about the astonishing experimental vitality and generic originality of *Cane.*

Toomer was right when he said that Anderson would get no beauty from such ideas. Anderson was a man deeply committed to binary thinking, and any deviation from strict differentiations between men and women, heterosexual orientation and "fairies," or black and white caused him considerable anxiety. In 1926, when watching a crew of African Americans unloading a ship in New Orleans, he lamented "what I would not give to be a man, not the shadow of a man" (Quoted in Helbling, "Sherwood Anderson" 119). Man and not-man, authentic and inauthentic, potent and impotent, man and his shadow, pepper his work; and yet his consistent desire not to "impose my own will on the people of my imaginative world" perpetually challenges these polarized ideals of categorization (*Triumph* 300). As can be seen in *Winesburg, Ohio* in particular, Anderson was often drawn to expressing the desire that "in every little thing there must be order," that the creative artist be allowed to organize and categorize his environment with an authoritative hand (100). Yet it is in the space between this desire and the actuality of the lived environment, between polarized categories of identity, and in the textual gaps that are so structurally central to *Winesburg, Ohio,* that Anderson's work is at its most interesting. Waldo Frank and Jean Toomer certainly seemed to think so, as their attempts at the short story cycle attest: yet it was only Toomer who realized that Anderson's textual ellipses gave readers a greater self-consciousness about the endeavor of reading. These ellipses are central to Anderson's fascinating insight into the nature of white American masculinity in the late 1910s and 1920s, particularly the response of this masculinity to the historical traumas of the Great War and the industrial division of labor. Similarly, such ellipses would enable Toomer to deal with the unspeakable elements of American racial politics.

Following the "trauma" of the war, race became more and more fundamental to Anderson's imagination of gendered identities. Fearing that "modern man is losing his ability to retain his manhood in the face of the modern way of utilizing the machine," Anderson turned to an essentialized view of race to help prop up the ailing binary of what he called the "man-woman thing" (*Perhaps Women* 7). In *Dark Laughter,* he wrote scathingly of the postwar environment of Paris; his account focused on the debauchery of the Quatz' Arts Ball, which becomes a mire of freely expressed, brutal, and embittered sexual desire on the part of the men who have survived the battleground. In the frenzied style of the novel that would attract so much criticism, he raged about the "[s]tench of the trenches—in the fingers, the clothes, the hair—staying there—getting into the blood—trench thoughts, trench feelings—trench love. . . . Nudity now! Perversion—well, what of that?" (180). The polymorphic sexualities at the ball are caused by the trauma of warfare in a virtually incoherent scene of dystopian bacchanal, a situation glaringly counterpointed by the glowing and envy-laden descriptions of African American men and women earlier in the novel.

However, as writers such as Hemingway so brutally pointed out, this was a clumsy form of escapism, and one that could overlap into the commercialized fetishization of blackness that underpinned much of the "vogue of the Negro" of the mid-1920s. Anderson too was aware of this failing; as he wrote in 1931, "Time and again I had told the story of the American man crushed and puzzled by the age of the machine. I had told the story until I was tired of telling it. I had retreated from the city to the town, from the town to the farm" (*Perhaps Women* 112–13). Yet, albeit in a less assured and insightful way than in Toomer's writing, Anderson's work reveals much about racialization in early twentieth-century America: its intersectionality with the politics of gender; its complex relations with ideas about culture; the degree to which racial "Others" who were in some way "out of place" both fascinated and terrified the white imagination; and the ramifications of circumstances when "whiteness" becomes visible.

Yet Anderson's increasingly desperate, and disturbing, faith in racial essentialism also suggests a reason why he never returned to his "Winesburg form," just as Toomer would never return to the form of *Cane*. *Winesburg, Ohio* represents the spectacle of a set of dominant fictions of gender beset by historical trauma, yet with no new fictions ready to serve as a replacement. As soon as there were (and increasingly "blackness" came to provide them), the lacunae, uncertainties, and ambiguous relations between text pieces that characterize the short story cycle became inappropriate. Just so with Toomer; once his intellectual flexibility and uncertainties, especially around race, solidified into Gurdjieffian dogma, the formal strategies of *Cane* seemed too amorphous to him; in his plans for a follow-up novel he claimed that it would display "more depth of content and continuity of attitude than is usual in collections of short forms. It is, in a sense, at the opposite pole from Cane."[1] It was an innovation born of restlessness that characterizes the many merits of these texts, a restlessness and a desire for innovation that was informed by many new and challenging discourses of gender and race in the culture of early twentieth-century America. For both men, this was a restlessness that was to occur only once in a fruitful intersection of personal, historical, and intellectual circumstances.

NOTES

INTRODUCTION

1. This omission has begun to be rectified in Toomer criticism, especially in the work of Barbara Foley and Charles Scruggs and Lee VanDemarr.
2. See, for example, Charles Scruggs, "The Reluctant Witness: What Jean Toomer Remembered from *Winesburg, Ohio*"; Darwin T. Turner, "An Intersection of Paths"; Mark Helbling, "Sherwood Anderson and Jean Toomer"; and Mary Jane Dickerson, "Sherwood Anderson and Jean Toomer: A Literary Relationship."
3. For an extended discussion of the importance of the Young American critics to the Harlem Renaissance, see George Hutchinson, *The Harlem Renaissance in Black and White,* 94–105.
4. Anderson would publish the essay "New Orleans, The *Double Dealer* and the Modern Movement in America" in the March 1922 edition of the *Double Dealer,* and several of his "New Testaments" also sporadically appeared in the magazine; Toomer's "Nora" (later retitled "Calling Jesus,") "Storm Ending," and "Harvest Song" appeared in the magazine in 1922.

5. See Scruggs and VanDemarr, 83–134. This influence is also extremely evident in the recently published collection of Toomer's letters.
6. Early literary histories that served to obscure the contribution of the Young Americans to American modernism included Malcolm Cowley's *Exile's Return* and *A Second Flowering* and Frederick Lewis Allen's *Only Yesterday*. In his introduction to *Structures of the Jazz Age,* Chip Rhodes gives a trenchant critique of several of the myths around American literature of the 1920s that such histories served to promote, particularly the narratives of escape/expatriation and apoliticism that have often marked criticism of this subject. George Hutchinson has made a similar point about the critical fate of the Young Americans; see his foreword to *Jean Toomer: Selected Essays and Literary Criticism,* x.
7. See Diggins's chapter on the "Lyrical Left" in *The American Left in the Twentieth Century*. The best account of the politics and aesthetics of the Young Americans can be found in Casey Nelson Blake's *Beloved Community: The Cultural Criticism of Randolph Bourne, Van Wyck Brooks, Waldo Frank, and Lewis Mumford.*
8. For example, in his registration at the University of Wisconsin he listed himself as a person of "French Cosmopolitan" heritage. See Foley, "Washington" 290. He also described himself as white when registering his daughter at a Quaker school in Pennsylvania in 1947; see Kerman and Eldridge, 292–93.
9. "The Individual in America," box 51, folder 1111, Jean Toomer Papers, James Weldon Johnson Collection, Beinecke Rare Book and Manuscript Library, Yale University (hereafter abbreviated to JTP).
10. George Hutchinson has discussed the significance of theories of cultural pluralism—pioneered by Horace Kallen—on figures such as Alain Locke and the impact this had on Locke's editorial policies as one of the key figures of the Harlem Renaissance. See his *The Harlem Renaissance in Black and White,* 78–93. For a contrasting view, which sees Locke as affiliated not to a sociological practice of cultural pluralism but to a pragmatic pluralism quite different from Kallen's model, see Ross Posnock's *Color and Culture: Black Writers and the Making of the Modern Intellectual,* 185–219. Toomer would famously castigate Alain Locke for including sections of *Cane* in *The New Negro* anthology (1925), allegedly without his permission. See *The Wayward and the Seeking,* 132–33.
11. Anderson outlined this view of national identity and gender most directly in his collection of essays *Perhaps Women* in 1931.
12. "The Negro Renaissance," box 1, folder 10, Wallace Thurman Papers, James Weldon Johnson Collection, Beinecke Library.
13. More recently, Alice Walker has commented that "I could not possibly exist without [*Cane*]." This appears on the cover of the 1993 Liveright reissue of *Cane*.
14. Quoted in Susan Garland Mann's *The Short Story Cycle: A Genre Companion and Reference Guide,* ix.
15. Cowley also offered an incipient contribution to the formal theory of the short story cycle in his review of Faulkner's *Knight's Gambit,* stating that it belonged "to a genre that Faulkner has made peculiarly his own by the artistic success of such earlier volumes as *The Unvanquished* and *Go Down, Moses*." Quoted in Mann, ix–x.

16. For a thorough critical history of the short story cycle and an extensive list of twentieth-century examples of "composite novels," see Dunn and Morris's *The Composite Novel: The Short Story Cycle in Transition.*

17. This is despite recent attempts to introduce alternative terms; Dunn and Morris re-introduced the term "composite novel" to allow for a more flexible formal category, as they felt the term "short story cycle" was unable to accommodate text-pieces that were not short prose fiction. "Composite novel," they argue, is a more inclusive formal category capable of absorbing poetry, history, autobiography, letters, and even recipes into a composite medium whose essential mode is prose fiction. Their contention is that this broadening of terms is necessary; they see it as a way of accommodating the growing number of contemporary works that include nonfiction in their overall design.

18. In addition to Kennedy's article, another notable exception to the "unificatory" tendency in short story criticism is Susan V. Donaldson's "Contending Narratives: *Go Down, Moses* and The Short Story Cycle."

19. Duff comments: "It is probable . . . that the concept of genre will continue to be put in question by more open-ended models of textuality, both those that stress the instability of all linguistic systems and those that emphasise the potentially unlimited scope of intertextuality" (16–17). For two of the most incisive deconstructions of genre of the stripe Duff refers to here, see Jacques Derrida's "The Law of Genre" and Roland Barthes's "From Work to Text."

20. These social understandings are to a considerable degree analogous to Jauss's concept of "horizons of expectation." Jauss's theory of genre has been important for my methodological approach, as I shall discuss later.

21. These are the two dominant trends in the history of genre criticism. For an overview—and critique—of this history, see "Magical Narratives: On the Dialectical Uses of Genre Criticism" in Fredric Jameson's *The Political Unconscious* and "The Sociology of Genres" in Tony Bennett's *Outside Literature.*

22. In choosing the term "pragmatism," however, I do not intend to follow through the rigorous pragmatism of Adena Rosmarin as outlined in *The Power of Genre.* My objections to her method can be best exemplified through her treatment of H. R. Jauss's theory of genre. Rosmarin claims that Jauss's theory, which explains generic codes as a key signifier in the "horizons of expectation" that structure all literary reception, is in fact a diluted form of pragmatism that uses deductive notions of genre but cannot admit that this is the case. Rosmarin goes on to suggest that the benefit of her method lies essentially in its honesty about genre being an inherently deductive concept. Yet arguably what she fails to take sufficient account of is that the concept of genre—whether deductive or not—has always had a significant role to play in the way in which works are written, materially produced, and read. The notion of "genre" may not exist in any rigorously defensible form outside of its particular use in a specific example of critical practice, but genres do have a constitutive function in social interaction and inform a shared range of understanding about literary typology within specific communities of readers and writers. Using inductive conceptions of genre may not be tenable, but examining ways in which genre is socially operative clearly is.

23. The question of whether *Cane* should be considered within a canon of African American literature is a debate that largely falls outside the scope of this argument, although my approach of assessing the interracial debates and contexts surrounding *Cane* with the view of creating a less racially bifurcated picture of literary production in the 1920s clearly has a bearing on this issue. Moreover, it is a debate that has recurred in *Cane*'s critical history, as Toomer's refusal to allow his text to be associated with "Negro" literature indicates. Henry Louis Gates Jr. has usefully considered these questions with reference to *Cane;* see his "The Same Difference: Reading Jean Toomer, 1923–1982," in his *Figures in Black,* 196–224.
24. This review is held in the Beinecke Rare Book and Manuscript Library clippings file on Jean Toomer, classmark JWJ Zan T619 + 1.
25. Benjamin F. McKeever's "*Cane* as Blues" also assesses *Cane* according to the critical parameters of the Black Aesthetic.
26. Quoted in J. Martin Favor's *Authentic Blackness: The Folk in the New Negro Renaissance,* 53.
27. Abdul Janmohammed has discussed the significance of recognition to what he calls the "Manichaean Allegory" of the master-slave relationship, which represents an "ideal context" in which the basic paradigm of desire, namely "to impose oneself on another and be recognized by the other," is fulfilled (20). See also Homi K. Bhabha, "Remembering Fanon," for a detailed assessment of the importance of Manichaean recognition in the process of identity formation within colonialism, an essay that draws extensively on Fanon's *Black Skin, White Masks.* For a selection of the other works that have been significant in my understanding of processes of racialization and of the relationship between race and representation, see Henry Louis Gates Jr., "'Race,' Writing and Difference"; Anthony Appiah, "The Uncompleted Argument: Du Bois and the Illusion of Race"; David Theo Goldberg, *Racist Culture and Racial Subjects: Writing on Race in America;* Felipe Smith, *American Body Politics;* Joel Williamson, *New People: Miscegenation and Mulattoes in the United States;* Kevin K. Gaines, *Uplifting the Race: Black Leadership, Politics, and Culture in the Twentieth Century;* Peter Stallybrass and Allon White, *The Politics and Poetics of Transgression;* Richard Dyer, *White;* Sander L. Gilman, *Difference and Pathology: Stereotypes of Sexuality, Race, and Madness;* Eric Lott, *Love and Theft: Blackface Minstrelsy and the American Working Class;* and Toni Morrison, *Playing in the Dark: Whiteness and the Literary Imagination.*
28. Posnock quotes Michael Lind's *The Next American Nation* here.
29. See Robert B. Jones's edition of *Jean Toomer: Selected Essays and Literary Criticism* and Frederik L. Rusch's *A Jean Toomer Reader: Selected Unpublished Writings.*
30. One good recent example of such a reading is J. Martin Favor's *Authentic Blackness: The Folk in the New Negro Renaissance,* which examines the way in which Toomer interrogates notions of "authentic" black subjectivity in African American intellectual discourse of the time, which tended to configure such subjectivities as rural, southern, and working class. Another is the collection of essays *Jean Toomer and the Harlem Renaissance,* the introduction to which announces "it is

Toomer's complex and contradictory involvement in the intricacies of the identity question that makes him resonate with contemporary preoccupations and provides for infinite readings of his creations" (Feith and Fabre, 9).

31. As Shelley Fisher Fishkin has noted, Ralph Ellison's comment in 1958 about the "true interrelatedness of blackness and whiteness" has only recently been applied to assessments of American identity, culture, and the American cultural field. Since the early 1990s, however, there has been a wealth of research undertaken in this area, which taken together constitutes a "remapping" of American culture (428). Her bibliographic essay provides an excellent introduction to this area.
32. See Kerman and Eldridge, *The Lives of Jean Toomer,* 126.
33. See her *Patterns for America: Modernism and the Concept of Culture.*
34. This link between women and the "natural" life to be found in the rural South is common in early Toomer criticism. For example, Patricia Chase opines, "If it is difficult for us to understand these women, and the way they react, it is because we live in a society and a century in which there is little left which is spontaneous and natural, where plastic reigns supreme god, and where the price of freedom is death" (397). Cancel sees the male/female divide in *Cane* to be absolute; the female characters possess "all the primitive instincts and lust for life that [refuse] to be contained in a sterile and mechanistic world. In contrast to the male, the female in Toomer is rich with sensibility, beauty, and fertility" (419). The most crassly misogynistic comment of this type of criticism, however, must fall to William J. Goede; he feels that Toomer's presentation of women in part 1 "reveal[s] the mystery of the Negro woman: a deep, natural child who, though made for love, should not be unthinkingly violated" (361).
35. See, for example, Alice Walker's assessment that the women in part 1 of *Cane* "seemed to Jean Toomer [like] exquisite butterflies trapped in an evil honey, toiling their lives away in an era, a century, that did not acknowledge them, except as the 'mule of the world.' They dreamed dreams that no one knew—not even themselves, in any coherent fashion—and saw visions that no-one could understand" ("Mothers' Gardens" 232). Nellie Y. McKay has a similar view; see her *Jean Toomer, Artist,* 90–93.
36. See also Laura Doyle's work on the figure of the "race mother" in *Cane,* in her chapter "Swan-Song for the Race Mother: Late Romantic Narrative in *Cane,*" which appears in her *Bordering on the Body: The Racial Matrix of Modern Fiction and Culture.*
37. See Martin Summers, *Manliness and its Discontents: The Black Middle Class and the Transformation of Masculinity, 1900–1930,* 160–66.

1. NARRATIVE, GENDER, AND HISTORY IN *WINESBURG, OHIO*

1. Also pertinent to this discussion is Robert Kraft's unpublished thesis, "Sherwood Anderson, Bisexual Bard: Some Chapters in a Literary Biography" (1969). While clearly of its time and therefore without the insights of feminist, gay, or queer theory on the nature of gendered identity, the significance of

homosociality both to Anderson's sense of masculinity and his self-conception as an artist is clearly brought out in his discussion (see chap. 1 in particular).

2. One of Chauncey's insights is that the hetero/homosexual binary—definitions determined by sexual object choice—is a categorization of sexuality that has been dominant in the United States only since the Second World War. Before this, which gender one "acted" was the primary determinant, which as Chauncey explains meant that many men had sexual encounters with other men without ever feeling their masculinity had been threatened. See his *Gay New York: Gender, Urban Culture, and the Making of the Gay Male World, 1890–1940,* and his earlier "Christian Brotherhood or Sexual Perversion? Homosexual Identities and the Construction of Social Boundaries in the World War I Era." For a similar thesis, but applied to early twentieth-century British society, see John Marshall's "Pansies, Perverts and Macho Men: Changing Conceptions of Male Homosexuality," particularly 134–37. For a shorter account of the growth of visible gay subcultures in U.S. cities at the turn of the century, see John D'Emilio and Estelle B. Freedman's *Intimate Matters: A History of Sexuality in America,* 223–35.
3. Also relevant to this discussion is Sharon R. Ullmann's work on the popularity of female impersonators on the Vaudeville circuit in the early twentieth century, particularly the celebrity of Julian Eltinge. She argues that "impersonation seemed to offer men the opportunity to take power over representations of femininity" but that the performers had to continually police and reinforce the boundaries between performance and "reality" to avoid charges that they themselves were becoming feminized, charges that normally spelled disaster for their careers. She finds that Eltinge's success was due in no small part to his ability to have a high media profile outside of his performances, a profile that stressed an aggressive and heterosexual masculinity (53).
4. See their *Before Stonewall: The Making of a Gay and Lesbian Community;* see also D'Emilio and Freedman, 228.
5. Anderson's choice of "Little Eva" as a name also recalls the child-heroine in Harriet Beecher Stowe's *Uncle Tom's Cabin;* her death scene has been seen as an archetypal moment of Victorian sentimentality. Not only was this a female name, then, but it had connections to what Anderson doubtlessly perceived as the excesses and "inauthenticity" of Victorian sentimentality and mass culture, both of which (as Ann Douglas has argued) were intimately involved with Modernist complaints about the "feminization of culture." The use of the name therefore suggests feelings of self-abasement by adopting the name of a woman, a pejorative view of female influence on cultural production, and arguably a view of mass culture as "feminized" and thus degraded. See Douglas's "The Legacy of American Victorianism: The Meaning of Little Eva," in *The Feminization of American Culture.*
6. Sherwood Anderson to Waldo Frank, Feb. 1919. Box 1, folder 15, Sherwood Anderson Collection, Newberry Library, Chicago (hereafter abbreviated to SAC). In all letters quoted from archival material, the spelling has been silently corrected, unless the reading is conjectural.
7. For assessments of Lawrence's sexual politics and the history of their reception, see Helen Simpson's *D. H. Lawrence and Feminism* and Drew Milne's

"Lawrence and the Politics of Sexual Politics." For an interesting view of Lawrence's investigation of the sublimation of homosexual desire within the army, a topic to which Anderson was drawn on several occasions, see Hugh Stevens's "Sex and the Nation: 'The Prussian Officer' and *Women in Love*." For a classic account treating Lawrence's ideal of sexuality as a critique of industrial capitalism, which contains much that is also applicable to Anderson, see Raymond Williams's chapter on him in *Culture and Society, 1780–1950,* 199–213. For comparisons between Anderson and Lawrence, see Irving Howe's chapter "In the Lawrentian Orbit" in his *Sherwood Anderson* and also Armin Arnold's *D. H. Lawrence and America,* 172–73. Wyndham Lewis discussed them together in unfavorable terms (particularly with respect to Anderson) in criticizing their primitivistic views; see the selection from *Paleface* in *Enemy Salvoes: Selected Literary Criticism,* 118–31.

8. "Small Black Notebook #2," SAC folder W-39, box 1. In the review of D. H. Lawrence's *Assorted Articles,* entitled "A Man's Mind," Anderson returned to this point, remarking "You young men . . . you want to know about the machine age . . . what it is doing to men . . . the way out. Here is a man who found a way out. He lived" (22).
9. Elsewhere in an unpublished autobiography Anderson recalled going flower picking and subsequently being ridiculed as a "sissy" by a friend. He retorted to the friend that "it was only men who were somewhat in doubt of their own maleness who were afraid of sissiness." "Book of Days." SAC box W-9, folder 5.
10. A similar argument about drag is made by Garber in "Spare Parts: The Surgical Construction of Gender," 239–42.
11. Dollimore has discussed the work of Leo Bersani in regard to gendered associations of passivity and activity. Bersani had identified similarities between fears of male homosexuals with AIDS in the 1980s with those voiced about venereal disease in female prostitutes in the nineteenth century; Dollimore suggests that this evinces patriarchal culture's fear of passive, promiscuous sexuality and indeed treats it as a metaphor for self-destruction (*Dissidence* 263). This echoes some of Chauncey's work about gay subculture before the war—that masculine sexuality was organized around "the phallocentric presumption that a man's sexual satisfaction was more significant than the gender or character of the person who provided that satisfaction" through being penetrated (*Gay New York* 85).
12. This is an assumption Sandra M. Gilbert has discussed within her examination of a strand of misogynist thought about authorship that allocates "generative literary power" exclusively to men. Gilbert observes that, within this tradition, often "if a woman lacks generative literary power, then a man who loses or abuses such power becomes like a woman" (490). For an alternative discussion on sexual role and its relation to writing in Anderson's work, see D. Sebastian's dissertation, "Sherwood Anderson's Theory of Art."
13. Toril Moi's gloss on Cixous is instructive: "Proper—property—appropriate: signalling an emphasis on self-identity, self-aggrandisement and arrogative dominance, these words aptly characterize the logic of the proper according to Cixous" (110–11).
14. JTP box 3, folder 84.

15. See Gilman's *Difference and Pathology: Stereotypes of Sexuality, Race, and Madness.*
16. Similar episodes occur in "Death," "The New Englander," "Death in the Woods," and "Like a Queen."
17. Several critics have made this assumption. See Rigsbee, 184; Papinchak, 24; Simolke, 59.
18. Wolfgang Iser has also discussed a variant on what Eco terms "inferential walks"; Iser talks in terms of the reader having to surmount the blockage of expected connections within a text, noting that "whenever the flow is interrupted and we are led off in unexpected directions, the opportunity is given to us to bring into play our own faculty for establishing connections—for filling in the gaps left by the text itself." It is in this process that "the dynamics of reading are revealed" (79–80).
19. Considerations of *Winesburg, Ohio* as a Kunslerroman or a Bildungsroman are given in Irving Howe's *Sherwood Anderson,* 102; see also Ray Lewis White's *Winesburg, Ohio: An Exploration,* 44–45. For a more critical approach to establishing "self-centered" narrative continuity in the short story cycle through the Bildungsroman tradition, see Sandra A. Zagrell, "Narrative of Community: The Identification of a Genre," 513.
20. For a similar argument, see Colquitt, "Motherlove," 95–97.
21. This foregrounding of the reading process provoked by *Winesburg, Ohio*'s use of the short story cycle genre recalls Wolfgang Iser's comments on the formal strategies of modernism; he remarked that "they are often so fragmentary that one's attention is almost exclusively occupied with the search for connections between the fragments; the object of this is not to complicate the 'spectrum' of connections, so much as to make us aware of the nature of our own capacity for making links. In such cases, the text refers back directly to our own preconceptions—which are revealed by the act of interpretation that is a basic element of the reading process" (80).
22. See Ray Lewis White's introduction to *Marching Men* for a consideration of the time of its composition.
23. The politics of *Marching Men* have unsurprisingly prompted disquiet among Anderson's critics. As Ditsky notes, "if *Marching Men* is meant to warn us about fascism—or totalitarianism by any name—then it is we who provide the counter-argument. Not Anderson" (113–14).
24. See David Forgacs, "Fascism, Violence and Modernity" 10–15; and Sandra M. Gilbert and Susan Gubar, *No Man's Land: The Place of the Women Writer in the Twentieth-Century,* 22, for assessments of the gender politics of Modernist associations with proto-fascism at this time. Anderson's position here partially validates claims that many of the emergent modernisms of this period were expressly misogynistic, that the aesthetics of many male authors were geared to gendering modernism as masculine. This is the argument of Ann Douglas in *Terrible Honesty: Mongrel Manhattan in the 1920s,* which contends that the impulse of much of American modernism was "matricidal," aimed at the rejection and supplanting of a "feminized" Victorian literary culture. See also Gilbert and Gubar's chapter "Tradition and the Female Talent: Modernism and Masculinism."

25. In particular, Forgacs discusses Giovanni Papini, who converted to Catholicism during the war in a crisis of guilt over his earlier opinions (13).
26. Christopher Looby's comments on the military and its negotiation of homosociality and homosexuality are pertinent here; he remarks that "*esprit de corps* or *camaraderie* of the group effectively absorbs and redirects the homoerotic energy that otherwise might find direct sexual expression. . . . the military context coercively *prescribes* the intensification of male-homosocial affective attachments, while at the same time it punishingly *proscribes* the physical expression of homosexual desires. It thus excites male-male emotional bonding to the highest pitch of intensity short of avowed homosexual love . . ." (75).
27. Many historians have examined the links between the First World War and gender identity. Important for my understanding have been Michael C. C. Adams, *The Great Adventure: Male Desire and the Coming of World War One;* Paul Fussell, *The Great War and Modern Memory;* Elaine Showalter, "Male Hysteria: W. H. R. Rivers and the Lessons of Shell Shock"; Donald J. Mroezek, "The Habit of Victory: the American Military and the Cult of Manliness"; T. J. Jackson Lears, "The Destructive Element: Modern Commercial Society and the Martial Ideal," in his *No Place of Grace: Antimodernism and the Transformation of American Culture 1880–1920;* Joanna Bourke, *Dismembering the Male: Men's Bodies, Britain, and the Great War;* and Sheila Rowbotham, *A Century of Women: The History of Women in Britain and the United States,* 64–118. See also the special issue of *Modernism/Modernity* devoted to the first world war and gender (vol. 9, Jan. 2002).
28. See Waldo Frank's essay of the same title, published in the *Seven Arts* in 1916.
29. For the effect of the war on American socialism, see John P. Diggins, *The American Left in the Twentieth Century,* 73–106; Richard Edwards's chapter "Until the Battle is Fairly Won: The Crisis of Control in the Firm," in his *Contested Terrain: The Transformation of the Workplace in the Twentieth Century,* 48–71; and David M. Kennedy's *Over Here: The First World War and American Society,* 258–79.
30. Historical contextualizations of *Winesburg, Ohio* have tended to examine the detrimental effect on community caused by the expansion of industrialized production in the 1890s. See J. Gerald Kennedy's "From Anderson's *Winesburg* to Carver's *Cathedral:* The Short Story Sequence and the Semblance of Community"; Thomas Yingling's "*Winesburg, Ohio* and the End of Collective Experience"; and Glen A. Love's "*Winesburg, Ohio* and the Rhetoric of Silence."
31. Silverman's precise definition of history is "a force capable of tearing a hole in the fabric of the dominant fiction, and so of disrupting its internal economy. In short, I will identify it with *trauma*" (116).

2. SHERWOOD ANDERSON AND PRIMITIVISM

1. Jerome Blum was a Chicago-born painter and friend of Anderson's; this letter was sent in early July 1920. *Letters of Sherwood Anderson,* 55–57.
2. Recent work assessing Anderson's links with these figures, and with other "Young Americans," includes Casey Nelson Blake's *Beloved Community: The*

Cultural Criticism of Randolph Bourne, Van Wyck Brooks, Waldo Frank and Lewis Mumford; George Hutchinson's chapter "Cultural Nationalism and the Lyrical Left" in his *The Harlem Renaissance in Black and White;* and Susan Hegeman's *Patterns for America: Modernism and the Concept of Culture.*

3. To H. L. Mencken, June 25, 1922. Quoted in David Levering Lewis's *When Harlem Was in Vogue,* 99. The original letter is in the H. L. Mencken Collection at the New York Public Library.
4. Primitivism correlated closely to the eight "ideas" characterizing the belief system of Greenwich Village Bohemians that Cowley lists in *Exile's Return,* 60. However, Cowley gives a dismissive—and conventional—account of primitivism when he remarks that it was a form of escapism, a faddish desperation that explained "the enthusiasm of tired intellectuals for Negro dances and music, the spirituals, the blues, Black Bottom and *The Emperor Jones*" (236).
5. For example, Torgovnick devotes a chapter to Freud and Bronislaw Malinowski in her *Gone Primitive: Savage Intellects, Modern Lives;* Julian Stallabrass considers Freud and several British anthropologists, as well as Margaret Mead, in his "The Idea of the Primitive: British Art and Anthropology 1918–1930"; and Ann Douglas also briefly considers these contexts in her *Terrible Honesty: Mongrel Manhattan in the 1920s.*
6. Susan Hegeman discusses the role of anthropology in making American culture "visible": See her *Patterns for America: Modernism and the Concept of Culture,* especially chapter 2: "Dry Salvages: Spatiality, Nationalism, and the Invention of a "National" Culture." The degree to which Boas's theoretical framework represented complete "cultural relativism" is often questioned; as Handler notes, he refused to countenance scientific discourse as carrying the potential for ethnocentrism. Hegeman describes his position as "moral relativism" (7).
7. The *locus classicus* for this type of critique remains Edward Said's *Orientalism.* See also James Clifford, *The Predicament of Culture: Twentieth-Century Ethnography, Literature, and Art,* 4; and his introduction to *Writing Culture: The Poetics and Politics of Ethnography,* 23–24.
8. Quoted in Torgovnick, 201.
9. Larsen's text deals very differently with the issue of primitivism than the white writers mentioned, and it is important to briefly indicate why. In a novel centrally concerned with how black female sexuality can be adequately recognized and delimited after centuries of abuse and commercialization, the quotation above represents only a temporary and unsustainable release for Helga's sexual energies. Far more significant is Helga's trip to Denmark, a trip in which she is treated as a "primitive" curiosity and through this discourse becomes objectified as a figure of male fantasy. As a result, Larsen's text prefigures Huggins's point that "for the purposes of ethnic identity, primitivism is particularly limited. It is especially a male fantasy" (188).
10. Anderson, of course, was not the only white American writer to be linked with primitivism or to be repeatedly drawn to primitivistic representations of African Americans. Others included Hart Crane, e. e. cummings, Waldo Frank, Eugene O'Neill, and Carl Van Vechten, as well as "professional primitivists" such as DuBose Heyward, Julia Peterkin, Clement Wood, and Paul Green.

11. The "racetrack stories" comprise "I Want to Know Why," "I'm a Fool," "The Man Who Became a Woman," and "An Ohio Pagan." All appeared in *Horses and Men* (1923) aside from "I Want to Know Why," which appeared in *The Triumph of the Egg* (1921).
12. Anderson to Crane, n.d., 1920, SAC box 2, folder 3.
13. Anderson to Waldo Frank, n.d., 1920. SAC box 2, folder 6; and Elizabeth Anderson and Gerald R. Kelly, *Miss Elizabeth: A Memoir*, 72. Elizabeth Anderson goes on to remark that "Sherwood had a deep and affectionate feeling for Negroes but not, I think, the kind that would be acceptable in these times" (72).
14. See Darwin T. Turner, "An Intersection of Paths: Correspondence between Jean Toomer and Sherwood Anderson," and Anderson's own "Negro Singing."
15. See Sander L. Gilman, *Difference and Pathology: Stereotypes of Sexuality, Race, and Madness*, especially chapter 1: "What Are Stereotypes and Why Do We Use Them?"
16. This echoes a point made by Terry Eagleton about F. R. Leavis and *Scrutiny* in the 1930s; see his *Literary Theory: An Introduction*, 36.
17. *Evening Standard*, July 20, 1922.
18. For example, he wrote to Marietta Finley on November 23, 1917, that "within me there is much of the primitive, the thing that could kill or save. The dreary time of the asking of questions passes and for a moment I stand forth, a naked man in a world clothed and choked by custom and habits of thought." *Letters to Bab*, 87.
19. See Hoffman's chapter "Sherwood Anderson" in his *Freudianism and the Literary Mind*. In a newspaper interview in 1925 Anderson stated, "Psychology? Never read a book on it in my life." *Toledo Blade*, Nov. 19, 1925, 3.
20. See Kim Townsend's discussion of Anderson's relationship with Burrow and how this is represented in "Seeds," in *Sherwood Anderson*, 138–41.
21. George Hutchinson has discussed this aspect of Whitman's cultural nationalism and its relevance to sexual liberation in the 1920s avant-garde; see his *The Harlem Renaissance in Black and White*, 109–10.
22. Good assessments of the Young Americans and their relationship with the "Lyrical Left" can be found in Diggins's *The American Left in the Twentieth Century*, 73–106; see also Hutchinson's chapter on "The Lyrical Left and Cultural Nationalism" in his *The Harlem Renaissance in Black and White;* Hegeman's discussions of Waldo Frank and Van Wyck Brooks in her *Patterns for America: Modernism and the Concept of Culture;* Helge Norman Nilsen's assessment of Frank in his "Waldo Frank and the Idea of America"; and Scruggs and VanDemarr's discussion of Frank's *Our America* in their *Jean Toomer and the Terrors of American History*, 85–100. The best treatment, however, is Blake's *Beloved Community: The Cultural Criticism of Randolph Bourne, Van Wyck Brooks, Waldo Frank, and Lewis Mumford.*
23. Hegeman has discussed Brooks's attachment to Arnold's formulation of culture, 72–76. However, despite this attachment, Brooks recognized the potential for Arnold's formulation to become merely a demarcation of class identity rather than a genuine force for social regeneration. See his "The Culture of Industrialism," 196–97.

24. The widespread support for the eugenics movement was very diverse, as were the political opinions of those scientists and public figures most closely involved with it. Equally, "eugenic" was a nebulously defined term that was employed in a variety of different contexts. For a more rounded and detailed picture than I am able to give here, see Marouf Arif Hasian Jr., *The Rhetoric of Eugenics in Anglo-American Thought;* Daniel Kevles, *In the Name of Eugenics: Genetics and the Uses of Human Heredity;* Ian Dowbiggin, *Keeping America Sane: Psychiatry and Eugenics in the United States and Canada, 1880–1940,* especially chapters 2 and 4; Martin S. Pernick, "Defining the Defective: Eugenics, Aesthetics, and Mass Culture in Early Twentieth-Century America"; and Diane B. Paul, *Controlling Human Heredity 1865 to the Present,* especially 97–114.
25. Stoddard's remarkable broadside against the contemporary arts echoed criticisms Max Nordau had made against early modernist writers in his 1883 text, *Degeneration*. The avant-garde in both texts is expressly linked to degenerate or atavistic bodies; Stoddard accounts for the "Lure of the Primitive" expressed in the writings of Rousseau and Tolstoy by maintaining that Rousseau was "born of unsound stock" and that Tolstoy came from "eccentric stock" (119–21).
26. In using the term "hard-line," taken from Marouf Arif Hasian Jr., I refer to those figures who supported policies of "negative" or coercive eugenics such as the sterilization of the "unfit" and statutory prohibition on miscegenation: they also tended to support a reduction in social welfare budgets for the underprivileged, and tough immigration control. This is in contrast to those who merely advocated an awareness of hereditary factors when selecting a marital partner (so-called "positive" eugenics). Hasian, 68.
27. As early as 1916 Walter Lippmann was criticizing Brooks for his "preoccupation with America's intellectual deficiencies" (Paul F. Bourke, 195). This was also Frank's criticism of him (*Our America* 197). See also Hegeman, 73–76, and for a more positive assessment of Brooks's theories, Blake, 113–21. In a 1924 letter Anderson remarked to Paul Rosenfeld, *apropos* of Brooks's two biographies (of Mark Twain and Henry James), that "unlike Brooks I cannot feed myself on other men's failures" (*Letters* 130).
28. See, for example, Frank's chapter "The Land of the Buried Cultures" in *Our America,* and Randolph Bourne's "Trans-National America."
29. Notably, for an example of how Anderson's construction of race was integral to his conceptualization of gender—an issue I shall return to later—he continues this letter: "When you get at your Mark Twain . . . you must do a chapter on the American going East into that thin, tired, New England atmosphere and being conquered by its feminine force" (43).
30. "Negro Singing Again." SAC box W-37, folder 4.
31. Both Yingling and J. Gerald Kennedy discuss the significance of Benjamin's theory to the nostalgia Anderson generates around the practice of storytelling in *Winesburg, Ohio.* As Michael Kimmel has noted, much of the discussion about masculinity in the era was marked by such antimodernism and nostalgia. See his *Manhood in America,* 81–221.
32. Carby also gives the salutary caution that the brutal and ritualistic practice of lynching must "be recognized as the ever-present underside of artistic or

philosophical imaginings of black masculinity as tropes of utopian possibility" (*Race Men* 47). As I shall investigate later in this chapter, Anderson's "utopian" models of black masculinity had their own underside of anxiety and fear which found expression in destructive fantasy.

33. As I mention in chapter 2, Anderson's patriarchalism has been roundly, and rightly, criticized. Recent works on Anderson and gender include Marilyn Judith Atlas, "Sherwood Anderson and the Women of Winesburg"; Nancy Bunge, "Women in Sherwood Anderson's Fiction," and T. J. Jackson Lears, "Sherwood Anderson: Looking for the White Spot." In many ways Anderson's thinking reflects what Carrigan, Connell, and Lee have identified as "one dimension of the recent politics of capitalism," namely "a struggle about the modernization of hegemonic masculinity" (599).
34. Casey Nelson Blake notes that "In his political and cultural criticism of the 1880s and 1890s, Morris insisted that the craft tradition . . . would have to inform a qualitatively new organization of labor if socialism were to mean more than a change in administrators. By making the reintegration of art and labor, of culture and society, his highest goal, Morris offered Brooks a radical lineage that both sought an organic synthesis of aesthetic, moral, and practical experience and challenged the fundamental premises of industrial capitalism" (109). As he observes elsewhere, all of the Young Americans decried the "industrial division of labor, which, in destroying craft, had separated practical activity from the creative imagination" (230).
35. "Negro Singing Again." SAC box W-37, folder 4.
36. For discussions of such stereotypes, see Michael Kimmel, 90–94; Felipe Smith, 37–47; and Gail Bederman, 16–23.
37. Anderson's distinction between these two words is not as conceptually clear as Bederman's (unsurprisingly), but he did display different attitudes toward them. In an essay on D. H. Lawrence, he commented, "I think, and have always thought, that is what talent is . . . it's manhood . . . the essence of manhood . . . masculinity if you please" (*No Swank* 100). This rather offhand dismissal of the term "masculinity" seems to imply that Anderson regarded it as faddish, devoid of a type of moral dignity he associated with "manliness."
38. Anderson to Paul Rosenfeld, August 19, 1922. SAC An Ap 11 (7).
39. Morrison discusses this last point; after discussing the centrality of individualism to the American sense of self, she notes, "Eventually individualism fuses with the prototype of Americans as solitary, alienated, and malcontent. What, one wants to ask, are Americans alienated from? What are Americans always so insistently innocent of? Different from? As for absolute power, over whom is this power held, from who withheld, to whom distributed? Answers to these questions lie in the potent and ego-reinforcing presence of an Africanist population" (45).
40. For example, Anderson wrote to Jerry and Lucile Blum in late 1920 that "I know you'll both get a story and a damn big one out of the nigger. He's somebody nobody knows a hell of a lot about yet." SAC box 2, folder 5.
41. Eric Lott, *Love and Theft: Blackface Minstrelsy and the American Working Class;* Langston Hughes, "Big Meeting," 1625.

42. "The South," 61; *Southern Odyssey,* 197.
43. Douglas, *Terrible Honesty;* Hutchinson, *The Harlem Renaissance in Black and White;* Lemke, *Primitivist Modernism.* For a more critical argument about the ways in which white modernism defined its own radical nature through the appropriation of black cultural forms—specifically speech—see Michael North's *The Dialect of Modernism.*
44. "Negro Singing Again." SAC box W-37, folder 4.
45. Dyer notes that "it was not spirituality or soul that is held to distinguish whites, but what we might call 'spirit': get up and go, aspiration, awareness of the highest reaches of intellectual comprehension and aesthetic refinement" (*White,* 23). The ability of the "spirit" to transcend the body is also advanced to whiteness alone.
46. This of course has relation to Judith Butler's theory of performativity, her view of gender as a type of citationality; she sees performativity as "always a reiteration of a norm or set of norms, and to the extent that it acquires an act-like status in the present, it conceals or dissimulates the conventions of which it is a repetition" (12).
47. As Kadlec has discussed, Hurston believed "'Negro folklore' was vibrant not because it was authentic or indigenous to any people or place but because it was '*still* in the making'" (482).
48. The Boas-trained anthropologist Melville Herskovits offers a basic definition of this shift, from the Arnoldian sense of "culture" to one of culture as social practice: "By the word culture I do not mean the refinements of our particular civilization which the word has come to connote, but simply those elements of the environment which are the handiwork of man himself" ("Americanism" 356). This issue of shifting definitions of "culture" is explained in much fuller detail in Hegeman's *Patterns for America.*
49. Schuyler, "Negro-Art Hokum," 97; Herskovits, "Father" 353.
50. Ann Douglas discusses the dance pioneer Martha Graham, a resident of Greenwich Village in the 1920s, in this context. One of Graham's frequent sayings was "Bodies never lie"; she also declared that dancing was "animal in its source." She studied "Indian and Negro dances" to develop her choreography, and "she was the first amongst the pioneers of modern dance to include people of colour in her dance troupe" (*Terrible Honesty* 51–52). Sieglinde Lemke also discusses the significance of dancing to primitivism in the 1920s with a discussion of the aesthetics of Josephine Baker's *Danse Sauvage.* See chapter 4.
51. For example, as Anderson wrote to Jean Toomer, "The negro life was outside me, had to remain outside me" (Turner, "Intersection" 107).
52. Žižek has discussed this in relation to ethnic conflict in eastern Europe; he argues that the consolidation of a sense of group identity—whether racial or national—is often premised on a feeling of shared enjoyment but an enjoyment that resists precise definition and that is particular only to that group, a force he calls the "nation Thing." The function of the "Other" in this paradigm is both the threat that "they" may steal "our" enjoyment and the "peculiar way it organises its enjoyment: precisely the surplus, the 'excess' that pertains to it—the smell of their food, their 'noisy' songs and dances, their strange manners, their attitude to work" (54).

53. For example, Jerome Blum wrote to Anderson in 1920 that "you can walk around quite nude and let your body have a great time. . . . [the indigenous population] are really *grandes enfants*—they have no reason for anything they just act because it is the thing to do. . . . dates mean nothing to them, nor time nor place." Jerome Blum to Sherwood Anderson, SAC box 4, folder 45. Anderson, a lifelong admirer of Gauguin, in 1931 wrote a review of Beril Becker's biography of the artist, *Paul Gauguin: The Calm Madman*. See Enniss, "Sherwood Anderson and Paul Gauguin: A Forgotten Review."
54. Anderson to Frank, n.d., winter 1920–Jan. 1921. SAC box 2, folder 7. Anderson to Frank, n.d., early 1920. SAC box 2, folder 2.
55. Felipe Smith argues that "if national history builds on the dynamics of ethnic communities thrust into conflicts over space, the prevailing modes of distinguishing 'us' from 'them' will necessarily shape the imagined nation" (35). One such mode is to imagine the different ethnic groups occupying different *times*. Accordingly, in late nineteenth century racial discourse it was argued that African Americans occupied an earlier stage of evolutionary time, one that had not progressed into individuation. This separation in times was therefore used to argue for the separation of bodies, i.e., segregation. Smith calls this technology the application of "undifferentiated difference" (44–46).
56. Toomer wrote this to Waldo Frank in January 1923. However, even before then—albeit to different people—Toomer was expressing his doubts about Anderson. On November 4, 1922, he wrote to Gorham Munson that "Anderson is all prose, not a thought one can bite into. . . . If his creativity is thinning to a middle-aged pleasure in rambling, soft-toned words, well, he is still readable" (*Letters* 93).
57. The phrase is Randolph Bourne's, from "Trans-National America." See Casey Nelson Blake, introduction.
58. Michael North, in a fascinating reading of the craze for all things Egyptian following the excavations of Tutankhamen's tomb in 1922, sees the use of an "exotic" past within a consumerist economy as typical of the cultural network of the age: "[I]t is . . . obvious that the 'aura' thus preserved to [the excavated objects] was consumed in the very process of celebration, that the unique, the traditional, the sacred, the old very quickly became the new, the secular, and the manufactured—so quickly, in fact, that interest in them was almost immediately exhausted." This—in true modernist style, and typical of both "high" and "mass" culture in 1922—makes "the past . . . nothing more than a magazine of references useful only in that ironically infinitesimal moment when their past obscurity is perfectly balanced against their coming banality" (*Reading 1922,* 24, 26).
59. To Burton Emmett, Nov. 10, 1930. *Selected Letters*, 128. *Dark Laughter* was his best-selling book on publication and made him $8,057.63 for the 21,487 copies sold by December. Two years later Liveright Publishing Co. listed sales of 28,681 copies of the regular edition and 15,043 of the reprint. See James Schevill, *Sherwood Anderson: His Life and Work,* 208.
60. "I Build My House." SAC box 11, folder W-22.
61. Nathan Huggins discusses this aspect of *Banjo,* as well as the novel's significance for African nationalist intellectuals. See his *Harlem Renaissance,* 172–78.

A fine discussion of Banjo's critique of nationalism, international capitalism, and Western civilization can be found in Brent Hayes Edwards's *The Practice of Diaspora,* 187–240.

62. This was particularly true of Charlotte Osgood Mason, patron at one time or another to Langston Hughes, Zora Neale Hurston, Alain Locke, Aaron Douglas, and others. For a discussion of her relationships with—and demands upon—these writers, see Lewis, 151–55, 256–59. Hughes presented a fictional version of Mason in his story "The Blues I'm Playing."
63. Gorham Munson wrote to Jean Toomer as early as November 11, 1922, that "I have never been an Andersonian, though for a long time I could not make up my mind either to accept or reject him. At length, I decided upon rejection. I believe now that there is taking place a very marked shift in his audiences. Louis Untermeyer, who has written enthusiastically about Anderson, also congratulated me warmly upon my letter [to the *New Republic*, criticizing Anderson] and my friend, Hart Crane, who positively worshipped the man, is balking at *Many Marriages.* On the other hand, A. is now selling stories at tremendous prices to *Harper's* and *Pictorial Review.*" JTP box 6, folder 183.
64. See De Lauretis, 112. Also see Peter Brooks's *Reading for the Plot,* 103–4, for a discussion of false endings.
65. Torgovnick also discusses this trope of immanent demise; it is often found within anthropology as a mode of self-justification, investing the task of "preserving" a culture with an immediacy in which urgent action is the only way of countering the imminent disappearance of the culture under observation (184). This also tends towards the static, and objectified, view of culture I discussed earlier as a recurrent feature of primitivist representation. Marcus and Fischer have remarked that the "narrative motif of salvage . . . is so important in the justification of anthropology as a modern scientific endeavor" (134).
66. Hurston uses this trope of salvage as a legitimation for her own exercise in her study of African-American folktales and Hoodoo practices in the South, *Mules and Men.* In that text, when asked by one of the locals why she is collecting the "lies" that the black community of Eatonville enjoy telling each other on the store porch in the evening, she replies, "We want to set them down before it's too late. . . . Before everybody forgets all of 'em" (24). However, as my earlier discussion of her commitment to a dynamic view of African American culture illustrates, this view must be seen as largely conditioned by the particular anthropological discourse within which she was working at Barnard College at the time. Jean Toomer, too, claimed that the lyrical beauty of the southern African American cultural tradition presented in *Cane* represented a "swan song": "The folk-spirit was walking in to die in the modern desert. That spirit was so beautiful. Its death was so tragic" (*Wayward* 123). Schuyler's *Black No More* imagines the invention of a machine that is able to convert black people into white, resulting in the almost total "whitening" of the African American population. Felipe Smith discusses white supremacist fantasies of racial death in chapter 1 of his *American Body Politics.*
67. For a similar discussion of African American racial extinction through absorption into whiteness, see *Sherwood Anderson's Memoirs: A Critical Edition,* 471.

68. The African American population of Chicago increased by 148.2 percent between 1910 and 1920, from 44,103 to 108,458, with the majority of the migrants arriving after 1917. By 1930, the figure was 233,903. See David Levering Lewis, 20, and Theodore Kornweibel's "An Economic Profile of Black Life in the Twenties," 309. Also see James R. Grossman's *Land of Hope: Chicago, Black Southerners, and the Great Migration,* particularly 3–9.
69. Anderson to Alfred Stieglitz, Nov. 10, 1923. Alfred Stieglitz/Georgia O'Keeffe Archive, Beinecke Rare Book and Manuscript Library. YCAL Mss. 85, box 2, folder 37.
70. See Felipe Smith, chapter 4.
71. In *Sherwood Anderson's Notebook,* he describes being told an anecdote by a white southern man about the abduction and mutilation of a black man falsely accused of assaulting a white woman.

3. DOUBLE DEALING IN THE SOUTH

1. Assessments of Frank's *Our America* can be found in Hegeman, chapter 4; Walter Benn Michaels's *Our America: Nativism, Modernism, and Pluralism,* 135–36; and Robert L. Perry's *The Shared Vision of Waldo Frank and Hart Crane,* 5–16. The excellent analysis of how Toomer absorbed the arguments of *Our America,* given in Scruggs and VanDemarr's *Jean Toomer and the Terrors of American History,* informs much of this section (83–108).
2. See George W. Stocking Jr.'s "The Ethnographic Sensibility of the 1920s and the Dualism of the Anthropological Tradition" for a discussion of ethnographical fieldwork in the American Southwest in the 1910s and 1920s. Particularly significant was the fieldwork of Boasian anthropologists such as Ruth Benedict, Elsie Clews Parsons, and Robert Redfield.
3. Frank to Anderson, Oct. 19, 1920. SAC box 10, folder 26.
4. Frank to Anderson, Dec. 1920. SAC box 10, folder 36.
5. Frank to Stieglitz, Mar. 14, 1920. Alfred Stieglitz Collection, Beinecke Rare Book and Manuscript Library. YCAL Mss. 85, box 19, folder 445.
6. Assessments of their relationship can be found in Kathryne V. Lindberg's "Raising Cane on the Theoretical Plane: Jean Toomer's Racial Personae"; Michael North's account in *The Dialect of Modernism: Race, Language, and Twentieth-Century Literature,* 162–74; and, for the fullest account, Scruggs and VanDemarr's *Jean Toomer and the Terrors of American History,* 82–134.
7. Draft Fragment. JTP, box 48, folder 1010.
8. "Outline of the Story of the Autobiography," 60–61. Draft, n.d. JTP box 20, folder 514.
9. This assessment of cultural pluralism is at the center of Walter Benn Michaels's argument about racism in American modernism in his *Our America: Nativism, Modernism, and Pluralism.* See also Werner Sollors's "A Critique of Pure Pluralism."
10. See Duffey's *The Chicago Renaissance in American Letters,* particularly his chapter "The Dispersal," 258–62; Dale Kramer's *Chicago Renaissance: The Literary Life in the Midwest 1900–1930,* especially his chapter "War Troubles and After," 309–30; and also Eric Homburger's "Chicago and New York: Two

Versions of American Modernism." Malcolm Cowley discusses the phenomenon of generational difference within Greenwich Village, and the distinctions he noticed between pre-1917 and post-1917 bohemia (66–73).

11. For critical histories of the *Double Dealer,* see Thomas Bonner Jr.'s "The *Double Dealer* and the Little-Magazine Tradition in New Orleans"; Violet Harrington Bryan's *The Myth of New Orleans in Literature: Dialogues of Race and Gender,* chapter 4; and Frances Jean Bowden's "The New Orleans *Double Dealer* 1921–1926, a Critical History." For considerations of Anderson's relationship to New Orleans, see Walter B. Rideout's "'The Most Cultural Town in America': Sherwood Anderson and New Orleans," and Kim Townsend's *Sherwood Anderson,* 185–202.
12. JTP box 3, folder 84.
13. *Double Dealer* 7: 91–99.
14. Hegeman's study is the most detailed assessment of the links between anthropology and the literary figures of American modernism. On Boas's significance to the Harlem Renaissance, see George Hutchinson's chapter "The Americanization of 'Race' and 'Culture'" in his *The Harlem Renaissance in Black and White;* work dealing with the textuality of ethnography includes Krupat's *Ethnocriticism,* James Clifford's *The Predicament of Culture: Twentieth-Century Ethnography, Literature, and Art,* and *Writing Culture: The Politics and Poetics of Ethnography,* ed. Clifford and Marcus.
15. Clifford outlines six features which characterized the new ethnography's claims to authority; see *Predicament,* 30–32.
16. For fuller accounts of the development of participant observation as the major methodology for ethnological fieldwork in the 1920s, as well as the way in which it constituted its authority, see Clifford, *Predicament,* 21–54. For discussions of Malinowski and Mead, see also George W. Stocking Jr.'s *The Ethnographer's Magic and Other Essays in the History of Anthropology,* 40–59, 239–75, and Torgovnick, 227–43.
17. Walter Benn Michaels's thesis in his *Our America: Nativism, Modernism, and Pluralism* is pertinent here. He argues that a culture only becomes viewed as "authentically" belonging to a person when it is based on grounds outside of culture, which in the 1920s was predominantly race. Therefore, what "your" culture was depended on your race, and reconnecting with an ancestral culture was always based on reaffirming your "genuine" racial identity. Culture therefore becomes a technology for talking about race; indeed, Michaels argues that it forms a significant development in racist thought. For counter arguments, see Hegeman 204–9, and Douglas Mao's review essay "Culture Clubs."
18. Scruggs and VanDemarr also discuss this letter, 121–22.
19. Waldo Frank to Jean Toomer, July 26, 1922. JTP box 3, folder 83.
20. Sapir wrote numerous literary reviews and poems, and several considerations of the relationship between anthropology and aesthetics. For an assessment of this material, see Richard Handler's "The Dainty and the Hungry Man: Literature and Anthropology in the Work of Edward Sapir."
21. Jean Toomer to Jesse Moorland, July 28, 1922 (*Letters* 54–55). Handler notes Sapir's objection to this kind of view of culture within anthropology; in "reify-

ing this [cultural] model," it treats it "as a real world existent and then [uses] it to explain the very interactional data from which it has been abstracted" (Handler, "Dainty" 226).

22. Jean Toomer to Waldo Frank, July 19, 1922 (*Letters* 43). Toomer to Moorland, July 28, 1922 (*Letters* 55).
23. Frank was born into an affluent Jewish family and grew up in upper-West-side Manhattan, followed by an education in Lausanne and Yale. His family was not particularly religious, but Frank's memoirs deal with the strains of being Jewish at Yale; see 35–56.
24. See Levine's *Black Culture and Black Consciousness.* Indeed, in his preface he notes that such indirection and discretion in African American culture undoubtedly influenced the process of collecting the folk materials that his study was drawn from, in terms of the reluctance of black singers and storytellers to speak candidly to folklorists, both black and white; he cites a "song sung by generations of Negroes": "Got one mind for white folks to see, / 'Nother for what I know is me; / He don't know, he don't know my mind" (xiii).
25. Toomer stated that he had never "passed," as the term implied lying about one's racial ancestry, which he claimed never to have done. However, given his family background, he would have been classed as a Negro for legal purposes, and on many occasions, for example when enrolling his daughter at school, he classed himself as white. See his "The Crock of Problems," 58; Kerman and Eldridge, 293.
26. Frank's language of "travelling" into blackness foreshadows perhaps the most famous recent example of white-to-black "passing," John Howard Griffin's account of southern racial attitudes during the Civil Rights movement in *Black Like Me.* At the point when he undergoes the "transformation" from white to black, Griffin writes, "I was imprisoned in the flesh of an utter stranger, an unsympathetic one with whom I felt no kinship. . . . I looked into the mirror and saw reflected nothing of the white John Griffin's past. No, the reflection led back to Africa, back to the shanty and the ghetto, back to the fruitless struggles against the mark of blackness. . . . I had gone too far" (11).
27. Such fantasies of assuming blackness, or interracial masquerade, are inseparable from the heritage of blackface minstrelsy to American culture, as Eric Lott has shown. In his book *Love and Theft: Blackface Minstrelsy and the American Working Class,* he discusses how the minstrel show functioned as a cultural practice that figured and mediated white working-class fears over class formation and interclass tension, anxieties over their own racial and gendered status, and sexual desire. The shows served "less a sign of absolute white power and control than of panic, anxiety, terror, and pleasure" (6), and he also notes the long tradition of attraction to the black body on the part of bohemian groups such as those in which Frank, Anderson, and Toomer moved (50–51).
28. See my discussion of Anderson's depiction of African Americans in the northern United Stated in the section "The Stories and Spaces of Primitivism" of chapter 2. Frank discussed the difference between southern, rural African Americans and northern, urban dwellers in his essay "In Defence of Our Vulgarity." He remarked upon "the Negro peasant in Alabama" who "in his native

state . . . draws from the soil and the sky in whose cycles he is seasoned, a grace which is refinement even if it be unconscious like the grace of a flower." This was in contrast to the African American in Harlem: "Hand him a little money and a good dose of our contemporary eighteenth-century notion of Equality. Now, his absence of refinement will grow aggressive. He will be vulgar" (109).

29. Toomer discusses this in his autobiography; see *The Wayward and the Seeking,* 125–27. Toomer's affair with Margaret Naumberg, Frank's wife at the time, did not help matters.

4. "THINGS ARE SO IMMEDIATE IN GEORGIA"

1. The term "mulatto" is clearly a problematic and in many ways unsatisfactory one. I use it here for the following reasons: phenotypic distinctions that formed the basis for social divisions *were* frequently made within the African American community. These included the degree of "white" characteristics exhibited, and the community at large used the term "mulatto" to designate such individuals. "Mulatto" thus has a historical and a non-pejorative sense that I am keen to preserve in this discussion.
2. This is a considerable simplification of Du Bois's position, especially as the last chapter of *The Souls of Black Folk* deals with a celebration of "The Sorrow Songs," or spirituals, which Du Bois "knew. . . as of me and of mine. . . . full of the voices of my brothers and sisters, full of the voices of the past" (204–5). I would argue, however, that folk tradition and oral culture had taken a much more central place in African American thought about forging a distinctive African American culture by the time of the New Negro Renaissance. For further discussion, see Darwin T. Turner's "W. E. B. Du Bois and the Theory of a Black Aesthetic"; Tommy Lott's chapter on Du Bois's concept of African American cultural identity in 1897 in his *The Invention of Race: Black Culture and the Politics of Representation;* and, for a conflicting view, Anthony Appiah's "The Uncompleted Argument: Du Bois and the Illusion of Race." For an assessment of the significance of "the folk" to the New Negro Renaissance more generally, see J. Martin Favor's *Authentic Blackness: The Folk in the New Negro Renaissance* and George Hutchinson's chapter "Towards a New Negro Aesthetic" in his *The Harlem Renaissance in Black and White.*
3. See J. Martin Favor, *Authentic Blackness: The Folk in the New Negro Renaissance.* Both Favor and other commentators, such as Hazel Carby, have examined the way in which this mark of "authenticity," conferred on a specific geographical and class identity, erases or obfuscates difference within the African American experience. Carby is also critical of the stress on the folk in the New Negro Renaissance as it served to displace consideration of new, northern, and urban black subjectivities resulting from the great migration. See her "The Politics of Fiction, Anthropology, and the Folk: Zora Neale Hurston" and also her "The Quicksands of Representation: Rethinking Black Cultural Politics."
4. Toomer to the *Liberator,* Aug. 19, 1922 (*Letters,* 70–71). This letter has often been used to contend that Toomer's creativity, and his ability to write significant literature, are linked inextricably to "blackness" and specifically a version

of the rural black folk. This is particularly true of the criticism of *Cane* that immediately followed its republication in 1967 after being out of print for forty years, as I discussed in my introduction; as Houston Baker wrote in 1974, "an examination of the journey toward genuine, liberating black art presented in *Cane* reveals Toomer as a writer of genius and the book itself as a protest novel, a portrait of the artist, and a thorough delineation of the black situation" (*Singers* 54).

5. See Hutchinson, *The Harlem Renaissance in Black and White*, especially the introduction, for an account of the racial politics of the U.S. publishing industry at this time.
6. See here Byrd's discussion of Alain Locke's "appropriation" of Jean Toomer: Locke published sections of *Cane* in *The New Negro* without Toomer's consent because "of the prestige that Toomer would bring to his efforts to increase national interest in what was then a burgeoning arts movement" (217).
7. Jessie Redmon Fauset to Jean Toomer, Feb. 27, 1922. JTP box 1, folder 37.
8. Perhaps the most obvious example of this is Toomer's angry reaction to the suggestion of his publisher, Horace Liveright, that Toomer revise a biographical sketch submitted for publicity purposes to include "a note sounded about your colored blood." Toomer responded that "my racial composition and my position in the world are realities which I alone may determine." See Michael Soto, "Jean Toomer and Horace Liveright," 167.
9. "Preface to a Place and a Function in Society" (dated 1935). JTP box 51, folder 1116.
10. Gavin Jones has argued that a new concern with strategies for representing regional differences in speech during the postbellum period was not restricted to African American writing but was an important feature of much American writing in the Gilded Age. See his *Strange Talk: The Politics of Dialect Literature in Gilded Age America*.
11. See the chapter "Black Vernacular Representation and Cultural Malpractice" in Tommy Lott's *The Invention of Race*, which examines both Alain Locke's aesthetic assessment of black dialect poetry and more recent debates on the black vernacular around gangsta rap. Henry Louis Gates Jr. outlines the parameters of the debate over dialect in the New Negro Renaissance in the chapter "Dis and Dat: Dialect and the Descent" in his *Figures in Black*, and also in his chapter on Zora Neale Hurston in *The Signifying Monkey*. Gayl Jones discusses the politics of dialect in the work of several key New Negro Renaissance figures in her *Liberating Voices: Oral Tradition in African American Literature*. See also Sylvia Wallace Holton's *Down Home and Uptown: The Representation of Black Speech in American Fiction*, particularly the chapter "Black English in Fiction, 1900–1945."
12. Johnson had first outlined this position in a debate with Floyd Dell in the pages of the *Liberator* in 1918. However, by the time of the second edition of *The Book of American Negro Poetry*, published in 1931, the experiments by Langston Hughes and Sterling Brown with literary representations of Black English had caused Johnson to adopt a less hostile opinion on the use of dialect in African American literature. See Gavin Jones, 183. Du Bois also had

reservations about the use of dialect by the African American protagonists of his novels; see Holton, 110–14. Holton also sees intention as crucial in the evaluation of African American dialect (119).

13. See North's *The Dialect of Modernism: Race, Language, and Twentieth-Century Literature.* He notes that black dialect appealed to white modernists because of its "technical distinction, its insurrectionary opposition to the known and familiar in language," a situation where "[m]odernism . . . mimicked the strategies of dialect and aspired to become a dialect itself" (vii).
14. Eric Sundquist uses this essay of Boas's as his theoretical paradigm for discussing Charles W. Chesnutt's use of dialect in his short fiction; I would agree with him that the essay offers a "compactly formulated means of understanding both the difficulties of writing dialect, broadly understood, and the cultural differences it may represent" (313). Gavin Jones finds that Boas's essay was "related to a wider recognition, during the late nineteenth century, of the impossibility of quantifying and qualifying speech" (46).
15. Claude Barnett to Jean Toomer, Apr. 23, 1923; quoted in Benson and Dillard, 33.
16. An alternative reading of the "problem of speech" in *Cane* can be found in Karen Jackson Ford's *Split Gut Song: Jean Toomer and the Poetics of Modernity*, 87–88.
17. "The Individual in America." JTP folder 1111, box 51.
18. Pertinent here are some of Casey Nelson Blake's criticisms of Frank. He finds that "Frank's romantic-democratic stance for intellectuals threatened to strip the public of any real role except as an echo to the prophet's call" (175) and that "Frank's romantic vision of intellectual prophecy overburdened the intellectual's public role with an ideal of intuitive union with his audience that he could never achieve in any real political context" (177). At least equally problematic, for all his intellectual colleagues, was that "Frank's appeals to community and spiritual fellowship were belied by his overbearing ego" (255).
19. For an excellent discussion of how the politics of class affected the African American Community during this era, see Kevin K. Gaines's *Uplifting the Race: Black Leadership, Politics, and Culture in the Twentieth Century.*
20. See, for example, William J. Goede's "Jean Toomer's Ralph Kabnis: Portrait of the Negro Artist as a Young Man"; Michael North's *The Dialect of Modernism*, 174; Barbara E. Bowen's "Untroubled Voice: Call-and-Response in Cane," 201; Melvin Dixon, *Ride Out the Wilderness: Geography and Identity in Afro-American Literature*, 40; Scruggs and VanDemarr, 191–92; George Hutchinson's "Jean Toomer and American Racial Discourse"; and Karen Jackson Ford's *Split-Gut Song*, 118–43.
21. The other two locations are the wilderness and the mountaintop. According to Dixon, the potency of the image of the underground originated in slave songs, where it was a "region . . . that lies 'down in the lonesome valley' where individual strength is tested and autonomy achieved" (4). See introduction, *Ride Out the Wilderness.*
22. See Sherley Anne Williams's afterword to Verago's 1997 edition of *Their Eyes Were Watching God* for a discussion of this trope with reference to Hurston's novel.

23. My argument here has similarities to that of Charles T. Davis in his "Jean Toomer and the South: Region and Race as Elements Within a Literary Tradition." Davis argues that in *Cane* Toomer rejected three "forms of the South" that were available to him. The first was the plantation tradition of sentimental, nostalgic fiction; the second was Booker T. Washington's vision of a South of improving conditions for African Americans achieved through thrift, application, patience, and a nonconfrontational approach to politics of racial inequality; the third was Du Bois's view of a black South suffering under white oppression that could be alleviated through an alliance with an intellectual "talented tenth" (189–91).
24. See particularly Barbara Foley's "'In the Land of Cotton': Economics and Violence in Jean Toomer's *Cane*." Nathan Grant also discusses this possibility; see his *Masculinist Impulses: Toomer, Hurston, Black Writing, and Modernity,* 83–85.
25. See his *Black Culture and Black Consciousness.*
26. Melvin Dixon discusses the critical debates over *Cane*'s ending and the various responses to its final image of Kabnis carrying a bucket of dead coals out of The Hole, in his *Ride Out the Wilderness,* 34–35.

5. *CANE,* BODY TECHNOLOGIES, AND GENEALOGY

1. See, for example, Susan L. Blake's "The Spectatorial Artist in Part I of *Cane*" and Nathan Grant's chapter "Toomer's Male Prison and the Spectatorial Artist" in his *Masculinist Impulses: Toomer, Hurston, Black Writing, and Modernity,* 20–48.
2. Darwin T. Turner, the editor of this autobiography, dates it as either 1928 or 1929, with probable revisions in 1930 (*Wayward,* 10).
3. "Book X," second draft, 61. JTP box 11, folder 362.
4. See, for example, Laura Doyle's chapter on Jean Toomer in her *Bordering on the Body: The Racial Matrix of Modern Fiction and Culture;* Vera Kutzinski's "Unseasonal Flowers: Nature and History in Placido and Jean Toomer"; Siobhan Somerville's chapter on Toomer in her *Queering the Color Line: Race and the Invention of Homosexuality in American Culture;* and Nathan Grant's *Masculinist Impulses: Toomer, Hurston, Black Writing, and Modernity.*
5. This is a highly condensed summary of what is clearly a huge historical field. For more detail on histories of masculinity at the time, see T. J. Jackson Lears, "The Destructive Element: Modern Commercial Society and the Martial Ideal" in his *No Place of Grace: Antimodernism and the Transformation of American Culture;* Harold B. Segel, *Body Ascendant: Modernism and the Physical Imperative;* Kristin L. Hoganson, *Fighting for American Manhood: How Gender Politics Provoked the Spanish-American and Philippine-American Wars;* Gail Bederman, *Manliness and Civilization: A Cultural History of Gender and Race in the United States, 1880–1917;* Martin Summers, *Manliness and its Discontents: The Black Middle Class and the Transformation of Masculinity, 1900–1930;* Marlon B. Ross, *Manning the Race: Reforming Black Men in the Jim Crow Era;* E. Anthony Rotundo, "Body and Soul: Changing Ideals of American Middle-Class Manhood,

1770–1920"; Kenneth R. Dutton, *The Perfectible Body: The Western Ideal of Physical Development,* particularly the chapter "The Body Built"; and Kimmel's "Consuming Manhood: The Feminization of American Culture and the Recreation of the Male Body, 1832–1920" and *Manhood in America: A Cultural History.*

6. Masturbation had been a cause of concern for many years before this in medical discourse and conduct manuals, and this concern reached a particular intensity in the mid-1800s. This was tied to the "marketplace man" model of masculinity: male sexual energy became regarded in economic terms, and masturbation was seen as harmful in that it involved a "waste" of "man's vital energies" (Kimmel, 15–18).
7. "Book X," second draft, 1935. JTP box 11, folder 362.
8. Ibid. See also Kerman and Eldridge for a discussion of this phase of his life (50).
9. For a discussion of the representation of different races in *Physical Culture,* see Mullins.
10. For a discussion of Toomer's involvement with these various bodily disciplines, see Kerman and Eldridge, 383–84.
11. "The Book of Searching and Finding." Chapter of "Incredible Journey," 1924. JTP Box 19, Folder 503.
12. Toomer's annexation of a discourse of embodiment that had the most direct of links to a politics of racial essentialism and white supremacy in a fashion that came to challenge those politics is in some ways analogous to the enthusiasm for eugenics among sections of the African American community. As Daylanne English has discussed, this was particularly the case in the pages of the *Crisis* under W. E. B. Du Bois's editorship, wherein photographs of children and "race men" in particular came to construct a biologized narrative of race progress. The use of photographic subjects as racially representative in this way "inscribes and prescribes the parameters of *collective* modern 'Negro' subjectivity" (51). See the chapter "W. E. B. Du Bois's Family Crisis" in English's *Unnatural Selections: Eugenics in American Modernism and the Harlem Renaissance* (35–64).
13. JTP box 11, folder 362.
14. JTP box 20, folder 514. A full discussion of the politics and editorial policy of these two magazines in relation to machine aesthetics is given in Dickran Tashjian's *Skyscraper Primitives: Dada and the American Avant-Garde,* chapter 6. Also useful is Munson's account of the history of *Secession*, given in "A Comedy of Exiles." For a fuller treatment of the significance of aesthetics of "the machine" to the New Negro Renaissance in general and Jean Toomer in particular, see my "Jean Toomer, Technology, and Race."
15. Perhaps the fullest treatment of Toomer's involvement with "machine aesthetics" and *S4N* is given in Charles Scruggs's "Textuality and Vision in Jean Toomer's *Cane.*"
16. Gorham Munson to Malcolm Cowley, Feb. 20, 1923. Malcolm Cowley Papers, Newberry Library.
17. This type of criticism was leveled especially at Matthew Josephson; Tashjian discusses Edmund Wilson's critique of Josephson on these grounds (135–37).
18. "Notes for Novel," n.d. JTP box 48, folder 1002.

19. Steinman discusses this phenomena in her *Made in America: Science, Technology, and American Modernist Poets,* chapter 1.
20. For other discussions of how the ritual of lynching produces racial categories in this poem—through the superimposition of the burnt black body on the blazon-style list of the white woman's physical features—see Doyle, *Bordering on the Body: The Racial Matrix of Modern Fiction and Culture,* 87; and Hutchinson, "Jean Toomer and American Racial Discourse," 234.
21. Norman Fitts to Jean Toomer, Good Friday 1923. JTP box 3, folder 79.
22. Toomer also wrote several "Sound-poems," which are very similar to both Marinetti's theory of *Parole en Liberta* (or "Words in Freedom") and Hugo Ball's Dadaist sound poems. See Toomer's *Collected Poems,* 15–16.
23. A quite different, but sensitive and closely argued, reading of this poem is given in Karen Jackson Ford's *Split-Gut Song: Jean Toomer and the Poetics of Modernity.* Rather than seeing technology in the poem as a liberating set of metaphorical and dynamic figurations, Ford argues that the "analogy between urban landscape and human intimacy is lethal" and that "the lovers' world in part 2 of *Cane* is an anti-paradise, where light emanates from a vast industrial structure, not from God, and where light destroys rather than creates" (84, 85). Similarly, Nellie Y. McKay has argued that technology and urban space in *Cane* separates African American "people from the folk culture" and is an invidious part of a "Western culture, which, in its advanced stages of industrialization and mechanization, has become sterile, limiting, and destructive to the human spirit." See *Jean Toomer, Artist,* 126.
24. See Michael North's *The Dialect of Modernism* (170–71) for another reading focusing on the use of technology in this poem.
25. This dissolving of boundaries between organic and technological—and also the stress on bastardy that I discuss later—is similar in some ways to more recent strategies of resistance to dominant power structures; see especially Donna Haraway's "Cyborg Manifesto."
26. This appropriation of traditionally white religious iconography was not unique to Toomer in the New Negro Renaissance. Du Bois drew on the motif of the black Christ in his "The Second Coming," printed in *Darkwater* (1920)*;* Winold Reiss included a portrait of the black Madonna in *The New Negro* (1925); and Countee Cullen titled his 1929 book of poems *The Black Christ.* Indeed, as Felipe Smith argues, the black Madonna and the black Christ formed central tropes in the discourse of writers such as W. E. B. Du Bois and James Weldon Johnson (276–306).
27. Waldo Frank to Malcolm Cowley, Nov. 9, 1924. Malcolm Cowley Papers, Newberry Library.
28. Assessments of Frank's involvement with *unanimisme* can be found in Casey Nelson Blake's *Beloved Community,* 145–47; and Scruggs and VanDemarr, 79–80.
29. Charles-Yves Grandjeat notes that trains have a special significance in *Cane;* the train "acts not just as a link with the blues, but also as a connecting element from one story to the next —a symbolic vestibule or a key "conductor," to borrow one of Gaston Bachelard's illuminating metaphors—in a chain of images rippling through the text" (61–62).

30. I use the term "bastard" as it is the one that recurs in *Cane* and other texts at the time. However, I recognize its pejorative status and accept Zingo and Early's term, "non-marital children," as more socially acceptable (16).
31. This "hard" view of heredity as the major determining factor in an organism's characteristics was indebted to the theory of the "continuity of germ plasm" advanced by August Weismann and the recently revived work of Gregor Mendel on heredity. This differed from the "soft" heredity of Lamarck, which saw changes in organisms effected by the environment as being inheritable. For further discussion of the difference between these approaches, see Diane Paul, *Controlling Human Heredity: 1865 to the Present,* chapter 3. For an excellent account of the connections between eugenics, nativism, and the immigration restriction bills of the 1920s, see John Higham, *Strangers in the Land: Patterns of American Nativism, 1860–1925,* 264–330.
32. Paul discusses the use of the term "race suicide," 100–107.
33. Siobhan Somerville has discussed the trope of the "legible" body in the scientific racism of the nineteenth century; she finds that "supported by the cultural authority of an ostensibly objective scientific method . . . readings of the body became a powerful instrument for those seeking to justify the economic and political disenfranchisement of various racial groups within systems of slavery and colonialism" (23). Madison Grant's program was also inherently patriarchal; he opined that "women in all races . . . tend to exhibit the older, more generalized and more primitive traits of the past of the race" (27).
34. For details of the history of legislation in the United States prohibiting interracial marriage, see Werner Sollors's *Neither Black nor White yet Both,* appendix B.
35. The term "disorganized" is a quotation from E. W. Burgess's preface to E. Franklin Frazier's groundbreaking study *The Negro Family in Chicago,* 1932, quoted in Gutman, 433. For more detail, see Gutman's *The Black Family in Slavery and Freedom,* 72–84, and chapter 10, which discusses the adverse representation of the African American family in the history of American social science, along with some of the attempts to redress these assumptions.
36. See Laura Doyle; she sees the technique of the narrator here as "indulging his culture's predilection for racial-patriarchal melodrama" (96). Also see Janet Whyde, "Mediating Forms: Narrating the Body in Jean Toomer's *Cane,*" 45–46.
37. Schuyler's wickedly satirical novel also looks at technology—it imagines a revolutionary medical technique that allows black people to be transformed into white, which is then used by the entire population of black America. As the technique produces people who are actually "whiter than white," discrimination begins against extremely fair-skinned, blonde, and thin-lipped sections of the population.
38. See Williamson's *New People: Miscegenation and Mulattoes in the United States.*
39. JTP box 18, folder 491. Scruggs and VanDemarr also discuss this incident (209–24).
40. Butler proposes that *Passing* offers a way of starting to think about how sexual difference intersects with racial difference: "What requires radical rethinking is . . . what convergent set of historical formations of racialized gender, of gen-

dered race, of the sexualization of racial ideals, or the racialization of gender norms, makes up both the social regulation of sexuality and its psychic articulations" (182). Siobhan Somerville offers a slightly different version of the meanings of the word "Queer" in New York society in the 1920s (142–43).

41. Somerville's fascinating chapter examines this "vocabulary of 'queer'" in Toomer's writing in order to "raise . . . crucial questions about the position of discourses of race and racialization in queer reading and theorizing" (137).

6. *CANE*, AUDIENCE, AND FORM

1. See, for example, Patricia Chase's "The Women in *Cane*" or Rafael A. Cancel's "Male and Female Interrelationship in Jean Toomer's *Cane*."
2. See Favor's chapter on *Cane* for a fuller discussion of northern and southern interaction in *Cane* and also Monica Michlin's intriguing close reading of "Karintha."
3. These quotations are taken from Turner, "Intersection," 101; Toomer, *Wayward,* 120; and Anderson, *Selected Letters,* 220.
4. As Burke wrote in his 1924 essay "The Psychology of Form," "The psychology here [Act I Scene IV of Hamlet] is not the psychology of the hero, but the psychology of the audience. Or, seen from another angle, form is the creation of an appetite in the mind of the auditor, and the adequate satisfying of that appetite" (21).
5. Lola Ridge to Jean Toomer, Oct. 12, 1920. JTP box 1, folder 18.
6. JTP box 18, folder 491.
7. See Monica Michlin, 102–3; Karen Jackson Ford, 40; and Scruggs and VanDemarr, 136.
8. See Hutchinson's "Jean Toomer and American Racial Discourse."
9. This discussion—of how Toomer's formal strategies of division and disruption attempt to interrogate social division—has also been discussed in Joel B. Peckham's "Jean Toomer's *Cane:* Self as Montage and the Drive Toward Integration"; Frederik L. Rusch's "Form, Function and Creative Tension in *Cane:* Jean Toomer and the Need for the Avant-Garde"; and Michael North's *Dialect of Modernism,* 162–74.
10. Sollors discusses the issue of a "double audience" for U.S. writers who belong to minority ethnic groups and how it affects their modes of address and formal strategies, in his *Beyond Ethnicity: Consent and Descent in American Culture,* 237–58. See also Charles Scruggs's "'All Dressed Up but No Place to Go': The Black Writer and His Audience during the Harlem Renaissance."
11. Toomer felt that this "fusion" had not occurred within Johnson's editorial policy by 1931, when he refused permission for his poems to be included in Johnson's anthology of Negro poetry. Toomer explained in a letter to Johnson that he saw "our literature as primarily American art and literature. I do not see it as Negro, Anglo-Saxon and so on. Accordingly, I must with draw from all things which emphasize racial or cultural divisions" (*Toomer Reader* 106).
12. "This Harlem Renaissance." N.d. Wallace Thurman Papers, box 1, folder 10. See also Sterling Brown, "Our Literary Audience."

13. JTP box 3, folder 79.
14. Jessie Redmon Fauset to Jean Toomer, Feb. 27, 1922. JTP box 1, folder 37.
15. Press clipping contained in JTP box 26, folder 611.
16. Among regional publications this kind of bias was even starker; the *Ashville Citizen*'s review remarked that *Cane* "would seem to be in expressionist prose—a fact which means we never shall read [it]. There. That's prejudice for you!" JTP box 26, folder 611. A fascinating look at the publication politics of *Cane,* and how it was marketed by Boni and Liveright, is given by Michael Soto in his "Jean Toomer and Horace Liveright: or, a New Negro Gets 'into the Swing of It.'"
17. For further discussion of this antiphonal structure, see Lawrence Levine, "Slave Spirituals," and also Barbara E. Bowen, "Untroubled Voice: Call and Response in *Cane.*"
18. These comments come, respectively, from John McClure, *Double Dealer;* William Stanley Braithwaite, 84; and ads for *Cane* (quoted in North, *Dialect* 164).
19. For a discussion of the range of generic and formal sources of *Cane*, see Frederik L. Rusch's "Form, Function and Creative Tension in *Cane*: Jean Toomer and the Need for the Avant-Garde" and Robert B. Jones's *Jean Toomer and the Prison-House of Thought.*
20. Diana Williams has argued that this is an idea consistent with eugenic ideology and that Toomer drew many of his ideas about the future of racial groups in America from this movement. See her "Building the New Race: Jean Toomer's Eugenic Aesthetic."

CONCLUSION

1. Toomer to B. G. Tobey, Apr. 7, 1929. JTP box 1, folder 9.

WORKS CITED

MANUSCRIPT COLLECTIONS

Sherwood Anderson Collection, Newberry Library, Chicago, Illinois.

Malcolm Cowley Papers, Newberry Library, Chicago, Illinois.

Waldo Frank Papers, Special Collections, Van Pelt Library, University of Pennsylvania, Philadelphia.

Alfred Stieglitz/Georgia O'Keeffe Archive, Yale Collection of American Literature, Beinecke Rare Book and Manuscript Library, Yale University, New Haven, Connecticut.

Wallace Thurman Papers, Yale Collection of American Literature, Beinecke Rare Book and Manuscript Library, Yale University, New Haven, Connecticut.

Jean Toomer Papers, James Weldon Johnson Collection, Beinecke Rare Book and Manuscript Library, Yale University, New Haven, Connecticut.

PRIMARY AND SECONDARY MATERIALS

Adams, Michael C. C. *The Great Adventure: Male Desire and the Coming of World War One*. Bloomington: Indiana UP, 1990.

Alcoff, Linda Martín. Toward a Phenomenology of Racial Embodiment. *Race*. Ed. Robert Bernasconi. Oxford: Blackwell, 2001. 267–83.

Allen, Frederick Lewis. *Only Yesterday: An Unofficial History of the 1920s*. 1931. New York: Harper and Row, 1959.

Anderson, Elizabeth, and David R. Kelly. *Miss Elizabeth: A Memoir.* Boston: Little, Brown and Co., 1969.

Anderson, Sherwood. *Beyond Desire*. 1932. New York: Liveright, 1961.

———. *Dark Laughter.* 1925. New York: Liveright, 1960.

———. *The Egg and Other Stories*. Ed. Charles E. Modlin. London: Penguin, 1998.

———. *Horses and Men*. New York: Huebsch, 1923.

———. Introduction. *Leaves of Grass*. By Walt Whitman. New York: Crowell, 1933. v–vii.

———. "Lawrence Again." *No Swank*. 1934. Mamaroneck, NY: Paul P. Appel, 1970. 95–101.

———. *Letters of Sherwood Anderson*. Selected and ed. Howard Mumford Jones and Walter B. Rideout. Boston: Little, Brown and Co., 1953.

———. *Letters to Bab: Sherwood Anderson to Marietta D. Finley, 1916–1933*. Ed. William A. Sutton. Urbana: U of Illinois P, 1985.

———. "Look Out, Brown Man!" *Nation* 131, Nov. 26, 1930: 579–80. Rpt. in *Sherwood Anderson: The Writer at His Craft*. Ed. Jack Salzman, David D. Anderson, and Kichinosuke Ohashi. New York: Paul P. Appel, 1979. 101–5.

———. "A Man's Mind." *The New Republic* (May 21, 1930): 22–23.

———. *Many Marriages*. 1923. Critical ed. Ed. Douglas G. Rogers. Metchuen, NJ: Scarecrow P, 1978.

———. *Marching Men*. 1917. A Critical Text. Ed. Ray Lewis White. Cleveland: P of Case Western Reserve U, 1972.

———. *The Modern Writer.* San Francisco: Lantern P–Gelber Lilienthal, 1925.

———. "Negro Singing." *Hello Towns!* New York: Liveright, 1929. 146–47.

———. "New Orleans, The *Double Dealer* and the Modern Movement in America." *Double Dealer* 3, March 1922: 119–26. Rpt. in *Sherwood Anderson: The Writer at His Craft*. Ed. Jack Salzman, David D. Anderson, and Kichinosuke Ohashi. New York: Paul P. Appel, 1979. 281–92.

———. *No Swank*. 1934. Mamaroneck, NY: Paul P. Appel, 1970.

———. "Out of Nowhere Into Nothing." *The Triumph of The Egg*. 1921. New York: Four Walls Eight Windows, 1988. 171–267.

———. *Perhaps Women*. 1931. Mamaroneck, NY: Paul P. Appel, 1970.

———. *Poor White*. 1920. New York: Compass-Viking, 1966.

———. *Sherwood Anderson's Memoirs: A Critical Edition*. Ed. Ray Lewis White. Chapel Hill: U of North Carolina P, 1969.

———. *Sherwood Anderson's Notebook*. New York: Boni and Liveright, 1926. 131–35.

———. *Sherwood Anderson: Selected Letters*. Ed. Charles E. Modlin. Knoxville: U of Tennessee P, 1984.

———. "The South." *Vanity Fair* 27, Sept. 1926: 49–50. Rpt. in *Hello Towns!* New York: Liveright, 1929. 54–65.

———. *Southern Odyssey: Selected Writings by Sherwood Anderson.* Ed. Welford Dunaway Taylor and Charles E. Modlin. Athens: U of Georgia P, 1997.

———. *A Story Teller's Story.* 1924. New York: Viking, 1969.

———. "They Come Bearing Gifts." *American Mercury* 21, Oct. 1930: 129–37. Rpt. in *Sherwood Anderson: The Writer at His Craft.* Ed. Jack Salzman, David D. Anderson and Kichinosuke Ohashi. New York: Paul P. Appel, 1979. 325–40.

———. "This Southland." *Southern Oddyssey: Selected Writings by Sherwood Anderson.* Ed. Welford Dunaway Taylor and Charles E. Modlin. Athens: U of Georgia P, 1997. 187–95.

———. *Winesburg, Ohio.* 1919. Ed. Charles E. Modlin and Ray Lewis White. Norton Critical Edition. London: Norton, 1996.

Anderson, Sherwood, and Gertrude Stein. *Sherwood Anderson/Gertrude Stein: Correspondence and Personal Essays.* Ed. Ray Lewis White. Chapel Hill: U of North Carolina P, 1972.

Appiah, Anthony. "The Uncompleted Argument: Du Bois and the Illusion of Race." *Critical Inquiry* 12 (1985): 21–37.

Arcana, Judith. "'Tandy' at the Centre of Winesburg." *Studies in Short Fiction* 24 (1987): 66–70.

Armstrong, Tim. *Modernism, Technology, and the Body: A Cultural Study.* Cambridge: Cambridge UP, 1998.

Arnold, Armin. *D. H. Lawrence and America.* London: Linden P, 1958.

Atlas, Marilyn Judith. "Sherwood Anderson and the Women of Winesburg." *Critical Essays on Sherwood Anderson.* Ed. David D. Anderson. Boston: Hall, 1981. 250–65.

Baker, Houston A., Jr. *Singers of Daybreak: Studies in Black American Literature.* Washington, DC: Howard UP, 1974.

Bakhtin, Mikhail. *Problems of Dostoevsky's Poetics.* Ed. and trans. Caryl Emerson. Vol. 8 of *Theory and History of Literature.* London: U of Minnesota P, 1984.

Baldwin, James. "Everybody's Protest Novel." *Notes of a Native Son.* 1964. London: Penguin, 1995. 19–28.

Baldwin, James, and Margaret Mead. *A Rap on Race.* London: Corgi-Transworld, 1972.

Baldwin, William H. Rev. of *Dark Laughter. Opportunity* 3, Nov. 1925: 342. Rpt. in *The Critics and the Harlem Renaissance.* Ed. Cary D. Wintz. New York: Garland P, 1996. 137.

Balshaw, Maria. *Looking for Harlem: Urban Aesthetics in African American Literature.* London: Pluto P, 2000.

Barthes, Roland. *Camera Lucida: Reflections on Photography.* Trans. Richard Howard. London: Fontana, 1984.

———. "From Work to Text." *Image, Music, Text.* Ed. S. Heath. Collins, 1971. 155–64. Rpt. in *Modern Literary Theory: A Reader.* Ed. Philip Rice and Patricia Waugh. 2nd ed. London: Arnold, 1992. 166–72.

Bederman, Gail. *Manliness and Civilization: A Cultural History of Gender and Race in the United States, 1880–1917.* Chicago: U of Chicago P, 1995.

Bell, Michael. *Primitivism.* The Critical Idiom 20. London: Methuen, 1972.

Benjamin, Walter. "The Storyteller." *Illuminations.* Trans. Harry Zohrn. London: Fontana–Harper Collins, 1992. 83–107.

———. "The Work of Art in the Age of Mechanical Reproduction." *Illuminations.* Trans. Harry Zohrn. London: Fontana–HarperCollins, 1992. 211–44.

Bennett, Tony. *Outside Literature.* London: Routledge, 1990.

Benson, Brian, and Mabel Dillard. *Jean Toomer.* Boston: Twayne, 1980.

Berger, John. *Ways of Seeing.* London: BBC, 1972.

Berzon, Judith R. *Neither White nor Black: The Mulatto Character in American Fiction.* New York: New York UP, 1978.

Bhabha, Homi K. "Foreword: Remembering Fanon." *Black Skin, White Masks.* By Frantz Fanon. Trans. Charles Lam Markmann. London: Pluto P, 1986. vii–xxvi.

———. "Of Mimicry and Man: The Ambivalence of Colonial Discourse." *October* 28 (1984): 125–33. Rpt. in *Modern Literary Theory: A Reader.* Ed. Philip Rice and Patricia Waugh. 2nd Ed. London: Arnold, 1993. 234–41.

Bidney, Martin. "Anderson and the Androgyne: 'Something More Than Man or Woman.'" *Studies in Short Fiction* 25 (1988): 261–73.

Blake, Casey Nelson. *Beloved Community: The Cultural Criticism of Randolph Bourne, Van Wyck Brooks, Waldo Frank, and Lewis Mumford.* Chapel Hill: U of North Carolina P, 1990.

Blake, Susan L. "The Spectatorial Artist and the Structure of *Cane.*" *CLA Journal* 17 (1974): 516–34. Rpt. in Jean Toomer, *Cane.* 1923. Ed. Darwin T. Turner. Norton Critical Edition. New York: Norton, 1988. 217–23.

Boardman, Kay. "'The Glass of Gin': Renegade Reading Possibilities in the Classic Realist Text." *Gendering the Reader.* Ed. Sarah Mills. Hemel Hempstead: Harvester-Wheatsheaf, 1994. 199–216.

Boas, Franz. "On Alternating Sounds." *American Anthropologist* 2 (1889): 47–53. Rpt. in *The Shaping of American Anthropology, 1883–1911: A Franz Boas Reader.* Ed. George W. Stocking Jr. New York: Basic Books, 1974. 72–77.

Bonner, Thomas, Jr. "The *Double Dealer* and the Little-Magazine Tradition in New Orleans." *Literary New Orleans in the Modern World.* Ed. Richard S. Kennedy. Baton Rouge: Louisiana State UP, 1998. 23–35.

Bontemps, Arna. Introduction. *Cane.* By Jean Toomer. 1923. New York: Harper and Row, 1969. vii–xvi.

Bourdieu, Pierre. "The Field of Cultural Production, or: The Economic World Reversed." *The Field of Cultural Production: Essays on Art and Literature.* Ed. Randal Johnson. Cambridge: Polity P, 1993. 29–73.

Bourke, Joanna. *Dismembering the Male: Men's Bodies, Britain, and the Great War.* London: Reaktion, 1996.

Bourke, Paul F. "The Status of Politics 1909–1919: *The New Republic,* Randolph Bourne and Van Wyck Brooks." *Journal of American Studies* 8 (1974): 171–202.

Bourne, Randolph. "Trans-National America." *Atlantic Monthly* 118 (1916): 86–97. Rpt. in *War and the Intellectuals: Collected Essays, 1915–1919.* Ed. Carl Resek. New York: Harper, 1964. 107–23.

Bowden, Frances Jean. "The New Orleans *Double Dealer* 1921–1926, a Critical History." Diss. Vanderbilt U, 1954.

Bowen, Barbara E. "Untroubled Voice: Call and Response in *Cane*." *Black Literature and Literary Theory*. Ed. Henry Louis Gates Jr. New York: Methuen, 1984. 187–203.

Bradbury, Malcolm, and James McFarlane. "The Name and Nature of Modernism." *Modernism: 1890–1930*. Ed. Malcolm Bradbury and James McFarlane. London: Penguin, 1991. 19–55.

Braithwaite, William Stanley. "The Negro in American Literature." 1925. Rpt. in *The William Stanley Braithwaite Reader*. Ed. Philip Butcher. Ann Arbor: U of Michigan P, 1972. 68–84.

Bremond, Claude. "The Logic of Narrative Possibilities." Trans. Elaine D. Cancalon. *New Literary History* 11 (1980): 387–411. Rpt. in *Narratology: An Introduction*. Ed. Susana Onega and José Angel García Landa. Longman Critical Readers. London: Longman, 1996. 61 75.

Brooks, Peter. *Body Work: Objects of Desire in Modern Narrative*. Cambridge, MA: Harvard UP, 1993.

———. *Reading for the Plot*. Oxford: Clarendon–Oxford UP, 1984.

Brooks, Van Wyck. *America's Coming of Age*. 1915. Rpt. in *Van Wyck Brooks: The Early Years*. Ed. Claire Sprague. New York: Harper, 1968. 79–158.

———. "The Culture of Industrialism." *The Seven Arts* 1 (1917): 655–66. Rpt. in *Van Wyck Brooks: The Early Years*. Ed. Claire Sprague. New York: Harper, 1968. 192–202.

Broun, Heyward. Review of *Winesburg, Ohio*. *New York Tribune* May 31, 1919: 10. Rpt. in Sherwood Anderson, *Winesburg, Ohio*. Ed. Charles E. Modlin and Ray Lewis White. Norton Critical Edition. London: Norton, 1996. 160–61.

Brown, Sterling A. "A Century of Negro Portraiture in American Literature." *Black Voices: An Anthology of African American Literature*. Ed. Abraham Chapman. London: Mentor, 1968. 564–89.

———. "Our Literary Audience." *Opportunity* 8 (1930): 42–46, 61.

Bryan, Violet Harrington. *The Myth of New Orleans in Literature: Dialogues of Race and Gender*. Knoxville: U of Tennessee P, 1993.

Bunge, Nancy. "Women in Sherwood Anderson's Fiction." *Critical Essays on Sherwood Anderson*. Ed. David D. Anderson. Boston: Hall, 1981. 242–49.

Burke, Kenneth. "The Psychology of Form." 1924. Rpt. in *Perspectives by Incongruity*. Ed. Stanley Edgar Hyman and Barbara Karmiller. Bloomington: Indiana UP, 1964. 20–33.

Butler, Judith. *Bodies That Matter: On the Discursive Limits of Sex*. London: Routledge, 1993.

Byrd, Rudolph P. "Jean Toomer and the Writers of the Harlem Renaissance: Was He There with Them?" *The Harlem Renaissance: Revelations*. Ed. Amritjit Singh, William S. Shiver, and Stanley Brodwin. New York: Garland P, 1989. 209–18.

Calverton, V. F. "The Growth of Negro Literature." *Negro: Anthology Made by Nancy Cunard*. 1934. Ed. and abridged by Hugh Ford. New York: Continuum, 1970. 78–82.

Cancel, Raphael A. "Male and Female interrelationship in Jean Toomer's *Cane*." *Negro American Literature Forum* 5 (1971): 25–31. Rpt. in *Jean Toomer: A

Critical Evaluation. Ed. Therman B. O'Daniel. Washington D.C.: Howard UP, 1988. 417–27.

Carby, Hazel. "The Politics of Fiction, Anthropology, and the Folk: Zora Neale Hurston." *New Essays on* Their Eyes Were Watching God. Ed. Michael Awkward. The American Novel Series. Cambridge: Cambridge UP, 1990. 71–93.

———. "The Quicksands of Representation: Rethinking Black Cultural Politics." *Reconstructing Womanhood: The Emergence of the Afro-American Novelist*. Oxford: Oxford UP, 1987. 163–75.

———. *Race Men*. Cambridge, MA: Harvard UP, 1998.

Carrigan, Tim, Bob Connell, and John Lee. "Toward a New Sociology of Masculinity." *Theory and Society* 14 (1985): 551–604.

Carroll, Peter N., and David W. Noble. *The Free and the Unfree: A New History of the United States*. 2nd Ed. London: Penguin, 1988.

Carter, Erica, James Donald, and Judith Squires. Introduction. *Space and Place: Theories of Identity and Location*. London: Lawrence and Wishart, 1993. vii–xv.

Chauncey, George, Jr. "Christian Brotherhood or Sexual Perversion? Homosexual Identities and the Construction of Social Boundaries in the World War I Era." *Hidden from History: Reclaiming the Gay and Lesbian Past*. Ed. Martin Duberman, Martha Vicinus, and George Chauncey Jr. London: Penguin, 1991. 294–317.

———. *Gay New York: Gender, Urban Culture, and the Making of the Gay Male World, 1890–1940*. New York: Basic Books, 1994.

Chase, Patricia. "The Women in *Cane*." *CLA Journal* 14 (1971): 259–73. Rpt. in *Jean Toomer: A Critical Evaluation*. Ed. Therman B. O'Daniel. Washington, DC: Howard UP, 1988. 389–402.

Ciancio, Ralph. "Unity of Vision in *Winesburg, Ohio*." *PMLA* 87 (1972): 994–1006.

Cixous, Hélène. "The Laugh of the Medusa." Trans. Keith Cohen and Paula Cohen. *New French Feminisms: An Anthology*. Ed. Elaine Marks and Isabelle de Courtrivron. Brighton: Harvester, 1981. 245–64.

Clifford, James. *The Predicament of Culture: Twentieth-Century Ethnography, Literature, and Art*. Cambridge, MA: Harvard UP, 1988.

Clifford, James, and George E. Marcus, eds. *Writing Culture: The Poetics and Politics of Ethnography*. Berkeley: U of California P, 1986.

Colquitt, Clare. "Motherlove in Two Narratives of Community: *Winesburg, Ohio* and *The Country of the Pointed Firs*." *New Essays on* Winesburg, Ohio. Ed. John Crowley. Cambridge: Cambridge UP, 1990. 73–97.

———. "The Reader as Voyeur: Complicitious Transformations in 'Death in the Woods.'" *Modern Fiction Studies* 32 (1986): 175–90.

Cowley, Malcolm. *Exile's Return*. 1934. New York: Viking-Compass, 1956.

———. Introduction. *Winesburg, Ohio*. By Sherwood Anderson. 1919. Harmondsworth: Penguin, 1976. 1–15.

———. *A Second Flowering: Works and Days of the Lost Generation*. New York: Viking-Compass, 1974.

Crane, Hart. "Cape Hatteras." *Complete Poems of Hart Crane*. Ed. Marc Simon. New York: Liveright, 1993. 77–84.

———. "Sherwood Anderson." *The Double Dealer* 2 (July 1921): 42–45. Rpt. in *The Complete Poems and Selected Letters and Prose of Hart Crane*. 1933. Ed. Brom Weber. New York: Liveright, 1966.

Crang, Mike. *Cultural Geography*. London: Routledge, 1998.

Davis, Charles T. "Jean Toomer and the South: Region and Race as Elements Within a Literary Tradition." *The Harlem Renaissance Re-Examined*. Ed. Victor A. Kramer. Georgia State Literary Studies Series. New York: AMS Press, 1987. 185–99.

De Lauretis, Teresa. *Alice Doesn't: Feminism, Semiotics, Cinema*. London: Macmillan, 1984.

Dell, Floyd. "On Being Sherwood Anderson's Literary Father." *Newberry Library Bulletin* 5 (December 1961): 315–21.

D'Emilio, John, and Estelle B. Freedman. *Intimate Matters: A History of Sexuality in America*. New York: Perennial Library–Harper and Row, 1989.

Derrida, Jacques. "The Law of Genre." Trans. Avital Ronell. *Glyph* 7 (1980): 202–13. Rpt. in *Modern Genre Theory: A Reader*. Ed. David Duff. Longman Critical Readers. Harlow: Longman-Pearson, 2000. 219–32.

Dewey, Joseph. "No God in the Sky and No God in Myself: 'Godliness' and Anderson's Winesburg." *Modern Fiction Studies* 35 (1989): 251–59. Rpt. in *Winesburg, Ohio*. By Sherwood Anderson. Ed. Charles E. Modlin and Ray Lewis White. Norton Critical Edition. New York: Norton, 1996. 194–203.

Diggins, John P. *The American Left in the Twentieth Century*. The Harbrace History of the United States. New York: Harcourt, 1973.

Ditsky, John. "Sherwood Anderson's *Marching Men:* Unnatural Disorder and the Art of Force." *Twentieth-Century Literature* 23 (1977): 102–14.

Dixon, Melvin. *Ride Out the Wilderness: Geography and Identity in Afro-American Literature*. Urbana: U of Illinois P, 1987.

Dollimore, Jonathan. "Bisexuality." *Lesbian and Gay Studies: A Critical Introduction*. Ed. Andy Medhurst and Sally R. Munt. London: Cassell, 1997. 250–60.

———. *Sexual Dissidence: Augustine to Wilde, Freud to Foucault*. Oxford: Clarendon–Oxford UP, 1991.

Donaldson, Susan V. "Contending Narratives: *Go Down, Moses* and The Short Story Cycle." *Faulkner and the Short Story*. Ed. Evans Harrington and Ann J. Abadie. Jackson: UP of Mississippi, 1992. 128–48.

Dorris, Ronald. "Early Criticism of Jean Toomer's *Cane:* 1923–1932." *Perspectives of Black Popular Culture*. Ed. Harry B. Shaw. Bowling Green, OH: Bowling Green State U Popular P, 1990. 65–70.

Double Dealer. Vols. 1–8, 1921–26.

Douglas, Ann. *The Feminization of American Culture*. 1977. London: Papermac, 1996.

———. *Terrible Honesty: Mongrel Manhattan in the 1920s*. London: Papermac-Macmillan, 1997.

Dos Passos, John. *One Man's Initiation: 1917*. 1920. Rev. ed. Ithaca: Cornell UP, 1970.

Dowbiggin, Ian Robert. *Keeping America Sane: Psychiatry and Eugenics in the United States and Canada, 1880–1940.* Cornell Studies in the History of Psychiatry. Ithaca: Cornell UP, 1997.

Doyle, Laura. *Bordering on the Body: The Racial Matrix of Modern Fiction and Culture.* Oxford: Oxford UP, 1994.

Du Bois, W. E. B. "Criteria of Negro Art." *Crisis,* Oct. 1926. Rpt. in *The Portable Harlem Renaissance Reader.* Ed. David Levering Lewis. Viking Portable Library. London: Penguin, 1994. 100–105.

———. "The Damnation of Women." 1920. Rpt. in *The Norton Anthology of African American Literature.* Ed. Henry Louis Gates Jr. and Nellie Y. McKay. New York: Norton, 1997. 740–52.

———. *The Souls of Black Folk.* 1903. London: Penguin, 1989.

Duff, David. Introduction. *Modern Genre Theory: A Reader.* Ed. David Duff. Longman Critical Readers. Harlow: Longman-Pearson, 2000. 1–24.

Duffey, Bernard. *The Chicago Renaissance in American Letters: A Critical History.* East Lansing: Michigan State UP, 1956.

Duncan, Bowie. "Jean Toomer's *Cane:* A Modern Black Oracle." *CLA Journal* 15 (1972): 323–33. Rpt. in *Jean Toomer: A Critical Evaluation.* Ed. Therman B. O'Daniel. Washington, DC: Howard UP, 1988. 237–46.

Dunn, Maggie, and Ann Morris. *The Composite Novel: The Short Story Cycle in Transition.* New York: Twayne, 1995.

Dutton, Kenneth R. *The Perfectible Body: The Western Ideal of Physical Development.* London: Cassell, 1995.

Dyer, Richard. *White.* London: Routledge, 1997.

Eagleton, Terry. *Literary Theory: An Introduction.* Oxford: Blackwell, 1983.

———. *Marxism and Literary Criticism.* London: Methuen, 1976.

Eco, Umberto. *The Role of the Reader: Explorations in the Semiotics of Texts.* Bloomington: Indiana UP, 1984.

Edwards, Brent Hayes. *The Practice of Diaspora: Literature, Translation, and the Rise of Black Internationalism.* Cambridge, MA: Harvard UP, 2003.

Edwards, Richard. *Contested Terrain: The Transformation of the Workplace in the Twentieth Century.* London: Heinemann, 1979.

Eldridge, Richard. "The Unifying Images in Part One of Jean Toomer's *Cane.*" *CLA Journal* 22 (1979): 187–214. Rpt. in *Jean Toomer: A Critical Evaluation.* Ed. Therman B. O'Daniel. Washington DC: Howard UP, 1988. 213–36.

Ellison, Ralph. "Change the Joke and Slip the Yoke." 1958. Rpt. in *The Norton Anthology of African American Literature.* Ed. Henry Louis Gates Jr. and Nellie Y. McKay. New York: Norton, 1997. 1541–49.

———. *Invisible Man.* New York: Signet–New American Library, 1952.

English, Daylanne. *Unnatural Selections: Eugenics in American Modernism and the Harlem Renaissance.* Chapel Hill: U of North Carolina P, 2004.

Enniss, Stephen. "Sherwood Anderson and Paul Gauguin: A Forgotten Review." *Studies in American Fiction* 18 (1990): 118–21.

Fabre, Geneviève, and Michel Feith. Tight-Lipped Oracle: Around and Beyond *Cane.*" *Jean Toomer and the Harlem Renaissance.* New Brunswick: Rutgers UP, 2001. 1–17.

Fagin, N. Bryllion. "Sherwood Anderson and Our Anthropological Age." *Double Dealer* 7 (1925): 91–99.

Fanon, Frantz. *Black Skin, White Masks.* Trans. Charles Lam Markmann. London: Pluto Press, 1986. Trans. of *Peau Noire, Masques Blancs,* 1952.

Faulkner, William. *Absalom, Absalom!* The Corrected Text. New York: Vintage–Random House, 1990.

———. "Sherwood Anderson: An Appreciation." Rpt. in *Winesburg, Ohio: Text and Criticism.* By Sherwood Anderson. Ed. John H. Ferres. New York: Viking, 1966. 487–94.

Favor, J. Martin. *Authentic Blackness: The Folk in the New Negro Renaissance.* Durham, NC: Duke UP, 1999.

Findlay, Alison. *Illegitimate Power: Bastards in Renaissance Drama.* Manchester: Manchester UP, 1994.

Fishkin, Shelley Fisher. "Interrogating 'Whiteness,' Complicating 'Blackness': Remapping American Culture." *American Quarterly* 47 (1995): 428–66.

Fitzgerald, F. Scott. "Echoes of the Jazz Age." *The Crack-Up with Other Pieces and Stories.* London: Penguin, 1965. 9–19.

———. *The Letters of F. Scott Fitzgerald.* Ed. Andrew Turnbull. Harmondsworth: Penguin, 1968.

Foley, Barbara. "'In the Land of Cotton': Economics and Violence in Jean Toomer's *Cane.*" *African American Review* 32 (1998): 181–98.

———. "Jean Toomer's Washington and the Politics of Class: From 'Blue Veins' to Seventh-Street Rebels." *Modern Fiction Studies* 42 (1996): 289–321.

Ford, Karen Jackson. *Split-Gut Song: Jean Toomer and the Poetics of Modernity.* Tuscaloosa: U of Alabama P, 2005.

Forgacs, David. "Fascism, Violence and Modernity." *The Violent Muse: Violence and the Artistic Imagination in Europe, 1910–1939.* Ed. Jana Howlett and Rod Mengham. Manchester: Manchester UP, 1994. 5–21.

Foster, Hal. "Prosthetic Gods." *Modernism/Modernity* 4.2 (1997): 5–38.

Foucault, Michel. "Nietzsche, Genealogy, History." *The Foucault Reader.* Ed. Paul Rabinow. London: Penguin, 1991. 76–100.

———. *The History of Sexuality.* Vol. 1. Trans. Robert Hurley. London: Penguin, 1990.

Fowler, Alastair. *Kinds of Literature: An Introduction to the Theory of Genres and Modes.* Oxford: Clarendon–Oxford UP, 1982.

Frank, Waldo. "The Artist in Our Jungle." *In the American Jungle, 1925–36.* New York: Farrar and Rinehart, 1937. 149–53.

———. *City Block.* 1922. New York: AMS Press, 1970.

———. "Emerging Greatness." *Seven Arts* 1 (1916): 73–78. Rpt. in *The Achievement of Sherwood Anderson.* Ed. Ray Lewis White. Chapel Hill: U of North Carolina P, 1966. 20–24.

———. "For a Declaration of War." *Salvos: An Informal Book About Books and Plays.* New York: Boni and Liveright, 1924. 11–27.

———. "I Discover the New World." *In the American Jungle, 1925–36.* Farrar and Rinehart: New York, 1937. 3–15.

———. "In Defence of Our Vulgarity." *In the American Jungle, 1925–36.* Farrar and Rinehart: New York, 1937. 109–12.

———. *Memoirs of Waldo Frank.* Ed. Alan Trachtenberg. Amherst: U of Massachusetts P, 1973.

———. "The Mexican Invasion." *New Republic* Oct. 23 1929: 275–76.

———. *Our America.* New York: Boni and Liveright, 1919.

———. "Sherwood Anderson: A Personal Note." *Newberry Library Bulletin* 2 (1948): 39–43.

Franklin, John Hope, and Alfred A. Moss, Jr. *From Slavery to Freedom: A History of Negro Americans.* 6th ed. New York: McGraw-Hill, 1988.

Frazer, James George. *The Golden Bough.* Ed. Robert Fraser. London: Oxford UP, 1994.

———. Preface. *The Argonauts of the Western Pacific.* By Bronislaw Malinowski. 1922. Studies in Economic and Political Science 65. London: Routledge and Kegan Paul, 1953. vii–xii.

Freud, Sigmund. *The Freud Reader.* Ed. Peter Gay. London: Vintage, 1995.

———. "Thoughts for the Times on War and Death." *The Standard Edition of the Complete Psychological Works of Sigmund Freud.* Vol. 14. Trans. James Strachey, in collaboration with Anna Freud and assisted by Alix Strachey and Alan Tyson. London: Hogarth Press, 1957. 275–300.

———. *Totem and Taboo: Resemblances Between the Psychic Lives of Savages and Neurotics.* Trans. A. A. Brill. London: Routledge and Sons, 1919.

Fussell, Edwin. "*Winesburg, Ohio:* Art and Isolation." *Modern Fiction Studies* 6 (1960): 106–14. Rpt. in *The Achievement of Sherwood Anderson: Essays in Criticism.* Ed. Ray Lewis White. Chapel Hill: U of North Carolina P, 1966. 104–13.

Fussell, Paul. *The Great War and Modern Memory.* London: Oxford UP, 1975.

Gaines, Kevin K. *Uplifting the Race: Black Leadership, Politics, and Culture in the Twentieth Century.* Chapel Hill: U of North Carolina P, 1996.

Garber, Marjorie. "Spare Parts: The Surgical Construction of Gender." *Theorizing Feminism: Parallel Trends in the Humanities and the Social Sciences.* Ed. Anne C. Herrmann and. Abigail J. Stewart. Boulder, CO: Westview P, 1994. 238–87.

Gates, Henry Louis, Jr. *Figures in Black: Words, Signs, and the "Racial" Self.* Oxford: Oxford UP, 1989.

———. "'Race,' Writing and Difference." *Critical Inquiry* 12 (1985): 1–20.

———. *The Signifying Monkey: A Theory of African-American Literary Criticism.* Oxford: Oxford UP, 1988.

Gayle, Addison, Jr. "The Black Aesthetic: Introduction." Rpt. in *The Norton Anthology of African American Literature.* Ed. Henry Louis Gates Jr. and Nellie Y. McKay. New York: Norton, 1997. 1870–77.

Gilbert, Sandra M. "Literary Paternity." *Critical Theory Since 1965.* Ed. Hazard Adams and Leroy Searle. Tallahassee: Florida State UP, 1986. 486–96.

Gilbert, Sandra M., and Susan Gubar. *No Man's Land: The Place of the Woman Writer in the Twentieth Century.* Vol. 1. New Haven: Yale UP, 1988.

Gilman, Sander L. *Difference and Pathology: Stereotypes of Sexuality, Race, and Madness.* Ithaca: Cornell UP, 1985.

Goede, William J. "Jean Toomer's Ralph Kabnis: Portrait of the Negro Artist as a Young Man." *Phylon* 30 (1969): 73–85. Rpt. in *Jean Toomer: A Critical*

Evaluation. Ed. Therman B. O'Daniel. Howard UP: Washington D.C., 1988. 359–75.

Goldberg, David Theo. *Racial Subjects: Writing on Race in America*. New York: Routledge, 1997.

———. *Racist Culture: Philosophy and the Politics of Meaning*. Oxford: Blackwell, 1993.

Grandjeat, Charles-Yves. "The Poetics of Passing in Jean Toomer's *Cane*." *Jean Toomer and the Harlem Renaissance*. Ed. Geneviève Fabre and Michel Feith. New Brunswick: Rutgers UP, 2001. 57–67.

Grant, Madison. *The Passing of the Great Race, or the Racial Basis of European History*. Rev. ed. New York: Scribner's, 1918.

Grant, Nathan. *Masculinist Impulses: Toomer, Hurston, Black Writing, and Modernity*. Columbia: U of Missouri P, 2004.

Gray, Richard. *Writing the South: Ideas of an American Region*. Cambridge Studies in American Literature and Culture. Cambridge: Cambridge UP, 1986.

Griffin, John Howard. *Black Like Me*. Boston: Houghton Mifflin, 1961.

Grossman, James R. *Land of Hope: Chicago, Black Southerners, and the Great Migration*. Chicago: U of Chicago P, 1989.

Gutman, Herbert G. *The Black Family in Slavery and Freedom, 1750–1925*. New York: Pantheon, 1976.

Handler, Richard. "Boasian Anthropology and the Critique of American Culture." *American Quarterly* 42 (1990): 252–73.

———. "The Dainty and the Hungry Man: Literature and Anthropology in the Work of Edward Sapir." *Observers Observed: Essays on Ethnographic Fieldwork*. Ed. George W. Stocking. History of Anthropology, vol. 1. Madison: U of Wisconsin P, 208–31.

Haraway, Donna. "A Cyborg Manifesto: Science, Technology, and Socialist Feminism in the Late Twentieth Century." *Theorizing Feminism: Parallel Trends in the Humanities and the Social Sciences*. Ed. Anne C. Herrmann and Abigail J. Stewart. Boulder: Westview P, 1994. 424–57.

Hasian, Marouf Arif, Jr. *The Rhetoric of Eugenics in Anglo-American Thought*. University of Georgia Humanities Center Series on Science and the Humanities. Athens: U of Georgia P, 1996.

Hegeman, Susan. *Patterns for America: Modernism and the Concept of Culture*. Princeton: Princeton UP, 1999.

Helbling, Mark. "Jean Toomer and Waldo Frank: A Creative Friendship." *Phylon* 41 (1980): 167–78. Rpt. in *Jean Toomer: A Critical Evaluation*. Ed. Therman B. O'Daniel. Washington, DC: Howard UP, 1988. 85–97.

———. "Sherwood Anderson and Jean Toomer." *NALF* 9 (1975): 35–39. Rpt. in *Jean Toomer: A Critical Evaluation*. Ed. Therman B. O' Daniel. Washington, DC: Howard UP, 1988. 111–20.

Hemingway, Ernest. *The Torrents of Spring*. 1926. Harmondsworth: Penguin, 1976.

Herskovits, Melville. "The Negro's Americanism." *The New Negro*. Ed. Alain Locke. 1925. New York: Touchstone–Simon and Schuster, 1997.

———. "Does the Negro Know his Father?" *Opportunity* 4 (1926): 306–10.

Higham, John. *Strangers in the Land: Patterns of American Nativism 1860–1925*. Rev. ed. New Brunswick: Rutgers UP, 1988.

Hoffmann, Frederick J. "Sherwood Anderson." *Freudianism and the Literary Mind*. Baton Rouge: Louisiana State UP, 1957. 229–50. Rpt. in *The Achievement of Sherwood Anderson*. Ed. Ray Lewis White. Chapel Hill: U of North Carolina P, 1966. 173–92.

Hoganson, Kristin L. *Fighting for American Manhood: How Gender Politics Provoked the Spanish-American and Philippine-American Wars*. New Haven: Yale UP, 1998.

Holmes, Eugene. "Jean Toomer: Apostle of Beauty." *Opportunity* 10, Aug. 1932: 252–54, 260. Rpt. in *The Critics and the Harlem Renaissance*. Ed. Cary D. Wintz. New York: Garland P, 1996. 96–99.

Holton, Sylvia Wallace. *Down Home and Uptown: The Representation of Black Speech in American Fiction*. London: Associated UP, 1984.

Homburger, Eric. "Chicago and New York: Two Versions of American Modernism." *Modernism 1890–1930*. Ed. Malcolm Bradbury and James McFarlane. London: Penguin, 1991. 151–61.

Howe, Irving. *Sherwood Anderson*. 1951. Rev. ed. Stanford: Stanford UP, 1966.

Huggins, Nathan Irvin. *Harlem Renaissance*. Oxford: Oxford UP, 1973.

Hughes, Langston. "Big Meeting." 1931. Rpt. in *The Heath Anthology of American Literature*. Vol. 2. 3rd ed. Ed. Paul Lauter. Boston: Houghton Mifflin, 1998. 1621–29.

———. *The Big Sea*. 1940. London: Pluto P, 1986.

———. "The Blues I'm Playing." 1934. Rpt. in The *Norton Anthology of African American Literature*. Ed. Henry Louis Gates Jr. and Nellie Y. McKay. New York: Norton, 1997. 1271–82.

———. "The Negro Artist and the Racial Mountain." 1926. Rpt. in The *Norton Anthology of African American Literature*. Ed. Henry Louis Gates Jr. and Nellie Y. McKay. New York: Norton, 1997. 1267–71.

Huntington, Ellsworth. *The Character of Races*. New York: Scribner's, 1924.

Hurston, Zora Neale. "Characteristics of Negro Expression." 1934. Rpt. in *The Norton Anthology of African American Literature*. Ed. Henry Louis Gates Jr. and Nellie Y. McKay. New York: Norton, 1997. 1019–32.

———. *Mules and Men: Negro Folktales and Voodoo Practices in the South*. 1935. New York: Perennial Library–Harper and Row, 1970.

Hutchinson, George. Foreword. *Jean Toomer: Selected Essays and Literary Criticism*. Ed. Robert B. Jones. U of Tennessee P, Knoxville: 1996. vii–xi.

———. *The Harlem Renaissance in Black and White*. Cambridge, MA: Belknap–Harvard UP, 1995.

———. "Identity in Motion: Placing *Cane*." *Jean Toomer and the Harlem Renaissance*. Ed. Geneviève Fabre and Michel Feith. New Brunswick: Rutgers UP, 2001. 38–56.

———. "Jean Toomer and American Racial Discourse." *Texas Studies in Literature and Language* 35 (1993): 226–50.

———. "Jean Toomer and the New Negroes of Washington." *American Literature* 63 (1991): 683–92.

———. "The Whitman Legacy and the Harlem Renaissance." *Walt Whitman: The Centennial Essays*. Ed. Ed Folsom. Iowa City: U of Iowa P, 1994. 201–16.

Ingram, Forrest L. *Representative Short Story Cycles of the Twentieth Century: Studies in a Literary Genre.* The Hague: Mouton, 1971.

"Interview with Sherwood Anderson." *Toledo Blade* Nov. 19, 1925: 3.

Irigaray, Luce. "This Sex Which Is Not One." Trans. Claudia Reeder. *New French Feminisms: An Anthology.* Ed. Elaine Marks and Isabelle de Courtrivron. Brighton: Harvester, 1981. 99–106.

Iser, Wolfgang. "The Reading Process." Rpt. in *Modern Literary Theory: A Reader.* 2nd Ed. Ed. Philip Rice and Patricia Waugh. London: Edward Arnold, 1992. 77–83.

Jameson, Fredric. *The Political Unconscious: Narrative as a Socially Symbolic Act.* London: Methuen, 1981.

Janmohammed, Abdul R. "The Economy of Manichean Allegory." *Critical Inquiry* 12 (1985). Rpt. in *The Post-Colonial Studies Reader.* Ed. Bill Ashcroft, Gareth Griffiths and Helen Tiffin. London: Routledge, 1995. 18–23.

Jauss, Hans Robert. *Toward an Aesthetic of Reception.* Trans. Timothy Bahti. Theory and History of Literature, vol. 2. Brighton: Harvester P, 1982.

Jelliffe, Rowena Woodham. "The Negro in the Field of Drama." *Opportunity* 6 (1928): 214. Rpt. in *The Politics and Aesthetics of "New Negro" Literature.* Ed. Cary D. Wintz. Vol. 2 of *The Harlem Renaissance, 1920–1940.* New York: Garland P, 1996. 214.

Johnson, James Weldon. *Along this Way.* 1933. Harmondsworth: Penguin, 1941.

———. "The Dilemma of the Negro Author." *American Mercury* 15 (1928): 477–81.

———. Letter to the *Liberator. Liberator* 1, April 1918: 41–43.

———. Preface. *The Book of American Negro Poetry.* Ed. James Weldon Johnson. New York: Harcourt, Brace, 1922. vii–xlviii.

Jones, Gavin. *Strange Talk: The Politics of Dialect Literature in Gilded Age America.* Berkeley: U of California P, 1999.

Jones, Gayl. *Liberating Voices: Oral Tradition in African American Literature.* Cambridge, MA: Harvard UP, 1991.

Jones, Robert B. *Jean Toomer and the Prison House of Thought: A Phenomenology of the Spirit.* Amherst: U of Massachusetts P, 1993.

Josephson, Matthew. "Great American Novels." *Broom* 5 (1923): 178–80.

Kadlec, David. "Zora Neale Hurston and the Federal Folk." *Modernism/Modernity* 7 (2000): 471–85.

Kennedy, David M. *Over Here: The First World War and American Society.* 2nd ed. Oxford: Oxford UP, 2004.

Kennedy, J. Gerald. "The American Short Story Sequence: Definitions and Implications." *Modern American Short Story Sequences: Composite Fictions and Fictive Communities.* Ed. J. Gerald Kennedy. Cambridge: Cambridge UP, 1995. vii–xv.

———. "From Anderson's *Winesburg* to Carver's *Cathedral:* The Short Story Sequence and the Semblance of Community." In *Modern American Short Story Sequences: Composite Fictions and Fictive Communities.* Ed. J. Gerald Kennedy. Cambridge: Cambridge UP, 1995. 194–215.

———. "Toward a Poetics of the Short Story Cycle." *Journal of the Short Story in English* 11 (1988): 9–25.

Kerman, Cynthia Earl, and Richard Eldridge. *The Lives of Jean Toomer: A Hunger for Wholeness.* Baton Rouge: Louisiana State UP, 1987.

Kern, Stephen. *The Culture of Time and Space, 1880–1918.* Cambridge, MA: Harvard UP, 1983.

Kevles, Daniel. *In the Name of Eugenics: Genetics and the Uses of Human Heredity.* Cambridge, MA: Harvard UP, 1995.

Kimbell, Ellen. "The American Short Story: 1900–1920." *The American Short Story 1900–1945: A Critical History.* Ed. Philip Stevick. New York: Hall-Twayne, 1984. 33–69.

Kimmel, Michael. "Consuming Manhood: The Feminization of American Culture and the Recreation of the Male Body, 1832–1920." *The Male Body: Features, Destinies, Exposures.* Ed. Laurence Goldstein. Ann Arbor: U of Michigan P, 1994. 12–41.

———. *Manhood in America: A Cultural History.* New York: Free Press, 1997.

Kornweibel, Theodore, Jr. "An Economic Profile of Black Life in the Twenties." *Journal of Black Studies* 6 (1976): 307–20.

Kraft, Robert George. "Sherwood Anderson, Bisexual Bard: Some Chapters in a Literary Biography." Diss. U of Washington, 1969.

Kramer, Dale. *Chicago Renaissance: The Literary Life in the Midwest, 1900–1930.* New York: Appleton-Century, 1966.

Krupat, Arnold. *Ethnocriticism.* Berkeley: U of California P, 1992.

Krutch, Joseph Wood. "Vagabonds." *Nation* 121 (1925): 626–27.

Kutzinski, Vera M. "Unseasonal Flowers: Nature and History in Placido and Jean Toomer." *Yale Journal of Criticism* 3 (1990): 153–79.

Larsen, Nella. *Quicksand.* 1929. Rpt. in *Quicksand and Passing.* Ed. Deborah E. McDowell. London: Serpent's Tail, 1989. 1–135.

Lawrence, D. H. *Studies in Classic American Literature.* 1923. London: Penguin, 1971.

Lears, T. J. Jackson. *No Place of Grace: Antimodernism and the Transformation of American Culture.* Chicago: U of Chicago P, 1994.

———. "Sherwood Anderson: Looking for the White Spot." *The Power of Culture: Critical Essays in American History.* Ed. Richard Wrightman Fox and T. J. Jackson Lears. Chicago: U of Chicago P, 1993. 13–37.

Lemke, Sieglinde. *Primitivist Modernism: Black Culture and the Origins of Transatlantic Modernism.* Oxford: Oxford UP, 1998.

Levine, Lawrence. *Black Culture and Black Consciousness: Afro-American Folk Thought from Slavery to Freedom.* New York: Oxford UP, 1977.

———. "Slave Spirituals." *Slavery in American Society.* 3rd ed. Ed. Lawrence B. Goodheart, Richard D. Brown, and Stephen G. Rabe. Lexington, MA: Heath, 1993. 99–115.

Lewis, David Levering. *When Harlem Was in Vogue.* 1981. Oxford: Oxford UP, 1989.

Lewis, Wyndham. *Enemy Salvoes: Selected Literary Criticism.* Ed. C. J. Fox. London: Vision P, 1975.

Lind, Michael. *The Next American Nation: The New Nationalism and the Fourth American Revolution.* Old Tappan, NJ: Free Press, 1995.

Lindberg, Kathryne V. "Raising Cane on the Theoretical Plane: Jean Toomer's Racial Personae." *Cultural Difference and the Literary Text: Pluralism and the Limits of Authenticity in North American Literatures.* Ed. Winfried Siemerling and Katrin Schwenk. U of Iowa P: Iowa City, 1996. 49–74.

Locke, Alain. "Beauty Instead of Ashes." *The Critical Temper of Alain Locke: A Selection of His Essays on Art and Culture.* Ed. Jeffrey C. Stewart. New York: Garland P, 1983. 23–25.

———. "Negro Youth Speaks." *The New Negro.* 1925. Ed. Alain Locke. New York: Touchstone–Simon & Schuster, 1997. 47–53.

Looby, Christopher. "'As Thoroughly Black as the Most Faithful Philanthropist Could Desire': Erotics of Race in Higginson's *Army Life in a Black Regiment.*" *Race and the Subject of Masculinities.* Ed. Harry Stecopoulos and Michael Uebel. Durham, NC: Duke UP, 1997. 71–115.

Lott, Eric. *Love and Theft: Blackface Minstrelsy and the American Working Class.* Oxford: Oxford UP, 1993.

Lott, Tommy L. *The Invention of Race: Black Culture and the Politics of Representation.* Oxford: Blackwell, 1999.

Love, Glen A. "Horses or Men: Primitive and Pastoral Elements in Sherwood Anderson." *Sherwood Anderson: Centennial Studies.* Ed. Hilbert H. Campbell and Charles E. Modlin. Troy, NY: Whitston, 1976. 235–48.

———. "*Winesburg, Ohio* and the Rhetoric of Silence." *American Literature* 40 (1968–9): 38–57.

Luscher, Robert M. "The Short Story Sequence: An Open Book." *Short Story Theory at a Crossroads.* Ed. Susan Lohafer and Jo Ellyn Clarey. Baton Rouge: Louisiana State UP, 1989. 148–67.

MacFadden, Bernarr. *Encylopedia of Physical Culture.* 5 vols. New York: Physical Culture Publishing, 1912.

———. *Manhood and Marriage.* New York: MacFadden, 1916.

McKay, Nellie Y. *Jean Toomer, Artist: A Study of His Literary Life and Work, 1894–1936.* Chapel Hill: U of North Carolina P, 1984.

McKeever, Benjamin F. "*Cane* as Blues." *Negro American Literature Forum* 4. Rpt. in *Jean Toomer: A Critical Evaluation.* Ed. Therman B. O'Daniel. Washington: Howard UP, 1988.

Mackethan, Lucinda H. "Jean Toomer's *Cane:* A Pastoral Problem." *Mississippi Quarterly* 35 (1975): 423–34. Rpt. in *Cane.* By Jean Toomer. Ed. Darwin T. Turner. Norton Critical Edition. New York: Norton, 1988. 229–37.

Maclean, Marie. "The Performance of Illegitimacy: Signing the Matronym." *New Literary History* 25 (1994): 95–107.

McClure, John. Review of *Cane. Double Dealer* 6 (1924): 26–27.

Malinowski, Bronislaw. *Argonauts of the Western Pacific.* 1922. Studies in Economics and Political Science 65. Routledge and Kegan Paul: London, 1953.

Mann, Susan Garland. *The Short Story Cycle: A Genre Companion and Reference Guide.* New York: Greenwood P, 1989.

Mao, Douglas. "Culture Clubs." *Modernism/Modernity* 8.1 (2001): 159–72.

Marcus, George E., and Michael M. J. Fischer. *Anthropology as Cultural Critique: An Experimental Moment in the Human Sciences.* 2nd ed. Chicago: U of Chicago P, 1999.

Marinetti, Filippo Tommaso. "The Foundation and Manifesto of Futurism." 1909. Trans. F. W. Flint. Rpt. in *Art in Theory: 1900–1990.* Ed. Charles Harrison and Paul Wood. Oxford: Blackwell, 1995. 145–49.

———. "Futurism." Trans. Norman Fitts. *S4N* 26–29 (1923): n.p.

Marshall, John. "Pansies, Perverts and Macho Men: Changing Conceptions of Male Homosexuality." *The Making of the Modern Homosexual.* Ed. Kenneth Plummer. London: Hutchinson, 1981. 134–54.

Massey, Doreen. "Politics and Space/Time." *Place and the Politics of Identity.* Ed. Michael Keith and Steve Pile. London: Routledge, 1993. 141–61.

Maxwell, William. *New Negro, Old Left: African-American Writing and Communism between the Wars.* New York: Columbia UP, 1999.

Mead, Margaret. *Coming of Age in Samoa: A Study of Adolescence and Sex in Primitive Societies.* 1928. Harmondsworth: Pelican-Penguin, 1973.

Mencken, H. L. "The Sahara of the Bozart." *Prejudices: Second Series.* Knopf: New York, 1920. Rpt. in *Major Problems in the History of the American South.* Ed. Paul D. Escott and David R. Goldfield. Lexington, MA: Heath, 1990. 323–28.

Michaels, Walter Benn. *Our America: Nativism, Modernism and Pluralism.* Durham: Duke UP, 1995.

Michlin, Monica. "Karintha: A Textual Analysis." *Jean Toomer and the Harlem Renaissance.* Ed. Geneviève Fabre and Michel Feith. New Brunswick: Rutgers UP, 2001. 96–108.

Milne, Drew. "Lawrence and the Politics of Sexual Politics." *The Cambridge Companion to D. H. Lawrence.* Ed. Anne Fernihough. Cambridge: Cambridge UP, 2001. 197–215.

Moi, Toril. *Sexual/Textual Politics: Feminist Literary Theory.* 1985. New Accents. London: Routledge, 1995.

Morrison, Toni. *Playing in the Dark: Whiteness and the Literary Imagination.* London: Harvard UP, 1992.

Mrozek, Donald M. "The Habit of Victory: The American Military and the Cult of Manliness." *Manliness and Masculinity: Middle-Class Masculinity in Britain and America, 1800–1940.* Ed. J. A. Mangan and James Walvin. Manchester: Manchester UP, 1987. 220–41.

Mullins, Greg. "Nudes, Prudes and Pygmies: The Desirability of Disavowal in Physical Culture." *Discourse* 15 (1992): 27–48.

Munson, Gorham B. *The Awakening Twenties: A Memoir-History of A Literary Period.* Baton Rouge: Louisiana State UP, 1985.

———. "A Comedy of Exiles." *Literary Review* 12 (1968): 41–75.

———. "The Mechanics for a Literary Secession." *S4N* 22 (1922): n.p.

———. *Waldo Frank: A Study.* New York: Boni and Liveright, 1923.

Nagel, James. *The Contemporary American Short Story Cycle: The Ethnic Resonance of Genre.* Baton Rouge: Louisiana State UP, 2001.

Nicholls, Peter. *Modernisms: A Literary Guide.* Basingstoke: Macmillan, 1995.

Nilsen, Helge Norman. "Waldo Frank and the Idea of America." *American Studies International* 17.3 (1979): 27–36.

Nordau, Max. *Degeneration.* 1883. Lincoln: U of Nebraska P, 1993.

North, Michael. *The Dialect of Modernism: Race, Language, and Twentieth-Century Literature.* Oxford: Oxford UP, 1994.

———. *Reading 1922: Return to the Scene of the Modern.* New York: Oxford UP, 1999.

Papinchak, Robert Allen. *Sherwood Anderson: A Study of the Short Fiction.* Twayne's Studies in Short Fiction. New York: Twayne-Hall, 1992.

Parsons, Elsie Clews. *Folklore of the South Sea Islands, South Carolina.* Cambridge, MA: American Folklore Society, 1923.

Paul, Diane B. *Controlling Human Heredity: 1865 to the Present.* The Control of Nature Series. Atlantic Highlands, NJ: Humanities P, 1995.

Peckham, Joel B. "Jean Toomer's *Cane:* Self as Montage and the Drive Toward Integration." *American Literature* 72 (2000): 275–90.

Pernick, Martin S. "Defining the Defective: Eugenics, Aesthetics, and Mass Culture in Early Twentieth-Century America." *The Body and Physical Difference: Discourses of Disability.* Ed. David T. Mitchell and Sharon L. Snyder. Ann Arbor: U of Michigan P, 1997. 89–110.

Perry, Robert L. *The Shared Vision of Waldo Frank and Hart Crane.* Lincoln: U of Nebraska P, 1966.

Phillips, William L. "How Sherwood Anderson Wrote *Winesburg, Ohio.*" *American Literature* 23 (1951): 7–30. Rpt. in *Sherwood Anderson: A Collection of Critical Essays.* Ed. Walter B. Rideout. Englewood Cliffs, NJ: Prentice-Hall, 1974. 18–38.

Posnock, Ross. *Color and Culture: Black Writers and the Making of the Modern Intellectual.* Cambridge, MA: Harvard UP, 1998.

Reid, Ian. *The Short Story.* The Critical Idiom 37. New York: Barnes and Noble, 1977.

Rhodes, Chip. *Structures of the Jazz Age: Mass Culture, Progressive Education and Racial Disclosures in American Modernism.* The Haymarket Series. London: Verso, 1998.

Rhodes, Colin. *Primitivism in Modern Art.* London: Thames and Hudson, 1994.

Rideout, Walter B. "'The Most Cultural Town In America': Sherwood Anderson and New Orleans." *Southern Review* 24.1 (1988): 79–99.

———. "The Simplicity of *Winesburg, Ohio.*" *Shenandoah* 13 (1962): 20–31. Rpt. in *Winesburg, Ohio.* By Sherwood Anderson. Ed. Charles E. Modlin and Ray Lewis White. Norton Critical Edition. New York: Norton, 1996. 169–77.

Rigsbee, Sally Aidair. "The Feminine in Winesburg, Ohio." *Studies in American Fiction* 9 (1981): 233–44. Rpt. in *Winesburg, Ohio.* By Sherwood Anderson. Ed. Charles E. Modlin and Ray Lewis White. Norton Critical Edition. London: Norton, 1996. 178–88.

Roberts, Diane. *The Myth of Aunt Jemima: Representations of Race and Region.* London: Routledge, 1994.

Roediger, David. R. *The Wages of Whiteness: Race and the Making of the American Working Class.* London: Verso, 1991.

Rosmarin, Adena. *The Power of Genre.* Minneapolis: U of Minnesota P, 1985.

Rosenfeld, Paul. *Men Seen.* New York: Dial P, 1925.

———. "Sherwood Anderson." *Port of New York: Essays on Fourteen American Moderns.* New York: Harcourt, Brace, 1924. 175–98.

Ross, Marlon B. *Manning the Race: Reforming Black Men in the Jim Crow Era.* New York: New York UP, 2004.

Rotundo, E. Anthony. "Body and Soul: Changing Ideals of Middle Class Manhood, 1770–1920." *Journal of Social History* 16 (Summer 1983): 23–38.

Rowbotham, Sheila. *A Century of Women: The History of Women in Britain and the United States.* London: Penguin, 1999.

Rusch, Frederik L. "Form, Function and Creative Tension in *Cane:* Jean Toomer and the Need for the Avant-Garde." *MELUS* 17 (1991–2): 15–28.

Said, Edward W. *Culture and Imperialism.* New York: Vintage, 1994.

———. *Orientalism.* 1978. London: Penguin, 2003.

Sapir, Edward. "Culture, Genuine and Spurious." *American Journal of Sociology* 29 (1924): 401–29. Rpt. in *Selected Writings of Edward Sapir in Language, Culture and Personality.* Ed. David G. Mandelbaum. Berkeley: U of California P, 1949. 308–31.

———. "A Symposium of the Exotic." *Dial* 73, July–Dec. 1922: 568–571.

Sayn, Pierre. "Waldo Frank and Unanism." *S4N* 30–31 (1924): n.p.

Schaffer, Ronald. *America in the Great War: The Rise of the Welfare State.* Oxford: Oxford UP, 1991.

Schevill, James. *Sherwood Anderson: His Life and Work.* U of Denver P, 1951.

Schomburg, Arthur A. "The Negro Digs up his Past." *The New Negro: An Interpretation.* 1925. New York: Arno P and The New York Times, 1968. 231–37.

Schuyler, George S. *Black No More.* 1931. New York: Negro Universities P, 1969.

———. "The Negro Art Hokum." *Nation* June 16, 1926. Rpt. in *The Portable Harlem Renaissance Reader.* Ed. David Levering Lewis. Viking Portable Library. London: Penguin, 1994. 96–99.

Scruggs, Charles. "'All Dressed Up but No Place to Go': The Black Writer and His Audience during the Harlem Renaissance." *American Literature* 48 (1977): 543–63.

———. "The Reluctant Witness: What Jean Toomer Remembered from *Winesburg, Ohio.*" *Studies in American Fiction* 28 (2000): 77–100.

———."Textuality and Vision in Jean Toomer's *Cane.*" *Journal of the Short Story in English* 10 (1988): 93–114.

Scruggs, Charles, and Lee VanDemarr. *Jean Toomer and the Terrors of American History.* Philadelphia: U of Pennsylvania P, 1998.

Sebastian, D. "Sherwood Anderson's Theory of Art." Diss. Louisiana State U, 1972.

Sedgwick, Eve Kosofsky. "The Beast in the Closet: James and the Writing of Homosexual Panic." *Sex, Politics, and Science in the Nineteenth-Century Novel.* Ed. Ruth Bernard Yeazell. Baltimore: Johns Hopkins UP, 1986. 148–86.

———. *Between Men: English Literature and Homosocial Desire.* New York: Columbia UP, 1985.

———. *Epistemology of the Closet.* New York: Harvester-Wheatsheaf, 1991.

Segel, Harold B. *Body Ascendant: Modernism and the Physical Imperative.* Baltimore: Johns Hopkins UP, 1998.

Showalter, Elaine. "Male Hysteria: W. H. R. Rivers and the Lessons of Shell Shock." *The Female Malady: Women, Madness, and English Culture, 1830–1980*. London: Virago, 1987. 167–94.

Silverman, Kaja. "Historical Trauma and Male Subjectivity." *Psychoanalysis and Cinema*. Ed. E. Ann Kaplan. New York: Routledge, 1990. 110–27.

Simolke, Duane. *Stein, Gender, Isolation, and Industrialism: New Readings of* Winesburg, Ohio. San Jose: ToExcel, 1999.

Simpson, Hilary. *D.H. Lawrence and Feminism*. London: Croom Helm, 1982.

Sinfield, Alan. *Cultural Politics—Queer Reading*. London: Routledge, 1994.

Smith, Felipe. *American Body Politics: Race, Gender, and Black Literary Renaissance*. Athens: U of Georgia P, 1998.

Smith, J. David. *The Eugenic Assault on America: Scenes in Red, White, and Black*. Fairfax, VA: George Mason UP, 1993.

Sollors, Werner. *Beyond Ethnicity: Consent and Descent in American Culture*. New York: Oxford University Press, 1986.

———. "A Critique of Pure Pluralism." *Reconstructing American Literary History*. Ed. Sacvan Bercovitch. Harvard English Studies 13. Cambridge, MA: Harvard UP, 1986. 250–79.

———. *Neither Black nor White Yet Both: Thematic Explorations of Interracial Literature*. Cambridge, MA: Harvard UP, 1997.

Somerville, Siobhan B. *Queering the Color Line: Race and the Invention of Homosexuality in American Culture*. Durham: Duke UP, 2000.

Sontag, Susan. "Notes on Camp." *Against Interpretation and Other Essays*. New York: Delta-Dell, 1978. 275–92.

Soto, Michael. "Jean Toomer and Horace Liveright; or, A New Negro Gets 'into the Swing of It.'" *Jean Toomer and the Harlem Renaissance*. Ed. Geneviève Fabre and Michel Feith. New Brunswick: Rutgers UP, 2001. 162–87.

Stallabrass, Julian. "The Idea of the Primitive: British Art and Anthropology 1918–1930." *New Left Review* 183 (1990): 95–115.

Stallybrass, Peter, and Allon White. *The Politics and Poetics of Transgression*. London: Methuen, 1986.

Steinman, Lisa M. *Science, Technology, and American Modernist Poets*. New Haven: Yale UP, 1987.

Stevens, Hugh. "Sex and the Nation: 'The Prussian Officer' and *Women in Love*." *The Cambridge Companion to D.H. Lawrence*. Ed. Anne Fernihough. Cambridge: Cambridge UP, 2001. 49–66.

Stocking, George W., Jr. *The Ethnographer's Magic and Other Essays in the History of Anthropology*. Madison: U of Wisconsin P, 1992.

———. "The Ethnographic Sensibility of the 1920s and the Dualism of the Anthropological Tradition." *Romantic Motives: Essays on Anthropological Sensibility*. History of Anthropology, vol. 6. Madison: U of Wisconsin P, 1989. 208–76.

Stoddard, Lothrop. *The Revolt Against Civilization: The Menace of the Under-Man*. London: Chapman and Hall, 1922.

Stouck, David. "Anderson's Expressionist Art." *New Essays on* Winesburg, Ohio. Ed. John W. Crowley. Cambridge: Cambridge UP, 1990. 27–51. Rpt. in

Winesburg, Ohio. By Sherwood Anderson. Ed. Ray Lewis White and Charles E. Modlin. Norton Critical Edition. New York: Norton, 1996. 211–29.

———. "*Winesburg, Ohio* as a Dance of Death." *American Literature* 48 (1977): 525–42.

Summers, Martin. *Manliness and its Discontents: The Black Middle Class and the Transformation of Masculinity, 1900–1930.* Chapel Hill: U of North Carolina P, 2004.

Sundquist, Eric J. *To Wake the Nations: Race in the Making of American Literature.* Cambridge, MA: Belknap–Harvard UP, 1993.

Sutton, William A. *The Road to Winesburg: A Mosaic of the Life and Imagination of Sherwood Anderson.* Metchuen, NJ: Scarecrow P, 1972.

Tashjian, Dickran. *Skyscraper Primitives: Dada and the American Avant-Garde.* Middleton, CT: Wesleyan UP, 1975.

Taylor, Paul Beekman. *Shadows of Heaven: Gurdjieff and Toomer.* York Beach, ME: Samuel Weiser, 1998.

Taylor, Welford Dunaway. *Sherwood Anderson.* Modern Literature Monographs Series. New York: Ungar, 1977.

Tichi, Cecelia. *Technology, Literature, Culture in Modernist America.* Chapel Hill: U of North Carolina P, 1987.

Toomer, Jean. "The Americans." *A Jean Toomer Reader: Selected Unpublished Writings.* Ed. Frederik L. Rusch. New York: Oxford UP, 1993. 106–10.

———. *Cane.* 1923. Ed. Darwin T. Turner. Norton Critical Edition. New York: Norton, 1988.

———. *The Collected Poems of Jean Toomer.* Ed. Robert B. Jones and Margery Latimer Toomer. Chapel Hill: U of North Carolina P, 1988.

———. "The Critic of Waldo Frank: Criticism, an Art Form." *S4N* 30 (1924): n.p. Rpt. in *Jean Toomer: Selected Essays and Literary Criticism.* Ed. Robert B. Jones. Knoxville: U of Tennessee P, 1996. 24–31.

———. "The Crock of Problems." *Jean Toomer: Selected Essays and Literary Criticism.* Ed. Robert B. Jones. Knoxville: U of Tennessee P, 1996. 55–59.

———. "Germ Carriers." *A Jean Toomer Reader: Selected Unpublished Writings.* Ed. Frederik L. Rusch. Oxford: Oxford UP, 1993. 82.

———. *The Letters of Jean Toomer, 1919–1924.* Ed. Mark Whalan. Knoxville: U of Tennessee P, 2006.

———. "The Negro Emergent." *A Jean Toomer Reader: Selected Unpublished Writings.* Ed. Frederik L. Rusch. New York: Oxford UP, 1993. 86–93.

———. "Open Letter to Gorham Munson. " *S4N* 25 (March 1923). Rpt. in *Jean Toomer: Selected Essays and Literary Criticism.* Ed. Robert B. Jones. Knoxville: U of Tennessee P, 1996. 19–20.

———. "Race Problems and Modern Society." *Problems of Civilization.* Ed. Baker Brownwell. New York: D. Van Nostrand, 1929. 67–111. Rpt. in *Theories of Ethnicity: A Classical Reader.* Ed. Werner Sollors. New York: New York UP, 1996. 168–90.

———. "Waldo Frank's *Holiday.*" *Dial* 75 (1923): 383–86. Rpt. in *Jean Toomer: Selected Essays and Literary Criticism.* Ed. Robert B. Jones. U of Tennessee P, Knoxville: 1996. 7–10.

———. *The Wayward and the Seeking: A Collection of Writings by Jean Toomer.* Ed. Darwin T. Turner. Washington, DC: Howard UP, 1982.

———. "Why I Entered the Gurdjieff Work." *Jean Toomer: Selected Essays and Literary Criticism.* Ed. Robert B. Jones. Knoxville: U of Tennessee P, 1996. 106–9.

Torgovnick, Marianna. *Gone Primitive: Savage Intellects, Modern Lives.* London: U of Chicago P, 1990.

Townsend, Kim. *Sherwood Anderson.* Boston: Houghton Mifflin, 1987.

Trilling, Lionel. "Sherwood Anderson." Rpt. in *Winesburg, Ohio: Text and Criticism.* By Sherwood Anderson. Ed. John H. Ferres. Viking Critical Library. New York: Viking P, 1966. 455–67.

Turner, Darwin T. "The Failure of a Playwright." *CLA Journal* 10 (1967): 308–18. Rpt. in *Jean Toomer: A Critical Evaluation.* Ed. Therman B. O'Daniel. Washington, DC: Howard UP, 1988. 377–86.

———. "An Intersection of Paths: Correspondence between Jean Toomer and Sherwood Anderson." *NALF* 9 (1975): 35–39. Rpt. in *Jean Toomer: A Critical Evaluation.* Ed. Therman B. O'Daniel. Washington, DC: Howard UP, 1988. 99–120.

———. "W. E. B. Du Bois and the Theory of a Black Aesthetic." *The Harlem Renaissance Re-Examined.* Ed. Victor A. Kramer. Georgia State Literary Studies Series. New York: AMS Press, 1987. 9–30.

Ullmann, Sharon R. *Sex Seen: The Emergence of Modern Sexuality in America.* Berkeley: U of California P, 1997.

Walker, Alice. "In Search of Our Mothers' Gardens." *In Search of Our Mothers' Gardens: Womanist Prose.* London: Women's Press, 1984. 231–43.

———. "The Divided Life of Jean Toomer." *In Search of our Mothers' Gardens: Womanist Prose.* London: Women's Press, 1984. 60–65.

Watson, Steven. *Strange Bedfellows: The First American Avant-Garde.* New York: Abbeville P, 1991.

Weinstein, Arnold. "Anderson: The Play of *Winesburg, Ohio.*" *Nobody's Home: Speech, Self, and Place in American Fiction from Hawthorne to DeLillo.* New York: Oxford UP, 1993. 91–107.

Weiss, Adrea, and Greta Schiller. *Before Stonewall: The Making of a Gay and Lesbian Community.* New York: Naiad P, 1988.

Welty, Eudora. "Place in Fiction." *The Eye of the Story: Selected Essays and Reviews.* London: Virago, 1987. 116–33.

Whalan, Mark. "Jean Toomer, Technology, and Race." *Journal of American Studies* 36 (2002): 459–72.

White, Ray Lewis. Introduction. *Marching Men.* 1917. By Sherwood Anderson. A Critical Text. Ed. Ray Lewis White. Cleveland: P of Case Western Reserve U, 1972. xi–xxvii.

———. *Winesburg, Ohio: An Exploration.* American Masterwork Series. Boston: Twayne-Hall, 1990.

Whyde, Janet M. "Mediating Forms: Narrating the Body in Jean Toomer's *Cane.*" *Southern Literary Journal* 26 (1993): 42–53.

Williams, Diana. "Building the New Race: Jean Toomer's Eugenic Aesthetic." *Jean Toomer and the Harlem Renaissance.* Ed. Geneviève Fabre and Michel Feith. New Brunswick: Rutgers UP, 2001. 188–201.

Williams, Kenny J. *A Storyteller and a City: Sherwood Anderson's Chicago.* Dekalb IL: Northern Illinois UP, 1988.

Williams, Raymond. *Culture and Society, 1780–1950.* London: Penguin, 1971.

———. *Marxism and Literature.* Oxford: Oxford UP, 1977.

———. *The Politics of Modernism: Against the New Conformists.* Verso, 1989.

Williams, Rosalind. "Jules Romains, *Unanimisme,* and the Poetics of Urban Systems." *Literature and Technology.* Research in Technology Studies, vol. 5. Ed. Mark L. Greenberg and Lance Schachterle. London: Associated UP, 1992. 177–205.

Williams, Sherley Anne. Afterword. *Their Eyes Were Watching God.* By Zora Neale Hurston. 1937. London: Virago, 1997. 287–97.

Williamson, Joel. *New People: Miscegenation and Mulattoes in the United States.* 1980. Baton Rouge: Louisiana State UP, 1995.

Wilson, Trevor. *The Myriad Faces of War: Britain and the Great War, 1914–1918.* Cambridge: Polity Press, 1986.

Woodson, Jon. *To Make A New Race: Gurdjieff, Toomer and the Harlem Renaissance.* Jackson: UP of Mississippi, 1999.

Woodward, C. Vann. *The Strange Career of Jim Crow.* Rev. ed. New York: Galaxy–Oxford UP, 1957.

Woolf, Virginia. *A Room of One's Own.* Ed. Morag Shiach. Oxford: Oxford UP, 1998.

Yingling, Thomas. "*Winesburg, Ohio* and the End of Collective Experience." *New Essays on* Winesburg, Ohio. Cambridge: Cambridge UP, 1990. 99–128.

Zagrell, Sandra A. "Narrative of Community: The Identification of a Genre." *Signs: Journal of Women in Culture and Society* 13 (1988): 498–527.

Zingo, Martha T., and Kevin E. Early. *Nameless Persons: Legal Discrimination Against Non-Marital Children in the United States.* Westport: Praeger, 1994.

Žižek, Slavoj. "Eastern Europe's Republics of Gilead." *New Left Review* 183 (1990): 50–62.

INDEX